METHUEN'S HISTORY OF THE
GREEK AND ROMAN WORLD

General Editor: M. CARY, M.A., D.LITT.

VII
A HISTORY OF THE ROMAN WORLD
FROM A.D. 138 TO 337

A HISTORY OF
THE ROMAN WORLD
FROM A.D. 138 TO 337

BY

H. M. D. PARKER
M.A.

FELLOW AND TUTOR OF MAGDALEN COLLEGE, OXFORD

WITH FOUR MAPS

METHUEN & CO. LTD.
36 ESSEX STREET W.C.
LONDON

First published in 1935

PRINTED IN GREAT BRITAIN

PREFACE

IN preparing my manuscript for the Press I received valuable assistance from Mr. R. Meiggs of Keble College. The final proofs were read by Mr. R. H. Dundas of Christ Church, and the onerous task of compiling the index was undertaken by Mr. T. M. Knox of Jesus College. To each of them I take this opportunity of expressing my most sincere gratitude.

Magdalen College, Oxford
    August 29, 1935

H. M. D. P.

CONTENTS

PART V

ORIENTAL DESPOTISM

MAPS

THE EASTERN PROVINCES
GERMAN AND RAETIAN FRONTIER
CENTRAL EUROPE
THE DIOCESES OF THE ROMAN EMPIRE

These are drawn by Richard Cribb and will be found at the end of book.

INTRODUCTION

THE basis of the Augustan imperial organization was a federation of allied communities, all of which were bound in varying degrees of subjection to the central authority of Rome. Within this system of government citizen was differentiated from subject, Italian from provincial, ruler from ruled. The ideal of an Empire united in the possession of a common citizenship was to be realized not by an immediate and indiscriminate extension of privileges, but by a lengthy process of development in which the subjects, in proportion as they served Rome with loyalty and constancy, should be rewarded by a gradual advancement to the status of her full citizenship. The policy of Augustus was in part a legacy from the Republic, and in part a deliberate concession to the prejudices of Romano-Italian sentiment, which finds a parallel in the constitutional fiction by which he sought to disarm its fear and abhorrence of monarchy. During the first century of the Principate the traditional ideal that the Romans were a race of conquerors lingered persistently in conservative circles, and found vocal expression in the opposition to Claudius' proposal to introduce Gauls into the Senate-house. But this attitude, which recurs in the pages of Tacitus, was little more than a reactionary lament. The administrative demands of a growing Empire combined with a declining Italian population had necessitated the employment of an increasing number of provincials in the public services of the State. The beneficial effects of the more liberal conception of Imperialism which this policy entailed created a more educated and enlightened public opinion, which found its chief exponent in Hadrian, the true author of *The Golden Age of the Antonines*.

The main purpose of Hadrian's policy was the unity of the Roman Empire. With the conviction that Roman arms had already reached, if not overstepped, the margin of security, he set his face against further expansion and determined upon a programme of consolidation. The Eastern conquests of Trajan were given up and the existing frontiers were strengthened by the construction of artificial barriers, such as the *Pfahlgraben* in Germany and the Solway-Tyne Wall in Britain, and the erection of a large number of forts, which were garrisoned by auxiliary troops in advance of the second line of legionary defence. Within the Empire he sought to create an atmosphere of peace and prosperity by the elimination of racial and political differences and by fostering the idea of a common citizenship and a common service to the Empire. The favoured position of Italy was curtailed by the division of the peninsula into four districts in which commissioners of consular rank dispensed justice, while the welfare of the provincials was promoted by an extension of the municipal system and the encouragement of local patriotism. The Emperor's imperial idea is attested not only by the literary authorities and his own famous tours of the Empire, but also by the great province-series of coins which he struck during the last four years of his Principate. On the reverse-types of this series are personifications of no less than twenty-five countries and cities of the Roman World, and these represent no longer the military triumphs of Rome, but are a symbolical expression of the natural resources of each province and town and the particular contributions which they had to offer to the Empire. The coins thus reflect the ideal which Hadrian was trying to realize of a society of fellow-citizens developing under conditions of political equality their individual pursuits beneath the directing control of a beneficent imperial government.

The realization of these imperial ideas necessitated a supreme control by the Emperor of the internal organization of the Empire. Towards the Senate he adopted an attitude of deferential respect, but at the same time by encroaching upon its spheres of administration treated it as a negligible factor in the government. The instrument which he chose for his work was the civil service drawn from the equestrian order and bound to himself by personal ties of obligation. Its numbers were increased and its powers extended. The three Secretaries of State who in the past had been normally freedmen were now drawn from the ranks of the knights, an indication that the private service of the Emperor was synonymous with imperial officialdom. The new posts, which the reforms of the administration entailed, were filled from the same source, and the Emperor's most trusted subordinate, Q. Marcius Turbo, who with the nominal title of prefect of Egypt was given an extraordinary command on the Danube, was a knight and not a senator. Of great significance was the reconstruction of the imperial *consilium* to which knights were now admitted. Hitherto informal in its constitution, it now became a formal institution composed of members regularly appointed and salaried, who included in their number the leading lawyers of the day. With the help of the latter Hadrian elucidated and perfected the Roman system of Jurisprudence, and by his authority the praetor's edict was edited and given its final form by Salvius Julianus.

With his devotion to administrative problems Hadrian combined a wide range of individual interests—a personal synthesis which may be said to epitomize his imperial ideal. " A searcher-out of all strange things," as Tertullian calls him, he found in his travels a means of satisfying his artistic tastes. Throughout the Roman World monuments in the form of baths, temples and libraries commemorated his passion for architecture, and his villa at Tibur, an incongruous mass of strange buildings, served as a reminder of the scenes which he had visited in the East. His love of all things Hellenic was responsible for what is popularly known as the " Greek Revival " in Roman Art. This reassertion, as it has been recently called, of the value of the idealistic Art of classical Greece,[1] enriched by the experience of the realistic tendencies of the earlier Principate, provided the most suitable medium for giving expression to the spirit of the age. The representation of idealistic types on medallions and coins harmonized with the imperial conception which the Emperor was attempting to translate into the government of the Roman World.

Despite his great work for the Empire and the statesmanlike skill with which he brought to their logical consummation the ideas innate in the Augustan programme, Hadrian did not enjoy a personal popularity with the upper classes of society.

The Senate in particular could not forget nor forgive his deliberate encroachments upon its privileges. Like all pioneers he was opposed by the rigid upholders of tradition, and the dictum of his biographer, " he died hated of all," is but the exaggerated expression of the conservative Roman hatred of his progressive theory of Empire.[2]

PART I

THE ANTONINES

CHAPTER I

ANTONINUS PIUS

§ 1. EARLY HISTORY AND CHARACTER

TITUS AURELIUS FULVUS BOIONIUS ANTONI-
NUS was born at Lanuvium on 19th September, A.D.
86. His father's family belonged originally to Nemau-
sus (Nîmes) in Gallia Narbonensis, and had migrated to Rome
where its leading members followed a political career.
Antoninus' grandfather, Titus Aurelius Fulvus, had held the
consulship twice and the city prefectureship, while his father,
Aurelius Fulvus, had also attained consular rank before his
early death. His mother was Arria Fadilla, whose father,
Arrius Antoninus, had been twice consul, and is said to have
offered his condolences to Nerva when the latter was raised
to the Principate. The future Emperor thus came of a good
family—*genere claro sed non admodum vetere*[1]—which, if
provincial in origin, had been sufficiently long resident in
Rome to become familiar with its social and political
environment.

Antoninus' boyhood was spent at Lorium, some twelve
miles west of Rome, which in later life he always regarded
as his home, and his education was entrusted to his two
grandfathers. Under these influences he acquired the
character and tastes of a country gentleman, ready when
required to take his share in the political life of the State, but
without any ambition for a career of distinction, far less
for the crowning honour of the Principate. In his *Meditations* Marcus Aurelius describes his adoptive father as a man
of mild temperament and unchangeable resolution with a love
of hard work and with no vain glory in those things which
men call honours.[2] His sobriety, truthfulness and reserve
were characteristic of a Roman of the early Republic, and he
was popularly acclaimed a second Numa Pompilius.

3

In due course Antoninus began his career as a senator, passing through the quaestorship and praetorship[3] until in A.D. 130 he became consul with Catilius Severus as his colleague.[4] On laying down office he retired to his country estate, but before long he was appointed by Hadrian one of the *IV-viri consulares* charged with the dispensation of justice in Italy, and received Etruria and Umbria as his district.[5] How long he held this office, which acquired considerable importance during the Emperor's journeys abroad, is not known, but between A.D. 133 and 136 he was made proconsul of Asia. His governorship was distinguished by soundness of administration and particular attention to the material welfare of the provincials, and earned for him the reputation of being " the only man to excel his grandfather." Nor did his abilities escape the notice of the Emperor; for on his return to Rome he was appointed a member of the newly reconstituted imperial *consilium*. Antoninus was now one of the leading men at Rome and was able to acquire an intimate knowledge of the aspirations and grievances of the Senate, which was in later years reflected in his imperial policy.

On January 1st, A.D. 138, L. Aelius Verus, who had been adopted by Hadrian and marked out as his successor by the title of Caesar, died. His son Lucius Ceionius Commodus was but a boy of seven, and Marcus Annius Verus, upon whom the Emperor had already bestowed favours,[6] was only seventeen and considered too young to shoulder the burdens of government. Hadrian had, therefore, to look elsewhere for a successor, and his choice fell upon Antoninus, whose general popularity and administrative experience suggested that the Empire would be sanely governed till Marcus was of an age to assume its responsibilities. After long consideration Antoninus accepted the proposal, and on February 25th, A.D. 138, was adopted by Hadrian. At the same time Antoninus was compelled to adopt both his nephew Marcus and, as a consolation to the family of the Commodi, Lucius the son of the late Aelius Verus,[7] who, it was stipulated, should become the husband of Antoninus' second daughter Annia Galeria Faustina. The latter part of this arrangement was, however, not carried out; for after the death of Hadrian Faustina was betrothed to Marcus, and Lucius later married

Lucilla the daughter of Marcus. Immediately after his
adoption Antoninus was made a colleague of Hadrian in
the two chief imperial powers, the *tribunicia potestas* and the
proconsulare imperium, and his name appears on coins of the
early spring of A.D. 138 as Imp. T. Aelius Caesar Antoninus,
but without as yet the title of Augustus.[8] Yet despite this
technical inferiority, Antoninus was the actual ruler of the
State, while he attended upon Hadrian in the last months of
his illness with a true filial devotion, which is perhaps commemorated by the symbol of *Pietas* on his earliest coins.[9]
Early in July Antoninus left Rome in the care of young
Marcus and went to Baiae, where on the tenth day of the
month Hadrian died.

§ 2. THE PRINCIPATE OF ANTONINUS

(a) *His relations with the Senate.*

Antoninus' first care was for the memory of Hadrian. The
body of the late Emperor was brought from Baiae and laid
in the tomb which he had built for himself, and which now
bears the name of the Castello Sant' Angelo. The Senate,
however, which had resented Hadrian's progressive imperialism and had been embittered by the diminution of its
authority, was opposed to the deification of the dead
Emperor and at first resolved to refuse an official ratification
of his *Acta*. Antoninus, whose preferment had not met with
the universal approval of his fellow-senators, was thus faced
with the dilemma of vindicating or repudiating his adoptive
father's policy. For the present he chose the former alternative, and his decision is reflected in the provincial coin
series, resembling that of his predecessor, which was issued
by him on the occasion of the offer of the customary *aurum
coronarium*.[10] A compromise was reached with the Senate
which, partly from fear of the army and partly from grati-
fication at Antoninus' deferential attitude to itself, agreed,
in return for the abolition of the detested office of *IV-viri
consulares*, to the apotheosis of the dead Emperor and the
ratification of his remaining acts.[11] Upon Antoninus himself
it conferred the unusual title of *Pius*—a tribute to his
reverence for the gods—and upon his wife, Annia Galeria
Faustina, the imperial title of Augusta.[12] In the following

year, after the customary first refusal, Antoninus accepted
the title of *pater patriae*,[13] and held the consulship with
Bruttius Praesens.[14]   In A.D. 140 and 145 he again took
office, choosing as his colleague his adopted son, Marcus,
who was created Caesar in 139 and received in 146 the
tribunicia potestas and *proconsulare imperium*.[15]

   Throughout his Principate the relations between Antoninus
and the Senate were amicable.   Despite his vindication of
Hadrian's memory the new Emperor shared neither the
imperialistic enthusiasms nor the cosmopolitan tastes of his
predecessor.   His real love was Italy, and his coinage reflects
his aspirations of reinstating her as the sovereign country of
the Roman World—a policy which could not fail to win the
support of the Senate.[16]   To individual senators he made
presents to enable them to live in a manner becoming to their
rank, and no senator was put to death by his command.   At
the same time he made himself readily accessible by refusing
to surround himself with a coterie of freedmen and Court
favourites, and so discountenanced both the sale of favours
and the growth of delation.   The number of State officials,
which had assumed such great dimensions in the principate
of Hadrian, does not appear to have been further increased.[17]
Antoninus' policy was to keep good magistrates in the same
posts for a prolonged period.   We hear of provincial governors
remaining for seven and nine years in the same districts,
while Gavius Maximus held the praetorian prefecture for
twenty years and received the *ornamenta consularia*.[18]   Nor
were there any marked signs of discontent with Antoninus'
rule.   Catilius Severus, disappointed in his personal aspirations, was the spokesman of a small party dissatisfied at
Hadrian's choice of a successor, but the opposition seems to
have been quelled by the deposition of Catilius from his
office of *praefectus urbi*.   Later Atilius Titianus made an
unsuccessful attempt to seize supreme power and was condemned to death by the Senate, but Antoninus showed
his clemency by forbidding the Senate to search out his
accomplices.

   But, if the dignity of the Senate was thus enhanced, there
were few signs of a revival of its ancient powers, and the
restoration by Marcus of the *IV-viri iuridici*[19] suggests that
even its resumed administration of Italy was incompetent.

Antoninus with his long association with the Senate was alive
to its weakness and inefficiency and, while ready to flatter
its pride by rendering an account of his actions and inviting
its criticism, he reserved for his imperial *consilium* the
discussion of all matters of administrative importance. The
constitution of this privy council remained according to the
principles laid down by Hadrian. Its members fell into two
categories, senators and knights, and a select number of
jurisconsults among whom were the praetorian prefects, who
at this period were regularly prominent lawyers. Antoninus
appointed to the council the four praetorian prefects who
held office during his principate, Gavius Maximus, Tatius
Maximus, Fabius Repentinus and Cornelius Victorinus.[20]
Capitolinus states that the Emperor never made any decisions
on provincial matters without consulting his " *amici*," and
that numerous legal principles were laid down by him upon
the advice of his councillors. Among the former mention
may be made of the grant of Latin rights to the Catali and
Carni,[21] two tribes that were " attributed " to the town of
Tergeste, and among the latter of the simplification of the
laws of inheritance, the protection of the interests of minors,
and regulations governing manumission and the relation of
masters and slaves.[22] These latter measures, if containing
little that was new, were at least beneficial in elucidating
some of the obscurities of Roman law.

(b) *Rome and Italy.*

One of the earliest acts of Antoninus was to return to the
Italians the whole of the *aurum coronarium*,[23] which was the
customary offering on the accession of a new Emperor, and
the rest of his Principate was characterized by a wise economic
policy, which combined an avoidance of extravagance with a
generous assistance for public works of utility. The renovation of the mole of the harbour at Puteoli was completed,[24] a
harbour at Caieta and another at Tarracina were restored.[25]
A bridge was thrown across the Trerus near Fregellae,[26] and
the Aemilian Way some eighteen miles south of Pisa was
reconstructed.[27] If such expenditure assisted the commerce
of Italy, the social welfare of the people was not neglected.
The baths at Ostia begun by Hadrian were finished,[28] and
the amphitheatre at Capua was dedicated.[29] The charitable

endowments that had been inaugurated by Nerva and
Trajan were further developed by the institution of *puellae
Faustinianae* in memory of the Empress, who upon her death
in A.D. 140 received divine honours from the Senate. [30]

In his *congiaria* to the commons at Rome and in his
elaborate games and spectacles Antoninus may perhaps be
thought unduly indulgent and munificent. On the coins of
nine separate years his *Liberalitas* is recorded, and it is estimated that the total expenditure was at the rate of 800
denarii a recipient. [31] At the same time life in Rome was not
free from misfortunes. We hear of a famine, a disastrous fire
which destroyed 340 houses, and a collapse of the buildings
in the Circus involving the death of more than a thousand
spectators. Antoninus' generosity was not ill-judged extravagance, but a prudent attempt to restore and maintain
confidence in his government. A final proof that his
economic policy was sound is provided by the full treasury
which he bequeathed to his successor. [32]

(c) *Foreign Wars.*

Although the principate of Antoninus is associated with
peace rather than war, some of the provinces were harassed
by serious insurrections. The Britons, Capitolinus states,
were subdued by Lollius Urbicus, who after driving back
the barbarians erected "another wall of turf." [33] Although
the biographer gives no indication of the site nor length of
the new wall, numerous inscribed stones found between the
Forth and Clyde prove that it was here that the wall or
vallum was constructed, while two fragmentary tablets
supply the name of Lollius as governor of the province. [34]
His governorship began in A.D. 140, or a year later, and the
acceptance by Antoninus of an imperial salutation in A.D. 142
or 143 combined with the contemporaneous issue of coins
commemorating the subjugation of Britain makes it practically certain that it was at this time that the work was
begun. [35] The new *limes*, which extended over a distance of
more than thirty-seven miles, began at Bridgeness on the
Forth and ended at Old Kilpatrick on the Clyde. Its two
most formidable features were the Rampart and the Ditch,
along the southern side of which ran the Military Way.
At average intervals of approximately two miles forts,

nineteen in number, were erected on sites which Agricola had chosen for his *castella*. Most of these abutted directly on the *vallum* which served as their northern defence, and all of those that have been excavated were, with the exception of two, crossed from east to west by the Military Way. Compared with the Agricolan forts they were of much larger dimensions and more substantially built, while the *vallum* represents an innovation that had been exploited by Domitian in the Dobrudja and incorporated by Hadrian in the system of frontier defences. The combination of Rampart, Ditch and Fort gave the appearance of a solid barrier extending from sea to sea, but this aspect is liable to obscure their purpose. The Antonine *limes* does not fall into the category of fortifications known as " continuous lines." The army in Britain was not large enough to provide troops to garrison its whole length, apart from the wasteful expenditure of man-power that such a scheme would have involved. Further, such a conception was alien to the Roman theory of frontiers. A *limes* was an arrangement which was designed with thoughts of peace and not of war. Its functions were to a considerable extent political and administrative. The intention of the Antonine *limes* was the overawing of the barbarians that lived to the south as well as to the north of it, which is further attested by the strength of the southern defences of some of the forts. It was not anticipated that it could successfully withstand a massed attack in the event of an insurrection on a large scale. The forts were observation posts that could communicate with each other by fire-signals and give timely warning of raiding parties of cattle-lifters or smugglers. The Ditch by its clear demarcation of Roman territory was a warning to the barbarians to respect the sanctity of Roman soil and a foil to unauthorized wheeled traffic. The Rampart assisted the work of the frontier-police and protected the Military Way, along which supplies were continually being transported. The whole *limes* was a symbol of Roman sovereignty.[36]

The construction of the *limes* was not an incident in a campaign, but marked the end of a successful war. The work was allotted to squads drawn from the three British legions, while the auxiliaries acted as covering troops and built the forts that were to be their garrison-homes. As each squad completed the sector assigned to it, it erected at either end a slab dedicated to the Emperor and stating the amount of work that had been carried out.[37] On the terminal slab at Old Kilpatrick is depicted a figure of Victory in an attitude of deep repose, an indication that the power of the Caledonians had been temporarily broken by Lollius Urbicus and his army.[38] Other inscriptions show that when the *limes* was finished some of the legionaries remained behind for garrison duties. This unusual practice both indicates that there were insufficient auxiliaries available and furnishes clear proof that the Hadrianic line was not evacuated. What Lollius Urbicus did was not to replace one frontier by another, but to provide Britain with a double line of defence.[39]

This scheme was not an unqualified success. For although the Romans were able to maintain themselves in the northern isthmus for another forty years, they were faced with serious trouble in the country that lies between the two walls. In the governorship of Julius Verus the Brigantes broke into revolt. Birrens was destroyed and the conflagration in all probability spread to the Antonine forts. Reinforcements were sent from Germany, and it was only after three years that peace was restored and the damage to the forts repaired.[40]

In Transrhenane Germany important developments took place in the frontier defences, which have an interesting connection with the construction of the Antonine Wall in Scotland. For the first time detachments of Brittones organised in *numeri* are found in the Odenwald and along the line of the middle Neckar from Neckarburken to Benningen. These units in all probability were composed of Britons whom Antoninus evicted from the area lying between the two walls and transplanted to Germany, settling them as *coloni* on the crown domains along the Neckar, and probably also beyond the frontier, on condition that they assisted in the defence of the Empire. They were further distinguished by local names derived from the districts in which they were stationed, as for instance the Murrenses from the river Murr near Benningen. This settlement of Brittones had important results in the history of the German frontier. On the Odenwald line the older wooden towers were replaced by stone ones, and small stone forts were erected near the larger

cohort fortresses on the Neckar. Of even greater importance
is the pushing forward of the frontier and the construction
of an advanced line of defence. This new frontier, which
may have had for one of its purposes the protection of the
new British settlers, ran from Miltenberg to Haghof near
Lorch, and throughout the greater part of its length followed
a straight line. Seven forts, which with one exception were
of normal cohort size, were constructed at intervals, and
in front of them at distances varying from two hundred
yards to a mile a palisade with stone watch-towers was
erected.

The auxiliary cohorts were then moved forward from the
old forts on the Neckar to garrison the forts on the advanced
line. The new frontier was thus drawn so as to connect in as
straight a line as possible the northern terminus on the river
Main with its southern objective Lorch, where the Raetian
limes began. Here, too, extensive developments were
effected and the frontier reached its final limit. Similarly
constructed to the German *Pfahlgraben* it now ran from Lorch
eastwards through Buch and Dambach to its final limit at
Hienheim. The Domitianic forts, too, were in large measure
replaced by others situated on or a few miles to the south
of the new *limes*. Thus in the western section Aalen on the
Kocher took the place of Heidenheim, and Scherenhof on
the south bank of the Rems that of Donnstetten, while on
the eastern sector forts were constructed at Pfünz, Kösching
and Regensburg, which under Marcus Aurelius became the
camp of his new legion III *Italica*.[41]

The provinces of Numidia and Mauretania suffered from
the attentions of robbers and brigands, who in Antoninus'
principate seem to have become a serious menace to the
prosperity of the country. As early as A.D. 145 a detachment of VI *Ferrata* in Judaea was sent to reinforce the African
legion, and built a road across the hills behind Lambaesis in
an attempt to open up the *Saltus Arausius*, which afforded a
safe harbourage to the brigands, while Fronto speaks of the
danger of travelling in Mauretania.[42] The brigands were
gradually driven out of Numidia, but in Mauretania a general
revolt broke out which necessitated a vigorous campaign.
Reinforcements were brought from the Rhine and Danube
legions ;[43] Titus Varus Clemens was in command of *auxilia*

from Spain,[44] and cavalry detachments were sent from Upper and Lower Pannonia.[45] By A.D. 150 the Mauri seem to have been driven into the extreme west of Mauretania, and the revolt was sufficiently quelled to justify the discharge or return to their headquarters of the troops that had been drafted from Europe.

There is little more fighting that calls for special comment. Soon after the war in Mauretania a revolt broke out in Upper Egypt, which may have been caused by the severity of the λειτουργίαι imposed upon the natives ; for an edict of M. Sempronius Liberalis, prefect in A.D. 154, speaks of the flight of Egyptians from their homes.[46] On the Danube the Dacians revolted, and were put down by M. Statius Priscus in A.D. 158,[47] and, possibly as a result of this rebellion, Upper and Lower Dacia were divided into three districts known as Apulensis, Malvensis and Porolissensis, each under the control of an imperial procurator. Further east the semi-barbarous tribe of the Tauroscythae attacked the neighbouring town of Olbia, which was assisted by a detachment of Roman *auxilia*, while the Alani seem to have been molesting the petty states lying round the eastern end of the Black Sea. No details of their activities are known, but perhaps the institution of Pacorus as king of the Lazi by Antoninus may have been an attempt to curtail any further encroachments.[48]

The policy of the Emperor was to employ diplomacy rather than arms in settling any disputes that arose. A coin struck between the years A.D. 140–143 speaks of a king given to the Armenians,[49] and Capitolinus states that the Parthian King Vologeses III was deterred from upsetting this arrangement " *solis litteris*." This harmony between Rome and Parthia, however, was no more than a temporary compromise. In the last years of Antoninus' principate L. Neratius Proculus was sent to Syria with detachments " *ob bellum Parthicum*,"[50] and, although a peace was soon patched up, the danger was only postponed and not averted. Nor was Parthia the only problem in the East. Abgarus of Edessa had attacked one of the neighbouring princes, and was only deterred from further aggression by the admonition of Antoninus.[51] Although the Emperor's negotiations were successful in avoiding open hostilities, yet in a sense they played into the hands of his enemies, who were able to concentrate their resources and choose their own time for challenging the armies of Rome.

On March 7th, A.D. 161, Antoninus died peacefully at his palace at Lorium, after three days' illness.   In the presence of his prefects he entrusted the State to the care of Marcus, and to the tribune of the guard gave as his final watchword " Peace of Mind."   His body was laid to rest in the Mausoleum of Hadrian, and his memory was consecrated without a murmur of dissent by the Senate.[52]

CHAPTER II

MARCUS AURELIUS

§ 1. THE MEDITATIONS

THE principate of Marcus Aurelius marks the beginning of the decline of the Roman Empire. The peace that had prevailed with few interruptions under the equitable rule of Antoninus was succeeded by a period of incessant warfare. The northern frontier was overrun, and for the first time for three hundred years the sanctity of Italian soil was violated by German invaders. The legions returning from the Parthian war brought with them plague, that spread over the Western empire and decimated its population. Internally the State was brought to the verge of bankruptcy and, when on the death of the Emperor the government passed into the hands of his profligate son, the Principate, that curious blend of constitutional monarchy that had been founded by Augustus and developed by his successors, came to an end, and the way was paved for the advance of military despotism. But apart from these momentous factors in the history of Rome stands out the personal tragedy of Marcus himself, the sacrifice of a life intended by nature for the pursuit of learning to the demands of an active public service, the triumph of an indomitable spirit over physical weakness, the surrender of a soul to the Will of God. In the evening of Rome's greatness her ruler fittingly personified the virtues that had been her glory.

From his early years Marcus shewed an aptitude for learning, and at the age of fourteen, like many another Roman boy, began his training as an orator. His Latin tutor, M. Cornelius Fronto, for whom Marcus retained a sincere affection throughout his life, had high, if perhaps exaggerated, hopes of a brilliant career, but to his unconcealed disgust his pupil

14

abandoned oratory and sought out the society of philosophers.[1] Philosophy, since it had found a second home in
Rome, had abandoned metaphysical speculation and concentrated upon the formulation of a rule of life. Foremost
in promoting this change of interest was Stoicism, which had
modified its earlier teaching so as to effect a bridge between
belief and practice. For the impersonal " world-soul " had
been substituted a benevolent providence, which guides the
world to a " far-off divine event." The soul of man is a spark
of this world-spirit, and it is his duty to live in conformity
with its will. Stoicism had thus become a religious creed and
its exponents moral preceptors, more interested in directing
conduct than in arguing the metaphysical grounds from
which their ethical system was derived. Marcus received his
early education in Stoic principles from Junius Rusticus,
from whom he obtained the impression that " his character
required improvement," and from whom he learnt not to be
led astray into sophistic emulation nor to writing on speculative matters.[2] To him also he expresses gratitude for being
made acquainted with the teaching of Epictetus, whose
famous dictum " if thou art fascinated by speculative
problems, sit still and meditate thereon ; but never call
thyself a philosopher " seems to be reflected in the Meditations. Marcus himself was not a great philosopher but a
deeply religious man, who attempted to regulate his life in
accordance with the rules of the creed that he accepted.
    During the long campaigns on the Danube it was his
practice to seek relief from the noise of war in the quiet of
his own reflections, and in the volume of his *Meditations*,
which is less of a philosophy or an autobiography than a
book of devotions, he has described the faith that he held and
the rules that he sought to follow in his relations with God
and man. " Everything harmonizes with me which is harmonious with Thee, O Universe. Nothing for me is too early
nor too late, which is in due time for Thee. Everything is
fruit to me which Thy seasons bring, O Nature ; from Thee
are all things, in Thee are all things, to Thee all things
return. The poet says, Dear city of Cecrops, and wilt not
Thou say, Dear city of Zeus ? "[3] Again he puts forward his
ideal of conduct. " Take care that thou art not made into
a Caesar, that thou art not dyed with this dye ; for such

things happen. Keep thyself then simple, good, pure, serious,
free from affectation, a friend of justice, a worshipper of the
gods, kind, affectionate, strenuous in all proper acts. Strive
to continue to be such as philosophy wished to make thee
Reverence the gods, and help men. Short is life. There is
only one fruit of this life on earth, a pious disposition and
philanthropic acts. Do everything as a disciple of Antoninus."[4] " Be not ashamed to be helped ; for it is thy business
to do thy duty like a soldier in the assault on a town. How
then, if being lame thou canst not mount up on the battlements alone, but with the help of another thou art able ? "[5]
" When thou art troubled about anything, thou hast forgotten
this, that all things happen according to the universal nature ;
and forgotten this, that a man's wrongful act is nothing to
thee ; and further thou hast forgotten this, that everything
which happens, always happened so and will happen so, and
now happens so everywhere ; forgotten this too, how close is
the kinship between a man and the whole human race ; for
it is a community not of a little blood or seed but of intelligence."[6] And the last words of the book : " Man thou hast
been a citizen in the great world State : what difference does
it make to thee whether for five or three years ? For that
which is conformable to the laws is just for all. Where is the
hardship then, if no tyrant nor yet an unjust judge sends
thee away from the State, but Nature who brought thee
into it ?—just as if a praetor who has employed an actor dis-
misses him from the stage.—' But I have not finished the five
acts but only three of them.'—Thou sayest well, but in life
the three acts are the whole drama ; for what shall be a complete drama is determined by him who was once the cause
of its composition, and now of its dissolution ; but thou art
the cause of neither. Depart then satisfied, for he also who
releases thee is satisfied."[7]

Placed amidst surroundings that would try the strongest
faith Marcus lived true to his religious beliefs, and posterity
reverenced his simple goodness. But the spiritual aloofness
and self-sufficiency that were the pillars of the Stoic creed
left him devoid of that sympathetic understanding of human
nature which is essential to the good statesman. It is a tragic
irony that the noblest example of Roman virtue failed in the
task of governing the Roman World.

§ 2. HIS CAREER DOWN TO A.D. 161

Marcus, who was born at Rome on April 26th, A.D. 121, was called after his maternal great-grandfather, Catilius Severus. He was the son of Annius Verus, who died while holding the office of praetor in A.D. 130, and upon being adopted by his grandfather went to live in his house, which stood near the present site of the Lateran, and assumed the name of Marcus Annius Verus. His mother was Domitia Lucilla, the daughter of Calvisius Tullus. His father's family had come originally from Spain and both his grandfathers had the distinction of holding the consulship twice.[8] At an early age he attracted the attention of Hadrian who nick-named him *Verissimus,* and on assuming the *toga virilis* he was betrothed to the daughter of Aelius Verus, who was designated as the next Emperor. When Aelius died there is no doubt that Hadrian would have adopted Marcus as his successor but for the barrier of his youth. Instead, as we have seen, he chose Antoninus, but with the condition that he should also adopt Marcus. On passing into the family of Antoninus, Marcus took the names of Marcus Aelius Aurelius Verus Caesar,[9] but was commonly known as Marcus Aurelius Caesar.[10] In 139 he held the office of quaestor, and was appointed a *sevir turmarum equitum Romanorum.*[11] In the same year his engagement to Aelius' daughter was broken off, and contrary to Hadrian's arrangement he was betrothed to Antoninus' daughter Faustina, whom he married in A.D. 145. During Antoninus' principate he held the consulship twice with his adoptive father as colleague,[12] and in A.D. 146, after the birth of his eldest daughter, he was given the *tribunicia potestas,*[13] the *proconsulare imperium extra urbem,* and, according to Capitolinus, the *ius quintae relationis.*[14] The titles of *imperator* and Augustus, however, he did not possess and, although consulted by Antoninus on affairs of State, he always maintained an attitude of deference to his imperial position and of sincere respect for his statesmanship. On his deathbed Antoninus entrusted to him the care of the State.

§ 3. THE JOINT RULE OF MARCUS AND VERUS

Marcus' first act as Emperor was to assume L. Aurelius Commodus as his imperial colleague, and to give him the title of Augustus. For the first time in the history of Rome the principle of collegiality was extended to the title of Augustus—*tunc primum Romanum imperium duos Augustos habere coepit*[15]—and administrative measures were enacted under the joint authority of the two Emperors.[16] Marcus took the name of Antoninus and gave his own name Verus to his colleague, with whom he held the consulship of 161. On an inscription of A.D. 162 their titles appear as " Imperator Caesar Marcus Aurelius Antoninus Augustus trib. pot. XVI, consul III " and " Imperator Caesar Lucius Aurelius Verus Augustus trib. pot. II, consul II."[17] The inauguration of this new government was celebrated by a *congiarium* to the people and this was repeated, and a donative added for the soldiers, on the occasion of the betrothal of Marcus' daughter Lucilla to Verus. The system of charitable endowments was also further extended by the institution of *pueri ac puellae Lucilliani et Veriani*.[18]

The first two years of the new régime were clouded by misfortune. The Tiber flooded its banks, Cyzicus experienced an earthquake,[19] and famine was widespread in the province of Galatia.[20] More serious was the news from the frontiers. The Catti invaded the provinces of Germany and Raetia, a revolt broke out in Britain, and Vologeses entered Armenia and put Pacorus, a prince of the Royal House, upon the throne. Although peace was restored on the Rhine and in Britain by the provincial governors Aufidius Victorinus[21] and Calpurnius Agricola,[22] in the East disasters befell the Roman armies. M. Sedatius Severianus, the governor of Cappadocia, crossed the Euphrates to meet the advance of Vologeses, but was defeated and killed at Elegeia, where Trajan had received the submission of Parthamasiris.[23] The Parthians then turned south and invaded Syria, inflicting a second defeat on the Roman troops which were under the command of L. Attidius Cornelianus.[24] In this crisis the presence of an Emperor was imperative, and Marcus with the approval of the Senate appointed his colleague to the supreme command, hoping no doubt that the responsibilities of his position might bring out the finer qualities of his nature and curb his love of indulgence and amusement. Reinforcements were sent from Europe, and in addition to detachments from the army on the Danube three whole legions were dispatched to the war. I *Minervia*, under M. Claudius Fronto,[25] and V *Macedonica*, under P. Martius Verus,[26] were added to the army of Cappadocia, and put under the supreme command of M. Statius Priscus, who, as we have seen, had defeated the Dacians in A.D. 158, and had subsequently been governor of Britain,[27] while II *Adiutrix*, under Q. Antistius Adventus, reinforced the Syrian army.[28]

Verus left Rome on March 28th, 162, but partly through illness and partly through the pursuit of pleasure his journey was leisurely, and he did not reach Antioch before the beginning of the next year.[29] Fortunately for Rome his subordinates were able generals.

The war was waged in two separate stages and in two distinct areas, Armenia and Parthia. In A.D. 163 Statius Priscus invaded Armenia and succeeded in capturing Artaxata. The old capital was destroyed and a new city—καινὴ πόλις— the modern Etchmiadzin, was built in its place. This campaign was decisive. As both Emperors held the auspices in equal measure each received an imperial salutation. The title *Armeniacus* was conferred upon Verus, but Marcus' characteristic modesty led him to refuse its acceptance, in order that he might not detract from his colleague's glory, till A.D. 164, when the Armenian episode ended and the country was pacified by the coronation of the Achaemenid Sohaemus.[30] In the next year the Parthian War began. Avidius Cassius, the son of a Syrian rhetorician named Heliodorus,[31] had been put in command of the Syrian army, and during the Armenian campaign had, it may be supposed, been devoting his attentions to the restoration of discipline in the demoralized troops in the province.[32] When the restoration of peace in Armenia set free the corps under Priscus, his troops were concentrated with those of Cassius for the campaign against Parthia. It seems probable that hostilities opened with two separate invasions of Mesopotamia. Cassius with one army forced the crossing of the Euphrates at Zeugma, captured Edessa, where a Nabataean had been set up as king in place of the Roman vassal Mannos,

and pushed forward to Nisibis which capitulated. The other
contingent after a victory at Sura, on the right bank of
the Euphrates, crossed the river and stormed Nicephorium.
These victories were signalized by a third imperial salutation
for both Emperors and the title *Parthicus Maximus* for
Verus, which Marcus again forbore assuming till the following
year.[33] Probably the two armies wintered in Mesopotamia,
and in the following year the campaign was brought to a
triumphant conclusion by the capture of Seleucia and
Ctesiphon, which was razed to the ground, and perhaps by a
further demonstration in Media. Peace was made with
Parthia, and, although the Roman troops were withdrawn,
Mesopotamia, through the re-establishment of Mannos at
Edessa, became a Roman protectorate.[34] In view of the
complete success of the campaign the terms seem disappoint-
ing. But Rome's purpose was not the subjugation of Parthia,
but the assertion of her sovereign rights in Mesopotamia.
The inactivity of her rival for many years to come was the
justification of her policy.

Verus returned to Rome, and in the autumn of A.D. 166
both Emperors celebrated a great triumph.[35] To mark the
occasion the two young sons of Marcus, Commodus and
Verus, aged five and three, received the title of *Caesar* and
took part in the triumphal procession. But already the
storm clouds were gathering afresh. The legions returning
from the East brought with them plague, which is said to
have broken out at the storming of Seleucia.[36] Sweeping over
the Roman world it left many districts almost depopulated
and contributed perhaps more than any other factor to the
decline of the Empire. At the same time Italy was suffering
from famine, and the northern frontier was in a state of unrest.

The northern defences of the Empire had been weakened
by the withdrawal of large bodies of troops for the Parthian
War, and the tribes living beyond the Upper Rhine and
Danube, under pressure from the Germans of Central and
Northern Europe, saw in the dislocation of the Roman
frontier garrisons an opportunity of appropriating land for
a new home for themselves inside the Empire. Probably as
early as A.D. 165 news of their suspected intentions reached
Rome, and a levy was held in Italy by which two legions,
subsequently called II and III *Italicae*, were raised. These

were sent north as a protection for Italy and the Alps in the following year.[37] At length, about the time when the Emperors were celebrating their triumph, the storm broke. The barbarians swarmed into the provinces of Raetia, Noricum and Pannonia, and, perhaps in the spring of the following year, crossed the Alps, burned Opitergium and laid siege to Aquileia, which was only saved by the strength of its natural fortifications.[38] Fortunately there were able officers in charge of the provinces, Ti. Claudius Pompeianus in Lower Pannonia, M. Claudius Fronto in Upper Moesia, and the future Emperor Pertinax in Raetia.[39] By the early summer of A.D. 167 the danger in Pannonia seems to have been past, as the discharge of veterans and a fifth, if un-official, imperial acclamation indicate.[40] Some of the German tribes, however, turned east and seized the gold mines of Alburnum in Dacia. To meet this danger Dacia, which was raised to the status of a consular province by the addition of a second legion (V *Macedonica*), was added to the command of Fronto, who successfully stemmed the invasion.[41] Mean-while Pertinax was gradually beating back the more westerly band of invaders, and when the two Emperors, whose depar-ture from Rome had been delayed by the crisis created by the plague and shortage of food till the late autumn of A.D. 167, reached Aquileia, the barbarians withdrew and asked for a truce.[42] So satisfactory was the general situation by the summer of the next year that Verus favoured an immediate return to Rome.[43] But Marcus mistrusted the good faith of the invaders and crossed the Alps to inspire terror by a military demonstration. The Emperors returned to Aquileia for the winter, and when plague broke out afresh set out for Rome in the spring. On the journey Verus died of an apoplectic fit at Altinum. His body was taken to Rome and buried in the Mausoleum of Hadrian; his name was canonized.[44]

§ 4. MARCUS AS SOLE EMPEROR

The death of Verus was as salutary for the Empire as it must have been welcome to Marcus. His love of ease and luxury had rendered him incapable and untrustworthy in a position of independent responsibility, and so far from providing the driving power that his colleague lacked he had become a clog in the machine of government. The first experiment in joint-sovereignty had ended in failure.

Marcus remained in Rome till the autumn of A.D. 169, when the renewed activities of the Germans again necessitated his personal intervention.[45] The State was faced with a severe financial crisis and, rather than impose fresh taxation upon the provincials, the Emperor held an auction in Trajan's Forum of the crown jewels, the gold and crystal vessels of the palace, and his wife's gold and silk dresses.[46] His daughter Lucilla, Verus' widow, he gave in marriage to Pompeianus, and left Rome in his charge when he set out in company with his new praetorian prefect, M. Bassaeus Rufus, for the north. He was absent from Rome for the next eight years.[47]

It is impossible to follow the course of the new war in detail. The literary evidence is fragmentary and reliefs on the column set up in Rome after Marcus' triumph treat of interesting episodes in the campaigns, but do not provide a coherent narrative. It seems clear, however, that there were really two wars, the German and the Sarmatian. From A.D. 170–172 Marcus was engaged with the Marcomanni and their neighbours the Quadi, and made Carnuntum his base.[48] During the first year and a half there was continuous fighting, and it was not till late in A.D. 171 that a decisive victory over the Marcomanni at the crossing of the Danube, for which the Emperor accepted his sixth salutation, was gained.[49] The following year was spent in pacifying the country,[50] and, probably in the next winter, Marcus transferred his headquarters to Sirmium with the intention of crushing the Iazyges, who two years previously had defeated and killed Fronto, the governor of Dacia.[51] The work of subjugation was, however, interrupted by a renewed insurrection of the Quadi, and Marcus had to hasten back to the Upper Danube. It was probably in this campaign that the battle was fought which gave rise to the Christian legend of the Thundering Legion. The story goes that the Roman troops exhausted by heat and thirst were on the point of defeat when in answer to the prayers of the Christian soldiers of legion XII—subsequently called The Thunderer—the heavens opened, and while the parched throats of the Romans were slaked by kindly rain, the eyes of the enemy were dazzled by lightning and blinded by hail. It is unnecessary to expose the impossible elements in this picturesque romance, but the episode was so far authentic that it found a place on Marcus' column, where a giant figure is depicted dropping water from his hair and arms upon the weary Romans.[52] More important was the ensuing victory of the Romans in A.D. 174, which effectively broke the resistance of the Quadi.[53] Marcus was thus free again to deal with the Iazyges, and in the late summer of the next year a great victory, which was celebrated by an eighth imperial acclamation and the assumption of the title *Sarmaticus*, ended the Sarmatian War.[54] But before this final campaign had reached its triumphant conclusion news had reached Sirmium of the revolt of Avidius Cassius, who had been left as commander-in-chief in the East after the Parthian War, and although, as we shall see, the usurpation was of very short duration, it undoubtedly deterred Marcus from carrying out his contemplated project of two new provinces in Marcomannia and Sarmatia.[55] Instead he contented himself with a settlement, part of which was of grave import for the future of Rome. The Roman subjects, numbering not less than 160,000, that had been taken prisoners were restored ; the Marcomanni and Iazyges were ordered to move back a distance of some five miles and a neutral zone was established on the left bank of the Danube, while the trading rights of both peoples were sharply defined, the Iazyges being granted a right of way through Dacia to their kinsmen the Roxolani. Other tribes were settled in the depopulated areas of Pannonia, Moesia, Dacia and Germany, with limited rights of free movement. At the same time they were made liable for military service in defence of the frontiers, and Germans of fighting age were enlisted as Roman mercenaries.[56] The Roman provinces thus began to be populated with barbarian settlers in a semi-emancipated condition, and Germans were employed to fight Germans. Two precedents were thus established, which were imitated by subsequent Emperors, and which in time completely transformed the ethnical character of the Roman Empire.

During the Marcomannic War the peace of other parts of the Empire was disturbed by bands of marauders. In A.D. 170 the Costoboci left their home on the eastern slopes of the Carpathians and broke into the province of Lower Moesia, whose garrison was now reduced to a single legion,

by way of Adamklissi. Continuing their raid, perhaps by
sea, they penetrated as far as Elatea in Phocis and Eleusis,
where they stormed the shrine of the Mysteries.[57] L. Julius
Julianus was sent against them with a detachment of troops,[58]
and the Costoboci returned to their own country where an
unexpected fate awaited them. Their neighbours, the
Asdingi, in search of fresh land made a sudden incursion, and
driving out the Costoboci settled in their territory. Perhaps
the latter became later merged with the Thracian Carpi.[59]
In 172 a revolt of " the Shepherds " in Egypt was crushed by
Avidius Cassius,[60] and the Mauri made a series of piratical
raids on the coasts of Africa and Spain. Serious apprehension was felt for the safety of the corn-supply and the
trade of the Western Mediterranean. We hear of a contribution, defrayed in part by the generosity of one Gamala,
by Ostia towards the expenses of a " *bellum navale*,"[61] and it
may be that the establishment of a " *nova classis Libyca* "
dates from this time.[62] Baetica was temporarily handed over
to the Emperor in exchange for Sardinia,[63] and Julius
Julianus after his expedition against the Costoboci was sent
against " the rebellious Moors."[64] These measures seem to
have been effective ; for a diploma granting discharge to a
number of marines in A.D. 173 suggests that in that year
peace was at least temporarily restored.[65] These frequent
wars and the heavy loss of life caused by the plague necessitated extraordinary methods of recruiting. In addition
to the German mercenaries already mentioned, slaves
(*voluntarii*) and gladiators (*obsequentes*) were pressed into
service.[66] Dalmatian brigands were incorporated in cohorts
charged with the protection of the roads of Pannonia,[67] the
diogmitae or police-soldiers of Asia Minor were employed as
auxiliaries,[68] and it may be that a contingent was levied at
Sparta, which was normally exempt from the obligation of
furnishing troops, for Verus' Parthian campaign.[69]

According to Cassius Dio, Avidius Cassius, who had revolted
while Marcus was still waging the Sarmatian War, was
instigated by the Empress Faustina, because in anticipation
of the early death of her husband she was afraid lest Commodus should be passed over in the succession and she herself
in consequence robbed of her imperial position.[70] Whatever
the truth of this alleged complicity, there seems no doubt

that the salutation of Cassius as Emperor was hastened by a false report of Marcus' death. The news occasioned great alarm in Rome ; for although the governors of Bithynia and Cappadocia, Clodius Albinus and Martius Verus, were loyal, Cassius held Syria and Egypt, the chief granary of the city. Marcus summoned Commodus to the camp at Sirmium and, investing him on July 7th, A.D. 175, with the *toga virilis*,[71] prepared to go to the East in company with his wife and son, and supported by an army drawn from the Danubian legions. But before he had started news came of the murder of Cassius, and his head was sent to Marcus, who refused to have it brought into his presence and ordered it to be buried. Fearing, however, for the safety of Martius Verus, Marcus did not cancel his plans, but set out for Syria and Egypt, travelling overland by way of Byzantium, Ancyra and Tarsus.[72] At a village called Halala, lying at the foot of the Taurus Mountains, Faustina died and Marcus wrote to the Senate with instructions for her apotheosis, while the village was honoured by being raised to the rank of a colony.[73] Continuing his journey through Syria and avoiding Antioch, which was still holding out against Martius Verus, Marcus reached Egypt in the early spring of A.D. 176. Here he spent several months re-establishing the loyalty of the province and treating the accomplices of Cassius with his customary clemency.[74] His return journey was made by the coast of Syria and Asia Minor, whose towns sent loyal deputations to meet him. At Smyrna he made the acquaintance of the rhetorician Aelius Aristides, and at Athens, where he and Commodus were initiated into the Mysteries, he appointed through the agency of Herodes Atticus professors for the four great philosophical schools, whose stipends he fixed at 40,000 sesterces.[75] Reaching Italy towards the end of the year he celebrated on December 23rd a great triumph with his son, who as a qualification for a share in the triumph had received the title of *imperator* on November 27th.[76] In the following year Commodus held the consulship, and probably in February received the *tribunicia potestas*. At midsummer, when news of further trouble on the northern frontier had been received, the title of Augustus was conferred upon him, and in all probability the occasion coincided with his marriage with Crispina. Thus by gradual stages Commodus was advanced to a full share in the government of the Empire, and the second period of joint-rule began.[77]

§ 5. THE JOINT RULE OF A.D. 177–180

Towards the end of A.D. 177 some success seems to have attended the Roman army in its conduct of the second Germanic War, which, as we have seen, broke out in the summer of that year. At least both Emperors felt justified in accepting an imperial acclamation.[78] But in the following year the tide began to turn. The two Quintilii, who were probably the governors of the Pannonias, were in the words of Dio " unable to put an end to the war,"[79] and Marcus felt himself obliged once again to take the field in person with his son. With his customary deference to the Senate he obtained the permission of that body to draw money from the *aerarium* for the expenses of the war, and doubtless in the hope of securing a line of succession to the Principate, hastened on the marriage of Commodus with Crispina before leaving Rome on August 5th.[80] The next few months were spent in concentrating an army composed of detachments from the German and Danubian garrison legions, and in the summer of the following year Tarrutenius Paternus, prefect of the praetorian guard, gained a decisive victory over the Marcomanni.[81] Marcus, who received with Commodus a further acclamation,[82] determined upon the occupation of the country of the Quadi and Marcomanni in the hope of starving them into submission, and that the policy was bearing fruit is suggested by an abortive attempt of the Quadi to migrate into the land of the Semnones.[83] At last it seemed as if Marcus would realize his ambition of making Marcomannia and Sarmatia Roman provinces, when he became seriously ill. Realizing that his end was near, he sent for his son and charging him not to abandon what was left of the war, commended him to the care of his friends. On March 17th, A.D. 180, he died peacefully in his sleep.[84]

§ 6. THE HOME ADMINISTRATION OF MARCUS

In the sphere of administration the Principate of Marcus has left few signs of positive achievement, and perhaps its

most distinguishing feature is a further increase in bureaucracy. From this time the different officials in the hierarchy
come to be designated by titles peculiar to their rank. The
senator is regularly styled *vir clarissimus*, and the knight *vir
egregius*. The district judges of Italy were revived under the
title of *iuridici*, and were now drawn from senators of
praetorian instead of consular rank. An inscription of the
period records the name of Arrius Antoninus as the first
iuridicus of the Transpadane district.[85] The alimentary system
was centralized under a consular *praefectus* in Rome, and
the district *praefecti* were superseded by equestrian procurators,[86] while the *procurator a rationibus* and the *praefectus annonae* had understudies appointed with the titles of
procurator summarum rerum and *subpraefectus annonae*.[87]
We hear too of the institution of a *praetor tutelaris*, whose
function, which had previously been performed by the two
consuls, was to appoint guardians for minors in Italy under
the age of twenty-five in accordance with the provisions of
the Lex Plaetoria, which Marcus seems to have re-enacted.[88]

Towards the Senate the Emperor maintained an attitude
of studied deference, attending its meetings regularly and
remaining till the consul adjourned the house. He made a
practice of entrusting to it judicial cases which affected his
own person, as when he referred to it with a special com-
mendation to mercy the senators alleged to have been
involved in the revolt of Cassius.[89] In return he enacted that
no knight should be present when senators were tried before
his own court, but although anxious not to put any
senator to death, he refused to take an oath not to do so. His
general interest in justice led him to spend many days over a
single suit, and that equity should not be frustrated by haste
he increased the number of days in the year upon which the
courts could legally sit.[90] Further improvements were made
in the laws of inheritance, and by the *senatus consultum
Orphitianum* children were permitted to inherit property
from their mothers who died intestate.[91] The government
of Marcus may be accorded at least this meed of praise that it
continued unchecked the principles of equity laid down by
Antoninus and his legal advisers.

Posterity has criticized Marcus for entrusting the government of the Empire to a son who was the antithesis of

himself, a cruel and cowardly profligate. He should, it is
argued, have followed the best Stoic principles and have
adopted his son-in-law Pompeianus, a man of proved ability,
as his successor. In the light of subsequent events the justice
of this verdict cannot be denied ; but in defence of Marcus it
may be urged that his choice at the time it was made was not
necessarily as wrong-headed as it is represented. According
to Dio, Commodus was not naturally vicious ; [92] it was the
weakness of his will and the friends with whom he associated
that led him into his later extravagances of pride and
brutality. Marcus may well have hoped when in 177 he
raised his son to the rank of Augustus that co-operation with
himself and the influence of experienced advisers would
stimulate the finer qualities of his nature. Again, even if
in 180, as his dying words would seem to indicate, [93] Marcus
had become aware of a growing degeneracy in his son's
character, he also rightly realized that it was now too late to
change his plans and that to substitute his son-in-law as heir-
apparent was to bequeath to the Roman people an inheritance
of civil war. Such considerations, however, do not exonerate
the Emperor from blame. His confidence in Commodus was
a disastrous error of judgement, which is only mitigated by
its witness to the depth of his human affection. In the
Emperor Julian's satire on the Caesars, Silenus reproaches
Marcus with his choice of a successor, and the Emperor
replies : " As to my son, I have Jupiter's own reasoning ;
for he said to Mars : ' Long ago I would have smitten you
with my thunderbolt, were it not that I love you because
you are my son.' " [94]

The news of Marcus' death was received with genuine
sorrow in Rome. On the day of his funeral after the customary oration, his apotheosis was voted by acclamation
without waiting for the formal resolution of the Senate ;
the temple of Faustina was rededicated in their joint honour,
and the *sodales Antoniniani* added his cult to that of his
adoptive father. [95] The column decreed by the Senate after
his triumph still stands to-day in the Piazza that bears its
name as a memorial of his military successes ; the simple
nobility of his nature is enshrined in his own Meditations.

CHAPTER III

COMMODUS

§ 1. HIS ADMINISTRATION

W ITHIN a few weeks of his father's death and contrary to the advice of Pompeianus, Commodus concluded peace with the German and Sarmatian tribes. The terms were not dissimilar from those imposed by Marcus in 175. Deserters and prisoners were to be returned, contingents of mercenaries supplied, and regulations were made limiting the time and place of public assemblies, and forbidding intertribal warfare. In return Commodus agreed to the payment of a subsidy and the evacuation of all Roman garrisons from the areas which his father had occupied.[1] In themselves these conditions were not unfavourable to Rome if they could have been enforced, and still more if the policy of annexation were regarded as impracticable. Indeed it might be urged that the need for national economy necessitated the abandonment of any scheme of territorial expansion. But even if such a defence may be found for the reversal of Marcus' policy, there can be little doubt that the motives which actuated Commodus were dictated by considerations neither of political expediency nor of economic prudence, but by his own personal distaste for a continued absence from the pleasures and indulgences of life in Rome.

The conclusion of peace was regarded by Commodus as a suitable occasion for the acceptance of his fourth imperial acclamation.[2] In the autumn of 180 he started out on his journey to Rome. The municipal towns through which he passed greeted him with enthusiastic good wishes, and shortly after his arrival in Rome he celebrated a great triumph in which, as a foretaste of future events, his chamberlain Saoterus rode behind him on the triumphal car.[3] Vows were

taken by the Senate and army for the safety of the new
Emperor, and a *congiarium* was distributed among the
people.[4] Commodus further signalized his accession to the
sole government of the Empire by assuming the surname of
Antoninus and by substituting for his own name Lucius
that of his father Marcus.[5] On coins struck between A.D. 180
and 191 he is regularly styled Marcus Commodus Antoninus.

For the first two or three years of his rule Commodus
retained a few of his father's ministers. Tarrutenius Paternus
continued in his post of praetorian prefect and Aufidius
Victorinus, who had served with distinction in Germany,
had the honour of a second consulship in A.D. 183 with the
Emperor as his colleague.[6] But even at this early stage of
his principate Commodus had begun to show his determination to govern the Empire through his favourites and a
corresponding contempt for the dignity of the Senate. The
hatred which that body felt towards him found expression
in a plot which was formed to assassinate him towards the
end of A.D. 182.[7] The chief conspirators were Lucilla the
Emperor's sister and her cousin M. Ummidius Quadratus,
and the agent of their crime Cl. Pompeianus Quintianus, who
was probably Lucilla's son-in-law.[8] Drawing his sword
the young assailant rushed to meet the Emperor as he
entered the theatre, but, pausing to utter the words " the
Senate sends you this," he was overpowered before he could
strike a blow. The cry of the assassin reveals the origin of
the plot. It was not the personal immorality of Commodus
—Lucilla herself was very far from being a paragon of virtue
—but his open hostility to the senatorial order that drove
the conspirators to seek in the murder of the Emperor an
escape from further persecution.[9] The failure of the plot
served but to accentuate the evils which it had hoped to
destroy. Quadratus and Quintianus were executed; Lucilla
was banished to Capri and soon put to death; a reign of
terror ensued comparable to the later years of Domitian's
principate under the direction of a succession of imperial
favourites.

The fate of Tarrutenius Paternus was not long delayed.
His colleague was Tigidius Perennis, and until the overthrow
and murder of Saoterus, the Emperor's chamberlain, both
officers had acted in concert.[10] But when one of his rivals

was removed Perennis determined to be rid of the other.
Accordingly he arranged that Paternus should be relieved of
his post of praetorian prefect and " allected " into the
Senate, and, when this supposed honour had been conferred, proceeded to inculpate him in a charge of treason. It
was alleged not that Paternus had been privy to Lucilla's
plot, but that he had joined with Salvius Julianus in a second
conspiracy against the life of Commodus, and the betrothal
of his daughter to Julianus' son was cited as an additional
proof of his guilt.[11] Probably Paternus was innocent, but
the truth or falsity of his allegations was to Perennis a matter
of indifference, provided that his intrigue to secure control
of the government was successful. Commodus believed his
informant and ordered the execution of Paternus and
Julianus. In gratitude for his preservation he decided to
retire from public life and leave the administration of the
Empire to Perennis.[12]

The rule of Perennis which lasted till A.D. 185 is described
by Dio as " incorruptible and circumspect," but there is
little to support this favourable judgement, which may reflect
the historian's gratitude for personal advancement.[13] There
is no indication of any attempt to check the licentious
excesses of Commodus, and it may well be that Perennis was
instrumental in the banishment to Capri of Crispina who
was later put to death,[14] and the substitution of a concubine
Marcia, said to have been a Christian, as chief of the imperial
harem. Perhaps the best that can be said of his government
is that he attempted to counteract the Emperor's personal
extravagances by some measures of national economy. There
was no *congiarium* to the people of Rome between A.D. 182
and 186 and the payments under the alimentary system were
suspended in A.D. 184.[15] But such economies only served to
create discontent, and the sincerity of Perennis' intentions
was vitiated by his own increasing riches. At the same time
he waged continuous war against the Senate. Not only were
some of its leading members, such as the two Quintilii, put
to death on charges of treason, but an attempt was made to
supersede the *legati legionum* with officers of equestrian rank.
This proved the downfall of Perennis. Dio speaks of an
embassy, 1500 strong, from the mutinous army in Britain
which came to Rome to denounce Perennis to Commodus for

treason and demand his head in compensation.[16] But
Herodian's account of his death is the more probable.[17] At
the head of the Illyrian army in A.D. 185 stood one of the sons
of Perennis, both of whom had been entrusted with military
commands. This gave his enemies an opportunity to expose
his alleged design to make his son Emperor, and Cleander,
the new chamberlain, was not slow in fomenting an intrigue.
He prevailed upon the Illyrian soldiers in Rome, in whom
we may recognize the *frumentarii* or dispatch-bearers, to
denounce Perennis to the Emperor and demand his surrender.
With characteristic cowardice Commodus yielded to their
threats. The manner of Perennis' death is variously told.[18]
Most probably he was executed during the night by the
Emperor's command, while his son was induced by false
promises to come to Italy and was murdered on the way.
To commemorate his escape Commodus assumed the title of
Felix[19] in addition to that of *Pius* which he had taken in
A.D. 183, probably as a direct appeal to the memory of
Antoninus, but, as a mocking Senate preferred to say, in
honour of his mother's paramour whom he had nominated
for the office of consul.[20]

For the next four years Cleander was the true ruler of
Rome. By birth a Phrygian he had been sold as a slave and
brought to Rome, and on obtaining his freedom had risen to
the rank of chamberlain of the palace in succession to
Saoterus. On the death of Perennis he did not immediately
receive the office of praetorian prefect; for Commodus,
alarmed at the power which Perennis had wielded, once
again appointed two prefects.[21] In 186 or in the early months
of 187, however, realizing that the prefecture was essential
for his ascendancy in the State, Cleander secured his appointment, but to allay the suspicions of the Emperor nominated
two other prefects. Thus for the first time in the history of
Rome there were three prefects of the praetorian guard.[22]
The years of Cleander's government present in an intensified
form the same features as had characterized the rule of his
predecessor. The extravagance of Commodus in games and
luxuries emptied the treasury and, to compensate these losses,
Cleander resorted to a policy of selling state offices. Freedmen bought their admission to the Senate, and for 190 no
fewer than twenty-five consuls, including the future Emperor

Septimius Severus, were nominated.[23]   Part of the resulting
revenue Cleander handed over to the Emperor to defray his
personal expenses, but he also was successful in amassing a
large private fortune. At last in 189 his hated government fell.
Rome was suffering from a serious shortage of food, and M.
Aurelius Papirius Dionysius, the prefect of the corn supply,
seized the opportunity to inflame the anger of the people
against Cleander, the alleged cause of their sufferings, against
whom he had also perhaps a personal grudge for having been
deposed from his earlier post of prefect of Egypt. A riot
broke out in the Circus, and the mob forced their way despite
the opposition of the praetorians to Commodus' suburban
villa. Once again the Emperor played the coward, and on
the advice of his mistress Marcia handed over his favourite
to the people, just as four years previously he had surrendered Perennis at the bidding of the soldiers.[24]

Commodus next fell under the influence of Marcia, Eclectus
his chamberlain, and Aemilius Laetus who became praetorian
prefect in A.D. 191. His mind seems now to have become
deranged, and in the intoxication of Empire his cruelty was
as monstrous as his vanity was absurd. Attacks upon the
lives of leading senators broke out with renewed violence,
and their property was confiscated to provide resources which
an empty treasury could no longer yield for his senseless
extravagances.[25] Towards the end of A.D. 191 Commodus
reverted to his original names of L. Aelius Aurelius Commodus,[26] and in the last few weeks of his life adopted and
bestowed titles unprecedented alike in number and inanity.
The city of Rome was rebaptized *Colonia Commodiana*[27] and
the same surname was conferred upon the Senate, the legions,
the city of Carthage and the new African corn-fleet.[28] His
own full names and titles, which corresponded to the new
names given to the months, were Lucius Aelius Aurelius
Commodus Augustus Hercules Romanus Exsuperatorius
Amazonius Invictus Felix Pius.[29] Of these the most interesting is the identification of the Emperor with the god
Hercules, and its significance deserves attention.

The cult of Hercules, the great hero who had been rewarded
for his labours and sufferings by deification, had long been
venerated in domestic worship, and as a martyr to duty
he had become the symbol of the Stoic and Cynic creeds.

3

Emperors such as Caligula, Nero and Domitian, who coveted divine honour for themselves in their life-time, had identified themselves with the first man to be apotheosized, and the dynasty of the Antonines, although not pursuing this idea, had not neglected the worship of a hero who had devoted his life to the struggle between good and evil and had championed the cause of civilization which it was now their duty as Roman Emperors to maintain. Believing that an imitation of the life of Hercules would win for them the reward of deification, they set themselves to follow the particular aspect of his career which accorded with their own character. Thus while to Trajan Hercules is the world-conqueror, and to Hadrian the pioneer of travel, to Antoninus he becomes the wrestler with the monsters of Italy, and to Marcus the god of self-sacrifice and devotion to humanity. Commodus combined these different aspects. On his coins Hercules appears not only as the great warrior and victor but as the god of peace, the protector and companion of the Emperor. Finally, dissatisfied with his role as protégé of the god, Commodus, in his desire for apotheosis in his lifetime, allowed himself to be regarded as the incarnation of Hercules himself. Thus he adopts the garb and weapons of Hercules, and in inscriptions and coins of the last weeks of his life he is officially designated as Hercules Romanus.[30]

In order to perfect his identification with Hercules Commodus devoted himself to the calling of a gladiator. Games lasting a fortnight were celebrated in December, 192, at which the Emperor displayed his skill and left-handed prowess in shooting down the countless animals that were provided for his sport.[31] Finally he conceived the idea of appearing on New Year's day before the Roman people as both consul and gladiator.[32] This was beyond the limits of endurance. Marcia, Eclectus and Laetus sought in vain to dissuade him from his intention, and when through the agency of a boy in the palace they received a list of more projected murders,[33] they decided to rid Rome of further humiliation from the monster that was her ruler. When their attempts to poison him failed, they suborned the services of an athlete called Narcissus, who strangled him.[34] Senate and people united in condemning his memory; his statues were pulled down, his name erased from inscriptions, and his body only saved from a traitor's grave in the Tiber through the intervention of Laetus, who gave it secret burial till by the authority of the new Emperor Pertinax it was transferred to the Mausoleum of Hadrian.[35] Thus in the darkness of disillusionment ended the enlightened monarchy of the Antonines.

§ 2.   WARS IN THE PRINCIPATE OF COMMODUS

In this period of internal confusion the Roman Empire was fortunately assailed by only one serious barbarian invasion. After peace had been concluded with the German and Sarmatian tribes Marcus' generals, and in particular Clodius Albinus and Pescennius Niger, devoted their energies to pacifying the Dacians and strengthening the frontier defences.[36] An inscription found near Aquincum speaks of fortresses erected at suitable sites to prevent the inroads of bands of marauders, and, as the name of the general has been erased, it is probable that it refers to Perennis' son, who, as we have seen, had been put in command of the army in Illyricum and who was given the credit, so Lampridius says, for successes gained by his predecessors.[37] Such defensive measures seem to have been effective in stemming any further aggression on the Danube and, when Commodus contemplated a third expedition to the northern front, he was deterred by Senate and people from leaving Rome.[38] In Mauretania the construction of new towers and the restoration of old battlements suggest that the Mauri were again restive,[39] but it was in Britain that the most serious trouble occurred.

In A.D. 184 the Caledonians broke through the frontier defences on the Antonine Wall, annihilating a Roman force and its general and overrunning South Scotland. Ulpius Marcellus, who had been governor of Britain in Marcus' principate, was sent by Commodus against the invaders. Dio describes him as a stern disciplinarian, vigilant and incorruptible, and after three campaigns he successfully stamped out the revolt.[40] The effect of this rebellion upon Roman frontier-policy in Britain is still a controversial question among archæologists. It seems, however, probable that the Antonine *Vallum* was restored, and that a withdrawal to the Tyne-Solway line was delayed for a further twelve years.[41]

On the conclusion of Marcellus' successful campaigns a mutiny broke out in the army. Its cause is not known. Perhaps it was occasioned partly by Perennis' appointment of equestrian legionary commanders, and partly through disappointment that no donative was forthcoming to celebrate the victory. After Perennis' death Pertinax, who had been living in exile in Liguria, was recalled and sent to Britain to restore peace, and coins struck with the legends CONCORDIA MILITUM and FIDES EXERCITUUM show that by 186 he had succeeded in his task.[42] To conciliate the rebellious spirits of the provincial soldiers it is not improbable that Commodus officially sanctioned the worship of their native gods under Roman titles in the military sanctuaries. Thus the cult of Commodus and Hercules came to be associated with that of the supreme Celtic god.[43] Nor were these concessions confined to Britain ; for an altar was set up at Apulum in Dacia between the years A.D. 183 and 185 dedicated to Pater Liber, the Roman equivalent of the chief god of the Dacians.[44] This official recognition of native cults in the worship of the army indicates that the principle of local recruitment was now permanently established.

Spain and Gaul were also the scene of disturbances. A deserter called Maternus waged a successful guerilla warfare against the civil authorities, and flushed by his success conceived the bold plan of coming to Rome in disguise and murdering the Emperor at the festival of the Hilaria in A.D. 187. On the eve of the feast, however, he was betrayed by a friend and beheaded, and Commodus gave thanks for his escape by the splendour with which he celebrated the popular festival.[45] Perhaps the honorary titles ' *pia fidelis constans Commoda* ' conferred upon legion VIII *Augusta* at Argentoratum may be a further reflection of the rising of Maternus in which the legion had stood firm against the rebels, perhaps they have reference to some other unrecorded disturbance. However that may be, the strengthening and enlargement of the fortifications at Niederbieber and Osterburken indicate that the Germans, encouraged no doubt by the unsettled conditions across the frontier, were again threatening an invasion of the Empire.[46]

CHAPTER IV

THE ROMAN WORLD IN THE AGE OF THE ANTONINES

§ 1. THE STATE OF THE PROVINCES

DURING the years of peace which marked the principate of Antoninus Pius the Roman World reached the apex of its material prosperity. The provincials undisturbed for the most part by foreign wars, internal dissensions or epidemics of sickness were free to enjoy the benefits which the wide extension of Roman civilization had placed at their disposal, and apart from the normal imperial obligations were subjected to few additional burdens. To this general welfare, which was the fruit of the Hadrianic policy, Antoninus himself, if making no outstanding contributions, was at least not indifferent. The interest in good government which he had shown during his earlier administration of Asia was reflected in his care for the whole Empire. At the beginning of his principate he returned to the provincials half of the customary *aurum coronarium*—a benefaction which is commemorated in a series of coins struck in A.D. 139[1]—and while governors were retained for long periods in office a tighter check was kept on the imperial procurators. The burdens of the imperial post which fell upon the municipal towns were lightened, and relief was given to Rhodes and the towns of Asia Minor which had suffered from a severe earthquake,[2] and to Antioch, Narbo and Carthage which had been ravaged by fire.[3] Apart from the completion of works begun by Hadrian—an aqueduct for instance at Athens and an amphitheatre at Porolissum in Dacia[4]—the Emperor pursued the same policy of economy in public works which characterized his administration of Italy. Road-making and road-restoration, however, was encouraged as an aid to commerce, especially

37

in Gallia Narbonensis, a district to which Antoninus was
bound by family ties.[5]

Antoninus never left Italy during his Principate (the story
that he visited Syria and Egypt rests upon a misunder-
standing of a speech of Aristides and the unreliable evidence
of Malalas),[6] and this avoidance of imperial tours, if it prevented a personal acquaintance with provincial problems,
at least saved the municipalities the heavy expenditure of
housing and entertaining the Emperor and his retinue.
Instead we hear of embassies coming to Rome and pleading
their cases before the imperial *consilium*. A dispute over
the ownership of some territory between Thisbe and Coronea
was settled by the Emperor's arbitration, and Q. Cornelius
Zosimus, an *Augustalis* from the *pagus Lucretius* near Arelate
in Gaul, was successful in securing for his village through the
indulgence of the *sacratissimus princeps omnium saeculorum*
the use of the public baths from which its inhabitants had
been wantonly excluded.[7]

In his speech εἰς Ῥώμην, delivered perhaps in A.D. 144,
Aelius Aristides describes the state of the Roman Empire
in terms of glowing admiration.[8] The richness and happiness
of all the countries of the Empire testify to the excellence
of Roman government. Everywhere towns have been
founded or restored and a place of honour has been reserved
for Hellenic culture. The Roman World is administered as a
single household which enjoys a perpetual holiday, and is
safeguarded from external aggression by the discipline of
the Roman army. The reigning Emperor is the incarnation
of the spirit of equity. Such are some of the chief points
in a lengthy panegyric, which has been criticized and condemned by some historians as a worthless piece of rhetorical
plagiarism. But although Aristides' utterances have for the
most part little to commend either the veracity or the
originality of their author, the speech εἰς Ῥώμην seems to
come much closer to reality. Further, it is the only work
in which the theory of the power and munificence of Rome
is systematically expounded by a Greek, and in all probability it represents the educated opinion of the upper classes
in the city states of Asia Minor. The prosperity which he
describes is confirmed by many inscriptions set up by the
municipal towns of the Empire in honour of Antoninus Pius.[9]

This state of peaceful contentment did not long survive the death of Pius. During the principate of Marcus a combination of forces sapped the strength of the Empire. Long and expensive wars were waged on the eastern and northern frontiers; plague decimated the population; famine was widespread. At the same time a growth in bureaucracy, an increase in doles to the idle populace of Rome, and the extravagances of Verus helped to empty the full treasury which Antoninus had bequeathed, and to bring the State to the verge of bankruptcy. For this disastrous position the improvident statesmanship of Marcus, whose heart was stronger than his head, must bear a measure of responsibility, but the crisis exposes even more strikingly the superficial character of the Empire's prosperity and the unsoundness of its financial structure. In times of peace the normal revenues were more than sufficient to balance the outgoing expenditure, but little attempt seems to have been made to build up a capital reserve or create a sinking fund to meet an exceptional and unexpected situation. The Empire lived largely from hand to mouth, and consequently, when some extraordinary expense such as a prolonged series of campaigns arose, the necessary funds had to be raised by additional subsidies. Marcus was reduced to auctioning the crown jewels to procure money for his Marcomannic War, but it was the provincials who had to bear the heaviest burdens. These new impositions did not take the form of an increase in the regular taxation, a solution to which most of the Roman Emperors seem to have been opposed. Instead the inhabitants of towns and villages were called upon, on the model of the Greek and Egyptian liturgies, to perform voluntary services. These might be either pecuniary or personal, and the most burdensome were the provision of food, lodging and transport for the imperial troops.

The full effect of this policy was not felt till the next century, but indications of its influence upon the vitality of the municipalities, aggravated as it was by the desolation caused by the plague, were already apparent in the principates of Marcus and his son. The performance of liturgies fell hardest upon the richer citizens, that is upon the very class from which the local senates and magistrates were recruited. Not unnaturally it became difficult to find candidates

who were prepared to accept offices which entailed such
a heavy drain upon their resources; for in addition to
the demands of the imperial government a local senator or
magistrate was expected to contribute generously to the
welfare of his town.[10] At the same time the imperial
government began to encroach further upon the autonomy
of the provincial towns and to appoint an increasing number
of officials called *curatores reipublicae*, drawn from the senatorial or equestrian orders, to supervise their government.[11]
These *curatores*, or λογισταί as they were called in the
Eastern half of the Empire, were first appointed in the
principate of Trajan, and their chief duty was the control
of the financial administration of the municipality to which
they were attached.   In his correspondence with Trajan
Pliny draws a vivid picture of the confusion into which the
towns of Bithynia had fallen through extravagant and
improvident expenditure.   But, if the reason for the institution of *curatores* was primarily the mismanagement of local
funds, its development under Marcus was occasioned by
the additional burdens which a growing system of imperial
requisitions placed upon the financial officials in the municipal
towns.   Nor is the picture of country life a happier one.
To escape the burden of levies and taxation we hear of
Egyptians fleeing from their villages to the swamps of the
Delta,[12] and imperial tenants of the *Saltus Burunitanus* in
Africa complained to Commodus that their annual contribution of labour and produce had been raised beyond its
legal limit and its exaction enforced by the intervention of
soldiers.[13]   With this preponderance of the interests of the
State began the decay of municipal and private liberty,
which culminated in the fourth century in the organization
of the population of the Empire in compulsory associations
under the control of the imperial bureaucracy.

§ 2. THE CULTURE OF THE AGE

The peace and comparative prosperity which the Roman
World enjoyed during Antoninus' principate created a spirit
of false contentment. The government was conservative
and unprogressive ; religion was dormant ; literature was
a rtificial and uncreative. Upon the Empire had settled a

sense of self-satisfaction which found expression in dwelling upon the greatness of Rome's past achievement. This spirit was typified by the Emperor himself. In A.D. 147 he celebrated the 900th birthday of the city and marked the occasion by the issue of a series of coins depicting scenes connected with its origin, and by elevating the Arcadian village of Pallantium, the traditional home of Evander, to the status of a free town.[14] But alone the past glories of Rome were powerless to save her civilization. Renan in his study of Marcus Aurelius has described his reign as " the end of the ancient world," and this exaggerated estimate is serviceable as emphasizing the important transformation which the Roman Empire underwent. There is, of course, no question of a sudden or violent dissolution of the Graeco-Roman civilization which the Principate had inherited from the Republic. The political and military ascendancy of Rome still remained, but the period witnessed the early stages of the triumph of Eastern over Western ideas, which a century later reached their mature development. It was especially in the sphere of religion that these new influences were felt, and to understand the reason for their victory it is necessary to review the circumstances which favoured their extension and sympathetic reception in Western Europe.

(a) Religion

The external factor which facilitated the westward journey of the Oriental cults was the political unity of the Roman Empire, which embraced under a centralized government both the West, to which Rome had given her own civilization, and the Eastern Mediterranean basin, which since Alexander had possessed a common language and culture of its own. Within this vast domain, with its developed system of communications, ample opportunity was given for a free interchange not only of commodities but also of ideas and beliefs. But while the political and military preponderance lay in the West, the centre of the industrial world was in the East. From here emigrants set out for Europe. Some of them, not infrequently Syrian merchants from the Levant, established themselves in small trading communities as far distant as the north of Gaul; others were compelled to seek their fortunes abroad, by working as slaves on the large estates in

Italy or by serving in the houses of the wealthy and in the imperial palace itself. Merchant and slave alike brought with him his particular god, and in his new home remained true to his native religion. Nor was the propagation of these cults confined to the avenues of commerce. The Roman soldier when his unit was moved from East to West carried with him the faith which he practised, and it was the trans-ference by Vespasian of some of the Eastern legions to Europe which more than any other factor established the worship of Mithras in the West.

The tolerant attitude of the Roman government to these foreign religions further assisted their dissemination, nor did its condition of participation in the imperial cult offer any real obstacle to the votaries of such polytheistic creeds. But if the unity of the Roman Empire together with the policy of its government explains how the Eastern cults reached Italy, it does not provide a satisfactory answer to the question why they met with such a ready acceptance. A great religious conquest cannot, it would seem, be ac-counted for on other than moral grounds. Whatever the force of environment and example, in the end it is only personal conversion that can assure its victory.

Now Roman society was ready for a new faith. Among the educated classes there were signs of a reviving interest in ethical problems and a dissatisfaction with the scepticism that had been the pride of their fathers. If a few intellectuals were content like Lucian of Samosata to rest in the con-viction of uncertainty, or like Marcus Aurelius to embrace the cold gospel of Stoicism, there were many who in their despair were ready to accept a faith which professed its ability to justify its teaching. Among the masses the need of a religion was even more insistent. The imperial cult, whatever power it still retained to arouse a sentiment of loyalty to a ruler whose power was all but absolute, was wholly incapable of giving a personal faith. Belief, too, in the State deities was dead or dying and the old animistic religion, if it lingered in the country-side, offered neither hope of happiness nor assurance of immortality. Roman society was ripe for a religious revival and the Oriental cults answered its immediate psychological requirements ; for they appealed to the intellect no less than to the emotions and to conscience.

The civilization of the East, unlike that of Greece and Rome, was sacerdotal. As in Europe during the Middle Ages, so in Asia and in Egypt it was the priests who were the men of learning. In the temples discussion was not confined to ethical and eschatological problems, but mathematics, astronomy and history were also studied. Even if the latter researches were falsified by preconceived notions and scientific enquiry was thereby adversely prejudiced, nevertheless religion acquired from the pursuit of knowledge an influence which it never exercised in Greece and Rome. The philosophy which it preached was dualistic—the antithesis between spirit and matter, between light and darkness, between God and the world. Contrasted with the Greek conception of the immanence of God, it taught a doctrine of a transcendental uncreated deity from which the spirit in man has emanated, and to which after being released from the prison of the body it will return. This act of deliverance calls for a redeemer who shall rescue the soul from the body of death, and by sacramental grace strengthen it in its struggle to reach the light. The knowledge of such a saviour has been granted by revelation ; the power of his redemption is experienced by the faithful who have been initiated into his mysteries. The faith was thus presented with the illusion of profound learning and assured conviction.

The appeal to the emotions and to conscience was more directly compelling. Contrasted with the dull prosaic ceremonies of the State religion the Eastern cults inspired enthusiasm and awakened remorse. Alternating fear and hope, with their scintillating ritual and seductive music they proclaimed the promise of an after-life in which the soul emancipated from the tyranny of the body might lose itself in unending bliss. Towards the attainment of this blessed state they enjoined a rule of life in which self-discipline and penance were combined with symbolic acts of purification, which not infrequently were performed with the most grotesque and sensuous ritual. Thus conscience and emotion were each to play their part in the pilgrim's progress to everlasting salvation.

Of the countless forms of worship which were disseminated throughout the Roman Empire during the second century A.D.,

four stand out in importance. The first was the cult of
the Great Mother, which had been brought to Rome in
response to an oracle in 204 B.C. and officially recognized
by the government. During the remainder of the Republic,
however, its orgiastic licences and the self-mutilation of its
priests offended Roman sensibilities, and severe restrictions
were placed upon its public services. But despite this police
control the religion continued to live, with its votaries drawn
from slaves, freedmen and merchants, till most probably
at the instigation of Claudius the official ban was lifted and
apprehension gave way to pronounced favour. The *archigalli*
were in future chosen from among Roman citizens, and the
festivals of the Phrygian goddess were celebrated with
greater magnificence than in her native Pessinus. At the
spring festival the death and resurrection of Attis, the
beloved of Cybele, were dramatized, and while the masses
were enthralled by the weird elaborations of its ritual, the
cultured regarded it as a manifestation of a pantheistic
philosophy, which there is some reason to think the cult had
acquired under the influence of Judaism. In the second
century the religion of the Great Mother seems to have
become associated with Mithraism, and to this transformation
may be assigned the introduction of the Taurobolium or the
baptism of blood, in which the initiate descended into a pit
above which an ox was slaughtered, and after suffering the
drops of blood to fall on his face arose again washed from
his sins to live a life of regeneration.

The second cult of importance was that of the Egyptian
Isis with whom was associated Serapis. Introduced into
Italy during the last century of the Republic it was rigorously suppressed by the Senate and later by Augustus
because of Antony's connection with Egypt. Despite this
official opposition, however, it spread over Northern Italy
into Gaul and the Danubian provinces carried by merchants,
sailors, slaves and artisans till in A.D. 38 Caligula recognized
its claims and built a temple for Isis in the Campus Martius.
From this date Isis and Serapis enjoyed the favour of all
the imperial dynasties. The strength of this religion lay
neither in its theology, which was flexible rather than original,
nor in its standard of morals, which was anything but austere.
Its victory in the Roman World was won by the elaborate and

impressive ritual with which its daily services were performed, by the efficacy which it claimed for its prayers, and
by its promises of everlasting life. In place of the uncertain
and contradictory theories of philosophy on the destiny of
the soul it offered an assurance founded on divine revelation
and corroborated by the faith of countless generations of
believers.

By the end of the first century A.D. Italy had been invaded
by a host of divinities from Syria and the neighbouring
countries. Every Semitic tribe had, to begin with, its own
particular Ba'al, who, as his title " master " suggests, was
revered either as an Eastern monarch to whom his worshippers
stood as slaves, or as the proprietor of the land which he
watered with his springs and rivers, or even as the lord of
heaven whence thunder and storms descended upon the
earth. But under the influence of Babylonian astrology
these Ba'alim were transformed from merely local deities,
and Syria developed a distinctive theology which taught
that God was eternal, omnipotent and omnipresent, and
emphasized the great gulf which separated the divine from the
human. Despite this exalted conception of the deity the
Syrian cults, because of the grossness of their accompanying
ritual, made no great impression upon the masses. But their
doctrine of the universality of God had in the next century a
strong influence upon the syncretism of the pagan cults.[15]

But by far the most important of the Eastern cults was
the worship of Mithras. In origin the god of the light that
illuminates the heavens before the rising of the sun, he had
later become to the Iranian peoples of Asia Minor, when they
developed their doctrine of a continuous warfare between
Light and Darkness, the invincible leader of the hosts of
Ormuzd, the principle of Good, against Ahriman the prince
of Darkness. Further influenced by Babylonian astrology
and losing much of the pure Mazdean faith through its contact with the native cults of Asia Minor, Mithraism reached
the West in the time of Pompey and was more widely
established a century later. It was distinguished—and
herein lay the chief ground of its triumph—from all other
Eastern cults by its insistence on the principle of dualism,
and by its deification of the Power of Evil, whom it set up as a
rival to the Supreme God. This apparently simple account

of evil attracted the cultured as it captured the masses who found in it an explanation of their sufferings. Further, Mithraism held out the certain hope of salvation to all who, passing through baptism and the sacramental rites of purification, attained to the full participation in its mysteries, and enjoined a standard of conduct in which purity and truthfulness predominated. As the victorious general of the hosts of Light, Mithras became the favourite god of the soldiers, who carried his worship to the frontier provinces where the legions were stationed.[16]

Thus by the end of the 2nd century A.D. a new conception of worship had gained the ascendancy in the Roman Empire. The old religion of the city state, which was so closely interwoven with service to the community, was superseded by faiths which were personal and at the same time contained in themselves the elements of an universal religion. The way seemed open for the realization of pagan monotheism; none could have foreseen the triumph of Christianity.

Unlike the Oriental cults which made no exclusive claims upon their adherents and which permitted homage to the Emperor, Christianity asserted an uncompromising belief in the existence of One Supreme God who had revealed himself to the world in the Incarnation of Jesus Christ. Consequently it forbade the faithful to participate in any pagan ceremonies and offered a stubborn resistance, which preferred martyrdom to surrender, even to an outward recognition of the Imperial Cult. With such an unequivocal opposition the government could have no peace; for the absolute dominion which the Christians claimed for the Founder of their religion was a challenge to the constitutional authority of the Emperor. Christianity was therefore declared a *religio illicita,* and its profession was treated as a capital offence. Nor did it meet with a favourable reception in society. The masses were ignorant of its nature and despite an easy credulity disliked the moral standard which it demanded.[17] The Jews consistently misrepresented its teaching, and charges of atheism, Thyestean banquets and Oedipodean intercourse were made against the secret meetings of the faithful.[18] When the faith began to influence the educated classes contempt broke into open polemic either in the form of a reasoned invective like that of Celsus[19] or

in the light badinage of a Lucian.[20] Attempts were made by
Christian apologists to dispel misapprehensions of the
character of their religion. Aristides, the Athenian philosopher, and Justin both endeavoured to influence the known
clemency of Antoninus, but the Emperor had little sympathy
with the Christians.[21] A devout worshipper of the State
gods, he was prepared to let the law take its course, although
anxious to avoid bloodshed.[22] In his principate, for example,
Ptolemaeus and Lucius were condemned to death by the
city prefect, Lollius Urbicus, and the aged Polycarp was
martyred at Smyrna.[23] Under Marcus Aurelius persecution
was encouraged.[24] The Stoic Emperor, despite his devotion
to philosophy, shared the current superstitions of his age.
In the hope of saving his Empire from destruction he revived
obsolete ceremonies of the old Roman religion and ordered
the punishment of the Christians, whose recalcitrant attitude
he was prepared to think might be in part responsible for the
misfortunes of his reign. This persecution, whose course is
reflected in the accounts of the martyrdoms at Lyons and at
Scyllium in Numidia,[25] lasted into the principate of Commodus. During his rule, perhaps under the influence of his
concubine Marcia, the Church enjoyed a temporary peace.

(b) Literature and Art.

The Antonine Age may be called the second age of the
sophists. The leaders of literary thought professed an
acquaintance with every branch of learning and dressed their
erudition in the garb of rhetoric. Influenced by Hadrian's
acknowledged preference for Ennius over Virgil, and for
Cato over Cicero, they affected an admiration for the earliest
Latin writers and sought to break away from what they
regarded as the cramping effects of the Ciceronian tradition.
But their labours more often resulted in the revival of literary
archaisms than in the creation of a new and more lively
diction. The leader of this movement was Fronto, a native
of Africa, who was appointed tutor to Marcus Aurelius, and
who enjoyed the admiration of the intelligentsia of Rome.
Of his abilities as an orator there is insufficient extant material
to judge, but a great mass of his correspondence with his
imperial pupil survives and from this a fair estimate of his
mentality may be formed. The letters are conspicuous for

their poverty of thought and barrenness of original ideas.
They abound in citations from ancient authorities and the
sentences are tricked out with elaborate similes, pedantic
phrases and turns of speech. To Fronto erudition spelled
eloquence, but his taste and discrimination were deficient,
and not infrequently the search for the *mot juste* ended in the
choice of the bizarre. It is perhaps not surprising that Marcus
forsook oratory for philosophy.

In his *Noctes Atticae* Aulus Gellius, a disciple of Fronto,
carried a stage further the tendency that was immanent in
his master's work. No branch of learning escaped his enquiring mind, but his compositions are little more than an
uncritical epitome of the sources which he had studied
decked out with borrowed phrases and archaic words. Unwittingly he provides the best example of the contemporary
passion for retailed erudition.

The Greek counterpart of Fronto was Herodes Atticus,
the prince of public benefactors and a tutor of Marcus
Aurelius.[26] He came of a noble family, which claimed
descent from the Aeacidae of Aegina and which seemed
possessed of almost inexhaustible riches. Atticus' father
had made a liberal contribution in supplementing an imperial
subsidy towards a water supply for the Troad; the son's
generosity extended to towns in Italy in addition to Corinth,
Thessaly, Elis and Boeotia, not to mention his native Athens.
Here he lived in princely style in a house on the Ilissus,
spending his fortune freely on the restoration of old temples,
benefactions to his fellow-citizens and the erection of a theatre
at the foot of the Acropolis, which aroused the admiration of
Pausanias. If the fame of Atticus was due more to his
wealth than his learning, under the patronage of Marcus,
who endowed four professorships at Athens, ample opportunities for distinction were offered to the Greek sophist.
Not only was he the representative of his city at official
ceremonies, but his versatility as a speaker and writer made
him an acceptable member of the imperial cabinet.

The most interesting of the Greek writers is Lucian, a native
of Samosata. The wide range of subjects in which he dabbled
reveals his affinity to the sophists of the period, but at the
same time he stands apart like a spectator of the passing
show and observes current movements with the eye of detach-

ment. His works are a mirror of the tendencies of the age, reflecting its moral, intellectual and religious aspirations and, although his satirical comments are too frivolous, and were probably never intended, to influence society, his characters are models drawn from life, who must in many cases have unwittingly posed for their portraits. If the author betrays his Syrian origin by his vanity and exaggerated conceits, he atones for these defects by his acumen, his occasional flashes of wit and the grace and charm of his style. Altogether different are the writings of Apuleius, the only Latin author of distinction. Like Fronto he was a native of Africa and studied oratory, but unlike his compatriot he succeeded in extricating himself from the coils of a professional rhetoric. Ardent and rich in phantasy his writing suggests perhaps rather the Oriental than the African. His most famous work is his *Metamorphoses*, the forerunner of the romances of the Middle Ages. Although undistinguished by originality of conception the material is handled with richness of imagery, and the book despite its riotous and coarse realism contains much that is imaginatively beautiful. But Apuleius does not escape from the antiquarian fashion of the age, and his language betrays archaisms, which are less probably to be explained as provincialisms than as the fruit of a pedantic affectation.

The period witnessed the birth of a new form of literature, which in the next century assumed a greater importance. These Apologies for the Christian Faith, most of which were written in Greek, were attempts to dispel current misrepresentations of its teaching. Dialectical in form, dogmatic and frequently intolerant, their merit lies more in the sincerity with which the aims of Christianity are expounded than in the literary style of their composition. To this general criticism, however, the only Latin work of its kind affords an exception. The *Octavius* of Minucius Felix, which is a dialogue between a pagan and a Christian, both of whom were friends of the author, has a charm of its own, which harmonizes with its pleasant setting by the seashore at Ostia.

In the more specialized branches of learning mention must be made of Galen's treatises on medicine, of Pausanias' *Travels in Greece* and Ptolemy's *Geography and Astronomy*,

4

which till Copernicus remained the standard work. All this
varied literary output was the creation of provincials. In the
West, Africa deprived Spain of the proud position which it had
held in the Flavian epoch ; in the East, Syria, not Greece,
produced the only distinguished littérateur. Rome, like
Athens, had lost her spiritual ascendancy, and with her
dethronement the way was open for the gradual absorption
of Graeco-Roman culture in a wider and more cosmopolitan
civilisation.

In the history of Art, on the other hand, there is not the same
story of decadence.[27] The " Greek Revival " of Hadrian's
principate might seem to portend the same pedantic love of
the archaic as characterized so much of the current literature ;
in fact it was no mere return to a " sterile classicism." The
emphasis which it placed upon the value of idealistic forms
of expression not only curbed for a time the realistic tendencies
of the previous century, but it also breathed into Roman
Art a fresh love of symbolism and allegory, and endowed it
with a sense of composition and design. This new spirit,
which during the Antonine period continued to make
itself felt, is most clearly discernible in two branches of Art.
From the principate of Hadrian with the issue of a series of
bronze medallions, which was repeated by all his Antonine
successors, dates the genesis of the art of medal-engraving.
In contrast with coins, medallions were struck to mark some
special occasion and had only a limited circulation. Consequently the choice of types was much less confined, and a
wider scope was given for richness of allegorical allusion,
while more time and skill could be bestowed by the designers
upon the perfecting of their technique. Many of the extant
examples with their idealistic representations of mytho-
logical figures were executed with a fine delicacy and
a discriminating taste, which makes them comparable
with the most beautiful specimens of ancient coinage. Similarly the sculptured friezes on sarcophagi reveal a remarkable
sense of grouping and an attempt to portray difference
of character among the represented figures. Although the
episodes are regularly taken from mythology, the individuals
are realistic and contemporary portraits. This effort to
depict varying psychological moods is also found on the
friezes upon the Marcus Column. Although compared with

Trajan's Column the treatment of the campaigns is episodic and the continuity between scenes is largely lost, there is a much greater concentration upon individual portraiture, and at the same time a deeper and more human sympathy. It is no longer left to pictorial events to convey the appropriate message ; the faces and the pose of the people reveal the pathos of their fate.   Nor is this interest in human emotions confined to monumental sculpture ; it is also apparent in contemporary portraiture.   The young Marcus is represented with an abstracted expression of melancholy pensiveness, the young Commodus with a proud and sensual beauty, while the same subtle difference is discernible in the portraits of the younger Faustina and her daughter Lucilla.

The impulse given to architecture by Hadrian was not lost on his successors, and in the Antonine Age an extensive programme of building and restoration was carried out. Although the style in which such temples as that of Antoninus and Faustina in the Forum were executed was conventional and lacked the daring originality which is illustrated in the Pantheon and the Hadrianic Mausoleum, the private houses that were erected maintained and developed the improved standard of domestic architecture.   Again it was in the provincial towns that, thanks to the benefactions of its citizens and the sense of security that the peace of the Empire imparted, the most costly and magnificent buildings were erected.   Among these pride of place must be given to the Temple of Jupiter Heliopolitanus at Baalbek, while in North Africa the arch of Marcus at Tripoli is a forerunner of the numerous commemorative works that were erected in the province during the reign of its native Emperor, Septimius Severus.

PART II

THE DYNASTY OF THE SEVERI

CHAPTER I

SEPTIMIUS SEVERUS

§ 1. HIS ACCESSION

ON the death of Commodus the political situation in the Roman Empire bore a strong resemblance to the crisis that followed the assassination of Nero. Now, as then, the choice of a new Emperor lay with the army and not with the Senate. Just as in A.D. 68–69 the praetorians, and the armies in Spain, Germany and Syria had put up their rival candidates, so in A.D. 193 the lead was taken by the guards, and their arbitrary claim to depose and create the Emperor was followed by separate challenges from the provincial armies of Illyricum, Syria and Britain. Once again the secret had been discovered that an Emperor could be elected elsewhere than in Rome. But although the army became the dominant factor in the appointment of the emperors of the 3rd century A.D., and although the Senate, which in theory remained the constitutional source of the Emperor's powers, was forced in most cases to acquiesce in the army's choice, it is a mistake to suppose that the soldiers themselves had a highly developed political sense, or that by the salutation of their own particular general as Emperor they were seeking to vindicate an accepted principle of government. The legions of the late 2nd century A.D. in contrast with those of the Julio–Claudian period were, it is true, recruited from local sources and perhaps more from the peasantry than the city populations, but that does not imply that these soldiers identified themselves with the interests of the classes from which they were drawn, still less that they were prepared to wage war for the country against the town. What influenced the legionaries was their own immediate prospect of aggrandisement. If their own general seemed capable and trustworthy, then they were prepared to salute him Emperor in preference to the candidate of another army, and to remain loyal to him so long as he substantiated his promises of booty and donatives. Similarly each Emperor knew that his retention of power depended upon his ability to satisfy the unlicensed greed of his troops. Thus the Augustan system of government, which had concealed beneath a veneer of constitutionalism the military foundation of the Emperor's power, was transformed into a monarchy whose continuity and policy was undisguisedly controlled by a professional standing army.

The conspirators lost no time in making their choice of a successor to Commodus. During the night Laetus the praetorian prefect called upon P. Helvius Pertinax and asked him to accept nomination as the new Emperor, assuring him that his distinguished career in the service of his country would meet with the approval of Senate and Roman people. Pertinax, who was sixty-six years of age and who had probably not been implicated in the plot against Commodus, accepted the invitation and was hurried by Laetus to the camp of the praetorians. By the promise of a large donative he secured the support of the guards, although the final words of his speech left in their minds the uneasy suspicion that he would attempt to exercise upon them the same disciplinary measures that had made his name notorious among the legions. The new Emperor was then accompanied to the Senate where he was greeted with unfeigned enthusiasm and received the customary imperial powers and titles.[1]

During his short reign of less than three months Pertinax attempted to resuscitate the Augustan diarchy. He showed a courteous respect for the dignity of the Senate and revived for himself the ancient title of *princeps Senatus*.[2] At the same time he refused the Senate's offer of the title of Augusta for his wife and of Caesar for his son.[3] But his eagerness for reform carried him into precipitate actions, and his regulation giving seniority to those who had actually served as praetors over those who had been " allected " into that rank earned for him unpopularity in the Senate.[4] Again his measures for the restoration of national solvency were not above criticism. The sale of Commodus' instruments of vice and luxury was legitimate enough, but the trafficking in offices and appointments was not calculated to inspire confidence in his economic policy.[5] But even had Pertinax avoided offence in the Senate, his position as Emperor was insecure unless the praetorians lent him their loyal support. Instead their resentment steadily grew when he failed to pay them more than one-half of the donative he had promised. A conspiracy was formed during Pertinax' temporary absence from Rome to place the consul Falco on the throne, and though the Emperor returned in time to stop the pretender's condemnation by the Senate, the resentment of the praetorians was only increased by the execution of some of their soldiers on the evidence of a slave.[6] At last, on March 28th, at the instigation of Laetus a band of soldiers invaded the Palatine. The Emperor, deserted by all his retinue except Eclectus, advanced boldly to meet them and attempted in vain to conciliate them until he fell a victim to the spear of a Tungrian called Tausius, one of the imperial bodyguard.[7] Upon his tombstone might fittingly be inscribed Tacitus' epitaph for Galba " *capax imperii nisi imperasset.*"[8]

The murder of Pertinax left the Empire without a ruler. The assassins, who had not as yet decided upon a successor, retired to the praetorian camp and barricaded its gates. An extraordinary scene ensued. The praetorians declared the Empire for sale to the highest bidder. Two competitors attended the auction, Flavius Sulpicianus, prefect of the city and father-in-law of Pertinax, who happened to be inside the camp on other business, and M. Didius Julianus, a rich senator of some sixty years and of no great distinction, who approached the camp from outside, and if we may believe Herodian, climbed by means of a ladder on to the walls of the camp. Sulpicianus was the first to name a figure that was satisfactory to the guards, but, fearing lest his relationship to Pertinax would lead to vengeance for the latter's death, the soldiers knocked down the Empire to Julianus at the price of 25,000 HS a man.[9] The new Emperor was then conducted by an armed force to the Senate where the cowed and frightened senators ratified the praetorians' choice. By the populace of Rome the election was no less detested. On the following day the Emperor was besieged by an angry mob as he made his way under armed escort from his Palace to the Senate, nor did his offers of a rich donative in any way appease its fury. Seizing what weapons they could find the people thronged into the Circus where they continued, Dio says, the whole of the next night and day without food and drink. A resolution was passed calling upon Pescennius Niger, the governor of Syria, to come to their assistance, and at last wearied by hunger and sleeplessness they separated to their homes content to wait for help from abroad.[10] As in A.D. 69 the last word was to lie with the legions.

News of the murder of Pertinax quickly reached the headquarters of the Danubian army at Carnuntum. On April 13 Septimius Severus the governor of Upper Pannonia, who was a native of Africa and had served with distinction during the principate of Marcus, harangued his troops recalling the splendid services of Pertinax to the State in the German wars of Marcus Aurelius, and depicting the vacillating cowardice of the Guards. Finally he urged them to march on Rome and exact vengeance for the murder of the Emperor.[11] The reply of the soldiers of XIV *Gemina* was to salute Septimius as Emperor and their example was soon followed by all the Danubian and Rhenish legions, the initiative in Germany being taken by I *Minervia* at Bonn.[12] Whether Septimius had been plotting a *coup d'état* in the lifetime of Commodus must remain an open question. Certain it is that he lost no time in utilizing the murder of Pertinax as a pretext for an advance upon Rome, realizing that to pose as the avenger of the dead Emperor would both win the support of the Senate and people of Rome and enable him to stand as the liberator of the Constitution. Meanwhile opposition might be expected from two other sources. Even if Septimius could not yet have heard of the proclamation by the Syrian troops of Pescennius Niger as Emperor,[13] he must have been aware of the enthusiasm of the populace of Rome for his advent. Accordingly he determined to secure the loyalty of Europe to himself by conciliating his other possible rival Clodius Albinus, the governor of Britain. By a clever ruse he offered him the title of Caesar and the prospect of succession to the Empire, which Albinus with a strange lack of foresight accepted.[14] All was now ready for the expedition. Leaving some troops behind to protect his rear Septimius set out from Carnuntum late in April and by a series of forced marches crossed the undefended Julian Alps and descended upon Italy where his first success was the defection of the fleet at Ravenna and the voluntary surrender of the town.[15]

Meanwhile Julianus' position was daily becoming more desperate. The praetorians who had sold him the Empire had neither the will nor the ability to defend the State. In vain Julianus sought to convert the city into an armed camp by building walls and ramparts and even mobilizing the Circus elephants in the hope of causing a panic among the Illyrian soldiers. The praetorians refused to work or drill, nor did the grant of a huge donative to each soldier awaken a sense of loyalty and gratitude ; for Julianus had failed to pay the price he had bid for the Empire and the money which he now distributed was regarded by them as the belated discharge of a debt.[16] The marines, too, who were summoned from Misenum had neither discipline nor efficiency. The hopelessness of the situation seems to have robbed Julianus of such wits as he possessed. First he caused Septimius to be declared a public enemy and despatched an embassy of senators to recall the troops to their allegiance ; but many of the delegates seceded, and Vespronius Candidus who remained loyal narrowly escaped with his life.[17] At a second meeting of the Senate the Emperor first proposed that a deputation of Vestal Virgins should be sent to Septimius with an appeal *ad misericordiam*.[18] But when the augur Plautius Quintillus had sharply rebuked him, reminding him that no man is fit to be Emperor who cannot support his claims with the sword, he retracted and caused a resolution of the Senate to be passed by which Septimius was offered a share in the Empire as its joint ruler.[19] At the same time Julianus appointed a partisan of Septimius, one Veturius Macrinus, as a third praetorian prefect.[20] The new proposal was summarily rejected by Septimius and its bearer put to death. Septimius now opened negotiations with the praetorians, promising them their lives, if they handed over the murderers of Pertinax and remained inactive themselves. The appeal was successful and the praetorians deserted Julianus. When news of their defection reached the consul, Silius Messalla, he summoned the senators to the Athenæum, where a resolution was passed deposing Julianus and proclaiming Septimius Emperor.[21] Deposition carried with it the sentence of death, and Julianus who, after a fruitless attempt to arouse the sympathies of the aged Cl. Pompeianus, had sought a final refuge in his deserted palace, was murdered on June 1st.[22]

Immediately after the passing of the decree of the Senate an embassy of one hundred senators was sent to meet the new Emperor, who had reached Interamna, and conveyed to him the good wishes of the Senate. Its reception was hardly flattering. Septimius, surrounded with a bodyguard of six hundred, ordered each of the ambassadors to be searched for any concealed arms ; but their feelings were doubtless mollified by the gift next day of 100,000 HS each and permission, if they desired, to stay behind and enter Rome in his retinue.[23] Septimius reached Rome on June 9,[24] but before entering the city he meted out dramatic punishment to the praetorians. The soldiers were ordered to leave their arms in camp and meet him in parade uniform in the Campus Martius. On their arrival they were immediately surrounded by Illyrian legionaries, while others were sent to collect their arms from the praetorian camp. In a speech to the troops the Emperor emphasized his anxiety to avoid bloodshed at the beginning of his reign and at the same time the impossibility of overlooking the murder of Pertinax. Accordingly he dismissed the praetorians from his service and granted them their liberty as long as they did not approach nearer than the hundredth milestone from Rome. Such was the fate of a corps which had made and unmade the emperors of Rome.[25] In its place Septimius organized a new body of Guards, no longer drawn exclusively from Italians and Roman citizens from Macedonia, Spain and Noricum, but of legionaries from any part of the Empire. A few years later Italy was given for the first time a legionary garrison, which was established at Albanum just outside Rome. The effect of these and other reforms upon the character of the Roman army will be discussed in the next chapter.

The entry of Septimius into Rome was a memorable spectacle. The Emperor rode on horseback to the city gates where he dismounted and, as Vitellius had done before, changed his military cloak for the *toga*. Senators greeted him at the gates, and through streets gaily decorated with flowers and thronged with cheering crowds he led his troops in procession to the Capitol to offer sacrifice at the temple of Jupiter,

and thence to his palace on the Palatine. The next day he
attended the Senate and in a speech outlined his programme.[26]
His usurpation of supreme power he excused by emphasizing
his purpose of vindicating the memory of Pertinax, and as
a guarantee of good faith adopted himself the name of
Pertinax.[27] With greater speciousness he asked the Senate
to pass a decree making it illegal for the Emperor to put to
death a senator without its consent—a provision which he
subsequently observed neither in theory nor in practice.
In general, in the hope of conciliating a body which not so
long previously had voted him a public enemy, he promised
that he would administer the State in accordance with the
principles of Marcus, whom later he was to adopt as his father.

One of the first acts of Septimius was the funeral and
deification of Pertinax. The first part of the ceremony took
place in the Forum. Upon a platform was placed a richly
decorated couch upon which was laid a waxen image of the
Emperor as though asleep and not dead, a beautiful slave
keeping the flies from his face with a fan of peacocks' feathers.
When the mourning people had assembled, Septimius delivered an encomium on the dead Emperor's virtues and the
procession then moved off to the Campus Martius. Here a
magnificent pyre had been erected of gold and ivory and upon
it had been set up the gilded chariot which Pertinax had been
used to drive. On it was placed the couch, and after Septimius
and the near relatives of Pertinax had kissed the waxen image,
the consuls applied their torches to the pyre. The release of
an eagle signified that yet another Emperor had joined the
blessed company of heaven.[28]

Septimius had now to deal with his rival, Pescennius
Niger, who had been proclaimed Emperor by his Syrian
legions. But in order to consolidate his position in Rome
and relieve the people of anxiety at the presence of
armed troops he carried out a number of popular measures.
He distributed a *congiarium* to the people and exhibited
expensive games, while at the same time taking some practical
steps to ensure the food supply of the city.[29] With the Senate
he attempted to strengthen the bonds of goodwill by giving
in marriage his two daughters by his first wife Marcia to
Aetius and Probus, whom he nominated consuls for the next
year. On July 9 Septimius set out for the East.[30]

§ 2.   WAR AGAINST NIGER

Gaius Pescennius Niger Justus was of humble origin and belonged to an equestrian family. Born somewhere between A.D. 135 and 140 he had held the post of *primus pilus* and later a military command in Egypt. " Allected " by Commodus into the rank of praetorian senators he held the consulship in 190 with Severus as his colleague, and was next year appointed governor of Syria through the favour of Narcissus, the athlete who strangled Commodus. On hearing of the murder of Pertinax and perhaps encouraged by reports of popular enthusiasm at Rome he was proclaimed Emperor by his legions. His character is variously represented in the literary sources, and he seems to have combined a firm and energetic generalship with a tendency to dilatory procrastination, engendered perhaps by a love of amusement. [31]

For the struggle with Septimius, Niger started with certain material disadvantages. Geographically he was too far distant from Rome to have any chance of anticipating his rival's advance upon the city. He could count upon the support of nine legions from the Eastern provinces, but in number and quality they were inferior to those that Septimius could command, provided that Europe remained loyal to his cause. To counteract these initial disadvantages Niger endeavoured to secure foreign alliances. But Armenia chose to remain neutral ; Vologeses V of Parthia was too occupied with internal troubles in his State to do more than make a gesture of friendship, and only from Barsemius of Hatra were any troops obtained. [32] On the other hand Niger had a good ally in Asellius Aemilianus the governor of Asia, Egypt was favourable to his cause, and most important of all Byzantium voluntarily surrendered to him. [33] From here his policy was to win over Perinthus, which controlled the two main roads from Europe to Asia, and as a second line of defence he ordered the pass across the Taurus mountains through the Cilician Gates to be put in a state of defence. [34]

On the first day of his march from Rome Septimius had to face a mutiny of his troops at Saxa Rubra on the Via Flaminia, some nine miles north of the city. [35] The revolt, however, does not appear to have been serious, and the Emperor

was soon able to proceed overland for Byzantium, while
a section of his army was sent by sea to Dyrrachium.
Before leaving Rome he had made some preliminary plans to
counter Niger's move on Perinthus. He appointed his brother,
P. Septimius Geta, governor of the three Dacias, and ordered
L. Fabius Cilo to proceed to Perinthus with detachments
which were probably drawn from the Moesian legions.[36]
This advance guard reached Perinthus early in May, and after
a slight defeat was successful in preventing Niger from occupying the town, and in forcing him to fall back upon Byzantium,
the siege of which, entrusted to Marius Maximus, the commander of I *Italica*, began in June.[37] When Septimius arrived
at Perinthus, he entrusted the supreme command to his
general Claudius Candidus with instructions to cross the
Hellespont and land near Cyzicus, while he himself remained
behind at Perinthus.[38] A battle was fought outside the town
in which Aemilianus, Niger's commander-in-chief, was utterly
defeated and Cyzicus fell to Septimius. Niger now left
Byzantium and retreated with his troops into Bithynia where
he prepared for a second stand near Nicaea, while Septimius'
army occupied Nicomedia, the capital of the province and
the traditional enemy of Nicaea. A decisive battle was fought
in the plain between Cius and Nicaea, and only the approach
of night and the close proximity of the latter town saved the
forces of Niger from complete destruction.[39] Niger and the
remnants of the army fled across the Taurus mountains to
Antioch, and Severus received three acclamations for the
successes of his generals at Perinthus, Cyzicus and Nicaea
(winter of 193–4).[40] A month or so later Egypt revolted from
Niger, and on Feb. 13, 194, a festival was celebrated at
Arsinoe in honour of the victory of Septimius.[41]

The victorious army, now under the command of Valerianus
and Anullinus, followed its routed enemy through Dorylaeum
and Tyana to the Cilician Gates. Here for a time it was held
up by a rearguard of the Nigerians, a part of which was
stationed on the heights and poured down missiles on its
opponents as they advanced along the pass. At last Valerianus
made a détour with some cavalry and got round the rear of
the Nigerians. Further resistance was hopeless, the pass was
forced and the road to Antioch lay open to the victors.[42]
News of this disaster aroused Niger, who had been meting

out punishment upon some rebels in Syria, to make a final
effort to stay the advance of Septimius. Leaving Antioch
he concentrated his army at Issus, and on the site where
five hundred years before Alexander had won his great victory
the European legions of Septimius routed the Syrian army.
Niger himself escaped to Antioch, and on the approach of
Septimius fled towards the Euphrates, but before he could
cross the river he was overtaken by a squadron despatched
in pursuit, and executed. His head was brought to Septimius,
who in turn sent it to Byzantium as a silent herald of
his success and a warning of the fate that awaited his
opponents. At Tarsus games were celebrated in honour of
the victory, and Septimius received his fourth imperial
acclamation.[43]

Septimius spent the winter of 194–5 in Syria. Upon the
towns which had taken the side of Niger he inflicted severe
punishments. Antioch, as might be expected, suffered most.
Its theatres and buildings were razed to the ground, and the
town was reduced to the status of a village subject to its
rival Laodicea, which now became the *metropolis* of Syria
with the title of *colonia Severiana Augusta Septimia Laodicea
Metropolis*, and received the *ius Italicum*.[44] Other towns
that had lent money to Niger were fined four times the amount
of their contributions, while their rivals were honoured with
the title of Roman colonies, and received a subsidy towards
the restoration of their buildings.[45] From this year, too, in
all probability dates the administrative division of Syria into
Syria Coele and Syria Phoenice, the former including Com-
magene and garrisoned by two legions, the latter with one
legion and its capital at Tyre.[46] The motive for the change
lay in the determination to prevent as far as possible any one
provincial governor obtaining military power as great as
Niger's ; its influence upon later Roman provincial policy
will be presently discussed. To Niger's partisans in the
Senate Septimius showed a tactful clemency ; his position
was not yet sufficiently secure to alienate that body.
Accordingly, while confiscating the property of many of his
late rival's adherents (and thereby amassing great personal
riches), he ordered the death of no senator.[47]

Septimius spent the year A.D. 195 in punitive expeditions
against those Eastern peoples who had profited by the Civil

War to attempt fresh accessions of territory. These were the
Osroeni, the Adiabeni and the Scaenite Arabs who lived in
the Mesopotamian desert. The first two had attacked Nisibis,
and the embassies which they and the Arabs sent to Septimius
on the death of Niger gave such hollow excuses for their
conduct that the Emperor decided to invade their territory.
The army probably crossed the Euphrates at Zeugma, with
Nisibis as its objective. On its way it occupied Edessa, the
capital of Abgarus' kingdom of Osroene, and that king was
temporarily deprived of his territory, which was converted
into a Roman province under a procurator. On reaching Nisibis, Septimius rewarded the town for its loyalty by raising
it to the rank of a colony and making it the seat of the governor
of the new province.[48] After a second abortive embassy
from the Arabs he divided his army into three corps under
the command of Lateranus, Candidus and Laetus, which
seem to have done little more than ravage the country as
far as the Tigris. Later in the year under Laetus, Anullinus
and Probus a more vigorous strategy was pursued. The
Tigris was crossed and Adiabene invaded.[49] Here the
campaign ended, a formal peace was made with Parthia,
and Septimius accepted three imperial acclamations and the
titles of *Parthicus Arabicus, Parthicus Adiabenicus.*[50] But
it is doubtful whether the war was the success that Septimius
wished it to be believed. The necessity for a second war
only three years later shows the unsatisfactory nature of the
settlement that had been concluded. Not improbably
Septimius, who had a clearly defined Eastern policy of expansion, would have proceeded to strike a blow at the tottering
Parthian Empire, had he not been disturbed by the long
siege of Byzantium and disquietening news of his Caesar,
Clodius Albinus. In the winter of 195–6 he, therefore, started
for home, and before he had left Mesopotamia he received the
welcome report of the fall of Byzantium, which had been
starved into submission after a siege of some two and a
half years.[51] A punishment comparable to that of Antioch
was meted out on the city. Its fortifications were destroyed,
its citizens deprived of their property and the state itself
made tributary to Rome and subordinate to its neighbour
Perinthus. Some years later the Emperor, on the intervention of his son, repented of his vindictive spite and caused the

walls to be rebuilt, but the city did not recover its ancient glory till the reign of Constantine.[52]

Septimius returned to Europe by way of Byzantium and Perinthus and reached Viminacium probably in the spring of 196, where he began active preparations for the impending conflict with Albinus. He now took a significant step towards the founding of a family dynasty. His elder son Bassianus, commonly called Caracallus, by his second marriage with the Syrian Julia Domna, who was now eight years old, he raised to the rank of Caesar, and an edict issued on June 30 bears the name of the Emperor and the heir-apparent.[53] At the same time he changed his name to Antoninus in order to forge a further link with the family of Marcus Aurelius. For coins and inscriptions show that Septimius himself had in the previous year adopted the Stoic Emperor as his fictitious father and with him the whole of the Antonine house as his ancestry.[54] At the same time he had caused his army to apotheosize Commodus, as it was clearly unsuitable that the Emperor should have a " brother " whose memory had been condemned. It would be unfair to see in the adoption merely the vanity of an unscrupulous usurper ; it has also a religious significance which may be traced to the Eastern influence of Julia Domna. Septimius intended that both the Emperor and the Imperial House should receive the halo of divinity in the State. Thus in the army Emperor-worship takes the place of the worship of the standards, and in the *scholae* dedications are made to the Emperor and the *domus divina*. Most significant of all is the exalted place given to the Queen-Empress. Not only was she worshipped in the Camp as *mater castrorum*, but she received the title of *mater Augusti*, and later was identified with Juno Caelestis, when Septimius admitted his native Virgo Caelestis into the Roman Olympus.[55]

§ 3. WAR AGAINST CLODIUS ALBINUS

From the literary sources it is difficult to judge with whom the responsibility for the next phase of civil war should lie. It might be held that Albinus, disappointed in the hopes of succession which his acceptance of the title of Caesar had raised, took the initiative and in self-defence had himself proclaimed Emperor, and that only then did Septimius

make any move against him. On the other hand, it is more
probable that after Niger's death Septimius decided to be rid
of the burden of a colleague who was not a member of his own
family, and that the detection of treasonable correspondence
passing between Albinus and the Senate gave him the opportunity, while still in Mesopotamia, to have his rival declared
a public enemy by his troops.[56] Such an hypothesis gives
an explanation not only of the premature termination of
the Eastern campaign and the speedy withdrawal of the
European legions, but also of Septimius' adoption of the
Antonines as his ancestors and the elevation of his own son
to the rank of Caesar in place of Albinus.

Clodius Albinus, although born in Hadrumetum, is said
to have come of a noble family. During the reigns of Marcus
and Commodus he had had considerable military experience
as the commander of three different legions and later as the
governor of one of the German provinces and finally of
Britain. His elevation to the rank of Augustus probably
occurred in the summer of 196 as an answer to Septimius'
proclamation of him as a public enemy, and in the autumn
of that year he crossed into Gaul with his army of British
legionaries and auxiliaries and with the support of L. Novius
Rufus the governor of Tarraconensis, and established himself
in Lugdunum as his headquarters.[57] Probably his plan of
campaign was to attempt to win over the German legions to
his side, and then, counting on the support of a large body of
senators in Rome, to march straight into Italy. But despite
an early victory of a section of his army over Lupus, the
governor of Lower Germany,[58] the German legions remained
loyal to Septimius, and Albinus' further project of an invasion
of Italy was forestalled by his opponent.

Septimius and his army left Viminacium in late October or
early November. The route lay through Pannonia, Noricum,
Raetia and South-West Germany with Lugdunum as the
objective. The Emperor, however, did not accompany his
troops the whole way, but perhaps at Poetovio decided to
pay a hurried visit to Rome. This change of plan was probably in consequence of an embassy from his loyal supporters
at Rome warning him of the growing hostility to his cause in
the city.[59] Taking with him L. Fabius Cilo and some detachments of the army Septimius reached Rome at the beginning

of December. After compelling the Senate to proclaim Albinus
a public enemy he sought to ingratiate himself with that
body by a display of clemency to one of its members, Cassius
Clemens, who had been a partisan of Niger, while the people
were appeased by a *congiarium* which is commemorated on
coins. Meanwhile in anticipation of an invasion of Italy he
sent forward a detachment to block the passes of the Alps,
and about the turn of the year left himself for Gaul and
effected a junction with his main body, which was in all
probability encamped at Trinuntium.[60]

The decisive battle of the campaign was fought near Lugdunum on February 19, A.D. 197, and, according to Dio,
as many as 150,000 were engaged on either side. At first
the Albinians were victorious, their right wing using the device
of the concealed trench with much success, and we are told
that Septimius himself, through the loss of his horse, was in
danger of his life. The scale was finally turned by Laetus
and his cavalry and, whether it be true or false that that
general had waited in the hope that both leaders would be
killed and himself proclaimed Emperor, the credit for the
victory must be given to him. Lugdunum was plundered
and burnt, and never again regained its old importance as
the chief city of the Gauls.[61]

After the battle Septimius remained three months in Gaul
regulating the administration of the provinces which had
supported Albinus and taking steps to round up his adherents.
Albinus himself committed suicide. His body, with those of
his wife and children who were put to death, was thrown into
the Rhone ; his head was despatched by the Emperor to
Rome as a warning of the vengeance that was to come upon
those that had resisted his will. Meanwhile Claudius Candidus was sent to Spain to deal with L. Novius Rufus and his
Albinian confederates, and the thirteenth urban cohort,
which had formed the garrison at Lugdunum, was cashiered,
and its place taken by a detachment from the four German
legions.[62] To this year also belongs in all probability the
division of Britain into two provinces. The geographical
demarcation cannot be exactly determined, but seems to
correspond with the Mersey–Humber line. The upper or
southern province had two legions at Chester and Isca, the
lower was garrisoned by a single legion at York. The arrange-

ment was similar to the reorganisation of Syria and the motive was the same, to prevent the recurrence of provincial rebellions by limiting the size of the army at a governor's disposal.

Septimius returned to Rome at the beginning of June, and his entry was greeted by the Senate with an ill-concealed and justifiable alarm. In a speech to the fathers he eulogized the cruelties of Sulla and Marius and defended his apotheosis of Commodus, whose morals he compared favourably with those of some of his audience. A persecution followed of the adherents of Niger and Albinus. Sixty-four senators were brought to trial and twenty-nine condemned to death, and their property confiscated.[63] The motive for this cruelty is hard to discover and would seem to spring from nothing else than a determination to abase the Senate, which for three years he had found it politic to conciliate, but now was strong enough to despise and treat as an instrument of his autocracy.

§ 4.   SECOND PARTHIAN WAR

Septimius remained but a short time in Rome. The Parthians profiting by the civil war in Gaul broke the provisional treaty made in 195 and invaded Mesopotamia, attacking Nisibis, which was only saved by the valiant defence of Laetus. The Emperor left Rome in the late summer of 197 accompanied by his praetorian prefect, C. Fulvius Plautianus, and a body of the praetorian guard. The details of the other troops which were employed in the war are difficult to ascertain, but it is probable that three new legions bearing the names of I, II and III *Parthicae* were raised in Illyricum, and that detachments of the Danubian legions were ordered to proceed to the East, and join the Emperor at Antioch. On hearing of the arrival of Septimius in Syria the Parthian king withdrew from Nisibis and recrossed the Tigris. But the Emperor wasted no time and advanced into Mesopotamia. On reaching Edessa he received support and hostages from Abgarus, who was probably as a reward reinstated in his princedom. The grateful monarch adopted the name of Septimius, and at a later date visited his benefactor in Rome.[64] Leaving Edessa, Septimius proceeded to Nisibis, but finding that the siege had been raised determined upon an invasion

of Parthia. Turning south-west he marched back to the
Euphrates, probably by way of Rhesaena to Nicephorium.[65]
From here, accompanied by a fleet, the army marched south-
wards along the banks of the Euphrates till the royal canal
that connects that river with the Tigris was reached. Here,
perhaps, a division of forces was made, one army moving
south on Babylon, which was taken without a struggle, the
other proceeding up the canal against Seleucia, which was
found to have been deserted by the Parthians. The final
attack was on Ctesiphon, which fell after a short resistance,
probably about March, A.D. 198. The city was sacked by the
soldiers and, despite a considerable slaughter of the inhabitants, no fewer than 100,000 prisoners were captured.
Septimius, however, made no attempt to pursue Vologeses,
possibly because of an outbreak of dysentery among his
soldiers. Instead he turned his face northwards once again
along the Tigris with the probable intention of regaining
Nisibis. In honour of his victory he accepted the title of
Parthicus Maximus and his eleventh imperial acclamation,
and raised his elder son Caracallus to the rank of Augustus,
while bestowing on his younger brother Geta the title of
Caesar.[66]

On his return journey Septimius decided to make a détour
and attack the desert town of Hatra, where Barsemius refused
to acknowledge his sovereignty. Why the Emperor should
have been so anxious to capture this isolated place is difficult
to understand. True, it was wealthy and lay on an important
avenue of trade, but such considerations seem hardly likely
to have carried weight with Septimius ; more probably the
motive is to be found in his implacable hatred of Niger's
adherents, which could only be satisfied by their extermina-
tion. However that may be, the first attack, made perhaps
in the late summer of 198, was entirely unsuccessful and the
Emperor withdrew by way of Singara to Nisibis. The next
year a second attempt was made, but a mutiny among his
troops finally compelled Septimius to abandon the project.[67]
By the summer of A.D. 199 the Parthian War was finished,
and, although the Parthian king had escaped, Mesopotamia
was annexed as a Roman province, which was given two
legions and governed on the model of Egypt by an equestrian
prefect.[68] Another important result was the grant of colonial

status to the desert town of Palmyra, which in the course of the
next century rose to great heights of power and wealth, and
for a short time became the rival of Rome itself.[69]

Septimius did not return to Rome till the summer of
A.D. 202. The intervening years he spent in visiting Syria,
Palestine and Egypt. The chronology of this period is difficult
to recover with certainty, but the evidence of dateable papyri
and inscriptions makes it probable that he reached Egypt
before the end of A.D. 199. An amusing anecdote is told of his
entry into the Egyptian capital. On the city gate he found
inscribed : ' τοῦ κυρίου Νίγρου ἡ πόλις,' and in pardonable
indignation he demanded an explanation. But his wrath
was unexpectedly appeased by the ready wit of an Alexandrian who replied : ' σὺ γὰρ ὁ κύριος τοῦ Νίγρου.' [70] Two events
are recorded of Septimius' stay in Alexandria. One was
the sealing up of Alexander's tomb that no one might after
him see the embalmed body of the Macedonian conqueror,
nor read the sacred books—perhaps magic papyri—that were
stored in the precincts.[71] The other was of great administrative importance. In Egypt, unlike the other Roman
provinces, there were no self-governing municipal towns.
Alexandria, the seat of the prefect of Egypt, was under the
jurisdiction of the *iuridicus Aegypti*, the μητροπόλεις, such as
Hermopolis and Antinoe, were constitutionally villages under
a κοινὸν τῶν ἀρχόντων, and derived their name and importance
as the administrative centres of the adjoining nomes.
Septimius now gave Alexandria and in all probability the
μητροπόλεις councils of their own. But although these communities thus acquired autonomy in their local affairs,
financially they were the losers. Upon the shoulders of the
new councillors was placed the duty of raising the quota of
imperial taxation—a responsibility which in the end was to
lead to their individual and collective impoverishment.[72]

Leaving Alexandria, Septimius sailed up the Nile visiting
Memphis and Thebes, where he heard the famous statue of
Memnon " sing " at dawn, but unfortunately the restoration
of its head and neck, which the enthusiastic Emperor ordered,
resulted in the statue losing its vocal powers.[73] Journeying
further south Septimius had reached the borders of Ethiopia
when he fell ill, stricken perhaps by plague or smallpox,
and on recovery returned to Alexandria. Some time in the

course of A.D. 201 he left Egypt, and on New Year's day entered upon his third consulship with Caracallus his son as colleague.[74] From Antioch the Augusti returned to Europe by way of Thrace, and after visiting the camps of the legions on the Danube proceeded through Aquileia to Rome. In place of the usual triumph the victories of Septimius and the tenth anniversary of his accession were commemorated by one festival which lasted for seven days. Magnificent games and shows were exhibited, and a largess of fifty million *denarii* was distributed to the praetorians and people. A more permanent memorial to the triumph of the Emperor and his two sons is the huge arch which still stands to-day in the north-west corner of the Roman Forum.[75]

§ 5. THE YEARS 202–207 AND THE HOME ADMINISTRATION OF SEPTIMIUS

During the six years which followed the return of Septimius from the East the Roman world was untroubled by foreign wars. The internal peace of some of the provinces, however, was disturbed by the desultory opposition of those adherents of Niger and Albinus who had been punished for their politics by a confiscation of their property. In Gaul C. Julius Septimius Castinus, the commander of I *Minervia*, operated with detachments of the four German legions against " the rebels and traitors "; in Asia Minor police-troops called κολλητίωνες were organized as collectors of the *bona damnatorum*, while in Italy itself a certain robber-chief called Bulla successfully defied authority for two years.[76] In Africa the tribes in Tripolis were restive, and, whether on that account alone or from a desire to see his old home, Septimius spent part of the year A.D. 203 visiting the principal towns of Africa. Upon many he conferred the status of a colony with the not infrequent addition of the *ius Italicum*, while dedications from Lambaesis speak of improvements made in the camp and the construction of a *via Septimiana*.[77] Of administrative importance is the elevation of Numidia, which had previously ranked as a diocese of the province of Africa, into a separate and independent imperial province under the control of the commander of III *Augusta* and with a procurator to administer its finances.[78]

Apart from his visit to Africa Septimius did not leave Rome
till A.D. 208, and to this period in all probability belong his
administrative reforms and his building activities in the
City. The celebration of the Secular games in A.D. 204
heralded, as it were, the beginning of a new age, and in the
following year the consulship was jointly held by the Emperor's
two sons.[79]

The rule of Septimius marks an important stage in the
development of the powers of the equestrian order, which
finds its culmination under Gallienus. Although senators
were not dispossessed of the governorship of the provinces
and the command of the old legions, the new province of
Mesopotamia and the three newly recruited legions were
entrusted to the care of knights. Similarly the *comites
Augusti*, who had previously been drawn exclusively from
the senatorial, were chosen by Septimius also from the
equestrian order, and the titles of *perfectissimus* and *eminentissimus*, in addition to the less honourable *egregius*, begin to
figure on inscriptions.[80] More significant is the great increase
of power and the enlarged sphere of activities acquired by
the prefect of the praetorian guard. What the office lost
in military power it gained in judicial and administrative
authority. The prefect now became the supreme criminal
judge in Italy beyond the hundredth milestone from Rome,
while inside the radius the *praefectus urbi* exercised the same
functions. To him came appeals from the sentences of the
provincial governors and in the absence of the Emperor he
presided over the imperial *consilium*. It was in consequence
more than ever necessary to entrust this office to the leading
jurists of the day, and under Septimius Papinian is but the
first of a long series of prefects, which included in its number
the lawyers Paul and Ulpian. In addition to his judicial
activities the prefect acquired control of the corn-supply
in place of the *praefectus annonae*, whose work was now limited
to the duties of distribution in the city, and with this function
was in all probability combined the wider and more important
duty of provisioning the army.[81] It is no exaggeration to
say that the praetorian prefect ranked only second to the
Emperor in the powers and authority which he wielded, and
the career of C. Fulvius Plautianus, the Emperor's one and
only favourite, provides the necessary illustration.

Plautianus like the Emperor was a native of Africa, and is said to have been exiled by Pertinax on a charge of treason.[82] How he came into close contact with Septimius is not known, but in the course of the second Parthian War he gained the confidence of the Emperor and amassed a great fortune from the confiscation of the property of Niger's adherents. Appointed prefect of the praetorians he encompassed the downfall of his colleague Aemilius Saturninus, and subsequently exercised an almost autocratic power. Dio tells many stories of his boundless greed and arrogance and, what is even more remarkable, Septimius' trust and confidence in his loyalty. He received the *ornamenta consularia*, and in A.D. 202 reached the zenith of his career by the marriage of his daughter Plautilla to Caracallus. Next year he held the consulship with Geta as his colleague, and this he was permitted to count as his second consulship, the previous gift of the consular *insignia* being unprecedently regarded as equivalent to the holding of that office. Thus anomalously the same man was vested with the two highest appointments open to the senatorial and equestrian orders. Plautianus' influence over Septimius was much resented by the Empress Julia Domna, and the strained relationship between them broke into open hostility when the prefect had the effrontery to bring specific charges against her. Meanwhile statues were being erected all over the Roman world to Plautianus, but when he caused his own image to be placed among those of the imperial family he fell from the Emperor's good graces. However, his disgrace was short-lived, and those, who, like Racius Constans, the governor of Sardinia, had pulled down his statues indiscriminately, were later brought to trial. For another year Plautianus continued to enjoy the restored indulgences of the Emperor, but at the same time incurred the detestation of his son.[83] Caracallus' marriage with Plautilla had not turned out a success, and a combination of dislike for his wife and disgust at the arrogant cruelty and ambition of her father drove him to a plot against his life. He suborned a centurion called Saturninus to warn his father of an alleged plan to assassinate him. The Emperor believing the story sent for the unsuspecting prefect. When he had come into his presence he received him kindly, merely reproaching him for his ingratitude and enquiring why he wished to kill

him. Indeed, Plautianus might have escaped, had not
Caracallus, foreseeing this possibility, rushed forward and
struck him. With difficulty Septimius restrained his son from
administering the *coup de grâce*, which was entrusted to a
common soldier. Thus on January 22, A.D. 205, ended the
career of Plautianus, remarkable alike for the obscurity
of its origin and the influence which it exercised over an
Emperor himself by nature an autocrat.[84] In his place
Septimius appointed two prefects, Maecius Laetus, the hero
of Nisibis, to perform the military duties of the office, and
Aemilius Papinianus to execute its judicial functions. Plautilla and her brother Plautus he banished to the Lipari Islands,
and Dio records the death or banishment of Caecilius Agricola
and others apparently unconnected with the conspiracy.[85]

As the equestrian order gained in power and privilege,
so the Senate was treated with disdain and indifference.
Its constitutional right to confer the Emperor's powers and
titles was reduced to an enforced acceptance and ratification
of the honours conferred by the army. A senator could no
longer propose a decree, nor had he any control over the
appointment of magistrates and provincial governors. He
became the member of a claque whose duty it was to applaud
the proposals and messages of the Emperor, nor was he any
longer shielded from torture if prosecuted on a charge of
treason. In this policy of senatorial oppression Septimius
seems to have had the support of the lawyers, who put forward
the theory that the Senate had surrendered rather than dele-
gated its powers to the Emperor. The legal fiction of the
Augustan diarchy was thus exposed; absolutism was
condoned in theory as it was demonstrated in fact by the
autocracy of the Emperor. But in the reign of Septimius
there are few indications of the misuse of supreme power,
which was typical of so many of his successors. Although
naturally cruel and vindictive to his opponents, he cannot
fairly be accused of a disregard of the principles of humani-
tarianism. The laws that he passed reflect rather a mildness
and equity, a recognition of the value of human life such
as had characterized the legislation of Antoninus Pius.
To take but a few examples, laws were passed forbidding
abortion[86] and protecting the interests of minors;[87] liability
to torture became no longer the exclusive fate of the lower

classes,[88] the status of slaves was more clearly defined.[89]
In short, the principle was established that the law is no
respecter of persons, and in it we may see an illustration of
the cosmopolitan policy of Septimius, which sought to
eliminate differences of race and rank among the citizens and
subjects of the Empire.

In the sphere of financial administration important developments took place. There were nominally still two treasuries,
the *aerarium* of the Roman people, theoretically controlled
by the Senate, and the imperial *fiscus*. In addition there
had grown up the *patrimonium* of the Emperor, consisting
of a great number of domains throughout the Empire
administered by his procurators, which had come to be an
inalienable inheritance transmitted with the Principate.
But in Egypt a further distinction was made between the
" Royal lands " which fell to the Emperor as the successor of
the Ptolemies, and the "Estates," the revenues of which went
into his private purse. Septimius made Egypt his model for
the reorganization of the Empire's finances. The *aerarium*
was reduced to the level of a municipal treasury of Rome ;
the *fiscus* received the revenues of imperial and senatorial
provinces and the bulk of the Emperor's *patrimonium*,
while side by side with it grew up a new exchequer, the
res privata principis. This received its first subsidies from the
confiscated property of the partisans of Niger and Albinus,[90]
and as it was enacted that all future acquisitions made by the
Emperor should be paid into its account, it rapidly surpassed
the old *patrimonium*. The officer in charge received a salary
equal to that of the secretaries of State and ranked with the
controller of the *fiscus*, whose title was changed from
procurator a rationibus to *rationalis*.[91]

On the death of Commodus the Roman Empire was on the
verge of bankruptcy ; Septimius left to his successors an
immense fortune. Of his methods of raising money by the
confiscation of his enemies' property we have already had
occasion to speak ; the effects of his financial policy upon
prosperity of the provinces will be later reviewed. But
whatever our judgement of his ability as a statesman, we
cannot fail to be impressed by the lavish open-handedness
of his expenditure. With justice was he commemorated
on his coins as " *munificentissimus providentissimusque*

princeps." During his reign six *congiaria* were distributed
to the populace of Rome, estimated at a total of two
hundred and twenty million *denarii* ;[92] expensive and extravagant games were exhibited in A.D. 202 and 204 ; free corn
and oil was distributed, and we even hear of free medicine
given to the sick under the superintendence of Galen.[93]
The alimentary system, which had been stopped by Commodus, was revived, and the cost of the postal service which,
despite some alleviation by Antoninus Pius, was still felt as
a heavy burden by the municipalities, was transferred to the
fiscus.[94] The city of Rome was enriched with costly new
buildings. In addition to the triumphal arch in the forum, on
which scenes from the Emperor's campaigns were depicted in
the continuous style, magnificent baths were constructed, and
at the south-east corner of the Palatine Hill a new palace
was built, partly on the foundations of Hadrian's palace
and partly on an artificially constructed platform supported
by huge arches overhanging the Circus Maximus, which still
survive to-day. Standing apart from the palace was the
Septizonium or House of the Seven Planets, the first landmark
to attract the attention of the traveller approaching Rome
by the Appian Way. In reality it was a fountain rising in
three tiers with columns, behind which were niches adorned
with statuary, and was probably intended as a memorial
to the Emperor's faith in astrology, which had guided him,
so tradition said, to choose Julia Domna, a lady with a royal
horoscope, for his second wife. It further illustrates the
Oriental influences that permeated Roman Art during the
3rd century.[95] Lastly, to repair the damage of the great
fire of A.D. 191 extensive building operations were carried
out in the city. From the reign of Septimius dates the
restoration of Vespasian's marble plan of Rome, which
was used to face the eastern wall of the temple of the Sacred
City overlooking the Forum of Vespasian.[96]

§ 6. THE LAST YEARS AND THE WAR IN BRITAIN

Septimius was not destined to finish his days in peaceful
retirement in the neighbourhood of Rome and on the
Campanian coast. Since the death of Plautianus the enmity
of Caracallus and Geta had been growing in intensity, and

the attempts of their father to distract them from the pursuit of pleasure had failed to make any impression. Convinced that the only possible way of restoring them to a sense of imperial responsibility lay in the discipline of camp life Septimius, despite his advanced age and severe attacks of gout, decided upon the personal conduct of a war in Britain. In A.D. 208 accompanied by his wife, his two sons and the praetorian prefect Papinian he left Rome, and on his arrival in Britain made York his headquarters.[97] But if anxiety for the dynastic succession and the recognition of the necessity of securing the loyalty of the army to his sons were dominant factors in determining the Emperor's action, the state of Britain itself called for a vigorous reassertion of Roman sovereignty. To understand the causes of unrest in the country we must go back a few years.

After his defeat of Albinus at Lugdunum in A.D. 197 Septimius sent Virius Lupus to take over the command in Britain. A very serious situation confronted the new governor. To support him in his bid for supreme power Albinus had denuded the garrisons of the province, and the Maiatae, one of the tribes that had broken through the Antonine Wall in the reign of Commodus, profited by the weakening of the Roman army to overrun a great part of northern Britain. Hadrian's Wall was destroyed, and the military stations and other centres as far south as York and Chester were overthrown. Lupus was compelled to bribe the Maiatae to return home, and then began a systematic restoration of the damage. In his governorship and that of Alfenius Senecio the work of reconstruction made such good progress that the country up to and including Hadrian's Wall was recovered and a beginning made with the rebuilding of outlying posts to the north of it.[98] Septimius, however, decided that such defensive operations were not sufficient, and in the year 209 under his personal leadership, and in 210, under the command of Caracallus, the army penetrated into the very heart of Scotland. The difficulties which confronted it were enormous. The native Caledonians were no longer prepared to risk a pitched battle as they had done a century earlier against Agricola at Mons Graupius. Instead they adopted guerilla tactics, harassing Septimius' army on the march, attempting to cut his lines of communication and rounding off stragglers and foraging parties. Dio estimates the Roman losses at no less a figure than fifty thousand.[99] In the autumn of 210 a peace was patched up by which Septimius ceded a considerable tract of country to the Caledonians, but early in the next year the latter in company with the Maiatae again broke into revolt. The aged Emperor rose from a bed of sickness to punish the rebels, but he was not fated to lead a third expedition. Worn out by illness and broken in spirit by the unfilial conduct of his eldest son he died at York on February 4, A.D. 211.[100]

If the motive of the Scottish campaigns was annexation, as Dio suggests,[101] then the result was nothing short of a military fiasco, and the assumption by Septimius and his two sons of the title *Britannicus* a hollow sham.[102] But his intention was probably different. While the Caledonian campaigns were in progress the reconstruction of Hadrian's Wall was vigorously carried on. The Tyne–Solway line was once again to be the northern boundary of the Roman province; the Antonine Wall was abandoned. Consequently the Scottish expeditions may be more fairly regarded as displays of military strength designed to impress upon the natives the lesson that the Romans did not intend to limit their activities to the construction of fortifications. And even if the policy failed in its immediate objective and the Caledonians gained confidence in their superiority in guerilla warfare, it bore fruit in the next century. Invasions from the north ceased and the restored Wall of Hadrian gave Britain a century of peace.[103]

CHAPTER II

THE MILITARY REFORMS OF SEPTIMIUS

JUST as the accession of Septimius had been secured by the legions, so the permanence of the dynasty which he attempted to found depended upon their continued support. It is consequently no great surprise to find that his reign marks an important epoch in the history of the Roman army. Not only were the fighting forces of the state increased in number, but their character and composition were transformed. The qualifications for command were revised and the conditions of service rendered easier and more attractive to the common soldier. The purpose and nature of these reforms and their effect upon the later history of the Roman Empire, however, have been very differently judged by historians. Before attempting, therefore, any appraisement of Septimius' policy, it will be best to examine in some detail the changes and modifications which he introduced in the Roman army.

On the death of Marcus Aurelius there were thirty legions in existence, a total which, except for the year of the four Emperors, had not been exceeded since the Principate of Augustus. Septimius recruited three new legions numbered I–III and bearing the title *Parthicae*, a sufficient indication that they were intended and considered necessary for the carrying out of his expansionist policy in the East. When and in what order these new units were raised we have insufficient evidence to decide. It has been thought on the strength of an inscription, which describes a certain C. Julius Pacatianus as " *procurator provinciae Osroenae, praefectus legionis Parthicae, procurator Alpium Cottiarum,*" that I *Parthica* was enlisted before the two other legions and is here referred to simply as *legio Parthica*, because there were as yet no other " Parthian " legions in existence.[1] But little confidence can be placed in such an argument. As far as we know a regularly formed legion—a *iusta legio*—always bore a name and number, and it is much more probable that the number has been accidentally omitted from the inscription in question than that the first of Septimius' new legions was at first called *legio Parthica*, and only received a number when two more units with the same titles were raised. Further, the Second and not the First Parthian War is the most likely occasion for an increase in the legionary army. As we have seen, the First Parthian War was in the nature of an adjunct to the war against Pescennius Niger ; it was retaliatory rather than aggressive in character ; it was concluded without any serious campaign against Parthia, and a temporary peace was patched up by the deposition of Abgarus and the transformation of his kingdom into the procuratorial province of Osroene. On the other hand, after the defeat of Albinus preparations were made in earnest for a war with Parthia, and the resulting annexation of Mesopotamia indicates that the Roman policy was now definitely expansionist. It seems then most probable that the three Parthian legions were raised early in A.D. 197 for this Eastern campaign. The areas from which the recruits for II *Parthica* were raised were Illyricum and Thrace,[2] and, although there is no evidence for the provenance of the soldiers of the other two legions, it is not unreasonable to suggest the Danubian region. At least we may be tolerably certain that Septimius would not raise troops in a part of the Empire that was favourable to Niger, and if I *Parthica* was recruited in the First Parthian War it is almost necessary to hold that its soldiers were Orientals.

After the Second Parthian War I and III *Parthicae* were left to garrison the newly-formed province of Mesopotamia, but II *Parthica* was on the return of Septimius to Italy established in a camp at Albanum less than twenty miles from Rome itself. Thus for the first time Italy was given a permanent legionary garrison. The significance of this step may be easily misunderstood. Some historians would see in it the planting of " the despotism of the East in the soil of the West," or " the sacrifice of Mediterranean culture to a pitiless soldiery."[3] Such exaggerations stand self-condemned. The policy of Septimius was more practicable and

6

less drastic. It was his intention to break down the distinctions that still separated Italy from the rest of the Roman world and to treat Italy as one of the provinces of the Empire. This levelling process, which culminates in Caracallus' famous edict, may also be traced in Septimius' reform of the praetorian guard.[4]

As we saw in the last chapter, Septimius replaced the old praetorian guard, which had been recruited from Italians and Roman citizens from Macedonia, Spain and Noricum, by a new guard for which legionaries from any part of the Empire were theoretically eligible. In practice the majority of these new praetorians came from the Danubian legions, and we only know of one Eastern legion—VI *Ferrata*—which as a reward for its loyalty to Septimius in the local conflicts of Samaria and Judaea was given the privilege of providing soldiers for the new guard.[5] One effect of this reform is clear. Service in the praetorians becomes a prize which any legionary soldier may hope to win; it ceases to be the exclusive right of Italians and favoured provincials. And as the praetorians were a seminary for the centurions and officers of equestrian rank, promotion from the ranks became easier and more frequent than it had been before. A definite step had been taken in the democratization of the Roman army, a levelling down of distinction between praetorian and legionary and between officer and common soldier. On the other hand, the urban cohorts still continued to be recruited from Italians and thus the link which had existed until then with the praetorians was broken.[6] The corps of *vigiles* too, which had previously been composed of freedmen, began to draw its members from free Roman citizens.[7] Thus against the provincializing of the praetorian guard must be set the retention of a definitely Italian character for the two other units of the household troops.

This remodelling of the praetorian guard has, however, been regarded by some historians as a " barbarization " of the Roman army. It is claimed that Italians and Roman citizens from the Western half of the Empire were now excluded from the *militia equestris*, and that officers of equestrian rank were in future drawn from Illyrians, Asiatics and Africans; that Italians ceased to be centurions, and that the new guard consisted of Thracian and Illyrian peasants who hardly spoke

Latin at all.[8] These statements give the impression that definite evidence exists for determining the provenance of tribunes, prefects and centurions in the third century A.D. Unfortunately in this period officers very rarely give their birthplaces and, even when they do, the chronological determination of a particular inscription frequently remains uncertain.[9] With such unsatisfactory evidence generalizations must necessarily be hazardous, but, when they are made, we are entitled to ask that they should be consistent with such dateable material as is available. The statements cited about the origins of tribunes and centurions will not stand this test. Inscriptions are extant which show that Italians could and did continue to serve as centurions, prefects and tribunes both in the legions and auxilia, and it is significant that one of them is a tribune of Septimius' new legion II *Parthica*.[10] On the other hand, it may be admitted that, especially after the edict of Caracallus, provincials were employed in increasingly large numbers as officers in the army, but the process was gradual and parallel to the proportional increase in legionary soldiers from the provinces relatively to Italians which begins with the Flavians. Such changes may be recognized without committing ourselves to the arbitrary judgement that Septimius excluded Italian officers and Vespasian Italian soldiers from the Roman army.

It is further questionable whether the soldiers of Septimius' new guard were Illyrian and Thracian peasants who hardly spoke Latin at all. It must be remembered that a necessary qualification for legionary service was the Roman citizenship, and until the passing of Caracallus' edict recruits for the Danubian legions were drawn from among the citizens of Roman towns and the sons of veteran soldiers born out of wedlock during their fathers' period of service. This is attested by an extant list of veterans of legion VII *Claudia* who were enrolled in A.D. 169 and discharged in A.D. 195.[11] Recruiting is local, but the soldiers give either a Roman town or *castra* as their birthplace. During the third century A.D., it is true, peasants gradually superseded townsfolk as legionary soldiers, and this change doubtless weakened the Roman element in the army. But for this Caracallus rather than his father must bear the responsibility. The immediate effects of the altered composition of the praetorian guard and

the establishment of a legion near Rome were the disappearance of a privileged status in the army for Italians and
favoured provincials and the reduction of Italy itself to a
level with the provinces. For the " barbarization " of the
army we must look rather to the policy of settling barbarians
inside the frontiers of the Empire and employing them to
fight for its protection.

Perhaps the most noticeable reform introduced by Septimius in the organization of the army is the widening of the
powers of the equestrian order and the increase in the number
of officers holding the rank of knight. Each of the three
new legions was commanded not by a *legatus* from the
senatorial order, but by an equestrian *praefectus*.[12] This
praefectus was of the same rank as the commander of a legion
in Egypt. He was thus selected from ex-centurions who had
held the post of *primus pilus* twice, and on inscriptions he
is regularly styled *vir egregius ducenarius*, while in order to
differentiate him from the *praefectus* (*castrorum*) *legionis*, an
officer of much inferior rank, the expression *vice legati* is
sometimes added, as if to indicate " this is the *praefectus* who
commanded the legion instead of the senatorial *legatus*."[13]
In the sphere of provincial command too the knights gained
at the expense of the senators. Mesopotamia was on the
model of Egypt placed under a *praefectus* of very high rank,[14]
and a new practice was instituted in the appointment of
vicarii or substitutes for provincial governors. Whereas in
the first two centuries such *vicarii* only functioned when a
governor had to be absent from his province or when he died
in office, and were normally the next senior officers in the
province, in the third century *vicarii*, who were procurators,
were not infrequently appointed, because the Emperor
wished to entrust a province to a man who was not qualified
to become a regular governor because he was of equestrian
rank.[15] Thus, although Septimius did not withdraw senators
from the government of existing provinces or from the command of existing legions, his regulations for the control of
Mesopotamia and the command of his new legions prepare
the way for the separation of civil and military administration which culminates in the reign of Gallienus.

With this increase in the powers and functions of the
equestrian order was combined a widening of its ranks. In

addition to centurions, *principales* were now granted the right to wear the golden ring and might be promoted to the rank of a knight.[16]   Sons of centurions became knights, while sons of *primi pili* entered the ranks of the senatorial order in the capacity of *tribuni laticlavii*.[17]   At the same time the common soldier was given wider facilities for obtaining the centurionate, *speculatores* and *beneficiarii consularis* being promoted directly without, as previously, holding the intermediate post of a *cornicularius*.[18]   The old barrier which had been drawn between officer and soldier was broken down and the common soldier might now rise through the centurionate to the rank of tribune or prefect.[19]   Special privileges were also granted to veteran soldiers.   The doors of the civil service were opened to them and such equestrian procuratorships as those in charge of mines and the city corn were regularly filled by them.   At the same time on their retirement into private life they were excused personal service in their native towns,[20] while tribunes of the praetorians were exempted from the duty of acting as guardians for the children of their comrades.[21]   Veteran soldiers thus constituted a definite class in the State which enjoyed particular favours.   On the completion of their military service they still retained a privileged status relatively to that of the peasant or the citizen of a municipal town, and consequently both during and after their military career they had little inducement to interest themselves in the politics and rivalries of the town and country population.   The policy of Septimius was thus both militarist and democratic.   The army is the avenue to the civil service and in the army the common soldier is a potential officer.

In addition to the facilities for promotion which we have been considering, Septimius introduced a number of changes affecting the social life of the army.   In his reign we first hear of the origin and development of *scholae* or clubs formed by the junior officers in the legion.   Apart from the social amenities which they offered these clubs corresponded to a modern insurance society.   Members contributed a small subscription from their pay and, when they were discharged or fell ill or were promoted to a higher rank, or even degraded, received a lump sum from the bank of the society which was controlled by a quaestor.   The chief evidence for these institutions comes from Lambaesis, the camp of the African legion. Here were *scholae* of horn-players, corporals, clerks, and armourer-sergeants.[22] But the movement was not limited to the native province of the Emperor. Similar clubs are mentioned at Aquincum and Potaissa, and there is no reason to suppose that the institution was not common to the whole legionary army.[23]

In Septimius' reign new regulations were made for the marriage of legionary soldiers. Previously if a soldier was a married man at the time of his enlistment, he was given the alternative of living apart from his wife, or, if he preferred, of divorcing her. In no case was she allowed to accompany him on his service abroad. Further, if a soldier during his period of service formed an alliance with a native woman from the neighbourhood of his camp, his marriage was not legally recognized till his discharge and only the subsequent issue was legitimatized. If sons were born to him during his period of service, they did not receive the citizen-status of their father. They were said to be born *castris*, and only acquired citizen rights when they offered themselves for service in the legions.[24] The purpose of Septimius' regulation was to abolish this anomaly.[25] In future the alliance of a legionary with a native woman was recognized as a *iustum conubium* from the time of its contraction, and the children of the marriage were in consequence Roman citizens. Although the legal recognition of a soldier's marriage meant that he was permitted on occasions to live with his wife in a house or lodging in the neighbouring town, there is no justification for the view that Septimius' regulation was tantamount to the abolition of barrack-life.[26] If one may argue from present-day conditions, not more than one-half of the soldiers in a unit would be married men, and it is a reasonable conjecture that the latter would only be permitted the privilege of living out of camp when conditions on the frontier were undisturbed by threat of invasion. The frontier-legions were not yet reduced to the local militia of the fourth century A.D. On the other hand, Dio, Herodian and subsequent writers represent Septimius as having relaxed and subverted the discipline of the army, and some historians have singled out the new marriage regulations as illustrative of the change. Other grounds may, however, be suggested for this recrimination. We hear of not infrequent revolts, notably at Saxa Rubra and at Hatra, and the pacification of the restive troops by large donatives.[27] The behaviour, too, of Septimius' troops in Rome is contrasted unfavourably with the discipline of Pertinax' army. Further, Septimius increased the pay both of praetorians and legionaries. In Commodus' reign a fifth *stipendium* had been added making the annual pay of the praetorian 1250 and of the legionary 375 *denarii*. Septimius, it would seem, added 25 *denarii* to each of the five *stipendia* that the legionary received, making his annual pay 500 *denarii*, while the praetorian's pay was proportionally raised to the figure of 1700 *denarii*.[28] Here then was ample material out of which Septimius' opponents might frame a charge of subverting discipline. The Emperor was dependent upon his soldiers for the maintenance of his power, but to secure that support it was necessary to bribe them with frequent donatives and an increase of pay. Nor is the charge without justification. Military despotism, it may be conceded, was the most practical solution for the chaotic condition of the imperial government at the accession of Septimius, but, however hard the task, the inability of the founder of the new dynasty to control the licentiousness of his soldiers except by pandering to their demands meant in effect that the door was opened to a domination in which the army and not the Emperor was the true despot.

During the reign of Septimius many works of military importance were constructed in the provinces, as the frequent dedications to the Emperor and the *Domus Divina* set up by the troops engaged in their erection abundantly testify. In addition to the restoration of Hadrian's Wall in Britain, which, as we saw in the last chapter, had been destroyed by the Maiatae and Caledonians during Albinus' absence in Gaul, outposts were erected in Africa on the caravan routes south of the *Limes Tripolitanus*. Ruins of a fortress with four gates have been discovered at the oasis of Bondjem, some 200 miles south-east of Oea in Tripolis, and an auxiliary cohort has left a record of some similar fortification at Siaoun, which lies about the same distance to the south-west of Oea.[29] On the northern frontier of the Rhine and Danube a systematic strengthening of the defences was probably begun in the reign of Septimius and completed by his son.

To this date belongs the stone wall which begins at Hienheim on the Danube and runs to a point north-west of Lorch, where it joins the *Pfahlgraben*, which effects a junction with the Rhine.[30] In the East there was less activity, but we hear of the construction of a camp for public safety against the terror of the Scaenite Arabs of Mesopotamia.[31] Elsewhere there was an extensive rebuilding and restoration of garrisons. At Lambaesis the club-rooms of the newly formed *scholae* were erected ; waterworks were constructed at Ems and an armoury rebuilt at Roomburg near Leiden, while in Dacia the legate, Octavius Julianus, provided work for the auxiliary troops under his command in replacing with stone a turf wall in the district of Bumbesti.[32]

There are thus abundant signs of attempts to strengthen the defences of the Empire and repair the damage of war and time. For a brief period Rome enjoyed peace from external aggression.

CHAPTER III

CARACALLUS AND MACRINUS

§ 1. CARACALLUS AND GETA

ON his deathbed Septimius is reported to have ex-
horted his sons to live in peace with each other, to
enrich the soldiers and despise the rest of the world.[1]
That this advice, which so well epitomized the secret of his
own success, was scantily respected was his misfortune
rather than his responsibility.

On hearing of his father's death Caracallus, while lending a
nominal recognition to his brother's claim as Augustus to a
share in the government of the Empire, immediately put into
operation his plans for the acquisition of sole personal rule.
His first act was to make peace with the Caledonians and
evacuate such of their territory as was occupied by Roman
troops.[2] Although this policy proved in the sequel advan-
tageous both to Britain and the Empire, the motive which
actuated Caracallus was the expediency of an early return to
Rome for the consolidation of his own position. At the same
time he decided to rid himself of the irksome company of his
father's advisers and friends, who might be expected to
respect the late Emperor's scheme for the future of his
dynasty and consequently to support the cause of Geta.
Accordingly he deposed Papinian from his office of praetorian
prefect and put to death his old tutor Euodus and his father's
counsellor Castor, while his wife Plautilla, who had been
banished to the Lipari Islands, was a further victim of his
brutality.[3] To this list he would gladly have added the name
of his brother, but, just as his intrigues had previously been
foiled by his father in his lifetime, so now the army stood in
the way of his murderous designs. Apart from a reverence
for their late Emperor's commands, the soldiers of the
British legions felt a genuine affection for Geta, who seemed

89

to them to resemble his father in character no less than in appearance.[4]

In this state of mutual distrust and suspicion the two princes set out for Rome in company with their mother Julia Domna, and taking with them the ashes of their father. On the journey the jealousy broke out afresh. If Herodian may be believed, they refused to stay at the same inns or take their meals together for fear of poison, and both were eager to reach Rome, where each imagined that his personal safety would be secure.[5] On reaching the city in May they were greeted with enthusiastic cries of " Long live the Augusti " by the Senate and people, who did reverence to the remains of their late ruler. But after the funeral and apotheosis of Septimius the hatred of the two brothers was intensified. They chose different parts of the palace for their residence, and set soldiers to guard the entrances and to prevent any unauthorized intrusions.[6] A plan was even proposed for a division of the Empire, by which Geta should govern Asia and Caracallus Europe, with the Hellespont as the frontier of their domains, but it was frustrated by their mother, who perhaps saw in such a scheme a diminution of her imperial authority. " You may divide the Empire," she said, " but you cannot divide your mother."[7] At last after an abortive attempt by Caracallus to murder his brother at the Saturnalia, the end came in February A.D. 212. Caracallus asked his mother to invite his brother and himself alone to her house to effect a reconciliation. Geta accepted, but on entering his mother's room he was set upon by some centurions whom Caracallus had previously concealed. With the cry of " Save me, mother," he rushed into Julia's arms, and was murdered as he clung to her bosom.[8]

Caracallus, although it was evening, immediately left the palace and was conveyed by his bodyguard to the camp of the praetorians, proclaiming as he went to the astonished passers-by his narrow escape from assassination. On entering the camp he forestalled the curiosity of the soldiers by extravagant promises of higher pay and better rations, and by his professed anxiety to be regarded as one of themselves. " With you I pray to live or, if need be, die ; yours are all the treasures of the State." Mollified by these assurances the

praetorians welcomed him as their only Emperor and promised
their loyal support.[9] From the praetorian camp Caracallus
hastened to test the feelings of the legion stationed at
Albanum, and here his schemes were nearly wrecked. Mindful
of their promise to Septimius to show allegiance to both his
sons, the soldiers shut the gates of their camp and refused
the Emperor admission. But their good intentions were not
proof against bribery, and the snare of increased wages was
too strong for their honourable scruples. At length the gates
were unlocked and Caracallus entered the camp.[10] For the
moment he took no further notice of the legion's recalcitrant
attitude, but the soldiers, who are recorded by Dio among
the victims of his later vengeance, may not improbably have
belonged to II *Parthica*.[11]

Caracallus spent the night in the praetorian camp and next
day under armed escort attended a meeting of the Senate.
After a long speech in which the dangers that had beset his
life from his brother's machinations were magnified in
evidence of his own innocence and integrity, he sought to
win a measure of popularity by granting an amnesty to all
exiles.[12] But Rome had not long to wait for the revelation
of his true intentions. On returning to his palace from the
Senate Caracallus gave orders for a vigorous persecution of all
adherents of his brother Geta. Men and women of every
rank were put to death, and Dio states that no less than
twenty thousand fell before his vengeance.[13] The mere
mention of the name of Geta spelled death.[14] Among the
more notable victims may be mentioned Papinian, Pompeianus, a grandson of Marcus, and Helvius Pertinax, a son
of the late Emperor of that name, while Cilo, Caracallus'
former tutor, although rescued from the soldiers' insults by
his pupil's intervention, was spared, if we may believe Dio,
less from any affectionate regard for the old man than from
disgust that his murder had been so protracted.[15] Geta's
name was erased from inscriptions and his coinage was cancelled.[16] His body was cremated and the ashes deposited in
the Septizonium which his father had built on the Palatine
adjoining the palace.

§ 2. REIGN OF CARACALLUS

Caracallus did not stay long in Rome. Early in A.D. 213[17] he set out for Germany, and with the exception of a short visit to the capital at the end of that year was continuously abroad till his death. Like his father he realized that the army was the mainstay of his imperial power and concentrated upon winning its approval and loyalty. For his hero he chose Alexander the Great and sought to imitate and achieve his plans of conquest and schemes of Empire.[18] He dreamed of an Utopia in which Romans and Iranians should live in unity and together dispel the dark menace of barbarian invasions. But for the realization of such an ideal Caracallus had neither the personality nor the requisite statesmanship and gift of command. With his troops he sought to ingratiate himself by raising their pay and consorting with them on terms of equality, sharing their duties and conforming to their standard of living. In negotiating with his enemies he would employ intrigue and even treachery, if by those means he could more easily effect his purpose. He had neither dignity nor charm ; he was cruel, vindictive and cowardly. Such popularity as he enjoyed among his men was rather the fruit of his indulgences than a spontaneous tribute to his generalship. In the last three years of his life he was haunted by delusions and afflicted with bodily diseases, for which neither magician nor doctor could provide a remedy.

Despite, however, the moral degradation of his character and the vanity of his ambition it cannot be said that the reign of Caracallus was devoid of military distinction. If he lacked the power to command, he possessed some ability as a strategist and had the soldier's eye for fortresses and defensive sites. At least this may be said to his credit that the northern frontier successfully withstood the barbarian attacks for a further twenty years.

After his departure from Rome Caracallus first went to Gaul, where his biographer states he put to death the governor of Narbonensis upon some unrecorded charge.[19] He next proceeded into Raetia to make preparations for an attack upon the Alamanni, a tribe that under pressure from the barbarians in Eastern Germany had migrated westwards and, living on the right bank of the upper Rhine, is now for the first time mentioned among the enemies of Rome. An army of considerable size was concentrated for the campaign. Detachments were taken from the Danubian legions probably under the command of C. Julius Alexianus, and perhaps too from Germany under the command of Suetrius Sabinus,[20] while from the title *Germanica* granted to the Egyptian legion II *Traiana* it is probable that the whole of that unit was temporarily withdrawn from its province.[21] Meanwhile a systematic strengthening of the Rhenish-Raetian frontier was carried out. Faimingen on the Danube was fortified with stone walls, and many other fortresses were now for the first time built of stone or reconstructed and restored. To this year in all probability belongs the completion of the stone wall from Hienheim to Lorch and the final form and direction of the *Pfahlgraben* in Upper Germany.[22] Nor did Caracallus abstain from treacherous intrigue in order to diminish the resistance of his enemy. We are told by Dio that he invited the Alamanni to an alliance and offered mercenary service to their young men, but when they came to be enrolled they were surrounded and put to death.[23] On August 11th Caracallus crossed the Raetian *limes*, while the governor of Upper Germany set out from Mainz. The plan of attack was a converging movement not unlike that which was intended by Tiberius against the Marcomanni in A.D. 6, and the strategy was an entire success. In the neighbourhood of the river Main a decisive victory was won towards the end of September; Caracallus was hailed *imperator* for the third time and received the title of *Germanicus Maximus*.[24]

Elsewhere in Germany, however, the Roman arms were less successful. In a campaign against the Cenni, who may perhaps be identified with the Catti, great losses were suffered and the invaders had to be bribed to withdraw.[25] We hear, too, of embassies from tribes living near the mouth of the Elbe successfully proffering friendship in exchange for a subsidy in gold.[26] Thus peace was re-established in Germany, but at a price which the Empire could ill afford to pay and on a principle which was subversive of its prestige. At the end of the year Caracallus, accompanied by a German body-guard, returned to Rome afflicted with a disease that even

the waters of Baden-Baden had failed to cure.[27] As a token
of his admiration for the country which he had pacified he
introduced into Rome the long flowing cloak reaching to the
ankles, which has given him the nickname by which he is
generally known in history.[28]

In the early spring of A.D. 214 Caracallus once again set
out from Rome. This time the East was his objective, where
he hoped to realize his dream of an Empire that would con-
tain in peaceful co-operation the two great civilizing powers
of the world. But first in order to satisfy himself that the
Danubian frontier was adequately fortified to maintain
the peace of Europe, Caracallus went to Pannonia. Here he
inspected the legionary fortresses and made alterations in
the boundaries and military resources of the two provinces,
the details of which will be later described.[29] Continuing
his journey down the river the Emperor stopped for some
time in Dacia, exacting hostages from those natives that were
not subject to Rome as a guarantee of good faith.[30] The rest
of the summer he spent in the Balkans engaged partly in a
war with the Carpi,[31] and partly in perfecting his imitation of
Alexander and in reverencing his memory.[32] He caused
statues of the king to be set up in Rome and in the camps ;
he used himself drinking vessels and arms like those of his
hero and attired himself in Macedonian dress. Of more
practical importance was the organization of a phalanx
16,000 strong, which he caused to be equipped and drilled
in the Macedonian tradition, giving its commanders the
names of Alexander's generals.[33] Late in the year he crossed
the Hellespont, narrowly escaping drowning from shipwreck,
and visited Pergamum and Troy. At the former he sought
the help of Asclepius for his sickness ; at the latter he paid
honour to the tomb of Achilles and, if Herodian may be
believed, attempted to reproduce the burial of Patroclus at
the funeral of a favourite freedman called Festus, who
happened to die during his sojourn at the city.[34] The rest of
the winter he spent at Nicomedia partly amusing himself
with games and shows, which included on the occasion of the
Saturnalia a feast for senators at which the historian Dio was
present,[35] partly organizing his army for the Eastern War.
Detachments from the Rhenish and Danubian legions were
concentrated in Bithynia, and the Macedonian phalanx was

drilled in preparation for the coming campaign. Two huge
engines of war were constructed and transported by sea to
Syria,[36] and at length, after celebrating his birthday on
April 4th, the Emperor set out with his troops to Antioch,
where he was enthusiastically welcomed and joined by
further reinforcements, which included a detachment from
the African legion.[37]

The subsequent fighting falls into distinct areas and
stages. In A.D. 215 Theocritus, a freedman, who had won
fame as an actor and been promoted as a reward to a high
command in the army, was sent against the Armenians,
whose king on the plea of friendship Caracallus had treacherously made prisoner. The result of the campaign was a
severe defeat for the Romans and the consequent withdrawal of the army into northern Syria.[38] Against the Parthians on the other hand no active steps were taken.
Caracallus, we are told, had sought a pretext for war in the
demand for the restoration of two deserters, one of whom
was the cynic philosopher Antiochus, who had rendered
useful service to Septimius in setting an example of endurance
to his soldiers by rolling himself in the snow of the Taurus
Mountains, and had then requited that Emperor's pecuniary
reward by joining his enemies. But when Vologeses complied
with the demand impending hostilities were postponed.[39]
A more probable reason for Caracallus' delay may, however,
be found in events taking place in Egypt. As we have seen,
the legion of that province had been sent to Germany to
assist in the war against the Alamanni. Profiting by its
absence the people of Alexandria had broken into revolt,
perhaps as a protest against excessive taxation. The situation was serious enough to require the Emperor's personal
intervention with part of his army, and the punishment
meted out to the rebels, if unnecessarily severe, may be
regarded rather as a guarantee of security during the coming
Parthian campaign than, as the literary authorities suggest,
a mere exhibition of vindictive cowardice.[40] Towards the
end of A.D. 215 Caracallus returned to Antioch and his
army wintered in north Syria.[41]

Next year war was declared against Parthia. The *casus
belli* was the refusal of Artabanus, who had succeeded
Vologeses, to give his daughter in marriage to Caracallus,[42]

who doubtless hoped by this rather obvious stratagem to facilitate the genesis of his Romano-Iranian Utopia. The Emperor moved from Antioch to Edessa where Abgarus IX, king of Osroene, suffered the same fate as had befallen the Armenian monarch in the previous year.[43] Advancing into Media he sacked several fortresses, including Arbela, without encountering any opposition.[44] But learning that the enemy had retired in order to make preparations for a more effective resistance he withdrew his troops to Edessa. The winter was spent in planning a more vigorous offensive, but Caracallus was not destined to witness the effect.[45] On April 8th, A.D. 217, while journeying from Edessa to make a sacrifice in a temple of the Moon at Carrhae, he was killed by a common soldier called Julius Martialis, acting on the instructions of Opellius Macrinus. This Macrinus was a native of Africa, whose business capacities had attracted the attention of Plautianus. On the latter's fall he had been admitted a member of the imperial service, and after holding the office of administrator of the Emperor's private domains succeeded Papinian as prefect of the praetorians. At the time of Caracallus' murder this command was shared by Oclatinius Adventus, a man of no education and now advanced in years who had been promoted from the ranks. Macrinus' motive for the assassination of Caracallus would seem to have been fear for his own personal safety. The story goes that Flavius Maternianus, who was acting as viceroy in Rome, was informed by an astrologer of impending danger to the Emperor at the hands of Macrinus and his son Diadumenianus. Accordingly he dispatched a warning letter to Caracallus, but unfortunately when the bearer arrived the Emperor was watching a chariot race and handed the missive unopened to his prefect. Whether this story is authentic or whether Macrinus received a secret warning from a friend in Rome, no alternative remained for him but to fulfil the destiny which the astrologers foretold. Martialis was suborned as the agent of the crime, and after striking the fatal blow was captured and killed by the imperial German bodyguard. By these means and by a feigned sorrow for his master's death Macrinus successfully concealed his share in the plot until the soldiers after a delay of two days, during which the Empire had no ruler, saluted him as Emperor.[46]

§ 3.   THE ADMINISTRATION OF CARACALLUS

The home administration of Caracallus followed closely
the lines laid down by his father. Towards the Senate he
adopted an attitude of open disdain and hostility, and drew
his ministers from the equestrian order. His cousins, Julia
Soaemias and Julia Mammaea, the daughters of Julia Maesa,
were given in marriage to two knights called Sextus Varius
Marcellus and Gessius Marcianus,[47] and the former seems
for a time to have acted as the Emperor's viceroy in Rome,
combining the duties of praetorian prefect and prefect of the
city. Thus by an unusual accumulation of offices he, like
Plantianus, received conjointly the crown of both the equestrian and senatorial careers. In the sphere of jurisdiction
Caracallus himself, although not slow to take a point, showed
little personal interest, but was content to leave the hearing of
cases to others.[48] At the same time he encouraged delation
and his secret-service agents, *speculatores* and *frumentarii*
drawn from the legions, exercised a tyranny over all classes of
society, while Dio characterizes the ascendancy of an eunuch
called Sempronius Rufus as the deepest affront that had
yet been offered to the Senate and people of Rome.[49]

Developing still further Septimius' policy of levelling
distinctions of rank and race in the Empire Caracallus in
A.D. 212 issued his famous edict conferring citizenship upon
all subjects in the Empire. Consistently with this reform he
gave the right of criminal jurisdiction over Roman citizens
to all provincial governors, and appeal to Rome was only
permitted in exceptional cases.[50] Further, to make the
financial consequences of the enfranchisement more remuner-
ative he raised the taxes on inheritances and manumissions
to which all citizens were liable from 5 per cent to 10 per
cent.[51] But neither this increase in taxation nor the repeated
demands for the *aurum coronarium*[52] were sufficient to balance
the heavy expenses of the State and the Emperor's lavish
gifts to his soldiers and favourites ; while, in addition, the
supply of gold and silver was diminished by the export of
gold to India and silver to Germany. In A.D. 215 resort was
made to the pernicious expedient of inflating the coinage.[53]
During the previous century the debasement of the silver
in the *denarius* had been steadily on the increase, rising from

7

15 per cent under Trajan to almost 40 per cent under Septimius. Further depreciation was dangerous. The government therefore chose the alternative course of reducing the weight of the coins, and rather than experiment in this way with the *denarius*, which was still worth more as a coin than as metal, issued a new coin, the *Antoninianus* or double *denarius*, at less than the weight of two *denarii*. At the same time the weight of the *aureus* was reduced to one-fiftieth of a pound. The *denarius* was thus saved for a while from the melting-pot, but because the government made a greater profit out of the new *Antoninianus* and because the relative values of the two coins was never properly adjusted, it soon fell into desuetude. After Severus Alexander had cancelled the issue of *Antoniniani*, Balbinus and Pupienus in the urgent need for money that the civil war entailed revived the issue, and from then onwards the *Antoninianus* became the standard silver coin till in the crisis of Gallienus' reign the government put into circulation masses of billon that was hardly distinguishable from copper.[54] Thus the reckless expenditure of Caracallus, to which the ruins of his magnificent baths, with their extensive colonnades and richly decorated halls, to-day bear sombre testimony, precipitated the Empire upon the downward path that forty years later led to national bankruptcy.[55]

§ 4. REIGN OF MACRINUS

The reign of Macrinus marks the beginning of a new epoch in the history of Rome. He was the first Emperor who did not belong to the senatorial order,[56] and his rule foreshadows the long succession of " soldier-Emperors " who owed their position entirely to the favour of their troops. His elevation was, however, at first not unpopular. So great was the relief felt in Rome at the death of the hated tyrant that the choice of the army was without hesitation recognized and confirmed by the Senate.[57] But Macrinus had no natural gifts for administration. If devoid of any conspicuous vices, he lacked judgement and political insight, he was unbusiness-like, dilatory and fond of pleasure. He attempted to affiliate himself to the fallen dynasty by adopting the title of Severus and conferring that of Antoninus upon his son, and somewhat tactlessly insisted on the apotheosis of Caracallus under the

name of "Antoninus the Great."[58] With the Senate his
popularity was short-lived. For although he tried to secure
its support by granting an amnesty to political exiles and by
cancelling the increase in taxes that his predecessor had
imposed,[59] he offended that august body by assuming the
full imperial titles and privileges before they had been conferred by the customary decree, and by the appointment
of his former colleague Adventus to the post of prefect of
the city.[60] But failure to maintain good relations with the
Senate would have been negligible if he had been able to hold
the loyalty of the army. Macrinus was a poor general. An
invasion of Mesopotamia by Artabanus in retaliation for his
treatment by Caracallus forced him to take the field, and
after some indecisive fighting a peace was patched up, by
which Macrinus agreed to the surrender of the prisoners that
had been captured and the payment of a large indemnity.
At the same time Armenia passed out of Roman control,
although the son of the king deposed by Caracallus continued
a nominal recognition of Roman sovereignty.[61] Such an
inglorious settlement was not calculated to inspire the
soldiers with confidence in their Emperor, but the re-establishment of peace might have been turned to advantage, if
Macrinus had taken immediate steps to introduce a stricter
discipline in the army. It is true that he attempted some
retrenchment in military expenditure by reverting to Severan
rates of pay for new recruits, while retaining the advances
guaranteed by Caracallus for serving soldiers only.[62] But
he made a fatal mistake in keeping the European legions in
the East after the campaigns were completed.[63] Discontent
soon broke out, the recruits grumbling at their lower rate of
pay, the veterans despising the unwarlike temper of their
general and clamouring for a return to their own native
countries. Everything was ready for another transference
of the imperial power, and the initiative was taken by a
woman.

Soon after the death of her son Caracallus, Julia Domna
had died at Antioch either by her own hand or of the disease
with which she had long been afflicted.[64] Her sister, Julia
Maesa, was dismissed from the Court by Macrinus, but
was permitted to retire to her native city of Emesa,[65]
where her family held the hereditary priesthood of the god

Elagabalus, under which title the local Ba'al, believed to
be incarnate in a black conical stone, was worshipped.
Maesa had two daughters, Soaemias and Mammaea, each of
whom had a son.[66] The elder of these two boys, Bassianus,
who was now in his fifteenth year, was the chief-priest of
Elagabalus. In the magnificent temple of the Unconquered
Sun-God he performed the religious ceremonies of his office,
clad in long flowing garments embroidered in purple and
gold and adorned with costly jewels. Good-looking, effemi-
nate and profligate, this moral pervert was by a ruse selected
to mount the throne of the Caesars. The plot originated
with his grandmother, Maesa, supported by the women and
eunuchs who attended her. The story was put about that
the boy-priest was the natural son of Caracallus. With the
additional promise of a large donative the officers and men of
III *Gallica*, the legion which was stationed in the district,
accepted Bassianus as the rightful successor of the Severi,
and on May 16th, A.D. 218, proclaimed him Emperor under
the title of Marcus Aurelius Antoninus.[67] Against the
usurper Macrinus despatched a cavalry force under his
praetorian prefect Ulpius Julianus, but the troops deserted
to the pretender, murdered their commander, and sent his
head to Macrinus.[68] Antoninus' army at Emesa was thus
considerably reinforced, and soon the news of the " dis-
covery " of Caracallus' son spread further disaffection.
Macrinus left Antioch for Apamea, the headquarters of
II *Parthica*, and endeavoured to restore confidence by cancelling the reductions in the soldiers' pay, by the addition of
an enormous donative and by the elevation of his son,
Diadumenianus, to the rank of Augustus. Supported by the
praetorians and II *Parthica* he proceeded against Antoninus,
but in the ensuing battle the legion deserted and he was
compelled to retire hastily to Antioch.[69] All was not yet
lost ; for Marius Secundus, the governor of Phoenice, and
Julius Basilianus, the prefect of Egypt, remained loyal to
Macrinus.[70] But the issue was not long in doubt. Antoninus
was now strong enough to take the offensive and advanced
against Antioch. In a battle fought in the immediate
vicinity of the city after varying fortunes victory rested with
the pretender's army. Macrinus fled from the battle-field
and made for Europe with such speed as the imperial

post horses could travel. Eventually, however, he was
captured at Chalcedon, and soon afterwards put to death by
order of Antoninus, while a similar fate attended his son,
Diadumenianus, who attempted to find a safe refuge in
Parthia.[71]

From the day of the battle, June 8th, A.D. 218,
Elagabalus—for under this name he was known to his contemporaries through the Oriental custom of identifying the
priest with the god whom he served—reckoned the beginning
of his reign.

CHAPTER IV

ELAGABALUS AND SEVERUS ALEXANDER

§ 1. THE REIGN OF ELAGABALUS

AFTER his victory over Macrinus, Elagabalus entered Antioch and in a letter to the Senate, in which he assumed the normal imperial powers and titles and styled himself the son of Antoninus and the grandson of Septimius, professed his intention of governing according to the precepts of Augustus and Marcus Aurelius.[1] Through fear of the army the Senate reluctantly acquiesced and hailed its unknown boy-Emperor as the son of blessed Caracallus, whose memory not so many months back it had been eager to anathematize. Elagabalus was, however, in no hurry to reach Rome and despite the urgent entreaties of Maesa spent the winter at Nicomedia.[2] Here he indulged in his fanatical rites and practices with the fullest and wildest extravagance, and when his grandmother suggested that it would be politic to discard his priestly robes and don the soberer Roman dress before entering the capital he not merely declined but caused a picture of himself performing his priestly functions before the divine emblem to be sent to Rome and to be placed above the image of Victory in the Senate-house with the added instructions that his god should be worshipped before all other gods, and that Senate and people should invoke his name first in their prayers and supplications.[3] In these excesses Elagabalus was encouraged by his mother, Julia Soaemias. The cult of the god dominated and obsessed their minds to such an extent that everything was subordinated and sacrificed to his worship.[4] To the affairs of State they gave neither thought nor attention, and it was only through the shrewd abilities of Julia Maesa that any control of the Empire was retained in the Court. Nor were the soldiers slow in recognizing the error of their choice ; for the very legion which had been instrumental in raising Elagabalus to the throne within a few months attempted to supplant him by its commander Verus, and was cashiered as a punishment for its disloyalty.[5]

Elagabalus entered Rome in the spring of A.D. 219, and for three years the city was subjected to an unparalleled exhibition of immorality and debauchery, practised with all the fanatical zeal and superstitious fervour that the emotional cults of the East can inspire in their adherents. Excess of every kind was represented as paying God honour and doing him service. For the god himself two magnificent temples were built, one on the Palatine and the other in the suburbs of the city, and to enhance his glory the most sacred emblems of the other cults were moved from their own shrines and collected in his temple near the imperial palace.[6] The image of Pallas was removed from the custody of the Vestal Virgins, and the goddess offered in marriage to the new god, and when she was rejected as too warlike a bride, a partner was sought for him in the Carthaginian Urania. Thus the Syrian Sun was joined in wedlock with the Phoenician Moon.[7] At midsummer the great festival of the year was celebrated. The god was taken from his temple on the Palatine and was driven in a chariot richly adorned with costly jewels and drawn by six white steeds to his temple outside the city. No charioteer mounted the carriage, but the Emperor himself ran backwards in front of the chariot with his eyes fixed in silent adoration upon the god himself. Thus he continued along the richly strewn route of the procession, attended by a bodyguard to save him from stumbling in his backward pilgrimage, and accompanied by a vast throng of people, among whom when the religious rites were over he distributed the gold and silver, beasts and raiment that had been collected in honour of the deity.[8]

The Emperor himself was officially designated " Priest of the Unconquered Sun-God Elagabalus," and this title took precedence of all the other imperial titles.[9] In this role he permitted himself every form of licentiousness that his perverted imagination could represent as for the greater glory of his god. Within three years he married and divorced no fewer than five wives, including Acilia Severa, one of the Vestal Virgins.[10] He took delight in appearing in public as a dancer or a charioteer, and like his mother, Soaemias, descended to the most debased forms of religious prostitution.[11] This transplantation of the Syrian cult into Roman public life and the fanatical intensity with which its rites were openly practised by the Emperor-priest naturally aroused the deepest detestation and sense of degradation among the more educated classes, of which Dio Cassius is the spokesman, and if the soldiery and common people showed no marked disapprobation, the reason may be found in their unscrupulous venality. Nor was Elagabalus a mere religious fanatic ; he was cruel, extravagant and treacherous, without honour or responsibility. Gannys the eunuch, who had commanded his troops in the final battle with Macrinus, was speedily put to death,[12] and this fate was shared by several provincial governors. Chief authority in the State was exercised by a certain P. Valerius Comazon, an ex-actor who became praetorian prefect and held the consulship with the Emperor, and subsequently the post of prefect of the city on no fewer than three occasions.[13] A charioteer called Cordius was prefect of the fire-brigade, while the care of the corn-supply was entrusted to a hairdresser named Claudius.[14] Moral depravity was the passport to administrative preferment.

The Emperor's conduct not unnaturally gave Julia Maesa cause for great alarm and uneasiness. In the growing unpopularity of her grandson she foresaw the loss of her own personal ascendancy and the final overthrow of the dynasty of the Severi. To safeguard her own position and to retain the privilege which she had been accorded of a seat in the Senate, she accordingly determined that her other grandson, Alexianus, the son of Julia Mammaea, should be given an official standing in the government of the Empire, and that Elagabalus should adopt him as his son. Playing upon the Emperor's fanatical devotion to his god she artfully suggested that, if he were to adopt his cousin, he could hand over to him the mundane affairs of state and so free himself for a deeper concentration upon his priestly duties. The ruse was successful. In the summer of A.D. 221, and perhaps on July 10th, Elagabalus adopted Alexianus as his heir, and the young Caesar, who now took the names of M. Aurelius Severus Alexander, was made a partner in the imperial power.[15] In the following year the two cousins held the consulship.[16]

Alexander, who was only thirteen years of age, was in every way the antithesis of his cousin. Through the care of his mother, Julia Mammaea, he had been kept free from the contamination of Eastern fanaticism and had been given the rudiments of an European education.[17] Of a friendly and amenable disposition he soon became a favourite both of the people and the soldiers. Elagabalus, apprehending danger to himself in his cousin's popularity, wanted to revoke his act of adoption, and even conspired at his assassination; but his schemes were thwarted by the vigilance of his aunt and his grandmother. Finally by an opportune distribution of largess Mammaea prevailed upon the praetorians to give practical expression to their resentment at the slights and discourtesies to which Alexander was subjected through the jealousy of his cousin.[18] On March 6th, A.D. 222, Elagabalus and his mother were murdered in the praetorian camp; their bodies were dragged through the streets of Rome and thrown into the Tiber; their minions and ministers were put to the sword.[19] Alexander became sole Emperor of Rome.

§ 2.   THE ADMINISTRATION OF SEVERUS ALEXANDER

The reign of Severus Alexander is represented in the literary sources as a reaction from those which preceded it. Not only is it a revolt against the excesses of Elagabalus, but it is also a rejection of the principles which characterized the rule of Septimius and his son. In place of a policy favourable to the army and the equestrian order and hostile to the Senate and the privileged classes in Italy, Alexander, it is said, attempted to restore senatorial government. This theme, which is succinctly stated by Herodian, is elaborately developed by the Emperor's biographer with undiscriminating flattery.[20]

How far a resuscitation of senatorial authority was either the intention or achievement of Alexander and his advisers admits of no immediate answer. Apart from a reference in Herodian to the establishment by Maesa and Mammaea of a *consilium* of sixteen senators to advise the young prince during his minority, there is no record of administrative

changes in any of our literary sources except the *Vita
Alexandri*, and here, as always, the difficulty arises of discriminating between the authentic and the imaginary, and
between the facts as stated and the interpretation which is
offered of their significance.[21] At times epigraphy affords
confirmatory material, but frequently there is no other
criterion than probability. Against an uncritical acceptance
of the biographer's standpoint, however, we are put on our
guard by the speech which Dio makes Maecenas deliver to
Augustus.[22] Although the dramatic occasion is the establishment of the Principate, the historian is describing the
developed imperial system of the third century, and is
expounding his own theory of imperial government. Here
there is no question of a return to Republican government.
Monarchy is a recognized necessity,[23] and, although the
Emperor is represented as dependent upon the Senate and
not upon the army, and as sharing with the Senate the
functions of government, yet the Senate is regarded as " the
adornment of the State," as receiving fitting honour, if it is
given the *appearance* of supremacy.[24] Now Dio had been
engaged in imperial administration from the reign of Commodus till his second consulship with Alexander in A.D. 229,
and was in consequence well qualified to observe and appraise
the evolution of government over half a century, nor can he
be classed among the opponents of the Senate. Unless then
the improbable theory is accepted that the speech of Maecenas
was deliberately composed as a protest against the Emperor's
projected reforms,[25] it seems fair to regard it as representing
the most that a sane and prudent senator could expect, and
in all probability as expressing the ideal of Alexander himself.[26] This view gains support when the purpose and scope
of such reforms as may be held to be authentic are considered.

The two most important administrative changes affecting
the status of the Senate were the reorganization of the imperial *consilium* and an extension of the privileges of the
praetorian prefect.

In addition to the advisory body of sixteen senators
mentioned by Herodian alone, Lampridius records, perhaps
in supersession of the earlier council, the establishment
of a *consilium* of seventy members.[27] Within this body are
two distinct groups. The first comprises twenty jurisconsults,

among whom we may include the more important bureaucrats belonging to the equestrian order; the second, fifty
men of distinction invited by the Emperor to join with him
in deliberation. If, as seems undoubted, these fifty belonged
to the senatorial order, it follows that in the new *consilium*
the Senate had a majority, and in consequence the old
antagonism between the *consilium* and the Senate disappeared.
Indeed the *consilium* of Alexander recalls at first sight the
consilia of Augustus and Tiberius. But there are important
differences. Whereas the members of Augustus' or Tiberius'
consilium were delegates of the Senate elected by vote or by
lot, the fifty advisers of Alexander were a collection of *amici*
invited by the Emperor to form a *consilium*, and, although
drawn from the Senate, selected independently of the Senate.
Further, although the equestrian members of the *consilium*
were in a minority, yet with such men as Ulpian and Paul
taking part in its deliberations, it is difficult to believe that
they did not keep the control of the meetings in their own
hands. The reform is then to be regarded not as a restoration
of senatorial power, but as a recognition of the dignity of the
Senate, by conferring upon it external distinctions while
retaining necessarily the real power in the hands of the
professional civil servants.[28]

The second most important reform affected the status of
the praetorian prefect. " *Praefectis praetorii suis senatoriam
addidit dignitatem ut viri clarissimi et essent et dicerentur.*"[29]
The biographer proceeds to interpret this reform as the conferment of senatorial *ornamenta* upon the praetorian prefects,
which he says had rarely happened in the past. The falsity
of this interpretation needs no elaboration; Emperors had
frequently granted *ornamenta* to their prefects without the
latter having to relinquish office. On the other hand, there
was a definite incompatibility between membership of the
Senate and the praetorian prefecture, and exceptions to it
were rare, Sejanus in A.D. 31, Titus and his brother-in-law
in the principate of Vespasian, and Plautianus in A.D. 203.
The purpose, then, of Alexander's reform was to remove this
incompatibility, and the effect of it is seen when we review
the careers of later praetorian prefects as far as they can be
discovered from epigraphy. Praetorian prefects were not
automatically " allected " into the Senate; on the contrary,

a majority of those holding office in the following fifty years belonged still to the equestrian order.[30] But there is no longer any incompatibility between senatorial rank and the office of prefect. The prefect may be *vir clarissimus* or he may be still *vir eminentissimus*. Now the biographer goes on to say that Alexander wanted his prefects to be senators " ne quis non senator de Romano senatore iudicaret " and uses this reform as an illustration of the policy of the Senate-loving Emperor. But while it is true that Alexander respected the claim of senators to be tried only by their compeers, the effect of the reform was to extend the judicial powers of the praetorian prefect. For if there was no incompatibility between his status and that of a senator, there was no longer any objection to his sitting as a judge when a senator was on trial. Thus once again, while outwardly the prestige of the Senate was enhanced, the powers of the praetorian prefect were in fact so increased that as representative of the Emperor he could preside at senatorial trials.

Of less importance is the disappearance of the offices of tribune of the plebs and curule aedile from the senatorial *cursus honorum*.[31] This change was a natural outcome of the transference of their duties to other magisterial bodies, and may be regarded as a practical simplification. If the Senate lost anything by the disappearance of these two magistracies, it was more than recompensed by the establishment of a board of fourteen *consulares* as colleagues to the prefect of the city in the administration of the fourteen regions of Rome.[32]

It is impossible then to deny that there was a senatorial reaction in the reign of Alexander : at the same time its practical effects must not be exaggerated. The Emperor was friendly and courteous to the Senate ; he showed it respect and paid it honour. The Senate recovered something of its past prestige and became again, in the words of Dio, " the ornament of the State." On the other hand there was no resuscitation nor extension of the powers of the Senate, nor was there any attempt to break with the administrative practices of the earlier Severi. Civil servants who had served the Empire under Septimius and Caracallus with their anti-senatorial prejudices continued to hold office under Alexander with his senatorial sympathies. This degree of permanency in the bureaucracy is illustrated not only by such well-known

careers as those of Cassius Dio and Marius Maximus,[33] but
also by a number of less famous officials such as Suetrius
Sabinus and Annius Honoratus, and most remarkable of all
Valerius Comazon, who escaped the general execution of
Elagabalus' ministers and survived to hold the office of prefect
of the city for a third time.[34] Further, there are no indications that the power of the army was less felt in politics
under Alexander than under his predecessors. The soldiers
disliked the disciplinary severity of Dio, and the Emperor
in fear for his safety thought it prudent to advocate his
retirement from Italy during the year of his consulship to the
safety of his native Bithynia where his history was written.[35]
Similarly Ulpian, the praetorian prefect, became unpopular
with his troops because he was not their nominee, and he
was murdered in the palace before the very eyes of his
master.[36]

The reign of Alexander thus exhibited the same features
as had become prominent under the rule of his immediate
predecessors. The chief civil authority remained in the
hands of the praetorian prefect and of the imperial bureaucracy, recruited for the most part from the equestrian order ;
the power to maintain or overthrow the government was
still the army. The Senate recovered something of its dignity
but nothing of its ancient powers. The reign of Alexander
marks not the revival but the end of senatorial government. And just because with the death of Alexander there
set in the gradual decay of the Senate as a political body, so
round the last of the dynasty of the Severi grew up the legend
that he was the last defender of the ancient order of things,
the last to uphold the civil authority against the domination
of the army. Alexander became the hero of those who
believed that the only cure for the internal troubles of the
State was a restoration of senatorial power. From such
panegyrics grew up the historical novel, *The Life of
Alexander*.[37]

§ 3. ALEXANDER IN ROME

The first nine years of Alexander's reign are devoid of
any events of outstanding importance. Apart from the
undisciplined behaviour of the praetorians and some troubles
inside the Court little occurred to mar the peace of the city.

Control of the government was assumed by Julia Maesa, and after her death and apotheosis by Julia Mammaea who received the title of Augusta.[38] By her influence Ulpian was appointed prefect of the praetorians as colleague of Flavianus and Chrestus, who had taken the place of Elagabalus' ministers, and after the murder of his colleagues, for which Dio holds him responsible, acquired supreme and sole authority. His period of office was beneficial in the restoration of sane government, but the praetorians were restive under his strict command. From some futile cause a quarrel arose between the soldiers and the populace and for three days there was faction in the streets, which was only brought to an end through the people's fear that the troops would set their houses on fire. Later the soldiers sated their hatred of their commander by murdering him in the Emperor's palace.[39]

Mammaea, to whom her son was devoted, exercised a jealous supervision over his young life. In A.D. 225 she chose for him a wife from a patrician family named Sallustia Orbiana, who was given the title of Augusta, while her father was raised to the rank of Caesar. Before long, however, the Queen-Mother grew jealous of her daughter-in-law and compelled her son to banish her to Africa, while her father, who perhaps in self-defence had attempted a pronunciamento, was put to death. After this domestic tragedy Alexander remained unmarried, and Mammaea reigned in unchallenged supremacy.[40]

During this period the State recovered from the economic crisis into which it had been precipitated by the excesses of Elagabalus. The taxes were lightened and deficiencies in revenue made good by duties placed on luxuries. The Emperor himself was thrifty and careful in his personal expenditures, while his mother acquired the reputation of being avaricious.[41] Despite this, however, *congiaria* were distributed five times to the people,[42] and Rome was beautified by new public works. In the Campus Martius the Neronian Baths were extended and renamed the Baths of Alexander, and water was brought to them by a newly erected aqueduct, while the huge baths of Caracallus were finally completed.[43] Throughout Italy and the provinces bridges, water-courses and baths illustrate the Emperor's care for his subjects, and we read of alleviation in taxation granted to communities that were undertaking works of public utility.[44] Nor were the military interests forgotten. In the Danubian district in particular road-making and road-restoration were actively pursued,[45] and these preparations proved of great service during the following five years when the peace of the Empire was broken by wars on the eastern and northern frontiers.

§ 4. WAR AGAINST PERSIA

During the preceding century the power of the Arsacid kings of Parthia had been on the wane, and the invasion of Septimius Severus had not only lowered their prestige, but had also weakened their hold upon their subject-kingdoms. Amongst their vassals were the princes of Persepolis, the ancient home of the Achaemenids, who were ever ready to put forward their claim to be regarded as the rightful heirs to the Empire of Darius. Profiting by the weakness of Parthia Ardashir (Artaxerxes), who had subdued the neighbouring country from the Persian Gulf to Ispahan, rebelled against the suzerainty of Artabanus V. Proclaiming himself the restorer of the Achaemenid Empire and of the true Zoroastrian faith, he invaded Parthia and by a decisive victory, won on April 28th, A.D. 227, overthrew Artabanus, and assumed the title of "King of Kings."[46] The next three years were spent in the consolidation of his position in Media; in A.D. 230 news reached Rome that Artaxerxes had overrun Mesopotamia and was threatening Syria and Cappadocia, and that he was asserting his claim to all the Empire that had belonged to Darius as far west as the Aegean Sea.[47]

After a futile attempt at negotiations Alexander gave orders for the mobilization of an army to avert this challenge from the East. Levies were made in Italy and the provinces; a new legion was raised, and given perhaps the title of IV *Italica*, and detachments from the Danubian legions were concentrated in readiness for the march to the East.[48] In A.D. 231 Alexander and his mother left Rome for Antioch, where they were joined by the European legions.[49] A second embassy was as fruitless in its results as the first, and Artaxerxes countered with an ultimatum ordering the Romans to evacuate the territory that rightfully belonged to the Persian Empire.[50] Meanwhile mutinies broke out among the Eastern troops. The legions of Mesopotamia revolted and put to death the governor of the province Flavius Heracleo, and we hear of attempts to put up rival candidates for the Empire, and of unrest among the troops brought from Egypt.[51] When these troubles had been settled, Alexander prepared for a campaign in the spring of A.D. 232. He divided his army into three divisions. The left column was ordered to march into Armenia, where the Arsacids were still offering some resistance, and then to invade Media. The centre column was commanded by Alexander himself, and was to operate in northern Mesopotamia, while the right received instructions to move south-east and attempt to turn the left flank of the enemy. The exact results of the campaign are difficult to ascertain from our sources. It would seem that the southern army met with great disaster, and that Alexander in the centre failed altogether to carry out his part of the scheme, perhaps because his European troops suffered from disease due to the strange climatic conditions. The northern army, on the other hand, after crossing Armenia successfully invaded Media, and appears to have been able to maintain its position until Alexander decided upon a retirement to Antioch, and recalled the division, which during its retreat suffered severely from the cold of the Armenian highlands. However, even though the Romans met with severe losses, it is clear that they must also have inflicted heavy casualties upon their enemy and have shattered for the time being Persian confidence.[52] At any rate Roman Mesopotamia was recovered, Artaxerxes made no fresh move for four years, and Alexander on his return to Rome in September, A.D. 233, celebrated a magnificent triumph.[53]

§ 5. WAR IN GERMANY AND THE DEATH OF ALEXANDER

Alexander did not stay long in Rome. Profiting by the weakening of the legionary garrisons the Germans had crossed the Rhine and Danube and destroyed a number of fortresses on the *limes*. They were now reported to be threatening Illyricum and even Italy itself, and the presence of the

Emperor was felt by the generals entrusted with the northern defences to be essential. Alexander and his mother accordingly left Rome probably early in A.D. 234.[54]

This speedy departure from the capital was perhaps not unexpected, for, if we may believe Herodian, news of the German danger had already reached the Emperor's ears while he was still at Antioch.[55] Indeed this may have been a decisive reason for abandoning the Persian War. Alexander, Lampridius tells us, had, following a precedent set by Marcus Aurelius, granted the officers and soldiers of the frontier forces parcels of land as freehold property on condition that they and their sons continued to serve in the armies of Rome.[56] The Illyrian soldiers were in consequence not unnaturally perturbed at the news of the barbarian invasion and, disgusted as they already were with the unwarlike qualities of their Emperor, clamoured to be taken back home. Probably, then, Alexander ordered the European troops to proceed direct to Germany, while he himself, accompanied perhaps by the Moorish and Osroenian archers and Persian deserters[57] who formed part of his expeditionary force, went to Rome to celebrate his triumph. However that may be, the army was concentrated in A.D. 234 near Mainz, which Alexander chose as his headquarters and a pontoon bridge was thrown across the Rhine.[58] But Alexander was no general, and before beginning his campaign attempted to negotiate with the Germans and buy peace from them.[59] This was a fatal miscalculation. The soldiers judged this pacific policy mere humiliating cowardice. In place of a general who had already shown himself afraid to fight, in place of an Emperor who was under the domination of his mother, they looked for a leader with energy, courage and determination. Perhaps, too, they were incensed by the report that Mammaea favoured the abandonment of the German campaign and a return of the army to the East,[60] and in jealousy of the favouritism shown by Alexander to the Eastern troops decided to find an Emperor who was a compatriot. Their choice fell on C. Julius Verus Maximinus, a Thracian peasant, who owed his promotion from the ranks to his enormous physical strength and his soldierly qualities, and who was in command of some recently conscripted Pannonian levies.[61] In March, A.D. 235, his soldiers invested him with the purple, and soon afterwards

Alexander and his mother, deserted at the last by the Oriental troops that had promised to defend them, were murdered at their camp near Mainz.[62]

Thus the dynasty of the Severi ended with the death of a prince who was the antithesis of its founder. Once again the army had asserted its power to make and unmake the Emperors of Rome.

CHAPTER V

THE PROVINCES UNDER THE SEVERAN DYNASTY

THE purpose of this chapter is an attempt to discover the measure of prosperity enjoyed by the provincials under the military despotism of Septimius and his son, and a formulation of the policy which engendered these conditions. The evidence at our disposal is almost entirely archæological, but the inscriptions are both plentiful in number and comprehensive in their sources and distribution, while for the history of Egypt recently discovered papyri give an intimate picture of the state of society in that province. The subject may be conveniently approached from two different angles. On the one side we must consider the attitude of the imperial government as reflected in the reforms and administrative measures which were put into execution, on the other side the internal conditions of the towns and villages of the provinces, the duties and functions which they were called upon to perform, and the methods by which they sought to discharge their obligations. These two aspects may then justify some general conclusions upon the provincial policy of the Severan dynasty and the economic structure of the Empire under its rule.

In the sphere of administration two reforms stand out in importance, the subdivision of some of the larger provinces and the introduction of a new title for provincial governors. After the defeats of Pescennius Niger and Albinus the provinces of Syria and Britain were each divided into two, the former into Syria Coele and Phoenice, the latter into an upper and lower province with the line of demarcation running approximately from Mersey to Humber. This policy was carried a step further by Caracallus. In A.D. 212 or early in 213 a reorganization took place in Pannonia. The frontier between the two provinces was altered so that Brigetio the camp of I *Adiutrix*, which had previously belonged to the upper province, was now assigned to the lower, and its governor became a legate of consular rank.[1] The main purpose of this levelling down of provincial legionary garrisons was undoubtedly to diminish the powers of the senatorial governors, and consequently their opportunities to revolt against the imperial house, and it is certain that the changes in Britain and Syria were the outcome of the civil wars with Albinus and Niger.[2] But the reform has also significance in the military history of the Empire. Of the 32 legions[3] stationed in the provinces 24 were now assigned in pairs to 12 provinces, while the remaining 8 were distributed singly in less important areas. No province had now more than two legions. This principle of distribution was adhered to throughout the 3rd century. When new legions were raised they were assigned to those provinces that had only a single legion, so as to make a pair with the existing unit,[4] and, when Diocletian added so greatly to the number of frontier-legions, the Severan precedent was not abandoned but extended by a further division of the existing provinces into smaller units of administration.[5] Thus the reform of Septimius, even if it was instituted purely from motives of immediate expediency, survived throughout the ensuing century as a guiding principle of military organization.

The second reform is nominal but again has a prospective significance. In provinces such as Sardinia and the two Mauretanias the title of the governor is no longer merely *procurator*, but *procurator agens vices praesidis* or just simply *praeses*.[6] So far the change calls for little comment, for *praeses* like *procurator* is an equestrian title. But in Macer's book *De Officio Praesidis*, written in the reign of Caracallus, *praeses* is recognized as the generic appellation—the *nomen generale*—for governors, both of senatorial and imperial provinces.[7] If, in addition to this change in official nomenclature, we recall the practice mentioned in an earlier chapter of appointing equestrian *vicarii* as substitutes for senatorial governors, it becomes clear that the road was open towards the gradual elimination of senators from provincial commands.[8]

During the reigns of Septimius and Caracallus there was considerable activity in the reconstruction and restoration of roads in the provinces. The main purpose of these works

was doubtless to facilitate the transit of troops from one part
of the Empire to another, but the improvements in communication inside the different provinces were also calculated
to promote the economic welfare of their inhabitants. A few
illustrations will suffice. In Africa many milestones are
adorned with the names of Caracallus or his late father, and
in the neighbourhood of Lambaesis,[9] the camp of III *Augusta*,
and also at Sitifis[10] extensive road repairs were carried out.
In the Danubian district between the years 198 and 201 the
road along the right bank of the river was reconstructed
almost throughout its entire length,[11] while in the eastern
provinces mention may be made of systematic restorations
in Cappadocia under C. Julius Flaccus Aelianus,[12] and
further south in Syria of repairs carried out in the road running north and south through Sidon and in that running east
to Palmyra under the direction of the governor Venidius
Rufus.[13] Lastly, milestones in Lusitania commemorate work
executed on the road from Emerita to Salmantica,[14] while
several bilingual inscriptions record road-making in Cyprus.[15]
The last two examples afford at least some evidence that
improvements in communication were not associated exclusively with the military campaigns of the Emperors.

The reforms and developments which we have so far been
considering may be regarded as characteristic of any great
imperial power. They suggest qualities of statesmanship, but
do not afford any evidence which enables us to differentiate
the Severan epoch from the earlier periods of the Principate,
nor to form any clear estimate of the welfare of the Empire
as a whole. We must therefore turn to the relationship of
the government with the towns and villages of the provinces.

The policy of the Roman government in the first two
centuries of the Principate was to administer the provinces
on the basis of urban communities. Towns formed centres
for local administration, for the dispensation of justice, for
the registration of census returns and for the assessment and
collection of imperial taxation. In return the privileges of
Roman citizenship were gradually extended, so that by the
end of the 2nd century A.D., especially in the western half
of the Empire, there was a large number of communities
possessing either the full Roman citizenship or that partial
degree known as Latin rights, by which the local magistrates,

and sometimes the local senators as well, in virtue of their office obtained the full citizenship for themselves and their families. In contrast with the towns the country was on a lower plane of civilization and privilege. Some of the country folk lived in villages situated on the territory of towns and subject to them for administration and taxation while sharing in few or any of their imperial privileges. Others worked on estates owned sometimes by Roman senators or knights, sometimes by rich citizens of the neighbouring provincial towns. Others again found work on the great imperial domains, which with the vicious policy of imperial confiscation were gradually absorbing the private estates. In the 2nd century A.D. attempts were made to improve the conditions of life upon the land and to develop the natural resources of the country, but little was done to bridge the gulf between town and country. The Roman government was still essentially town-minded.

In some respects the provincial policy of Septimius and Caracallus follows the precedent set by previous Emperors. In the East and in their native province of Africa a considerable number of towns receive the status of Roman colonies with the not infrequent addition of *ius Italicum*, which exempted the citizens from the payment of tribute. In Mesopotamia Nisibis and Rhesaena, the camp of III *Parthica*, were thus honoured,[16] and from Syria comes a list which includes Tyre, Laodicea and Emesa.[17] In Africa new colonies were established at Vaga, Cuicul and Thugga,[18] and *ius Italicum* was granted to Carthage, Utica and Leptis Magna.[19] In Dacia Apulum and Potaissa were promoted to colonial status,[20] while, as we have seen, Alexandria received a council of its own and local autonomy.[21] An interesting letter of Septimius and Caracallus to the people of Tyras in Lower Moesia confirms to them the privilege of exemption from customs dues.[22] At the same time to guard against abuses, the right of the city, which apparently it had interpreted in too liberal a sense, to extend its citizenship to foreigners is curtailed and made subject to the approval of the governor of the province. Lastly, mention must be made of the foundation of a number of *castella* or *stationes*, which were garrisoned by the agricultural population. If the main purpose of this policy was to supplement the military resources of the Empire, it also achieved a considerable urbanization of the life of the peasants. These forts were established notably in the region of Sitifis, which was a huge imperial domain, and also in Upper Germany and in Thrace. As an illustration we may cite the extant edict of the Emperor's legate Q. Sicinius Clarus about the foundation of Pizus.[23] This settlement lay on the imperial highway from Philippopolis to Hadrianopolis, and its inhabitants were drawn from the neighbouring villages, being induced to migrate by the promise of exemption from such public liturgies as the *angary* or compulsory provision of animals and drivers for the transport of imperial troops and merchandise. Pizus, it would seem, was to serve as a model for other *stationes* in the province.

The treatment of towns in the provinces was not, however, of an uniform beneficence. The hatred felt by Septimius for the adherents of Niger and Albinus died slowly. Upon the cities of Antioch, Byzantium and Lugdunum he meted out a harsh vengeance, razing their buildings to the ground and depriving them of their urban status, and even though at the intervention of Caracallus the first two were subsequently pardoned, that did not diminish the social and economic distress to which their citizens had been reduced. Nor did the retaliatory measures stop here. Imperial officials were appointed to search out the partisans of the Emperor's late rivals and confiscate their property as a punishment for their political opinions. In Asia Minor a police-force of *colletiones*[24] was instituted for this purpose, while the procurators of Mauretania and Baetica, with their special title *a cognitionibus*,[25] supervised in their respective areas the collection of the *bona damnatorum*. The provinces became full of homeless men who joined themselves together in rebel bands, and eked out a precarious livelihood by brigandage. Not till A.D. 208 were these insurrections stamped out, and two inscriptions from Ephesus and Sicca Veneria in Africa record the satisfaction of their inhabitants that the imperial house has been set free from the snares of its public enemies.[26]

If these repressive measures fell heavily upon the propertied classes in the Empire, the lot of the country-folk at least in Asia Minor was no better. Four petitions addressed to the Emperor by the peasants living upon the imperial estates have recently been found in Lydia.[27] In each of the

documents the burden of their complaints is the same. The
villagers are being ruined by the intolerable exaction of
goods and by the immense expenditure which they are forced
to make upon the entertainment of *colletiones* and other
imperial officials. To escape further trouble they have been
obliged to bribe these agents of the Emperor's will, and when
unable to produce a satisfactory sum have been imprisoned
and in some cases put to death. Agricultural work is in consequence at a standstill, and, unless the Emperor intervenes,
there is no alternative but to abandon the imperial domains.

In Egypt the fate of the village population is little better,
although here it is the heaviness of taxation and public
service and the opposition of the property-owners which are
the chief causes of distress. In desperation the peasants
abandoned their homes and took to brigandage. In A.D. 201–2
Septimius granted an amnesty to all fugitives, and the
prefect Subatianus Aquila in connection with the census of
that year issued an edict calling upon the peasants to return
to their homes.[28] Compliance with this proclamation,
however, did not end the trouble. On reaching their native
village of Socnopaei Nesus the peasants took up leases on the
public lands along the shore, but soon an attempt was made
to dislodge them by an influential local family, which proposed to pasture its flocks upon their land. In despair the
peasants addressed a petition to the *strategus* to bring these
men to justice and to prevent themselves being forced once
again to abandon their homes.[29] This practice of deserting
their native villages had become almost chronic,[30] and, when
as in A.D. 200–1 the Emperor with his large staff and retinue
was present in the country, the temptation to use this
remedy for oppression became too strong to resist. Septimius
intended to make a tour of inspection of the whole country.[31]
This meant a great additional burden upon the population,
and both cities and country had to make proportional
contributions to defray the expenditure. Lodgings had to
be found for the Emperor, his staff and his soldiers, and if
these were provided largely by the towns, the country had
to supply meat, corn, and wine for their visitors' con-
sumption. In A.D. 215 we are met with a similar situation
to that of A.D. 201. Once again there has been an exodus of
peasants from their homes, and some of them have flocked

into Alexandria. Caracallus ordered the prefect to send
" the foreigners " with the exception of the traders back to
their native villages.[32] Upon the citizens of Alexandria he
meted out a punishment which in the literary sources is
represented as cowardly vindictiveness. He ordered the
younger generation to be secretly and treacherously put to
the sword. An explanation, if not an excuse, for this
violence may, however, be found in a rebellion which the
Alexandrians had started, profiting by the temporary
absence of II *Traiana*, the Egyptian legion, in Germany.
Caracallus decided that not only must the rebels be punished,
but steps be taken to guarantee as far as possible the loyalty of
Alexandria during his projected campaign against Parthia.[33]

The picture that these illustrations give of the condition
of the provinces does not suggest a period of widespread
prosperity. At the same time we must be on our guard
against making a general condemnation of the government
of the Severi, and some factors of importance must be borne
in mind. In the first place our evidence for the condition of
the country population is drawn exclusively from Asia
Minor and Egypt, and it would be rash to infer that the same
distress was necessarily experienced by the peasants of the
western Empire. Secondly, the retaliatory measures taken
by Septimius against the partisans of Niger and Albinus
represent a temporary episode, and it is probable that in
the last years of his reign more settled conditions had been
re-established. Thirdly, we must not minimize the significance of the great number of inscriptions placed beneath
altars and statues erected in honour of Septimius, his wife
and sons. Although the authors of these dedications are most
commonly officers and soldiers or private individuals, a
considerable number was set up by municipal towns or their
senates. The distribution of these inscriptions is interesting.
Africa, as might be expected of the Emperor's native country,
provides the largest number of inscriptions, and although
the army and private enterprise is responsible for most, the
comparative paucity of urban dedications may be balanced
by the large number of triumphal arches erected in honour
of the Imperial House.[34] Compared with Greece and Asia
Minor the other provinces of the West offer a somewhat
meagre total of urban inscriptions, which in the case of Gaul,

Spain and Britain finds perhaps an explanation in their loyalty to Albinus. In Pisidia on the other hand there is, considering its size, a considerable expression of loyalty to Septimius,[35] and the cities of Greece proper are loud in their praises of Caracallus.[36] Even granted that these expressions of enthusiasm are largely flattery and adulation, it is surely not wrong to read into them a measure of sincere gratitude for the beneficence of the Emperors. The state of the Empire therefore under the rule of Septimius and his son cannot be praised or condemned without qualification. Different provinces were differently affected according as they won the approval or met with the disapprobation of the Emperor. Thus in Africa, and Syria because of its associations with Julia Domna, the towns enjoyed a period of prosperity which was shared by those of Asia Minor and to a lesser extent of Egypt. By contrast the rural population was oppressed and poverty-stricken. In the West the provinces, which had espoused the cause of Albinus, recovered slowly from the retributory justice that visited them, while the Danubian provinces probably suffered from the effects of compulsory recruitment for the wars in the East.

When, however, we come to look at the methods adopted by the imperial government for the provision of the necessary public services and the collection of its revenue, the prosperity that is apparent in certain parts of the Empire becomes in large measure illusory, and we are confronted with evidence that gives unmistakeable indications that the economic foundations of the Empire were unstable and insecure.

It was a principle of city-state government that in time of crisis the citizens should assist the State by personal or pecuniary service. Even more firmly established was the doctrine that the rich could be required to furnish supplementary contributions, such as money for equipping an army or fitting out a fleet. In the municipal towns of the Roman Empire this system of liturgies is early apparent. The local magistrate paid a *summa honoraria* in gratitude for his election to office, and during his year of service was expected to contribute generously to schemes of local welfare. At first these obligations were undertaken with enthusiasm, but gradually the number of *munera* falling upon the local magistrate became so onerous that it was difficult to find

candidates at the elections, and, as we saw in an earlier
chapter, the home government was obliged to send out
officials from the imperial bureaucracy to supervise local
administration. Two causes may be assigned for this great
increase in *munera*. Firstly, many towns embarked upon
building schemes which were extravagant and unproductive.
Secondly, and more important, the imperial government in
the course of the first two centuries A.D. made ever-increasing
requisitions upon its provincial communities. In times of
peace the state revenue was sufficient to meet the cost of
administration, nor is there much reason to suppose that the
normal taxation was excessive. But in times of crisis when
war was inevitable the income of the Empire was inadequate
to meet the additional strain. This was strikingly apparent
in the principate of Marcus Aurelius with its long campaigns
in the East and in Germany. After the extravagant rule of
Commodus and during the civil and foreign wars of the
reigns of Septimius and Caracallus the problem was no less
pressing, nor was the situation made any easier by the
increase in the size of the army, the raising of its pay and the
pernicious practice of largess and donatives. In the absence
of a system of a national debt there were two main alter-
natives open to the government, increase of taxation or the
extension of the principle of compulsory requisitions. Both
Marcus and the Severi chose the latter course, while
Caracallus to give the impression of an artificial prosperity
resorted in addition to a depreciation of the coinage. To
meet these additional demands the system of liturgies
inevitably was enlarged. Towards the end of the second
century boards of the ten richest men called *decem primi* or
δέκα πρῶτοι who were responsible for the collection of the
taxes begin to appear in the municipalities of West and East.
In the third century they become a permanent feature.[37]
The principle of compulsory service too affected rich and
poor alike, and under the guidance of the lawyers received
legal recognition. It is no accident that two of these jurists,
Papinian and Callistratus, were contemporaries of Septimius.

Municipal liturgies were classified under three headings,
munera personalia, *munera patrimoniorum* and *munera
mixta*.[38] The difference between the first two types was that
munera personalia did not require any expenditure of money,

while *munera patrimoniorum* were a form of taxation on the property of the incumbent.[39] The third class was so called because, though normally personal, it might in an emergency demand an outlay of money. Under this heading came the liturgy of the ten richest men charged with the collection of the taxes, who might not infrequently be obliged to make good a deficiency out of their own pockets.[40] The personal liturgies were largely menial tasks, which were performed by the poorer residents in the towns and by the villagers living on territory owned by the town. They included such duties as the care of aqueducts, temples and public buildings, the provision of grain, corn and oil, the convoying of recruits, horses and other beasts of burden for the imperial service, in short, any public service required by their local senate or imposed upon their town by imperial officials.[41] *Munera patrimoniorum* comprised such liturgies as the holding of priesthoods, the provision of transport for the imperial army or of billets for troops that were temporarily stationed in the town.[42] While every inhabitant of a town, whether a citizen or temporary resident, could be required on a system of rotation[43] to take his share in these public services unless he had secured exemption, it is clear that the burden fell most heavily on the propertied classes from which the local senators were drawn. For not only did they contribute out of their incomes the major portion of the imperial taxes imposed upon the town, but in the performance of liturgies were also subjected to what was in effect a form of capital levy. When Septimius gave Alexandria and the *metropoleis* of Egypt municipal councils he transferred to them responsibility for the arrangement and classification of liturgies, which had previously been controlled by the officials of the nomes. Liturgies, it is true, were no novelty in Egypt ;[44] Rome had received them as a legacy from the Ptolemies. But the action of Septimius, even if it imposed no fresh public services, placed upon the shoulders of the new councillors a responsibility for their performance, which not infrequently they were forced to discharge themselves. Thus in Egypt as in the rest of the Empire the honour of belonging to the local senate became indistinguishable from a compulsory public service.

From these municipal public services certain classes of people received exemption. Immunity might be granted in

virtue of age or personal status.   Thus personal liturgies
were not imposed upon those over seventy, upon women, nor
upon the fathers of five or more living children.[45]   On the
other hand, such grounds did not excuse the owners of
estates subject to *munera patrimoniorum* from carrying out
their obligations.[46]   Exceptions were also made in virtue of
other public services to the State.   Under this category came
the following classes : members of the imperial nobility,
officials in the State bureaux, *conductores* or agents employed
in the collection of taxes from the imperial estates, members
of certain *collegia* such as *navicularii* and *centonarii* (firemen),
who were employed in carrying on the necessary services of
the State, and the *coloni* or tenants on the estates of the
Emperor.[47]   In addition, veterans enjoyed immunity from
personal but not from patrimonial liturgies,[48] and serving
soldiers were immune from both.[49]   Finally, doctors and
schoolmasters, with the exception of elementary teachers,
were excused personal services,[50] and the same privilege was
extended to professors of philosophy ; but, as all true
philosophers despise riches, it was doubtless considered
that it would be an inducement to hypocrisy if they were
also exempted from liturgies which fell upon their estates.[51]

The ground upon which most exemptions from municipal
services were granted was thus the performance of some other
work of public utility for the State.   Of chief interest in this
connection is the mention of guilds or corporations of ship-
owners, merchants and firemen.[52]   These *collegia*, as they were
called, were in origin voluntary associations formed by
men engaged in the same trade or occupation, in order that
in times of emergency they might act together for the protection of their interests.   During the second century A.D. the
State had begun to make an extensive use of these ready-made
organizations for maintaining such important public services
as the fire-brigades and the transport of troops and commissariat.   Indeed it is not improbable that the exemptions
which were now granted to their members were an answer to
such protests as that of the shipowners of Arelate[53] against
excessive demands upon their services.   But it is important
to observe that the State does not as yet recognize a collective
responsibility of the *collegia*.   The exemptions are granted
to individual members of the guilds[54] and emphasis is

laid on the necessity that such members must be *bona fide* practising traders, shipowners and firemen, before they can claim the enjoyment of these privileges.

Of the other classes of the population that were excused municipal liturgies no more than a passing mention is necessary. The most highly favoured are the imperial officials and the soldiers, the former as the instruments and the latter as the necessary condition of a military despotism. The tenants of the imperial estates are protected that their services may be available for the development of the imperial domains and the upkeep of the revenues derived from them by the imperial Treasury. Doctors and schoolmasters are recognized as essential to the welfare of the communities ; in the extension of privileges to philosophers utility is emphasized as the motive. But although these exceptions may have been equitable and necessary, at the same time they aggravated the misfortunes of the depleted ranks of municipal citizens who had to maintain the liturgies of their towns. The constant requisitions upon their capital led to the impoverishment of the middle classes, which had been one of the chief pillars of the economic structure of the Empire.

In A.D. 212 Caracallus issued his famous edict granting citizenship to all *peregrini* inside the Roman Empire, of which a very mutilated papyrus found in Egypt is almost certainly a Greek translation.[55] Unfortunately the number and identity of the recipients of this privilege are alike obscure and controversial, and the motives suggested for the reform in Dio and the papyrus are different. It is, however, probable that Caracallus bestowed the franchise upon members of all tax-paying communities, urban and rural alike, but withheld the concession from the *dediticii*, a term which may denote such conquered barbarians as had been settled by Marcus Aurelius inside the Empire, and also the lowest class of freedmen as defined by the *Lex Aelia Sentia* of A.D. 4.[56] This grant would increase, as Dio says, the amount derived by the imperial exchequer from the tax on inheritances, to which only Roman citizens were liable. But it had also an important bearing on the history of municipal liturgies. Previous to the edict, Roman citizens who were domiciled in a non-Roman town were almost certainly exempt from the performance of its local services. In Egypt this exemption was also extended to Alexandrian citizens.[57] After the issuing of the edict, this privileged position of Roman citizens in non-Roman towns was automatically removed ; for all members of the community had now the same legal status and became equally liable for public services.[58] The edict of Caracallus may, then, from one aspect be regarded as a further stage in the levelling process of citizen and subject which was inaugurated by his father. But, on the other hand, even though it removed certain legal disabilities under which the new recipients had previously suffered, it did not decrease their liability to compulsory state service, except in so far as there was now a greater number to share the responsibilities.

A theory has recently been advanced that the keynote to the policy of Septimius and his successors in the third century A.D. is to be found in their championship of the cause of the peasants, from whom the army was recruited, against the interests of the provincial towns.[59] In support of this view emphasis is laid, on the one hand, upon the punishment meted out by Septimius upon the cities of Antioch, Lugdunum and Byzantium, and by Caracallus upon Alexandria, and upon the evil effects of the system of liturgies on the middle classes in the towns. On the other hand, imperial favour to the peasants is inferred from the protection given to tenants on the domain land, from the petitions addressed to the Emperors themselves by the villages of Lydia, and from identifying the interests of the rural population with those of the army from which it was recruited. Against this theory, however, there are, it would seem, certain fatal objections. The attitude of Septimius and Caracallus towards the provincial towns was not uniformly hostile : while some suffered, others received imperial favours. Indeed, the difference of treatment is so marked that, so far from reflecting a settled policy towards towns as such, it finds rather its explanation in the sensibility of the two Emperors to flattery and correspondingly their implacable intolerance of opposition. Secondly, it may be admitted that the extended system of liturgies was most detrimental to the citizens of municipal towns, but that does not warrant the further assumption that it was deliberately invented to lower the pride and prestige of the towns. Compulsory service was not limited to the population of urban communities ; it was common to almost every class in the

Empire, and in the circumstances was necessitated, as we have seen, by the nature of the military despotism. Thirdly, although there are signs of improvement in the condition under which the peasants worked in Africa, Thrace and Germany, the plight of the villagers in Egypt does not seem to have been materially ameliorated. Lastly, and most important, the petitions addressed to Septimius from the peasants in Lydia are from workmen on imperial estates protesting against the intolerable tyranny of soldiers and imperial officials, that is, against the very class whose interests are supposed to be identical with their own. Of course, they complained to the Emperor ; he was their only hope against the brutality of his servants, and the adulatory language which they employ is less the measure of their confidence in his beneficence than the expression of their own distress.

Septimius was the patron of neither town nor country. The army was the factor that determined his imperial policy. Upon the army depended his personal safety, upon the army the dynasty that he had founded. Upon the maintenance of its loyalty were concentrated his abilities and his energies. The soldiers' pay was raised, their numbers were increased, donatives were lavished upon them and special privileges were their reward on discharge. By the overthrow of his civil enemies and an expansionist policy in the East, Septimius sought to impress upon his troops his character and role of soldier-Emperor. But to maintain this policy the normal revenues of the Empire had to be increased. Discarding a possible solution in an increase of the tribute, Septimius chose instead to organize all the available resources of the Empire on the principle of compulsory public service. Into this scheme town and country alike were drawn ; the Empire was organized, no matter the cost, no matter the unsoundness of the system, on a basis of state-socialism. The example set by Septimius was followed and further developed by his son. To counteract his personal extravagance, his foreign wars and the increase in the centurions' pay, he resorted to a depreciation of the coinage, while his edict by which he extended Roman citizenship to foreigners may perhaps find at least one explanation in the extension of the system of liturgies. The dynasty of the Severi was followed by half a century of military anarchy, and with the advent of plague, famine and barbarian invasions, the provinces of the Empire were ransacked and destitute.

CHAPTER VI

RELIGION AT ROME UNDER THE SEVERI AND THE CIRCLE OF JULIA DOMNA

THE age of the Severi marks not only a radical alteration in the character of the imperial government, but also a further evolution in the transformation of Roman Society which had begun in the Antonine Age. The Principate was superseded by a military despotism, the recognized superiority of the Italian over the provincial and of the citizen over the subject was undermined, if not entirely eliminated ; Roman law was developed on the lines of equity and humanity ; Graeco-Roman civilization was more deeply blended with Oriental culture ; society became cosmopolitan. The effect of these changes was to weaken patriotism and diminish enthusiasm for politics. At the same time, and partly in consequence of them, there were signs of a growing interest in literature and art, in philosophy and religion. Education was officially encouraged and professors and teachers were welcomed at Court. Among the educated classes doubt was giving place to faith, indifference to curiosity, and despite the persistence of practised cruelty, there were aspirations for a higher moral standard founded on justice and equity. To meet these new interests neither Stoicism, the creed of the cultured, nor any one of the prevalent religions, apart from Mithraism, provided a satisfactory outlet. The former preached a gospel that was too detached, remote and unsympathetic to answer the felt need for God, the latter by their very multiplicity tended to perplex rather than to inspire. " Our world is so full of *numina*," complained Quartilla, " that you can more easily find a god than a man."[1] New deities had been flocking in with such rapidity that even the Olympians themselves had to legislate against the importation of aliens.[2] The westward spread of the Oriental

9   129

cults had marked the first stage of a religious revival. The time had now arrived for a further step forward in the direction of monotheism. The age of the Severi witnessed the development of a paganism that was national, local and particularist, into a paganism that was cosmopolitan, universal and syncretist.

The path to this syncretism was smoothed by the ease with which the gods of the different races that composed the Empire could be identified, and this process was facilitated by the similarity of their symbols and functions. Isis, by the multiplicity of her attributes, had her Roman counterpart in Ceres or Proserpine, in Juno or Venus ;[3] Serapis, as the protector of health, resembled Aesculapius or Apollo Salutaris ;[4] again, as the god of the underworld, he performed the same functions as Pluto,[5] while in his character of sun-god he tended to be merged into Jupiter[6] or Mithras.[7] Jupiter himself appeared with a great variety of titles, such as Damascenus,[8] Heliopolitanus[9] and Dolichenus,[10] and these are merely different local personifications of the same universal Sun-deity. Again, different gods might have common temples, such as Isis and the Great Mother, and the same priests act as the servants of different cults.[11] Among the common people this syncretism was natural and unreflecting, the expression of an instinctive desire for a completer satisfaction of their religious needs. For them religion was no longer merely family duty nor the participation in some state function, but a means of personal salvation with purity and holiness as its ideals and a future life as its promised goal. Among the philosophers the process was eclectic, and out of the fusion of different philosophic systems two schools predominated that exercised a considerable influence upon the development of religion, Neo-Pythagoreanism and Neo-Platonism.

The religions which were elements in this process of syncretism may be divided into two categories, the national or state religions and the Oriental cults. Of the former the worship of the Olympians claimed the fewest adherents, but at the beginning of the third century it was not yet quite defunct. In particular we may notice a revival of the old Italian cults of Silvanus and Minerva, to the latter of whom Septimius himself built a temple,[12] while the worship of the

Lares, Penates and Manes still persisted, and religious brotherhoods such as the Salii and Arvales lasted into the fourth century. In connection with these was the cult of spirits or daemons, which attended upon a man in his lifetime and continued in a nebulous existence after his death. Apuleius thinks of them as guardian-angels,[13] and Celsus compares them with satraps and proconsuls, and reproaches the Christians, who regarded them as evil spirits, with failure to worship them.[14] Even the Neo-Platonist philosopher Plotinus peoples the spheres between heaven and earth with a legion of daemons, eternal as the gods, mediating between God and man, answering prayer and having direct relations with the souls of men after death.[15] But of the state-religion emperor-worship still continued the most vital element, and was extended so as to include the *domus divina*. Julia Domna, the wife of Severus, for example, received the title of *mater deorum* and was worshipped in her lifetime as Juno Caelestis.[16] Not without significance as reflecting the approach of religion to morality is the title *sanctus* assumed by the Severan Emperors.[17]

More widespread and popular were the religions that had come to Rome from the East, introduced into the life of the city by slaves, traders and soldiers. Unlike their counterparts in the national religion, the priests of these eastern cults were not civil administrators, but attended exclusively to their specific functions of worship and preaching. In consequence they became experienced propagandists and attracted many converts to their gods. The four cults which predominated in the Antonine Age still continued to enjoy the greatest popularity. The Magna Mater aroused the deep devotion of both Commodus and Severus Alexander,[18] while Caracallus built a sanctuary for Isis near the Colosseum.[19] Among the Syrian gods Jupiter Dolichenus was held in high honour by the soldiers and his worship was carried to such distant provinces as Britain, Dacia and Africa,[20] while the Syrian goddess, whose rites are described by Lucian, had a temple in Rome.[21] But above all these stood out the worship of Mithras with its dualistic doctrine of Good and Evil and its ascetic standard of conduct, and it is its influence that is most clearly discernible in the religious revival of the age.[22]

Three different attempts to promote religious syncretism

may be noticed. The first is closely connected with Neo-
Pythagorean philosophy, in which, in contrast with Neo-
Platonism, the religious vein of thought predominated over
the philosophic. This is reflected in the frequent appeals
made by its exponents to recorded sayings of Pythagoras and
in their attempts to formulate a discipline of daily life in
accordance with his precepts. The writings attributed by
them to the Master were extremely eclectic. Many of them
were taken from Stoics as well as from Plato and Aristotle, but
these coincidences were explained by the assertion that these
philosophers had themselves borrowed their ideas from
Pythagoras. Towards sages and poets the Neo-Pythagoreans
showed a respectful veneration, although many of them, such
as the Brahmins and Buddhists, were only known by hearsay
or repute. From all religions except Christianity they professed to distil an elixir, and yet it was from the Church, which
they sought to discredit by impugning the veracity of its
claims, that they borrowed ideas with which to breathe fresh
life into their moribund Hellenism.[23]

The first reform may be said to have been inaugurated
under the aegis of Julia Domna. Although outwitted in the
political world by the Emperor's favourite, Plautianus, the
Empress reigned supreme in her *salon*. Cultured and intelli-
gent, endowed with wit and beauty, and combining the
credulousness of the East with powers of sane reasoning
that a philosophical training had developed, she was not
undeservedly called ἡ φιλόσοφος Ἰουλία.[24] Around her she
gathered a large coterie of savants, among whom practically
every branch of learning and letters had its representative.
Here might be found the doctors Galen and Serenus Sam-
monicus, the historian Diogenes Laertius, the naturalists
Aelian and Oppian, and the lawyers Papinian, Ulpian and
Paul. Besides there was a group of rhetoricians and sophists
which included the learned Athenaeus, author of the *Deip-
nosophistae*, and most important of all, Philostratus. In this
assembly conversation ranged over a wide variety of subjects.
But the *salon* produced little that bears the stamp of originality or rises above the level of mediocrity. The discussions,
if erudite, were pedantic and artificial. The Latin element
tended to be subordinated to the Syrian, and this is most
clearly to be discerned in the writings of Philostratus, whose

Life of Apollonius was the most important contribution to the promotion of religious syncretism.[25]

Apollonius himself is a historical figure. He was a Pythagorean thaumaturge who lived in the first century A.D. at Tyana in Cappadocia. Philostratus' account of his career purports to be founded on a diary kept by his disciple Damis, which somehow had come into the possession of Julia Domna and which she gave to the sophist to be re-edited. The biography which we possess is less of a philosophic treatise than a gospel. Apollonius is represented not as a god or a magician, but as the personification of the highest spiritual nobility to which man can hope to attain. He is the incarnation of a reformed paganism, the concrete historical expression of the Neo-Pythagorean ideal. In many ways the account resembles the story of the Gospels, with its virgin birth and annunciation, parables and miracles of healing, the appearance of Apollonius before the judgement-seat of Domitian, his disappearance from earth and subsequent appearance to confirm the faith of his disciple Damis.

It is, indeed, the story of the Gospel emended so as to depict Christ as the enlightened circle of Julia Domna thought he should have been. The portrait is carefully copied, but with one important omission ; there is no crucifixion. To the Sun-worshipper such a degradation seemed incompatible with the nature of the " divine " man. The romance, too, represents the limits to which the authorities, by whose sanction it was published, were prepared to go in the way of concessions. Apollonius refuses to attend a sacrifice of blood and contents himself with burning incense on the altar of the Sun. He denounces the worship of idols and preaches against the savagery of the amphitheatre. On the other hand, he loyally accepts the Emperor as Head of the Church and State, and believes in monarchy as the only form of government suitable to the age. Such were the conditions offered to the Christians which, if they had been accepted, would have protected them from the enmity of the heathen priests, whose no less embittered opposition Apollonius was able to defy.

That the new gospel failed to win many converts is not surprising. By its lack of logical consistency it falls short of a philosophical system, by its exaggerated emphasis on the miraculous it produces scepticism rather than reverence. It has little or nothing of the sincerity and simplicity of the Christian faith ; the personality of its " divine " man is an artificial creation ; the pagan Christ has neither the compelling charm nor the living reality of the Christian God. The Neo-Pythagorean cult had a short-lived vogue. Its philosophy was superseded by Neo-Platonism, its religious appeal was transcended by the teaching of Christianity.

The religious policy of Elagabalus and his mother Julia Soaemias stands in contrast to the reforms which preceded and succeeded his reign. By the introduction of the Syrian Sun-god into Rome and by the subordination of all other cults to his worship, an attempt was made to create a sort of pagan Catholicism. Whereas Neo-Pythagoreans and Neo-Platonists sought to establish a universal religion by a combination of all existing cults, Elagabalus refused to recognize any god but his own. In place of a confederation of all the creeds, syncretism was now based on the assertion of an absolute monarchy, which should command universal homage and allegiance.[26] That the attempt was a failure is sufficiently explained by the character of the religion itself. Eastern in its ritual and ceremony, with all the accompanying excesses of fanatical devotion, it was both incomprehensible to the minds and repellent to the sensibilities of educated Roman society, and, if the masses offered at first no pronounced opposition, their acquiescence was but proof of their corruptibility. Yet the attempted reform is not without significance. The arrival of the Syrian Sun-God in Rome is the first triumph of a jealous god in the western world, and to that extent he is the precursor of official monotheism. And this at least may be added in defence of his fanatical priest, that it was for his god, and not for himself, that he sought the worship of his subjects.

The reign of Severus Alexander saw both a reaction from the Oriental fanaticism of Elagabalus and also a further development in religious syncretism, the nature of which, as before, owed much to the influence of a woman. Just as Julia Domna had been the inspiration of her *salon*, and Julia Soaemias had encouraged the wild excesses of the Syrian cult of the Sun-God, so now Julia Mammaea exercised a dominating control over her Court and over her son. Unlike her sister, she was a woman of almost saintly character, educated and refined in her tastes, and if she lacked the intellectual acumen of her aunt, she atoned for that shortcoming by the sincerity and nobility of her ideals. Under her direction Alexander was protected from the infection of his cousin's licentiousness, and was brought up in an atmosphere and environment that was essentially Roman. But though virtuous and honest, he was vacillating and ineffective, and this innate weakness was accentuated by the almost possessive devotion of his mother.

One of Alexander's first acts was to order the return of the Syrian Sun-God to his native Emesa, and the restoration of the gods, whom Elagabalus had gathered together in his temple, to their own shrines. With this banishment of the jealous Eastern god and the rehabilitation of the worship of the other deities that had found a home in Rome, he inaugurated a religious reform, which is characterized by a spirit of toleration, that extended, despite the protests of his legal advisers, even to the Christians. Each cult was to be recognized as a particular expression of the truth common to all religions, each god as partaking in the nature of the One Supreme and Universal Deity. For the practice of this eclecticism Alexander had two oratories in his palace, where he caused to be set up statues of heroes, sages and prophets. To the upper hierarchy belonged Orpheus and Abraham, Christ and Apollonius, to the lower, Virgil and Cicero, and such of the Emperor's ancestors as were reputed to have benefited the cause of humanity.[27] To each of them Alexander sought to accord fitting reverence and worship in a manner not altogether dissimilar from the Christian invocation of the saints.

This form of syncretism in all probability owed much to the philosophic writings of the Platonic School, which was designed to defend paganism against the attacks of Christianity. Celsus, in his *True Word against the Christians*, written towards the end of the second century A.D., visualized the problem as the reconciliation of philosophical theism with the diversities of national worship. The solution which he proposed postulated the existence of a Supreme Deity, which had assigned different regions to subordinate divine powers, to which the Greeks gave the name of gods or daemons, and the Jews of angels. While to the Supreme God as pure Reason only the worship of the mind should be offered, nothing need

hinder the address of hymns to visible powers like the Sun
or to mental attributes such as Wisdom, which is represented
in Greek mythology by Athena. Piety is made more perfect
when it pays respect to all the varied manifestations of
divinity in the world.[28] In a similar vein was the teaching of
Numenius of Apamea, who, influenced by the Christian
Gnostics, expounded a theory of the Trinity, in which the first
member was the Father, changeless and therefore uncreative,
the second the Maker, and the third the World, or that which
is made. The interest of this cosmology lies not only in the
distinction of the Supreme God from the Creator of the World,
but also in its anticipation of the teaching of Plotinus, who
may be called the founder of Neo-Platonism.[29]

Born in Egypt at the beginning of the third century A.D.,
Plotinus was a pupil of the Alexandrian philosopher
Ammonius Saccas, with whom he studied for eleven years. A
desire for acquaintance with Persian and Indian philosophy
led him to join Gordian's expedition to the East in A.D. 242.
After a narrow escape from death he went to Antioch and
soon afterwards came to live in Rome, where he gave instruc-
tion in philosophy. In the first year of Gallienus' reign
he began to write books on such topics as had arisen in his
lectures, and these were subsequently collected and arranged
by his pupil Porphyry in nine volumes (*Enneades*). In his
metaphysical system, which is sometimes called the Neo-
Platonic Trinity, Plotinus gave final expression to the revival
of Platonism which had begun before the Christian era.
Above Thought and Being is the One, to which the name of
God is applied in a peculiar sense in that everything after It
which is called divine is derivative from It. The second
member of the Trinity is the divine Mind, which is identical
with its object, " the intelligible world." Lowest in the order
of supramundane causes is the Soul of the Whole produced
by Mind, whence is the descent to the world of particular
souls and changing things. Thus the Platonic Trinity
presents God in his threefold aspect as the Absolute, Thought
and Action.[30] The historical importance of Neo-Platonism
lies in its unification of all that survived of a distinctively
Greek type of thought. For three centuries it became the one
philosophy of the Graeco-Roman world, and although it was
not destined to be the directing force in the civilization of the

future, yet it succeeded in imparting to Christianity, its victorious rival, much of its distinctive teaching.

Under the Severan dynasty the Christian Church enjoyed a comparative freedom from official persecution. Septimius himself was, in the early years of his reign, by no means unfavourably disposed towards the new religion, and his son Caracallus was entrusted to the care of a Christian nurse.[31] Fear, however, of the proselytising activities of the Christians and, perhaps, an exaggerated estimate of their number and ubiquity led him, about A.D. 200, to revise his policy. The form which this took was not a persecution of existing Christians, but a ban against further conversions. Just as the circumcision of any one who was not a Jew by birth had for long been strictly forbidden, so now a veto was placed on the baptism of pagans.[32] The effects of this legislation were felt most strongly in Egypt and in Africa. At Alexandria the Catechetical School, over which Origen presided, was dispersed, and in A.D. 203 Perpetua and her companions, who were neophytes, were martyred at Carthage.[33] But with the death of Septimius the persecution died down, and the peace of the Church was not again officially disturbed till Maximinus, in hatred of Severus Alexander and his friends, issued edicts which were directed principally at the leaders of the Church. Although the Bishop of Rome and Hippolytus, the head of a schismatic party in the capital, were arrested and deported to Sardinia and some church property was destroyed, yet the edicts, even in the Emperor's lifetime, do not appear to have been rigorously carried out, and after his death they ceased to be enforced.[34]

During the same period the unity of the Church was weakened by the appearance of a number of heretical sects. These represented a reaction to the teaching of the great Gnostic Schools of Syria, Egypt and Pontus, which, by their dualistic doctrines and the limitation of the possibility of redemption to an aristocracy of enlightened souls, had preached a creed which was imcompatible with an orthodox belief in the Incarnation. The most important of these heresies were Montanism and Monarchianism. The former, beginning in Phrygian Mysia as a form of ecstatic and prophetic revivalism with a belief in the imminence of the Second Advent, developed in Africa into a rigid asceticism under the

leadership of the great apologist Tertullian, who, despite his
vigorous denunciations of heresies, was converted to its cause
about A.D. 205. The latter, although Catholic in its affirm-
ation of the Unity of the Godhead, was heterodox in its
contention that both the Son and the Holy Spirit were
derived from the Father as separate activities of a single
Monad.[35] These doctrinal differences belong, it is true, to the
realm of theology, but they have also an historical importance.
In the first place they were an incentive to the orthodox
Church to formulate a clear statement of its faith, and
secondly, they show that Christianity was beginning to draw
its converts from the educated classes of the Empire. In
Alexandria in particular the Church and the lecture-room were
already being brought into connection. As successive heads
of the Catechetical School, Clement and Origen gave instruc-
tion to converts and enquirers, while their own researches
were fruitful of learned works on biblical criticism and Christian
apologetics.[36]

PART III
THE YEARS OF ANARCHY

CHAPTER I

MAXIMINUS AND THE GORDIANS

§ 1. MAXIMINUS

THE accession of Maximinus marks a further development in the militarization of the government which had been inaugurated by Septimius Severus, and is the prelude to a long series of local revolutions which culminated in the disintegration of the Empire under Gallienus. Maximinus was the first barbarian to ascend the throne of the Caesars. A native of Thrace, he had attracted the attention of Septimius by his great physical strength and powers of endurance, and had been promoted to the rank of centurion.[1] By the time of Severus Alexander he had entered the equestrian order, and after holding the posts of commander of the Egyptian legion,[2] and probably of governor of Mesopotamia,[3] was on the death of that Emperor in charge of some recently recruited levies from Pannonia.[4] His position was, therefore, similar in many respects to that of Macrinus. Like him, he was of equestrian and not of senatorial rank ; like him, he owed his elevation entirely to the votes of his soldiers.[5] But whereas Macrinus had held the important civil post of prefect of the praetorian guard, Maximinus' career had been exclusively military. He was the first Roman Emperor who rose from the ranks. His success was won by his own military abilities, which at the critical moment contrasted so favourably with the pusillanimity of Severus Alexander. Whether Maximinus was also the first to vindicate the right as opposed to the power of the soldiers to make Emperors without reference to the Senate as the constitutional source of imperial authority must remain doubtful.[6] We do not know in what terms he chose to announce his elevation in the despatch which he sent to Rome. Nor is the question of much historical importance. For whether an Emperor chosen by the army sought to legitimatize his position by soliciting the Senate's recognition or whether he contented himself with announcing the *fait accompli*, the Senate was powerless to offer any opposition to the soldiers' choice. Even if Maximinus may have offended its susceptibilities by the dictatorial tone of his letter, the Senate was compelled, however reluctantly, to acknowledge him as their Emperor. Most probably there was little difference except in manner between the attitude of Maximinus and Macrinus towards the Senate, and if the former's reign was stigmatized as a tyranny, that was less because it was a constitutional novelty than because the Emperor, during the three years of his reign, was never seen in Rome, and in promoting the interests of the army was indifferent to the lives and property of the civil population.

Maximinus' first care was the prosecution of the German war which Alexander had shelved by a fatal attempt at negotiations. But before he could set out on his campaign the Emperor was faced by two mutinies. The first was planned by a number of centurions and officers of senatorial rank who were partisans of Alexander. The scheme was to wait till Maximinus had crossed the Rhine and then to cut off his only retreat by breaking down the bridge. Having thus rid themselves of the usurper the conspirators intended to put in his place a man of senatorial rank called Magnus. But the secret leaked out, and Maximinus, without the preliminaries of a trial, put to death all whom he in any way suspected of complicity in the plot.[7] Despite the severity of this punishment, however, a second revolt broke out. This time the ringleaders were the Osroenian archers who, devoted to the memory of Alexander and resenting the action of the European troops, invested a consular friend of the late Emperor, called Quartinus, with the purple. But the plot came to a premature end by the treachery of a supposed friend and former officer of the Osroenians called Macedo, who murdered Quartinus in his tent, and in his turn was put to death by Maximinus whose approval and gratitude he had hoped to win.[8] Such mutinies naturally embittered the innate brutality of the Emperor. He removed all officers of senatorial rank from his army and replaced them with his own promoted soldiers.[9] Throughout his whole reign he waged warfare against the nobility, dismissing from their offices all who were suspected of friendship with the late Emperor and encouraging delation as a safeguard against further rebellions.[10] At the same time his financial agents were despatched into the different provinces to collect money to pay for the expenses of war and for the increase which he made in the soldiers' pay,[11] and it was the excessive exactions of one of these officers that, as we shall see later, was the indirect cause of his downfall.

After quelling the two revolts, Maximinus crossed the Rhine and invaded Germany. His army, in addition to legions, consisted of Moorish archers and light-armed troops that Alexander had brought with him from the East, including, according to Herodian, the recently rebellious Osroenians, who later paid the penalty for their infidelity by being disbanded in disgrace.[12] Plundering the country and burning the villages, Maximinus drove the Germans to seek refuge in their forests and swamps. Near Würtemberg a battle was fought in a bog in which the Emperor displayed great personal courage by riding breast-high into the water and shooting down the enemy who were opposed to him on the farther side.[13] If the Romans suffered severe losses, the German casualties were even heavier, and Maximinus, with the approach of winter, was able to retreat in safety. He made Sirmium his winter quarters, in preparation for a campaign on the Danubian frontier where the barbarian tribes were restless.[14] Meanwhile he sent a dispatch to the Senate and ordered a picture to be displayed before the Senate-house to impress the populace with the magnitude and difficulty of his victory. His son he raised to the rank of Caesar, coins were struck with the legend VICTORIA GERMANICA, and the Emperor assumed the title of *Germanicus Maximus*.[15]

The German victory was the high-water mark of Maximinus' career. During the next two years his attention was fully occupied with wars in the Danubian area, and any plans that he may have made for an invasion of Germany were frustrated. Gravestones record the deaths of soldiers in Dacia,[16] and Maximinus assumed the complimentary titles of *Sarmaticus Maximus* and *Dacicus Maximus*.[17] In the spring of A.D. 238 his headquarters were still at Sirmium when news came of a rebellion in Africa.[18]

§ 2. AFFAIRS IN AFRICA

The immediate cause of this revolt was the unscrupulous policy of one of Maximinus' procurators, who in his desire to curry favour with his master attempted to confiscate the wealthy landowners' property in the country. In self-defence some young nobles formed a conspiracy and, supported by labourers from their estates, assassinated the procurator. Their next move was to give their private enterprise an official character and to rouse the whole province in revolt.[19] Accordingly they approached the proconsul of Africa, who was living at Thysdrus, and invited him to become Emperor. Gordian, who was already in his eighty-first year, traced his descent on his father's side from the Gracchi, while his mother was a relative of the Emperor Trajan. He was a man of great wealth and long administrative experience and was, except for his age, endowed with qualities that were likely to commend him to the Senate and Roman people as a suitable liberator of the Empire from the tyranny of Maximinus. At first the aged proconsul declined the invitation of the young nobles, but realising that his refusal would mean immediate death, and spurred perhaps by ambition to finish his days amid imperial honours, he finally consented and was duly proclaimed Emperor.[20] After a few days' delay he moved to Carthage, and assuming his son as a colleague in the imperial powers, prepared to send an embassy to Rome consisting of his active young quaestor and some centurions and soldiers.[21] The chief obstacle in the way of Gordian's success was the prefect of the praetorian guard, Vitallianus, a partisan of Maximinus. Instructions were accordingly given to the embassy that they should first secretly remove Vitallianus, and then present to the Senate Gordian's dispatch in which a programme of constitutional government with the abolition of delation and the promise of a donative to the troops was outlined. The young quaestor played his part well. Vitallianus was assassinated by a clever deception, and the Senate joyfully accepted the two Gordians as the rightful Emperors of Rome, while declaring Maximinus a public enemy.[22] Amid the general rejoicings of the populace the Senate acted with unusual vigour and foresight. It appointed a board of twenty men *reipublicae curandae causa*, and assigned to them different parts of Italy with instructions to take vigorous measures for their defence against the anticipated invasion of Maximinus.[23] At the same time embassies were sent to the provincial governors ordering them to throw off their loyalty to the tyrant,[24] and with the exception of Spain, Dacia and Pannonia the rest of the Empire ranged itself on the side of the Gordians.[25]

Meanwhile events took a sinister turn in Africa. Capellianus, whom Gordian had attempted to remove from his office of governor of Numidia, rose in rebellion. Whether his motive was loyalty to Maximinus or whether he hoped to become Emperor himself is of little importance. The strength of his position was the command which he held over the only regular troops in the country, against which Gordian could muster but a volunteer militia. When Capellianus moved upon Carthage, Gordian sent his son out to oppose his advance. But against the disciplined efficiency of the regular army the local levies had no chance. Gordian II was killed in battle, and on hearing of his son's death his father committed suicide.[26] The reign of the two Gordians had lasted only twenty-two days,[27] but its significance cannot be fairly gauged by the shortness of its duration. While the initiative of the aged proconsul provided the necessary stimulus to a cowed and dejected Senate to assume a fresh responsibility for the government of the Empire, the failure of the revolution emphasised the supremacy of the army in politics. Without the support of the soldiers the civil population was powerless to maintain an Emperor in power. The lesson of Capellianus was soon to receive a further confirmation in Rome itself.

§ 3.   GORDIAN III

On receiving news of the deaths of the two Gordians, the Senate chose two members of the commission of twenty to be the next Augusti. The names of the two new Emperors were D. Caelius Calvinus Balbinus and M. Clodius Pupienus Maximus, the former coming from a distinguished family, the latter of humbler origin, but an officer of experience.[28] The constitutional position of these two Emperors was unique in the history of Rome. Neither had precedence over the other, and each of them was given the dignity of *pontifex maximus*.

10

The settlement was probably an intentional imitation of the consulship, but with this important difference, that the duties of government were divided between the two Emperors, Balbinus being entrusted with the civil administration and Maximus appointed to command the army against Maximinus.[29] But the decision of the Senate to appoint two of its own members Augusti did not meet with the approval of the soldiers and common people in Rome. If the former regarded the reviving initiative of the Senate as detrimental to their accustomed control of the administration, both parties were more closely actuated by the fear that they would lose the material advantages that were offered them by the wealth of the Gordian family. After some rioting a compromise was reached and M. Antonius Gordianus, a grandson of Gordian I by his daughter Maecia Faustina, was raised to the rank of Caesar.[30]

On hearing of the rebellion in Africa, Maximinus, after a short delay, decided upon an immediate invasion of Italy. His army consisted of the troops which he had concentrated for his projected invasion of Germany, and included some irregular German contingents serving probably as mercenaries.[31] On reaching Emona he found the city deserted by its inhabitants and its stores of food removed or destroyed. If the abandonment of the town was a lucky omen for the success of the campaign, the absence of commissariat was an unlooked-for misfortune which aroused a mutinous temper among the soldiers.[32] But it was Aquileia that offered the first real obstacle to Maximinus' advance. The gates of the city were barred and through the energy of Menophilus and Crispinus, two members of the commission of twenty, the defences had been strengthened and preparations made for a long siege.[33] At first Maximinus attempted negotiations, and when these proved fruitless, decided upon storming the town. But to reach his objective he had first to cross the Isonzo, some 16 miles from Aquileia, which was in high flood with snow-water, while the bridge over it had been broken down by the enemy. After a delay of two or three days a pontoon bridge was constructed and the army proceeded to the siege of the town.[34] But despite the energy of Maximinus, no success attended his efforts. The defenders put up a desperate resistance, encouraged both by the abundance of the food

supply and by the belief that their native god, Belenus, had
promised them victory.[35] Meanwhile Maximinus' troops
were becoming enfeebled from starvation and disheartened by
failure. At last the soldiers of II *Parthica*, whose garrison-
town was at Albanum near Rome, where they had left their
wives and children, took the initiative and executed Maximinus and his son as they were taking a siesta after the mid-
day meal.[36] Their heads were sent to Rome under cavalry
escort, while news of their death was promptly despatched
to the besieged in Aquileia. The gates of the city were not,
however, opened, but, as a test of loyalty, portraits of either
Balbinus or Pupienus Maximus and Gordian were hung over
the walls and the besiegers were invited to do reverence to
them. The response was immediate ; so great was the famine
among the soldiers that even the Pannonian troops did not
hesitate to acclaim the Emperors elected by the Senate. In
return the defenders provided a market outside the walls from
which the besiegers might satisfy their hunger.[37]

Maximus had reached as far north as Ravenna and was
concentrating his army there when the horsemen bearing
the heads of Maximinus and his son arrived. The Emperor
sent the escort on to Rome and himself proceeded to Aquileia,
accompanied by a bodyguard of Germans who had joined him
as allies in token of their gratitude for his earlier administration as governor of Germany.[38] The people of Aquileia
received him with open gates and Maximinus' soldiers gave
him a feigned welcome. After an address to the troops,
Maximus sent back his late enemy's army to their respective
provinces, and with his German bodyguard returned to
Rome.[39] He was met at the gates of the city by Balbinus and
young Gordian and received an ovation from the Senate and
people. For a few days the joint government worked with
apparent smoothness. But soon jealousy broke out between
the two Emperors, while the soldiers in the city resented
Maximus' German bodyguard and disliked being governed by
Emperors elected by the Senate.[40] Indeed even earlier a riot
had taken place, in which two senators called Gallicanus and
Maecenas had been involved with the soldiers left behind by
Maximus for the garrisoning of the City.[41] At length the
latent opposition found open expression. The praetorians
entered the palace and proceeded to drag the two Emperors

through the streets of Rome to their camp, adding insults to bodily injuries. When the Germans came to the rescue, the praetorians murdered their victims, leaving their bodies bruised and disfigured in the roadway. They then took young Gordian and proclaimed him the Emperor of the Roman people's choice.[42] Thus after three months ended the experiment of senatorially-elected Emperors. Once again the soldiers had triumphed, even though their candidate for the Empire was no more than a boy of thirteen.

The reign of Gordian III was clouded by almost continuous warfare, especially on the north-eastern and eastern frontiers of the Empire. Already under Maximus and Balbinus the Goths had entered Lower Moesia and destroyed the town of Istros, while the Carpi had invaded Roman territory higher up the river Danube.[43] Against these tribes the Romans seem at first to have met with little success, and it was three years before the situation was effectively improved. Two other events deserve a passing mention. In August, A.D. 239, Viminacium in Upper Moesia started to issue coins marking a new era of chronological reckoning,[44] and this may imply that the town was raised to the status of a colony and had perhaps been used as the headquarters of the army during the Sarmatian War, which had begun under Maximinus and which was terminated in this year. In Africa the legion III *Augusta*, which had supported the rebellion of Capellianus, was cashiered in disgrace before the end of A.D. 238.[45] Its soldiers were drafted into the German and Raetian legions, but the unit itself was not reinstated till the reign of Valerian.[46] How the military arrangements in Numidia and Africa were carried on in the intervening years is not known. Most probably the country was denuded of regular garrison-troops ; for when Sabinianus, the governor of Africa, revolted in A.D. 240 the rebellion was crushed by the governor of Mauretania with an army largely, if not entirely, composed of auxiliaries.[47]

Of the early administration of Gordian we know little or nothing. Clearly his youthfulness necessitated the conduct of affairs by relatives or advisers, and if Capitolinus' narrative may be trusted, the government was at first in the hands of eunuchs and favourites of the Empress Maecia Faustina. We hear of a Felicio as prefect of the guard and a Sarapammon in command of a legion.[48] Whatever truth or exaggeration there may be in this tradition, in A.D. 241 the situation underwent a complete change by the appointment of C. Furius Sabinus Aquila Timesitheus to the post of praetorian prefect, and by the Emperor's marriage to his daughter.[49] Like most officials of the period Timesitheus had risen from the ranks and passed by way of the centurionate into the equestrian order.[50] His career is remarkable for its accumulation of procuratorial appointments and for the number of times in which their holder acted as a substitute for a senatorial governor. Under Severus Alexander, Timesitheus had been controller of the commissariat during the Persian War,[51] and had later served in a financial and military capacity in Germany. On the death of the young Emperor, for whom he showed no marked loyalty or aversion, he passed as a willing instrument into the service of Maximinus and acted as his financial agent in Bithynia, raising funds to defray the cost of his German War. He successfully weathered the storm that followed his master's murder, and under Gordian held the procuratorship of Lugdunensis before the marriage of his daughter and his elevation to the highest post of the equestrian service. About the character of this remarkable man the sources are silent. Probably he was no better or worse than most of his contemporaries, and for the good fortune that attended his career had to thank his own unscrupulous abilities and dominating personality. It is perhaps no accident that in the Latin writers his name is constantly given as Misitheus.[52] However that may be, his influence over Gordian was complete, and for nearly three years the Roman Empire was virtually under his rule.

In the spring of A.D. 242 Gordian, for the last time in Roman history, ceremoniously opened the doors of the temple of Janus and set out for war against Persia.[53] In the reign of Maximinus, Artaxerxes had captured Carrhae and Nisibis, and now his son, Sapor I, had invaded Syria and was threatening Antioch.[54] The Roman army was probably concentrated at Viminacium, but did not leave Europe till the following year. The summer of A.D. 242 was spent in re-establishing the Danubian frontier. After some successful fighting the danger from the Goths was averted.[55] While Gordian and Timesitheus made their winter quarters on the coast of the Black Sea, Tullius Menophilus, the defender of Aquileia, was

left as governor of Moesia to deal with the Carpi. For the
next three years he successfully warded off any fresh invasions,
and already by the spring of A.D. 243 the situation was
sufficiently well in hand for the main army to proceed on its
way to the East.[56] Most of its soldiers were probably transported by the imperial fleet from Misenum and Ravenna,[57]
and at Antioch fighting began in earnest. The Roman arms
were victorious; Antioch was saved, Carrhae and Nisibis
recovered and the retreating Persian army was decisively
defeated at Rhesaena.[58] At Nisibis arrangements were made
for the administration of the re-won territory and a descendant
of Abgarus was established as king of Osroene.[59] It was now
intended to push forward with Ctesiphon as the objective,
when Timesitheus, who had directed the campaign, died of
illness in the winter of A.D. 243-4.[60]

In his place Gordian appointed his understudy Julius
Verus Philippus, a native of Arabia, to be his praetorian
prefect.[61] The change in personnel was, however, of grave
import to the safety of the young Emperor. For whereas
Timesitheus had been content to exercise his extraordinary
power as guardian and adviser of Gordian, Philip soon
showed that his ambitions would only be satisfied by the
imperial authority itself. Nor had he long to wait for his
opportunity. Making use of a scarcity of food due to the
non-arrival of the corn-ships he fomented the indignation of
the soldiers against Gordian as the alleged author of their
misfortunes. The helplessness of the young Emperor was
pathetic. He offered to resign, to serve as Philip's Caesar,
to take any subordinate post, if only his life were spared.
Philip appealed to the soldiers and their answer was decisive.
They wanted a man and not a child for their ruler. To Philip,
too, the presence of a possible rival in his entourage was
fraught with danger, and led him to give the order to his troops
to murder their young Emperor. Gordian fell a victim to their
ruthlessness at Zaitha, some four miles from Circesium, on
February 25th, A.D. 244.[62]

Philip sent an official dispatch to Rome announcing
Gordian's death from natural causes and his own proclamation
by his army, which the Senate subsequently confirmed. At
the same time he caused the late Emperor to be deified by the
soldiers and asked the Senate to decree his canonization and

to grant his family relief from the performance of state obligations, in both of which requests that body acquiesced.[63] At the scene of Gordian's death a tombstone was erected inscribed, it is said, with the following words: "*Divo Gordiano, victori Gothorum, victori Sarmatarum, depulsori Romanarum seditionum, victori Germanorum, sed non victori Philipporum.*"[64]

CHAPTER II

PHILIP AND DECIUS

§ 1. HISTORY OF PHILIP'S REIGN

THE first act of Philip's reign was the conclusion of peace with Persia. The terms of the treaty were not unfavourable to Rome. Mesopotamia and Lesser Armenia remained inside the Roman Empire, and the only disadvantage which Rome suffered was that the dependence of the client-king of Greater Armenia was nominal and not actual. Philip appointed his brother Priscus governor of Mesopotamia, and himself accepted the title of *Persicus Maximus*.[1] He then set out for Rome in company with his son, M. Julius Philippus, whom on his own accession he had raised to the rank of Caesar. Before leaving the East, however, he conferred privileges upon some of the towns in the district. Neapolis in Syria was given the status of a colony and the title *Colonia Julia Sergia Neapolis*, and on the site of his own birthplace he founded Philippopolis and gave it the rank of a colony, while Bostra was honoured with the title of *Colonia Metropolis*.[2] Making his return journey through Thrace, where he conferred the status of a colony on the other Philippopolis, and Macedonia where games were held in his honour at Beroea, Philip reached Rome not later than July 23rd, A.D. 244.[3] With the Senate he was immediately successful in establishing good relations, which continued throughout his reign, and by the strength of his personality he was able to allay the suspicions that the sudden death of Gordian had aroused. At the same time he showed a particular interest in the fortunes of his own family. He caused his father Marinus to be apotheosised by the Senate and, in addition to the already mentioned appointment of Priscus in Mesopotamia, gave the command in Moesia and Macedonia to his brother-in-law Severianus.[4]

Either in A.D. 245 or 246 the Carpi who, as we have seen, had been held in check by the ability of Menophilus, once again crossed the Danube. Neither Prastina Messalinus, the governor of Lower Moesia, nor his superior officer Severianus seem to have been a match for the invaders. Indeed the situation was so serious that Philip himself left Rome to take command of the army on the Danube. His presence in July A.D. 246 in Dacia is attested by the right of coinage granted to that province, which appears to have reckoned the years of its new chronological era from about the twentieth of the month.[5] At the same time the mints in Macedonia, Lower Moesia and Thrace were closed down, perhaps because they had been stormed by the barbarians. In the same year there was probably some fighting with German tribes on the Danube as the Emperor assumed the title of *Germanicus Maximus*.[6] Next year saw a decisive victory over the Carpi. Defeated in battle, some of the barbarians retreated to a fortress where they were besieged, and when, on observing that others of their band who had been scattered in flight were rallying again outside, they attempted a sortie, they were overcome by the Moorish archers and sued for peace.[7] Philip granted them terms and returned to Rome to celebrate a great triumph, which was further enhanced by the elevation of his son to the rank of Augustus, and the assumption by the victor of the title *Carpicus Maximus*.[8]

In A.D. 248 Philip entered on his third consulship with his son as colleague and consul for the second time.[9] On April 21st the thousandth birthday of Rome was commemorated with all the pomp and magnificence that was normally associated with imperial celebrations. Games were held on an extravagant scale in the Circus Maximus, in which a number of wild beasts that Gordian had collected for his Persian triumph were brought into the arena.[10] A *congiarium* was distributed to the people and Rome had the air of a nation in peace and prosperity. This was the pinnacle of Philip's fame.

In the early summer news reached Rome of a rebellion on the Danube, where the legions invested with the purple one of their officers called Ti. Claudius Marinus Pacatianus.[11] Profiting by the ensuing confusion inside the Empire and incensed at not receiving the annual tribute which Gordian

had agreed to pay, the Goths supported by the Carpi, Peucini
and Asdingian Vandals invaded Lower Moesia under the
command of Argaithus and Gunthericus, and besieged
Marcianopolis, the capital of the province. But thanks to
the bravery of the Roman governor, a Thracian called
Maximus, and to the fortifications which Menophilus had
erected, two barbarian attacks were successfully warded off,
and such severe casualties were inflicted on the second army
of assault that the whole project was abandoned.[12]

About the same time as the rebellion in Moesia, trouble
also broke out in the East. After his governorship of
Mesopotamia, Priscus had been promoted commander-in-
chief of the army of the East with the title of *praefectus
praetorio rectorque Orientis*.[13] His oppressive administration,
and in particular the vigorous measures which he employed
in the collection of taxes, led to the proclamation as Emperor
of a certain Iotapianus, who claimed to be a descendant of
Alexander, by the soldiers of Cappadocia.[14] Meanwhile in
Syria yet a third pretender appeared, L. Aurelius Sulpicius
Uranius Antoninus, who maintained himself in power till
A.D. 253.[15]

This troubled state of the Empire, which so well exemplifies
the undisciplined power of the army, caused Philip the
greatest consternation. In his anxiety he turned to the
Senate for help. His offer to abdicate was received in silence,
and no senator had any advice to give till C. Messius Quintus
Decius expressed the opinion that Philip need feel no alarm,
as Pacatianus was unfitted to be an Emperor and would be
killed by his own soldiers. This prediction was soon afterwards fulfilled; not only Pacatianus but also Iotapianus
were murdered. But despite the removal of the two chief
usurpers Philip's fears were not allayed. He knew that the
army in the Balkans hated their officers, and so he prevailed
upon a reluctant Decius to take over the command in
succession to Severianus.[16]

On his arrival on the Danube, probably in the autumn of
A.D. 248, Decius, who was gifted with a statesmanlike ability,
immediately proceeded to restore order and discipline. The
Goths were forced back out of Roman territory and Romula
in Dacia was fortified and perhaps raised to the status of a
colony.[17] The mutinous legions were brought back into a

state of loyalty, partly by the settlement of their arrears of pay, but more essentially by the vigorous discipline enforced by Decius. In the exercise of his command Decius remained faithful to Philip, and to dispel any suspicion that he coveted the post of Emperor forebore from striking any coins in his own name in Moesia.[18] But once again the soldiers took matters into their own hands. Impressed by the military capacities of their general and believing that under his leadership victory over Philip would be easily won, they invested Decius with the purple despite his protests in the winter of A.D. 248–9. Even now Decius attempted to disarm any suspicions about his motives. In a letter to Philip, which bears the impression of honesty, he attempted to remove the Emperor's anxiety for his own safety by promising on his return to Rome to give up the insignia of Empire which his soldiers had compelled him to assume.[19] But Philip mistrusted the sincerity of his professions, and marched out from Rome towards the end of June to oppose the anticipated attack of the usurper. Some time in September a great battle was fought at Verona.[20] Details of the fighting are scarce, but two things favoured the cause of Decius, the confidence of his troops, although outnumbered, in their commander's tactical abilities and the enfeeblement of Philip by old age. Both Zosimus and Zonaras state that the younger Philip fell with his father in the battle : another tradition asserts that he was put to death afterwards in the praetorian camp when news of Verona reached the City.[21] Neither Philip nor his son was deified.[22]

§ 2. PHILIP'S ADMINISTRATION

The five and a half years of Philip's reign provide a clear illustration of the forces which were undermining the stability of the Roman Empire. An almost continuous succession of foreign wars not only sapped the wealth of the provinces which were exposed to invasion, but also put an enormous strain upon the resources of the whole Empire. To pay for the cost of campaigns and the maintenance of the army taxation became increasingly oppressive and compulsory state services were more rigorously imposed. If these burdens fell mainly on the upper and middle classes, the lot of the peasants, as a petition from the tenants of an imperial estate in Phrygia shows,[23] was in no way better than it had been under the dynasty of the Severi. The civil population was being ground down by the tyranny of a militarized bureaucracy. At the same time the soldiers were undisciplined and mutinous. Indifferent to politics, they cared only for their own interests. Their loyalty extended no further than the promptings of their personal greed and ambition, and with ruthless inconsistency they changed their allegiance from one general to another, indifferent to the welfare of the rest of the community provided their own fortunes were temporarily enhanced.

Despite this troubled state of the Empire, it cannot be said that Philip's government was bad nor that he was blind to the responsibilities of Empire. Although his accession was secured by connivance at the murder of his predecessor, his subsequent rule demonstrated his belief in constitutional government. His relations with the Senate were cordial; a general amnesty was granted to exiles,[24] and measures were taken for the protection of Italy and the welfare of the provincials. Against the activities of robbers and pirates a detachment of marines from Ravenna was stationed at Petra Pertusa in Umbria; an auxiliary contingent was established at Concordia and a detachment of XIII *Gemina* at Aquileia.[25] If these latter measures were unavailing against Decius, they do not detract from the strategical ability of Philip, which received a further confirmation in his victory over the Carpi. In the provinces numerous milestones attest the Emperor's care for roads and transport, and that his interests were not purely military is indicated by grateful dedications erected by provincials.[26] The people in Rome were kept contented by the distribution of three *congiaria*, and a reservoir was constructed in Trastevere.[27] In the speech of Pseudo-Aristides εἰς βασιλέα, which is now rightly held to be addressed to Philip, the orator describes his rule as based upon all the Stoic virtues.[28] Although the picture is clearly exaggerated and represents the ideal government visualized by the educated classes rather than its realization in the reigning Emperor, still such a rhetorical panegyric would not have been dedicated to Philip unless his administration had given clear indications of an honest, if unsuccessful, attempt to govern the Roman world upon statesmanlike principles.

Later tradition emanating from gossip recorded by Eusebius has selected Philip for the honour of being the first Christian Emperor of Rome.[29] This evidence is unhistorical and must be rejected. There is no mention of Philip's conversion in contemporary Christian literature; the letters of Origen addressed to him and his wife, while indicating the Emperor's interest in the faith, say nothing of his baptism.[30] Nor do Philip's activities suggest that he was converted, for it is difficult to believe that a man who deified his own father, appointed his son *pontifex maximus*, and celebrated the birthday of Rome with pagan rites, can have been admitted a member of the Catholic Church. In contrast with his successor Decius, Philip was undoubtedly tolerant and indulgent to the Christians, and we hear that he permitted Pope Fabianus to convey the ashes of his predecessor from Sardinia to Rome.[31] Such a story and the ensuing persecution of Decius are sufficient to account for the legend.

§ 3.   THE EARLY REIGN OF DECIUS

The victor at Verona was a native of the village of Budalia in Lower Pannonia, and was born about the beginning of the third century.[32] Of his parentage and early career few details survive. His father was either an officer stationed in the district or a native of the province; his wife Herennia Cupressenia Etruscilla belonged to an old Italian family.[33] He seems to have attained senatorial rank early in his career, if he is rightly identified with the governor of Lower Moesia between the years A.D. 234–8,[34] and may have passed through the normal *cursus honorum*. In the later years of Philip he was appointed prefect of the City, before being sent out to settle the disturbances caused by the rebellion of Pacatianus.[35]

Decius probably reached Rome early in October, as his name is attached to an edict promulgated on the sixteenth of the month. He is first mentioned as Emperor in Egypt on a papyrus dated November 28th.[36] His proclamation by his soldiers was confirmed by the Senate and he assumed the name of Trajan, partly as a personal recognition of his own military abilities and partly as a guarantee to the Senate of the friendly terms which he hoped to establish with it. His official title was thus Imp. Caesar C. Messius Quintus Decius Traianus.[37]

The first year of Decius' reign was a period of peace and reorganization. On December 28th a number of veterans who had served for twenty-eight years were discharged ; a *congiarium* was distributed to the people, and a series of coins bearing the legends AEQUITAS and ABUNDANTIA may indicate a care for the food supply.[38] The Emperor next turned his attention to the provinces. Realizing like all good generals that the most common cause of rebellion is the idleness of camp life, he set the soldiers to work on a scheme of road-reconstruction. As might be expected it was in the Balkan area that the greatest activity was first apparent. The military highway along the south bank of the Danube was repaired, its side-roads and bridges reconstructed.[39] Decius fully realized that here was the danger zone of the Empire, and his determination to re-establish discipline among the legions is attested by an inscription from Oescus which calls him *reparator disciplinae militaris*.[40] But his programme was not limited to the north-eastern frontier. Milestones from Spain, Britain and Africa in the West,[41] and from Syria and Galatia in the East,[42] indicate that the more peaceful provinces were included in his scheme of reconstruction. This evidence despite its fragmentary form is the greatest tribute to the statesmanship of Decius ; for it shows that while his attention was necessarily concentrated on the possibility of renewed invasions, he still had time to consider the welfare of the outlying provinces and to instil fresh life into their administration.

Early in his reign Decius created a special office which bears some slight resemblance to the old censorship, and appointed the later Emperor Valerian, who was of senatorial rank, to be its first holder.[43] There were two general intentions in this innovation. Decius wanted to emphasize his friendly relationship with the Senate, and secondly to have a trustworthy representative to whom he might entrust the care of Rome, if he were summoned to the front by the news of barbarian invasions. For his sons Herennius and Hostilianus were as yet too young to shoulder responsibilities and were not raised to the rank of Caesar till September and December A.D. 250, respectively.[44] The language of Zonaras suggests that the new post was primarily financial in its scope ($\epsilon\pi\grave{\iota}\ \tau\hat{\eta}$ $\tau\hat{\omega}\nu\ \pi\rho\alpha\gamma\mu\acute{\alpha}\tau\omega\nu\ \delta\iotao\iota\kappa\acute{\eta}\sigma\epsilon\iota$) and perhaps that author is not mistaken in his further contention that Valerian assisted Decius in his attempted revival of state religion with its concomitant persecution of the Christians.

In order to appreciate impartially Decius' intention it is necessary to rid our minds of modern ideas that are associated with a holy war or a religious persecution. To the Roman the state-religion was essentially political in character; its solidarity was the moral expression of the unity of the Empire, just as conversely indifference to its claims might call down divine vengeance in the form of civil disturbances or external invasions. Towards foreign creeds the government had always adopted an attitude of tolerance, provided that their adherents showed a fitting reverence to the religion of the State. But it was just this condition that the Christians with their strongly developed monotheistic faith were unable to accept. In the early years of the Christian era different Emperors had attempted to enforce compliance with the state demands, but for the most part the Christians because of the smallness of their number had been left unmolested. But now in the middle of the third century the Church had become an organized body and numbered among its adherents members of all classes of society throughout the Empire. Its proselytizing activities and its gospel of international peace might well cause alarm to an Emperor who had set himself the task of resuscitating the imperial greatness of Rome, and who believed that an essential condition of its realization was the recognition by all his subjects of the gods of the State. The danger of religious disintegration had further been brought home to him by riots in Alexandria in the last year of Philip's reign. For a whole year the mob had conducted a pogrom against the Christian community, which the late Emperor had been apparently powerless to control.[45] So, early in his reign, Decius issued a decree requiring of all Christians and those suspected of Christian sympathies a declaration of conformity

to the religion of the State. The terms of the edict have not
been preserved, but from Egyptian *libelli* we get some
information of the manner in which the enquiry was conducted.[46] In every town a commission, usually consisting
of five men, was established, before which the suspected
person was required to make a sacrifice or libation to the
gods of Rome among whom, it is worth observing, the
Emperor himself was not expressly included. If this was
carried out to the satisfaction of the judges, then a certificate
of conformity was issued which secured its possessor from any
further molestation. If, on the other hand, the Christian
held firmly to his faith and refused compliance,he was arrested
and kept in prison suffering the tortures of hunger and thirst
in the hope that he would apostatize. Capital sentences were
rarer, and this suggests that Decius' intention was less to
exterminate the Christian sect than to compel it to renounce
its creed and so increase the solidarity of the Empire by the
common recognition of its official religion. Under the pressure
of the persecution the courage of many Christians collapsed
and apostasies were rife. On the other hand, some of the
leaders of the Church were ready to face martyrdom in the
profession of their Faith.[47] In Antioch and Jerusalem Bishops
Babylas and Alexander were arrested and died in prison,
Origen escaped with his life, but died soon after from the
effects of his sufferings; in Rome Pope Fabian was put to
death on January 20th, 250, and so serious was the situation
that no successor was elected for fifteen months.

§ 4. THE GOTHIC WAR AND THE DEATH OF DECIUS

During the summer of A.D. 250, there was fighting both on
the Danubian and on the Rhenish frontiers. The former
campaign was brought to a successful conclusion, as is clear
from an inscription from Apulum dedicated to Decius without the Caesars as *restitutor Daciarum*.[48] Further west there
was considerable activity in the neighbourhood of Mainz,
and inscriptions from Ladenburg and Heidelberg inscribed to
Herennius as Caesar[49] show that fighting took place in these
districts in the later months of A.D. 250. At the end of the
year Decius discharged another set of veterans at Ravenna.[50]

These events in all probability preceded the invasion of the Goths, who under their chief Kniva may have taken advantage of the icebound Danube to enter Moesia.[51]   The invaders seem to have divided themselves into two armies.   One of them, after an unsuccessful attempt to storm Novae, from which they were driven off by Gallus, the military commander of the two provinces of Moesia, moved south and besieged Nicopolis ; the other besieged L. Priscus, the governor, in Philippopolis.[52]   Decius immediately sent his elder son to take command of the Illyrian army, elevating him in all probability at the same time to the rank of Augustus,[53] and on hearing of the gravity of the situation followed himself at the earliest possible opportunity.[54]   On reaching Moesia he was successful in relieving Nicopolis, but was too late to save Philippopolis, which was ruthlessly plundered with the massacre of its inhabitants.[55]   The Emperor with his lieutenant Gallus next attempted to cut off the retreat of the Goths, who on realizing his intentions made a fruitless effort at negotiations.   A great battle was fought about the beginning of July at Abrittus, not far from Adamklissi in the Dobrudja. At first Decius was successful in defeating two contingents of the enemy, but the issue was decided by the treachery of Gallus.   He signalled to the Emperor to advance against a third band of barbarians, and the latter, ignorant of the country and unsuspecting, was trapped with all his soldiers in a bog where they were shot down by the enemy.   Neither his body nor that of his son Herennius was recovered.[56] Such was the ill-fated end of an Emperor who in his short reign of two years had ruled wisely and well.

After the battle the soldiers proclaimed Gallus Emperor. The new ruler immediately made a shameful treaty with the Goths, by the terms of which they were not merely permitted to return home with their booty, but also to take with them the Roman prisoners, mostly of noble rank, whom they had captured at Philippopolis ; in addition they were promised an annual payment of tribute.[57]   Gallus then set out for Rome, where Hostilianus, the younger son of Decius, was residing.   In order to facilitate the acceptance of the story that the Decii had died in battle and that his own proclamation had been forced upon him by the army, the Emperor decided upon a compromise.   He raised Hostilianus to the rank of

11

Augustus and created his own son Volusianus Caesar.[58]
Before long, however, Volusianus was further elevated and
Rome had three Augusti as her rulers till Hostilianus died of
plague.[59] His death probably occurred in November; for
on an Egyptian papyrus of December 3rd, Gallus and
Volusianus appear as the joint rulers of the Empire.[60]

CHAPTER III

VALERIAN AND GALLIENUS

§ 1. INTRODUCTION

DURING the seventeen years between the accession of C. Vibius Trebonianus Gallus and the death of P. Licinius Gallienus, Rome passed through one of the darkest periods of her history. The forces which were gradually sapping her strength seemed to combine as it were for a concentrated and final attack upon her existence as an imperial power. The northern frontier was destroyed; barbarians poured into Italy and swept over the provinces of Gaul and Spain. The Persians overran Mesopotamia and Syria and returned home with a Roman Emperor as their captive. The seas were infested with pirates and robbers who devastated the rich coastal towns of Pontus and Asia Minor ; Africa was pillaged by hostile tribes from the Sahara. Italy and the Eastern provinces experienced the horror of a great earthquake, and plague beginning in Egypt spread to the West and decimated the population. Before this combination of external forces the unity of the Roman Empire collapsed. Local Emperors appeared in quick succession in almost every province, and, if some were speedily suppressed, others maintained themselves for a number of years in independence of the central government. On the death of Gallienus the Roman Empire extended no wider than Italy, Africa, Illyricum, Achaea, Asia Minor and Egypt, its resources were exhausted and its treasury bankrupt.

This disintegration of the Roman Empire may be attributed to two main causes which had been insidiously at work since the days of Septimius Severus. Owing to the system of local recruitment and to the introduction of barbarians into its ranks the Roman army had lost much of its disciplined efficiency. Encouraged by frequent donatives and increase pay its soldiers had come to look upon military service less as an honourable profession than an avenue to personal wealth and advancement. Consequently their loyalty to the reigning Emperor extended no further than their confidence in his ability to satisfy their demands and ambitions, and without any consideration of imperial questions they were ready without hesitation to substitute a candidate of their own choice. At the same time the grant of land to serving soldiers in the neighbourhood of the camps with the added permission, if married, to live outside barracks was prejudicial to the peace-time exercises of the army. Under a slack commander roads and fortifications were allowed to fall into disrepair, so that when the barbarians decided upon invasion the frontiers were inadequate to keep them out. Further, the practice inherited from the early Principate of withdrawing garrison troops to form an expeditionary force in another part of the Empire depleted the frontier provinces, notably on the Danube, of their necessary man-power. The Empire required both a mobile and a garrison army ; in the middle of the third century the organization, if not the size, of its military resources was inadequate for its safety.

The second main cause of the Empire's collapse was economic. With few exceptions the Emperors of the third century pursued a policy of wasteful expenditure. Personal extravagance, donatives to the populace at Rome, costly civil and foreign wars, in which a pandering to the greed of the soldiery was a condition of success, had drained the wealth of the provinces. To supplement the normal revenues of the State a system of compulsory state service had been introduced, and hardly any class of the civil population was exempt from financial and personal obligations, which were ruthlessly enforced by the officers and agents of the Emperor. No attempt was made to build up in time of peace a reserve fund to meet the extraordinary requirements of war. The conception of a national debt was as foreign to the Emperors of the third century as it had been to the statesmen of the Republic. Instead to give an air of superficial prosperity resort had been had to a policy of inflation. The gold coinage lost all stability and regularity, while debasement of the silver proceeded till Gallienus flooded the

market with a worthless billon. The State had virtually
declared itself bankrupt.

But although the crisis in the middle of the third century
may be regarded as the logical outcome of the military and
economic policies that had been characteristic of Rome
since the dynasty of the Severi, the suddenness of the disintegration of the Empire may seem to call for some more
immediate explanation. As so often in times of national
distress it was the incalculable and unforeseen factor that
contributed most to the misfortunes of Rome. It is difficult
to over-emphasize the disastrous effects of the plague which
raged with unabating force for fifteen years. Not only did
it undermine the Empire's powers of resistance, but it
carried off vast numbers of its population. Whole cities were
left desolate and fell a prey into the hands of the barbarian
invaders. Compared with this relentless scourge the sufferings
inflicted by the Goths seemed almost tolerable.[1]

Literary tradition delights to find a personal agent upon
whom to place the responsibility for a crisis and in this case
the Latin authors have selected Gallienus for their victim.[2]
In this and the following chapter we shall attempt to consider
the justice of this judgement and in particular whether the
policy adopted by Gallienus was, as it is represented, the
product of his own careless indifference to affairs of State,
or whether it may more fittingly be described as a prudent
and diplomatic handling of a situation for which he himself
was not primarily responsible.

§ 2.   GALLUS AND AEMILIANUS

The reign of Gallus and his son Volusianus, which lasted
a bare two years, was a period of disaster and misfortune
unrelieved, as far as our records go, by any notable successes
in public administration. The Persians again overran
Mesopotamia and advanced as far as Antioch, returning home
laden with spoils and booty.[3] The Goths crossed the Danube
and plundered the cities of Moesia and Thrace, while another
band of marauders moved into Asia Minor and ravaged the
country as far south as Ephesus.[4] Even more devastating
was the plague which coincided with the invasion and left
towns and villages denuded of their populations.[5] In the

face of these misfortunes Gallus seems to have taken no active steps with the exception of a revival of the Decian persecution of the Christians as a diversion for the populace of Rome. A new edict was issued compelling the Christians to sacrifice, and Pope Cornelius was imprisoned at Centum Cellae, where he died in the summer of A.D. 253.[6] A temporary success, however, was achieved against the Goths by the action of Aemilius Aemilianus, the governor of Moesia. Recalling his soldiers to a sense of the greatness of Rome and promising them a liberal donative in the event of victory he fell upon the enemy that were still in his province, and, after a considerable slaughter, carried the warfare into their own country, where the suddenness of his attack was rewarded with an unexpected success. This unlooked-for recovery of Roman prestige so impressed the soldiers with the strategical ability of their commander that they proclaimed him Emperor, and threw off their allegiance to Gallus. Aemilianus accordingly collected as strong an army as he could and advanced into Italy, hoping to join battle before his opponent had time to make his preparations. On hearing of the rebellion, Gallus sent orders to P. Licinius Valerianus to come to his assistance with an army drawn from the legions on the Rhine. But before he could arrive Aemilianus had established himself in Italy and advanced as far south as Interamna, some twenty miles north of Rome. Here a battle was fought, in which the soldiers of Gallus realizing their own numerical inferiority and despising the careless apathy of their commander, murdered him and his son and took the oath of allegiance to Aemilianus.[7] The latter, however, was only permitted a short reign of some three months.[8] Valerian undaunted by the news of Gallus' death continued with his plans for an invasion of Italy, and in Raetia was proclaimed Emperor by his troops.[9] Prominent in the movement were the soldiers of III *Augusta* who, when their legion had been cashiered by Gordian, had, as we have seen, been drafted to Germany. Their action was rewarded by Valerian, who reinstated their old regiment and sent it back to Africa.[10] News of the proclamation of Valerian sealed the fate of Aemilianus. His soldiers, realizing his unfitness to rule and anxious perhaps to avoid further civil war, murdered him and took the oath to Valerian.

§ 3. REIGN OF VALERIAN AND GALLIENUS

The action of the army in Raetia was welcomed with satisfaction by the Senate and, perhaps on its own initiative, it created Valerian's son, P. Licinius Egnatius Gallienus, who was living in Rome, Caesar.[11] When Valerian reached the capital in the autumn of A.D. 253 he received from the Senate the customary imperial powers and adopted his son, who was raised to the rank of Augustus, as a partner in the Empire.[12] The first months of the new reign were comparatively peaceful, but soon news reached Rome of great unrest among the German tribes. The fear of local insurrections determined Valerian to entrust the command on the Rhenish frontier to his son, and in the latter half of A.D. 254 Gallienus set out from Rome. During the first three years of his command his army, which was reinforced by detachments from Britain, won several victories which are commemorated on coins.[13] Some of the Germans were prevented from reaching the Rhine, others were defeated as they attempted to cross the river, while to counteract the numerical superiority of his opponents Gallienus made an alliance with one of the German chiefs— a diplomatic move which he was later to repeat in other parts of the Empire.[14] It was probably also at this time that repairs were carried out at a number of Roman fortresses on the left bank of the Rhine. Cologne was walled, Neuss (Novaesium) was refortified, while Andernach (Antumnacum) was transformed into a garrison town and Trier fortified so as to serve as a second line of defence.[15]

In A.D. 256 or 257 Valerian left Rome for the East and appointed his son ruler of the Western Empire.[16] About this time the tide of success in Germany began to turn. The Franks broke through the northern *limes*, overran Gaul and Spain, destroying Tarraco, and penetrated in a pillaging raid as far as the coast of Mauretania Tingitana.[17] Further south the Alamanni were continuously attacking the forts on the Germano-Raetian *limes*,[18] and in A.D. 258 invaded Italy by way of the Brenner Pass. Gallienus himself left Gaul and won a great victory over the invaders at Milan, for which he received his fifth imperial salutation.[19] Having saved Italy the Emperor returned to his task of safeguarding the frontier from further assaults, but in the next year news came from Pannonia of the rebellion of Ingenuus, who was supported by the Moesian legions.[20] Gallienus decided to entrust the command on the Rhine to M. Cassianius Latinius Postumus, and left his second son P. Cornelius Licinius Saloninus at Cologne under the care of his praetorian prefect Silvanus.[21] He himself with an army, which included the British detachments, set out for the scene of the revolt.

Even before the rebellion of Ingenuus the situation on the Danubian frontier had been serious. Barbarians were attacking along the whole length of the river, Pannonia being threatened by the Marcomanni, Quadi and Sarmatae, Dacia by the Goths and Carpi. In such a crisis a successful rebellion might well have meant the surrender of Roman sovereignty at one of the most vulnerable parts of the Empire. This disaster was averted by the prompt action of Gallienus. With an army, in which were detachments from the two Dacian legions which had fought for him at Milan,[22] he and his general Aureolus, who commanded the cavalry, crushed Ingenuus at Mursa. The danger was not, however, over. The remnants of Ingenuus' army attempted to continue the rebellion by investing Regalianus with the purple.[23] The new usurper, who associated with himself a Roman lady called Dryantilla, maintained himself in power at Carnuntum for a number of months, but in A.D. 260 unity was restored by Gallienus in Illyricum.[24] To protect the district from foreign aggression he also made an alliance with Attalus, king of the Marcomanni, ceding to him parts of Pannonia in return, it is said, for his daughter Pipa as his concubine.[25]

During Gallienus' absence there were sinister developments in Gaul. Postumus and Silvanus quarrelled and the former marched on Cologne. Saloninus and his guardian were captured and put to death, and Postumus was proclaimed Emperor by his troops (A.D. 259).[26] In the next year his sovereignty was recognized by the German legions, and soon the armies in Spain and Britain followed their example.[27] To meet this challenge Gallienus returned to Gaul, and for the next year and a half waged an indecisive warfare against the usurper and was wounded in attempting to besiege one of his fortified towns (? Trier).[28]

Meanwhile in the East Valerian had by A.D. 257 established his headquarters at Antioch and repelled a further invasion

of Syria by Sapor.[29]   Asia Minor, however, was suffering
from a series of piratical raids by the Goths and their neighbours. The Borani were the first to engage in this form of
brigandage. They obtained their ships from the Bosporan
kingdom which lay to the north of the Black Sea. Previously
its native kings had been friendly to Rome and prevented the
barbarians from gaining access to the sea, but the overthrow
of the monarchy had resulted in internal confusion, and fear
rather than judgement dictated a policy of compliance with
their neighbours' demands. The Borani were thus enabled
to cross to the east coast of the Black Sea, but in their eager
lust for plunder made no provision for the retention of the
fleet, which the Bosporani took back home with them. Their
first objective was the Roman outpost town of Pityus, but
thanks to the courage and ability of its governor, Successianus,
they were driven back with great loss, and seizing what ships
they could find retreated to their homes. A further attack
was not anticipated, and Valerian sent for Successianus and
rewarded his services by making him prefect of his guard.
But the Borani were not daunted by their initial failure.
Once again they crossed the Pontus, this time securing a fleet
for the duration of their campaign, and anchored at the mouth
of the Phasis. After plundering the shrine of Artemis they
once again attacked Pityus, which they were successful in
storming. Reinforcing their fleet with captives who were
skilled oarsmen, and profiting by an unusually calm summer,
they sailed to Trapezus, which after a short siege was captured
by a surprise night attack. Some of the defenders made good
their escape, but many were massacred and the city was
burned to the ground. Enriched by the booty which its great
wealth had provided the Borani returned home.[30]

Their example was soon emulated by their neighbours the
Goths, who chose a less circuitous and dangerous route for
their invasion. Their fleet moved down the west coast of the
Black Sea accompanied by an army which marched by way of
Tomi and Anchialus till it reached the marsh of Phileas,
which lies to the west of Byzantium. Here the troops were
embarked and crossed successfully to Chalcedon, which was
captured without opposition, its defenders having taken to
flight. The invaders next attacked Nicomedia, allured by
its wealth, some of which the inhabitants anticipating a

siege had conveyed away with them in their flight. Nicaea, Apamea and Prusa suffered a similar fate, but Cyzicus was saved by the river Rhyndacus being in flood. The Goths accordingly returned home with their rich spoils, setting fire to Nicomedia and Nicaea as they went.[31]

On hearing of the invasion of the Goths, Valerian sent one of his officers called Felix to take command at Byzantium, and himself advanced into Cappadocia with the further intention of bringing relief to Bithynia. But the expedition was abortive. Plague broke out in his army and carried away many of his soldiers, and news came that Sapor, king of the Persians, was once again advancing against Antioch. After an initial victory[32] Valerian crossed into Mesopotamia, but despairing of his power to wage a war with an army depleted by the ravages of the plague, he attempted negotiations. His emissaries returned with a request from Sapor for a personal interview, and Valerian trusting the good faith of his enemy set out with a small retinue for Edessa to discuss terms of peace. By a perfidious ruse Sapor effected his arrest and an Emperor of Rome was led off in triumph to die a captive in Persia (A.D. 260).[33] Roman prestige was eclipsed ; but a word of pity may be accorded to the author of her disgrace. Valerian was neither a fool nor a knave. In times of peace he might have governed with unoffending moderation ; for he was honest and well-intentioned. But the crisis in the third century demanded a statesmanship and courage that Valerian did not possess.

Of the internal administration of Valerian we possess little or no information with the exception of his religious policy. For the first three years of his reign the Christian Church enjoyed peace and tranquillity, but in A.D. 257 a new wave of persecution set in. Once again an attempt was made to enforce recognition of the state religion as a means of combating the dangers that were besetting the Empire, and war was declared upon the Church as the chief obstacle to this consummation. Two edicts were issued, one in August A.D. 257, and the other a year later. The former only affected the higher clergy, who were ordered to sacrifice to the gods of the State, but were not forbidden the worship of Christ in private. Thus was the principle of syncretism extended to Christianity. The second edict was promulgated in the East and addressed to the Senate with instructions for provincial governors. Its scope was much wider and its punishments more severe. Laymen in certain positions as well as clergy fell under its ban, and sentences, varying from death for clergy and confiscation of property for senators and knights to condemnation to the mines for tenants on the imperial estates, were laid down as the reward for recalcitrance. In the Western Empire many Christians suffered martyrdom in defence of their faith, of whom the most notable were St. Lawrence, who was burned to death at Rome, and St. Cyprian, who on his refusal to sacrifice was executed at Carthage. In the East the persecution seems to have been on a much smaller scale, perhaps because of the Gothic and Persian invasions, and with the death of Valerian the Church entered upon a long period of peace.[34]

CHAPTER IV

GALLIENUS AND HIS ADMINISTRATION

§ 1. THE EAST

THE capture of Valerian left the Eastern provinces at the mercy of the Persians. Antioch and Tarsus were taken and Caesarea in Cappadocia after a gallant defence by its commander Demosthenes was betrayed by a prisoner of war.[1] Meanwhile Macrianus, one of Valerian's generals, and Ballista, the praetorian prefect, rallied the remnants of the Roman army at Samosata and deliberated on what measures should be taken for the recovery of the lost provinces.[2] No help could be expected from Gallienus, who was busily engaged fighting Postumus. Macrianus himself was old and lame, and Ballista seems to have been averse from accepting imperial honours. The former, therefore, decided, with the approval of the soldiers, to proclaim his two sons Macrianus and Quietus Emperors, while he himself acted in an advisory capacity and Ballista continued to serve as prefect of the guard.[3] The centre of this new Empire was in Syria and its existence was spontaneously acknowledged by Asia Minor and Egypt :[4] but in character it was essentially Roman and was no more Oriental than was the Empire of Postumus Gallic. Hostilities were actively pursued against the Persians, and a victory of Ballista at Corycus in Cappadocia compelled Sapor to retreat to the Euphrates.[5] But Macrianus was not content with his position in the East. Lacking the wisdom of Postumus he determined to make a bid for the whole Empire. Consequently leaving Quietus and Ballista in Syria he set out in company with his elder son for Europe. Gallienus sent his general Aureolus against them and in a battle fought either in Illyricum or on the borders of Thrace Macrianus and his son were killed.[6] Further, one of his generals called Piso, who had been sent against Valens

Gallienus' proconsul of Achaea, and had assumed the purple, was put to death by his rival, who in his turn had himself proclaimed Emperor and maintained himself for a short time in power till he was murdered by his troops (A.D. 261).[7]

Despite his preoccupations in the West, Gallienus did not give up hope of reconquering the East, but a personal intervention or the dispatch of a Roman army from Europe was equally out of the question. In this crisis he found a valuable ally in Odenath of Palmyra.

The accession of the Sassanids to power had marked a turning-point in the history of Palmyra. Whereas the Arsacids had tolerated and even encouraged the caravan trade which constituted its wealth, the new masters of Central Asia had from the outset, by the annexation of Characene, shown their determination to establish economic as well as political domination by paralysing the commerce of Palmyra. Further, during the whole of the second and the early years of the third century peace had, except for two brief periods, governed the relations of Rome and Parthia, and the Palmyrenes had been able to assimilate Roman civilization without forgoing their friendship with Parthia. But with the advent of the Persians to power the situation was reversed. Wars were frequent and more often than not unfavourable to Rome. The Palmyrenes, who provided auxiliaries to the Roman army, came to realize the inability of the Romans to maintain their eastern frontier and the necessity, especially when an Illyrian Emperor succeeded their fellow-countryman Philip, of relying upon their own resources for self-defence against the ambition of the Sassanids.[8] Odenath's father had already attempted some years previously to establish his independence, but his schemes were discovered and he was put to death by Rufinus, who was governor of either Syria or Arabia.[9] He was succeeded first by one son, Septimius Hairanes, and then by another, Septimius Odenath, who in A.D. 258 was prince of Palmyra, bearing the honourable titles of *clarissimus* and *consularis*.[10] Daring and perspicacious, the young ruler knew how to make use of the crisis of A.D. 260. After making overtures to Sapor which were disdainfully rejected,[11] he turned to the side of Rome and proclaiming himself king of Palmyra collected an army from Arabia and Syria and marched to the Euphrates, where he inflicted a

severe defeat upon Sapor, which compelled him to retreat
to his own country, leaving prisoners and booty in the hands
of his victor.[12]

Odenath had so far acted on his own initiative, but Gallienus
was quick to show his gratitude for the defeat of Persia.
Turning a blind eye to the name of king he entrusted Odenath,
under the title of *dux*, with the supreme command of the
Roman forces in the East.[13] By this means he was able to
constitute an effective opposition to the Empire of Macrianus.
Nor was Odenath slow to execute his task. First he succeeded
in detaching most of the Syrian cities from their submission
to Ballista, and then attacking Emesa he conquered and
killed the praetorian prefect, while the townspeople put
Quietus to death.[14] Theoretically the unity of the Roman
Empire was re-established, actually Odenath became the
undisputed master of the East. Nothing could have prevented
his declaration of independence but the exceptional political
wisdom with which he was endowed. Personal advancement
was to him negligible beside the prosperity of his kingdom.
Visualizing a great Palmyrene Empire he saw also that the
conquest of Persia was the necessary condition of its realization. Without the army of Rome such a project was beyond
the native resources which he could command. So he was
content to remain the nominal mandatory of Gallienus, and
in this capacity contributed in no small measure to the later
reunification of the Roman Empire.

In A.D. 262 Odenath launched his attack upon Persia with
an army composed of Roman legionaries, and cavalry and
archers from his own kingdom, and for the next three years
he was engaged in active warfare. Great success attended
his campaign. Mesopotamia and probably Armenia were
recovered, and from Nisibis the army advanced to Ctesiphon.
Here, however, a stern resistance was put up by the Persians,
who had succeeded in rallying their scattered troops, and,
although the outskirts of the town were plundered, Ctesiphon
itself, despite two successive attacks, defied the conquering
invaders.[15] Odenath's purpose in making Ctesiphon his main
objective was not only to avenge the capture of Valerian, but
also to provide access for the caravans to and from the Persian
gulf, as an effective reply to the Persian occupation of
Characene ; and an inscription dated April, A.D. 266, suggests

that already one of his countrymen had been able to avail himself of this route.[16] Gallienus rewarded Odenath for his victories by granting him the title of *imperator*,[17] but the latter did not long survive this honour. In A.D. 266–7 he fell a victim to a dynastic plot and was assassinated together with his elder son. The scene of this intrigue cannot be decided with certainty. Zosimus places it at Emesa and makes the occasion a birthday celebration. Dexippus, on the other hand, associates it with an invasion of the Goths who had penetrated into Cappadocia, and states that Odenath, alarmed for the safety of the Taurus passes, had marched out against them with Heraclea in Pontus as his objective when he fell a victim to his assassin.[18] On his death the government of Palmyra passed into the hands of his second wife Zenobia and her infant son Waballath. Gallienus now showed his determination to prevent the Palmyrene dynasty establishing an independent power in the East. He conferred upon Waballath none of the titles which he had granted to Odenath. Legally Waballath was only king of Palmyra. But Gallienus was too weak to give effective expression to his policy. Zenobia and her son remained masters of the Eastern provinces with the exception of Asia Minor and Egypt, where a rebellion by Aemilianus was put down by Gallienus' general, Theodotus ; and when the Emperor attempted to deprive them of their position, his general, Heraclianus, was completely defeated. It was left to Aurelian to re-establish Roman sovereignty in the East.[19]

§ 2. THE WEST

Meanwhile Postumus was consolidating his position in Gaul. He made no attempt to re-establish the unity of the Empire for his own advantage, but contented himself with the control of the provinces which had acknowledged his sovereignty. The Franks and the Alamanni who had invaded Gaul were crushed and, although the northern *limes* was not recovered, a certain number of advanced posts in the Neckar valley were maintained.[20] On coins of A.D. 263 Postumus' victories are worthily commemorated by the legend VICTORIA GERMANICA, and the later legends RESTITUTOR ORBIS and SALUS PROVINCIARUM indicate, perhaps in flattering terms,

the completeness of his success.[21] Public works were also
carried out, to which the ruins of a palace at Trier bear
witness, and commerce revived, assisted by a coinage that
was less debased than that of Gallienus, and by the protection
of the coasts from pirates.[22] For ten years Postumus maintained his position in Gaul. In the last year of his reign
(A.D. 268) he was attacked by a rebel called Laelianus, whom
he successfully crushed, but his refusal to allow his troops
to plunder Mainz, which had assisted the usurper, led to his
own assassination. After a brief period of rule by Marius,
who is called by Eutropius " a workman of the lowest class,"
the Gallo-Roman Empire found a successor to Postumus in
M. Piavonius Victorinus, who had held under his predecessor
the post of a tribune of the guards that were stationed at
Trier.[23]

Gallienus, as we saw in the last chapter, had attempted to
suppress the rebellion in Gaul, but had been obliged to abandon the project owing to the usurpation of Macrianus. During
the remainder of his reign he never recognized the Empire of
Postumus, but circumstances and perhaps a realization of the
futility of the task prevented any effective intervention. In
A.D. 262 the plague extended to Italy and Africa and
devastated the population of Rome, carrying off, it is said, as
many as five thousand in a day.[24] The cities of Asia Minor
suffered from a severe earthquake, and a fresh invasion of the
Goths in the Balkans necessitated the Emperor's presence in
the East. The invaders ravaged Macedonia and Thrace, besieged Thessalonica, and moving into Greece attacked Athens,
which since the days of Sulla had experienced no assault.
As in the time of Xerxes' invasion the Peloponnesians built
a wall across the isthmus for the protection of the southern
peninsula. Finally the Goths were driven out of Greece, but
another band took to its ships and landing in Asia Minor
plundered the temple of the Moon at Ephesus. Probably
about the same time a mutiny broke out in Byzantium from
some uncertain cause, which was suppressed by the Emperor's
vigorous disciplinary measures.[25] By September, A.D. 262,
Gallienus was back in Rome and celebrated the tenth anniversary of his accession with festivities reminiscent of a triumph
in the days of the Republic. This military pageant was
staged by the Emperor to do honour to his army. If it

harmonized ill with the troubled state of the Empire, it was at the same time a symbol of an age when the goodwill of the soldiers was an essential condition for the maintenance of imperial power.[26]

During the next few years Gallienus made Rome his usual residence, leaving his officers to attend to the defences of Italy and Illyricum. The general confusion of the Empire seems for a time to have undermined his old vigour and determination and to have reduced him to a state of helpless acquiescence in the game which fortune was playing. Yet the stories which the Latin authors tell of his debauchery are probably without foundation, unconfirmed as they are by any Greek writer. Gallienus was very different from the soldier-emperors of his age and resembled rather the Antonines in character. He was a man of good education and refined tastes, interested in literature and art and with a special devotion to Hellenic culture. Like Hadrian, he had himself appointed archon at Athens, and, his biographer tells us, would fain have finished his days in peace as a member of the Areopagus.[27] He was initiated into the Eleusinian Mysteries and was attracted by religion and philosophy. Towards the Christians he showed a kindly tolerance,[28] and was on terms of such friendship with Plotinus that the philosopher had hopes of founding a Platonic state in Campania with the help of the Emperor and his wife Salonina.[29] If such were the characteristics of Gallienus, it seems probable that he spent the leisure which he perhaps wrongly permitted himself to enjoy, not in licentious indulgence, but in the cultivation of his literary and artistic interests.

The Emperor's holiday from war was ended by news of a fresh Gothic invasion, and once again he devoted his whole energy to dispelling the danger. The invaders, who were mostly Heruli, first crossed the Black Sea and devastated the Roman territory at the mouth of the Danube. Gallienus accordingly ordered two Byzantines, called Cleodamus and Athenaeus, to renovate the defences of the coastal towns and the barbarians were temporarily checked, while Venerianus inflicted a defeat upon them on sea. But when the latter had been killed in battle the Goths swept on, plundering Cyzicus and ravaging Greece. Beaten back from Athens by the *ephebi* under the command of the historian Dexippus, they

12

wandered, plundering as they went, through Epirus and Macedonia into Moesia.[30] Gallienus meanwhile had made his plans. Posting his general Marcianus so as to cut off the Goths' retreat and ordering Cleodamus and Athenaeus to destroy their fleet, he himself joined battle with the invaders on the banks of the Nessus.[31] The victory was decisive and might have ended in a rout, had not Gallienus been forced to abandon pursuit by news of the rebellion of his general Aureolus, whom he had left in charge of the defences of Italy. Accordingly he marched straight back and succeeded in driving Aureolus into Milan, which he began to besiege.[32] But treachery among his officers robbed him of a final victory. Heraclianus, the prefect of the guard, Marcianus, who had fought against the Goths, and Cecropius the commander of the Dalmatian cavalry hatched a plot to which the later Emperors Claudius and Aurelian were privy. The conspirators were all Illyrians, and their purpose was to substitute for Gallienus with his Hellenizing sympathies an Emperor who was a soldier and a native of the country from which the best troops in the imperial army were recruited. They informed Gallienus that Aureolus was making a sortie from the city. The Emperor rode out unarmed and unprotected to observe the alleged movements of his enemy, and the assassins seizing their opportunity fell upon their victim and murdered him.[33]

§ 3. THE REFORMS OF GALLIENUS

The reign of Gallienus marks an important stage in Roman military and administrative history, and paves the way for the reforms of Diocletian. This is most clearly to be discerned in his treatment of the senatorial and equestrian orders. In earlier chapters we saw that Septimius Severus with his anti-senatorial policy had entrusted the command of the new legions which he raised not to senatorial *legati*, but to equestrian *praefecti*, while both he and his successors had made frequent use of procurators as substitutes for the senatorial governors, a practice which is well illustrated by the career of Timesitheus. With Gallienus this development is carried a stage further. Aurelius Victor states that, to prevent the Empire passing into the control of the nobility,

he deprived the senators of the privilege of holding appointments in the legions, and would not allow them to have anything to do with the command of the army.[34] How this
enactment was put into effect is clear as far as the officers of
the legions are concerned, but is less certain with regard to
the governors of the provinces. From the time of Gallienus
onwards there is no record of any senatorial *legatus legionis*.
His place was taken by an equestrian officer with the title
of *praefectus legionis*. This new commander was distinguished
from the less important *praefectus (castrorum) legionis* by the
additional titles of *vir egregius*, or *agens vices legati*,[35] and in
all probability the previous qualification for such an office
was the same as for the command of the Egyptian legion,
namely, to have held the post of *primus pilus* centurion
twice.[36] With the *legatus* the other senatorial officers in the
legion, the *tribuni laticlavii*, also disappeared. The old
barrier, which had separated the higher from the lower
commands, was thus removed ; there was now nothing to
prevent the common soldier rising through the centurionate
to the command of his legion. The democratization of the
Roman army was complete.

Now if Gallienus' purpose was to deprive the Senate
entirely of military power and in this way to counteract
revolts by senatorial governors in the provinces, it is clear
that this end could not be attained simply by substituting
equestrian for senatorial commanders of the legions. For in
a province which was garrisoned by more than one legion
the governor was commander-in-chief of the troops, and the
commanders of the legions were subordinate to him. If then
a provincial governor was invested with the purple by his
soldiers, he would be able to make short work of any opposition
put up by his equestrian subordinates. Gallienus' reform
must surely in consequence have affected the position of the
senatorial governor, as it certainly did that of the senatorial
legionary commander. The simplest course would doubtless
have been to eliminate senators altogether from provincial
administration, but epigraphy shows that this was not the
effect of the reform ; for in the early part of Diocletian's
reign Syria Coele and Tarraconensis were still being governed
by senators.[37] It seems best to conclude that what Gallienus
did was to begin the separation of the military from the civil

functions of the provincial governor, which was gradually
extended throughout the Empire, when the independent
local Empires of his day were once again merged into an
united government.[38] The senatorial governors thus became
mere civil administrators, while the military command was
transferred to equestrian officers, at first perhaps called
praepositi and later *duces limitum*.[39] Nor were the senatorial
governors left undisturbed in the enjoyment of their depleted
authority. Gradually from the reign of Gallienus onwards
they were superseded by equestrian governors, who with the
title of *agentes vices praesidum* were at first represented as
acting on behalf of non-existent senatorial governors. The
institution of this " independent vicariate " facilitated the
final removal of senators by Diocletian from the administration of the provinces.[40]

Two further military reforms which were in all probability
instituted by Gallienus must be noticed. Beginning from
his reign the title *protector* or more fully *protector lateris
divini* begins to appear on inscriptions, and was conferred at
first upon *praefecti legionum* and tribunes of the urban
troops.[41] Before the end of the century, however, important
developments took place. The title was no longer conferred
upon senior officers, but was given to selected centurions and
decurions. Recipients of this honour entered, as it were,
the Staff College and, while some remained in Rome in
attendance upon the Emperor and the praetorian prefect,
others were appointed to commands in the army in the
provinces. The protectorate became the necessary avenue to
promotion, and there is little doubt that it was instituted to
counteract the lack of education among the centurions which
the barbarization of the army had produced.[42]

The Roman army of the fourth century A.D. may be
contrasted with that of the earlier Principate by the importance which cavalry had assumed in its organization. Not
only were its numbers enormously increased, but in honour
and reputation it took precedence over the legions of heavy-
armed infantry and the auxiliary infantry units. Towards
this change Gallienus made an important contribution. The
Byzantine writer Cedrenus calls him the founder of mobile
cavalry units,[43] and that he certainly raised contingents of
horsemen, distinct from the old auxiliary *alae*, in Dalmatia is

attested by Zosimus, who further gives Aureolus the title of commander-in-chief of the cavalry.[44] On an inscription from Grenoble, dated to the year after Gallienus' assassination, independent cavalry units called *equites* are recorded side by side with the familiar infantry detachments or *vexillationes*.[45] This process was further developed in all probability by Aurelian who separated the legionary cavalry, which Gallienus had perhaps increased in number, from the infantry and constituted them under the title of *promoti* as distinct tactical units. Administratively these new cavalry contingents still retained as late as the year A.D. 302 a relationship with the legions from which they were drawn similar to that of the old infantry *vexillationes* to their parent-body, and it was not till the reign of Constantine that they acquired complete independence.[46] Thus the changes in military organization, which were inaugurated by Gallienus and developed by his immediate successors, marked an important epoch in the history of the Roman army and laid a foundation upon which Diocletian and Constantine were later to base their reforms.

§ 4.   SUMMARY

Gallienus left the Roman Empire divided and disintegrated. In the West, Britain, Spain and Gaul were subject to Victorinus, in the East, Zenobia had successfully defeated Gallienus' attempt to recover the provinces which were under the control of Palmyra. The Raetian frontier had been broken through and the Alamanni were again threatening Italy, while the Goths, despite their defeat on the banks of the Nessus, were ready for a fresh invasion of the Danubian provinces. In Italy the situation was critical. Aureolus held Milan, the treasury was empty and the currency valueless.

In attempting to assess the responsibility of Gallienus for this crisis a distinction must be made between the first ten and the last five years of his reign, and the celebration of the *Decennalia* provides a convenient landmark. In the earlier period Gallienus acquitted himself with determination, vigour and diplomatic foresight. The Germans were defeated on the Rhine and in Italy, the Goths were checked, local insurrections were for the most part quickly suppressed, and the confusion ensuing upon the capture of Valerian was successfully handled by a timely, if fortunate, alliance with Odenath. In the last five years activity seems to give place to apathy, determination to acquiescence. Such attempts as were made to re-establish imperial unity ended in failure ; only against the Goths was any marked success achieved and this was offset by the revolt of Aureolus. Where did the responsibility lie for this growing weakness of the Imperial Government ? The reply of the Latin authors, whose account is coloured by their dislike of the Emperor's anti-senatorial policy, is to single out Gallienus as the culprit and to charge him with culpable negligence. But such a judgement would seem to minimize the factors against which Gallienus had to contend. The resources of the Empire were exhausted, plague had ravaged the population, the army at the disposal of the Emperor was altogether inadequate for the defence of Illyricum and Italy, if at the same time it had to provide an expeditionary force against Postumus or Zenobia, and as the defeat of Heraclianus indicated, nothing short of a campaign on a large scale could have any hopes of restoring the unity of the Empire. Gallienus, therefore, chose from necessity and not from apathy a policy of tacit acquiescence in the tripartite division of the Roman Empire and concentrated his energies on protecting those lands which were still loyal to himself ; and in this project he might have succeeded but for the treachery of his generals. The responsibility for the crisis of A.D. 268 cannot be fairly ascribed to the depravity and selfishness of the Emperor. His loss of vigorous resolution, his apparent helplessness and lack of initiative were the effects of a ruthless combination of forces, in face of which he continued to offer a passive resistance until engulfed in the general chaos which had seized hold of the Roman world.

PART IV

THE RESTORATION OF IMPERIAL UNITY

CHAPTER I

CLAUDIUS GOTHICUS

§ 1. INTRODUCTION

THE years which followed the death of Gallienus saw the reassertion of Roman military ascendancy. Under three soldier-Emperors, who were all natives of Illyricum, not only were the barbarians driven out of the northern provinces and the old frontiers in some measure at least re-established, but also the independent empires in Gaul and the East were brought to an end, and the authority of the central government was once more acknowledged throughout the Roman world. Further, and as a condition of these successes, a new spirit of loyalty was awakened in the army, with the result that local rebellions declined in number and in importance. For this transformation the chief credit must be given to Aurelian and Probus and in a lesser degree, because of the brevity of his reign, to their predecessor Claudius. Themselves keen and vigorous soldiers with few interests outside the careers which they had chosen they concentrated their energies upon the restoration of military discipline, and by their personal efficiency won the confidence of their troops in their leadership. Although their reigns were short and their fate assassination, the intrigues which brought about their fall were not the expression of the public opinion of the army, but were fomented by small cliques, either discontented with the disciplinary reforms which the Emperors had introduced, or alarmed for their personal safety and advancement.

The brilliant triumphs of the three Illyrian Emperors and the rapidity with which they re-established the unity of the Empire may once again suggest that the political disintegration which they inherited was a direct consequence of the unstatesmanlike administration of Gallienus. But this sudden

185

reversal of fortune cannot be simply attributed to changes in the personnel of government. There were other factors that assisted the restoration of Roman sovereignty, and two in particular are of outstanding importance. During practically the whole of Gallienus' reign the Gallo-Roman Empire was firmly consolidated; it was victorious in its foreign policy, it was unmolested by internal strife. When Aurelian came to the throne part of it had voluntarily returned to loyalty to Rome, and dissension was rife in such parts as still adhered to the local Emperor. Consequently, whereas Gallienus had been confronted by two rival and vigorous Empires, Aurelian was able to disregard Gaul and concentrate his energies upon the overthrow of Palmyra. Secondly, by the time of Aurelian the long succession of local rebellions had begun to bear fruit in the temper of the Empire. The provincials with the constant danger of invasions were alarmed for the safety of their homes and property, and were coming to realize that their salvation lay in the integrity of the Roman Empire. The soldiers, too, had found their temporary champions unavailing in the promotion of their personal interests, and in particular the Illyrian legions, which were the most efficient troops in the army, were eager for the restoration of unity. This change of spirit undoubtedly assisted the Illyrian Emperors in their determination to introduce a stronger discipline in the ranks. In short, the imperial situation in the reign of Aurelian had radically altered since the days of Gallienus. The latter had been obliged to combine diplomacy with military aggression, to sacrifice parts of the Empire in order to safeguard the rest, but within a few years of his death his policy had borne fruit. The stage was set for the reassertion of Roman military domination, and it was Rome's good fortune that at this crisis in her history she was ruled by Emperors whose lives and interests were devoted to the army.

§ 2. CLAUDIUS IN ITALY

The generals who formed the conspiracy against Gallienus had already decided upon his successor before the assassination took place.[1] The choice lay between M. Aurelius Claudius and L. Domitius Aurelianus, each of whom had risen from the ranks and had seen distinguished service in the armies of Gallienus. The decision in favour of Claudius was probably dictated by the uncertain temper of the soldiers who, it was anticipated, would take more kindly to an emperor of a courteous and mild disposition than to one whose reputation as a disciplinarian was already notorious. As it was, there was a rebellion when the report of Gallienus' death was announced, and the soldiers had to be placated by the promise of a donative of twenty *aurei* apiece.[2] After the suppression of the mutiny Claudius was adopted Emperor without further opposition (March, A.D. 268).

The new Emperor was confronted with a situation of great complexity and danger, and it is to his credit that he wisely decided to leave all question of the restitution of the Empire alone until he had freed Italy from the present invasion of the Alamanni, and the Balkans from the imminent menace of the Goths. The fate of Aureolus, whom Gallienus had driven into Milan, was quickly settled. On hearing of the accession of Claudius, the rebellious general had attempted first to secure terms for himself and, when his overtures were rejected, surrendered, probably on condition that his life was spared. But soon afterwards he was murdered, perhaps at the instigation of Aurelian, to appease the resentful temper of Gallienus' soldiers.[3] Meanwhile, news had reached Rome of Gallienus' death. The fate of their enemy was a welcome relief to the senators, and to signify their joy they prepared to persecute his relatives and partisans. From this programme, however, they were deterred by a dispatch from Claudius in the name of the army, enjoining a policy of clemency and asking for the deification of the dead Emperor.[4]

At the time of Aureolus' surrender the Alamanni, whose help he had perhaps invited, had already invaded Raetia and penetrated into Italy. Claudius sent forward some cavalry to oppose their advance, which through the rash action of its commanders seems to have met with a defeat.[5] The Emperor quickly remedied this set-back by deposing the unsuccessful generals and by appointing Aurelian commander-in-chief of the cavalry. He himself advanced with his legions and encountered the enemy not far from Lake Benacus, inflicting such a severe defeat upon them that only one-half of the invading army made good its retreat into Raetia.[6] Claudius

himself assumed the title *Germanicus Maximus*, and coins
were struck with the legend VICTORIA GERMANICA.[7] Having
freed Italy from invasion he set out for Rome, and there
received from the Senate the constitutional powers of Empire.

While these events were happening in Italy there were
signs of disintegration in the Gallo-Roman Empire. The
absence of any record of Postumus' successors in Spain, and
the existence of several inscriptions in honour of Claudius,
make it probable that the province broke off its allegiance to
the Gallo-Roman Empire soon after Postumus' death.[8] At
the same time there were dissensions in Gaul, which broke
out into open hostility at Augustodunum (Autun). To quell
the revolt, Victorinus, whose hand was perhaps forced by his
troops, marched against the city. A siege, which is said to
have lasted seven months, ensued and the inhabitants sent
for help from Claudius.[9] The latter, however, had no
intention of making a personal campaign in Gaul. Instead, he
contented himself with sending Julius Placidianus, commander
of the *Vigiles*, with a small force from Rome. The latter did
not cross the Rhone, fearing perhaps the inadequacy of his
force for the relief of Autun, but encamped at Grenoble in
order to protect Narbonese Gaul and Italy.[10] In A.D. 270
Autun fell, the soldiers plundered its possessions, and its
rich inhabitants, who included Arborius, the grandfather of the
poet Ausonius, were banished.[11] Soon afterwards Victorinus
was killed at Cologne,[12] and his mother, whose influence was
predominant, secured the election of Tetricus, the governor
of Aquitania, as his successor.[13] Thus the Gallo-Roman
Empire still comprised Britain and all Gaul, except for that
district of Narbonensis which is bounded by the Rhone and
the Alps, but with the defection of Spain and the outbreak
of internal disturbances it was no longer so pressing a problem
for the central government. Claudius had rightly decided
that the barbarians on the Danubian frontier must claim his
undivided attention.

§ 3. THE EAST

After their defeat by Gallienus, the Goths made preparation
for a renewed attack upon the Balkans on a greater scale than
on any previous occasion. Assisted by their neighbours the
Heruli and Peucini, they built a fleet of 2000 ships, and with

a host of 320,000 they set out from Maeotis in the summer of
A.D. 268.[14] Sailing along the Black Sea they first attacked
Tomi and Marcianopolis in Lower Moesia. On failing to
capture either place they moved into Propontis, where
many of their ships were lost through storms and the rapidity
of the current, and after a vain attempt on Byzantium and
Cyzicus, sailed through the Hellespont into the Aegean,
stopping at Athos to repair their ships. Passing Chalcidice
they then laid siege to Cassandria and Thessalonica.[15]
Claudius now set out from Rome[16] to meet the invaders, who,
on hearing of his approach raised the siege of the two towns
and decided upon a new plan of campaign. They divided
their forces into two separate bands. The larger of the two
abandoned the fleet and set out overland towards Naissus on
the road to Viminacium with the intention of reaching the
Danube and ultimately their own country. The other
contingent was to sail round the islands of the Aegean and
ravage the cities on the coast. To meet this situation
Claudius devised the following strategical plan. He ordered
Aurelian to post his cavalry on the borders of Dardania and
Macedonia to prevent the barbarians, if they abandoned the
valley of the Axius, from plundering Illyricum. He himself
occupied the valley of the Margus and blocked the road
leading to the Danube. In this way he hoped that the Goths,
shut off from the sea and the Danube, would be surrounded
by the Roman infantry and cavalry. The strategy was an
entire success. In a preliminary battle near Doberus, 3000
Goths were killed by an attack of Aurelian's Dalmatian
horsemen, and at Naissus where Claudius had encamped the
main issue was decided. At first the barbarians, who far
outnumbered their opponents, were victorious, but a Roman
contingent got round the enemy's rear and inflicted such great
losses that the Goths, leaving, it is said, 50,000 dead on the
field, retreated by the route by which they had advanced.[17]
Harassed in their retirement by the Roman cavalry and
suffering from famine, they were driven into the rugged and
uncultivated region of Haemus. Here, although surrounded,
they won a small success against some scattered Roman
troops, but the arrival of the Roman cavalry decided the
issue. Many Goths were captured or surrendered, and of
these, some were drafted into the Roman *auxilia*, while

others were settled by Claudius as *coloni* in Thrace, Macedonia and Moesia.[18] Of the remainder, some fell victims to plague, others in attempting to reach the Danube were overwhelmed.[19] Meanwhile, the other contingent of Goths had met with little success in their ravaging tour of the Aegean. The walls of the cities defied their assaults, and after a series of battles with the Roman fleet under Probus, the governor of Egypt, who had been assigned this special command, they retreated home.[20] Claudius assumed the title of *Gothicus Maximus*, and coins were struck in commemoration of his victory.[21]

Taking advantage of the Gothic War, Zenobia, in the name of her son Waballath, attempted to extend the Palmyrene Empire. Claudius had refused to grant Waballath the titles which Gallienus had conferred on his father Odenath, but his preoccupation with the Alamannic and Gothic wars prevented him from interfering with the actual control of the Eastern provinces by the Queen of Palmyra. Egypt and Asia Minor had remained loyal to Rome, and Zenobia now planned their annexation to her dominions. In order to mask her designs, she refrained from an open declaration of war and from the assumption of the imperial title for herself or her son, nor were any coins struck in the name of the Palmyrene Queen and her son. But during the winter of A.D. 268–9, before the outbreak of the Gothic War, she occupied Antioch and the issue of coins from that mint in Claudius' name ceased. All was now ready for the invasion of Egypt.[22] The command of the army, which numbered 70,000 and was composed of Palmyrenes, Syrians and barbarian contingents, was entrusted to Zabdas, and Egypt itself provided some allies led by a certain Timagenes. The task of the invaders was facilitated by the absence of the governor of Egypt who, as we have seen, had been appointed admiral of the Roman fleet which was operating against the Goths in the Aegean, and by the numerical superiority of their forces. After a hard battle victory rested with the Palmyrenes, and Lower Egypt came under the control of Zenobia, who decided to leave a garrison of 5000 in the country and to recall her army into Syria. Probus now returned to his province, ejected the garrison and, when the Palmyrenes made a second invasion, compelled them to retire once again. He further attempted to intercept their retreat into Syria by the occupation of a hill in the vicinity of Babylon, which lay to the south of Heliopolis. But his scheme ended in disaster. Timagenes, with a native's knowledge of the country, seized the top of the hill and fell upon the Roman army, which was not anticipating an attack. The Romans had many casualties, and Probus, to avoid capture, committed suicide. The Palmyrenes then re-occupied Egypt, but Alexandria, from which coins were issued in the names of Claudius and his brother Quintillus, remained till Aurelian's reign at least nominally subject to Rome.[23]

Zenobia now summoned her army to Antioch and prepared to carry out the second part of her programme, the occupation of Asia Minor. By the beginning of A.D. 270, Cappadocia and Galatia, including the city of Ancyra, had been added to the Palmyrene possessions, and Zenobia was intent on winning Bithynia and extending her Empire as far as Chalcedon.[24] This ambition was, however, never realized. Claudius had ordered the governor of the province, Velleius Macrinus, to strengthen the defences of Nicaea by surrounding it with a wall.[25] The city held out successfully, and in other parts of the province the invaders were repelled, so that Aurelian was able later to start his great offensive against Palmyra from Bithynia.

§ 4. THE LAST DAYS OF CLAUDIUS

Claudius was still engaged in rounding up the Goths in Haemus when news came that the Juthungi, who had been in alliance with Rome and received an annual subsidy, had crossed the Danube in search of fresh settlements and were threatening Raetia, and that the Vandals were about to invade Pannonia.[26] Accordingly he entrusted Aurelian with the supreme command against the Goths and returned to Sirmium.[27] But plague contracted from the barbarians broke out in his army and Claudius himself succumbed to the disease in January, A.D. 270, after a reign of twenty-one months.[28] His death was sincerely mourned both by the soldiers and the Senate. Towards the latter body he had shown courteous respect, and without diminishing his own imperial status had enlisted its co-operation in his work of liberating the Empire. In gratitude the Senate decreed him divine honours and erected a golden statue on the Capitol and a golden shield engraved with his portrait in the Senate-house to commemorate his reign.[29]

Claudius' civil administration calls for little comment. His short reign was largely devoted to military activities, and he himself was by nature a soldier and not a statesman. The reforms which Gallienus had introduced he left in force, and the senatorial order recovered none of its earlier privileges. Economically he had neither the time nor the resources to ameliorate the precarious position of the Empire. The billon coinage issued by Gallienus reached its greatest degradation, the coins being small, irregular in shape and hardly distinguishable from copper. The mints used by Claudius remained the same as in the last years of Gallienus, in Italy, Rome and Milan, for the Danubian district Siscia, and in the East Cyzicus in compensation for Antioch, which was controlled by Zenobia.[30] In the military sphere milestones attest a considerable activity in road-construction,[31] and, as an anticipation of later Roman policy, we hear of the drafting of captive Goths into the legions and the settlement of others as tenants on Roman soil, measures which were perhaps prompted by the depopulation caused by the plague.

The natural successor to Claudius was Aurelian, who had been appointed commander-in-chief of the Balkan army, but for a short time his succession was delayed. Claudius on leaving Italy had left his brother, M. Aurelius Claudius Quintillus, in command of the troops that were concentrated at Aquileia.[32] When the news of the Emperor's death reached the camp the soldiers invested Quintillus with the purple. Their choice met with a ready acceptance by the Senate, which anticipated that Aurelian would prove a second Gallienus. Therefore it decreed the customary imperial powers, and Quintillus was recognized in the provinces as the rightful heir of Claudius, coins being struck in his name at the mints at Rome, Milan, Siscia and Cyzicus.[33] But the new Emperor was but a pale reflection of his brother. If he showed the same courteous and clement disposition, he had none of his experience and ability as a commander of men, nor did he make any effort to come to Rome. Meanwhile Aurelian quickly finished off the Gothic War by defeating the barbarians when they attempted to storm the cities of Anchi alus and Nicopolis and cut their way home across the Danube.[34] He then moved to Sirmium, where he was proclaimed Emperor by Claudius' troops. For a few days there were two Emperors, but, when Quintillus attempted to oppose Aurelian's claims, his soldiers deserted him and in desperation he committed suicide. Aurelian was left as sole ruler of the Roman Empire.[35]

CHAPTER II

AURELIAN

§ 1. ITALY AND THE GERMAN INVASIONS

AURELIAN set out immediately from Sirmium against the Juthungi, who had already crossed the Alps by the Brenner Pass. On hearing of the Emperor's approach the invaders retreated from Italy in the hope of reaching home in safety with their rich booty. But Aurelian intercepted their movement in Raetia, defeated them in battle and pursued them across the Danube. The barbarians now sued for terms and sent an embassy requesting peace and a renewal of the former alliance. To create an atmosphere of terror the Emperor drew up his army in battle array and received the envoys seated on a raised platform and clothed in a purple cloak. Their proposals were summarily rejected and the embassy departed without having gained any concessions except permission for their army to return to its own country. This decision was probably a deliberate makeshift. Aurelian's presence in Rome was urgently required, not only for the ratification of his own position but also for deliberation on other questions of imperial importance.[1]

On his arrival in the capital the Senate decreed without opposition the customary powers, and during a short stay the Emperor made two decisions affecting the foreign and home policy of the government. Although anxious to restore the unity of the Empire he realized that the time was not yet ripe for a campaign against Palmyra. His army was weary with protracted warfare and was not yet sufficiently disciplined, while the Danubian provinces were again in danger of a barbarian invasion. He therefore decided for the present to recognize Waballath and conferred upon him the titles which Gallienus had granted to his father Odenath.

Coins were struck at Antioch with the portrait of Waballath on one side and of Aurelian on the other, and in the legends the Palmyrene prince was entitled *vir consularis, rex, imperator, dux Romanorum.*[2] This convention had at least this advantage that it maintained in appearance the sovereignty of Rome in the East but at the same time it gave Waballath much greater actual power than Odenath had wielded. For Egypt and most of Asia Minor were tacitly recognized as under his control. Future events, however, justified Aurelian's diplomatic gesture. Against Tetricus the Emperor took no further steps. Placidianus was kept at Grenoble,[3] and the Gallo-Roman Empire was left to effect its own disruption. The second decision of Aurelian was of economic import. In order to put an end to the thefts and fraudulent emissions that were being perpetrated by the mint officials, he closed the mint at Rome.[4] This measure was intended as a preliminary step towards the reorganization of the financial administration which he later hoped to introduce, but the reform was, as we shall see, productive of grave disturbances in the City.

While Aurelian was engaged with this administrative work news came that the Vandals assisted by the Iazyges had invaded Pannonia, probably between Brigetio and Aquincum. Aurelian ordered the governors of the two provinces to concentrate all available supplies in the towns in the hope of compelling a retirement of the invaders through lack of commissariat. This precautionary measure attained its purpose, and when Aurelian himself reached Pannonia he inflicted a severe defeat upon the Vandals, who sued for peace. The Emperor put the issue to his troops, realizing his own dependence upon the full support of the army, and when the soldiers voted for peace terms were arranged. The barbarians were guaranteed an unmolested retirement to their own country with the provision of commissariat as long as they were on Roman soil, on condition that their two kings surrendered their sons as hostages and furnished a contingent of 2000 horsemen for service in the Roman auxiliary forces. These terms were accepted, but during their retreat some 500 Vandals violated the treaty by a plundering raid away from the main body. Aurelian sent the Vandal cavalry which he had just received in pursuit, and the raiders were rounded up and killed to a man. The invaders then retreated peaceably to their own country.[5]

The peace which Aurelian made was timely and prudent. The Vandals had not yet recrossed the Danube when yet another invasion of Italy was reported. The Juthungi, disappointed at the outcome of their earlier expedition, united with the Alamanni and Marcomanni and poured through the Brenner Pass into Italy.[6] Aurelian hastened back from Pannonia with the intention of cutting the lines of communication of the enemy who had already reached Placentia. The plan was so far successfully carried out that Aurelian, with his army concentrated between the barbarians and the Alps, felt himself strong enough to propose their capitulation. The Germans replied that they would join battle the next day, but during the evening a party of them that had been lying in ambush fell upon Aurelian and inflicted a complete defeat. The situation was dangerous in the extreme and rumours went about that the Empire was lost.[7] To make matters worse serious disorders broke out in Rome. The labourers at the mint thrown into unemployment through Aurelian's action broke into open rebellion under the leadership of Felicissimus the *procurator summarum rerum*.[8] Probably their revolt had the sympathy of some members of the senatorial order, who accepted the defeat at Placentia as a proof of Aurelian's weakening authority and were ready to make use of any means that might add to his discomfiture and lead to his final overthrow.[9] In this crisis the Emperor attempted to stem a panic by ordering the Senate to consult the Sibylline books and to carry out a solemn purification of the City.[10] But Rome's salvation lay in the mistakes of her enemy. Elated by success the barbarians scattered in plundering bands about the country, and Aurelian was able to deal with them separately. In two battles fought at Fanum Fortunae and in the neighbourhood of Pavia the Germans were completely defeated and few of them succeeded in crossing the Alps.[11] Aurelian, however, abstained from pursuit, feeling that the situation in Rome demanded immediate rectification. Reaching the city he took vigorous measures against the conspirators. Some senators were put to death, others had their property confiscated. The mint-workers, who had entrenched themselves on the Caelian

Hill near their old headquarters, were attacked and overwhelmed. Their casualties numbered 7000 and their leader,
Felicissimus, was killed.[12]

Having thus restored peace in Rome and liberated Italy
from the invaders, Aurelian determined that for the future
the capital must not be left exposed to the possibility of
further barbarian attacks. The defence of Italy had previously
depended upon the ability of the legions to maintain the
northern frontier, but since the storming of the Germano-
Raetian *limes*, there was little to stop the German tribes
pouring through the passes of the Alps, and with the exception
of Aquileia and Verona there was not a town in Italy that
was adequately equipped to offer any effective resistance to
their advance.

In consultation with the Senate,[13] Aurelian decided to
enclose the City with a wall sufficiently strong to repel any
future massed raids from the north by barbarians who were
not provided with siege-apparatus. In A.D. 271 work was
begun.[14] The wall, whose circuit was twelve miles, was
designed to enclose as far as was consistent with defensive
strategy the fourteen city wards, and for a considerable part
of its length it followed the line of the old customs barrier.
It was built according to the standard of Roman defensive
walls and had a thickness of twelve and a height of twenty
feet. In one or two sectors, however, a different type of wall
with a loop-holed gallery supporting a rampart walk was
erected for no other apparent reason than that it was the
choice of a particular society of builders. At intervals along
the wall, towers of an uniform rectangular shape were constructed for the purpose of accommodating heavy artillery to
keep assailants at a distance from the wall; for the wall itself
was not designed to sustain a siege, nor were its defenders
intended to fight from its top. That the prospect of a siege
was not anticipated by Aurelian is further confirmed by the
number of gateways and posterns that broke the course of
the wall. There were eighteen gates, which were built with
protecting towers of an uniform style, with the exception
that the four principal gates which spanned the Via Flaminia,
the Via Appia and the two main roads to the sea were double-
arched. The simplicity and uniformity of the wall and its
gates may be explained by two considerations. First they

had to be constructed rapidly in case the Germans repeated
their recent activities, and secondly, in view of the projected
campaign against Palmyra, no soldiers could be spared for
building, which had in consequence to be carried out by the
civil population, which, unaccustomed to the erection of
military fortifications, could only be expected to execute
the simplest of designs. The work was entrusted to the
corporations of builders, which were in all probability at
this time transformed from voluntary into state organizations,[15] while other sections of the commons and slaves
provided the unskilled labour. Building continued throughout
the life of Aurelian, and it was not till the reign of Probus
that the wall with its towers and gates was completed.[16]

During Aurelian's stay in Rome a number of military
rebellions occurred in the provinces. Septimius was proclaimed Emperor in Dalmatia, and two other pretenders,
Urbanus and Domitian, of whom nothing is known except
their names, were put up in other parts of the Empire.[17]
Their revolts were, however, temporary and unimportant.
For the rest of his reign Aurelian was undisturbed by any
rival competitors for Empire.

§ 2. PALMYRA. FIRST CAMPAIGN

The German invasion of Italy and the attendant misfortunes
of Rome seemed to Zenobia a favourable opportunity for
breaking the convention which she had signed with Aurelian
the previous year. In the summer of A.D. 271 Waballath
assumed the title Augustus; the Emperor's portrait disappeared from the coinage at Antioch, and the Palmyrene
Queen and her son struck coins in their own names and
bearing their own effigies.[18] Aurelian accepted the challenge
and prepared for war. The Palmyrene Empire consisted of
two parts, the Roman provinces which had been governed
in Rome's name by Odenath, and the conquests of Zenobia
which included Egypt and Asia Minor as far north as
Bithynia. The task of recovering Asia Minor where the
Greek element prevailed was, despite the fact that Zenobia
had secured the services of the orator Longinus as her Prime
Minister,[19] not likely to present serious difficulties, while in
Egypt there was a considerable pro-Roman party. In Syria

on the other hand, where the Oriental element prevailed, a vigorous resistance might be expected, and Zenobia had attempted, to her cost as the sequel will show, to secure the sympathy of the Christians by her friendship with Paul of Samosata, the Bishop of Antioch.[20] Aurelian decided upon a double plan of campaign. The future Emperor Probus was entrusted with the conquest of Egypt; Aurelian himself took command of the other army, whose first objective was the reconquest of Asia Minor and North Syria.

Probus took the field first and by the autumn of A.D. 271 succeeded in recovering Egypt.[21] Probably he met with little opposition, as Zenobia had decided to concentrate her army in Syria. Towards the end of the year Aurelian left Rome and mobilized on the Danube his army, which consisted of detachments from the legions of Raetia, Noricum, Pannonia and Moesia, with their auxiliaries and the mobile cavalry contingents of Mauri and Dalmatians.[22] His progress was temporarily interrupted by an incursion of 5000 Goths under their leader Cannabas into Moesia, but the invaders were soon driven back across the river and Aurelian, assuming the title *Gothicus Maximus*, proceeded by way of Byzantium into Asia Minor.[23] Galatia had remained loyal to Rome and the Emperor entered Ancyra without opposition. The first resistance was offered at Tyana, which commanded the passes of the Taurus, but through the treachery of one of its citizens called Heraclammon, Aurelian was able to occupy a height overlooking the town, which then capitulated. In a fit of exasperation at the unexpected opposition he had promised his soldiers that he would sack the town and give them the booty, but on its surrender a more prudent judgement prevailed. Tyana was left unplundered, and this clement treatment of the first Greek town to oppose his advance created a most favourable impression of his policy.[24] After crossing the Taurus, Aurelian received the voluntary submission of the Greek cities in Cilicia,[25] and he was able to advance upon Antioch where Zenobia had determined to make her stand.

The main body of the Palmyrene army under Zabdas was stationed at Antioch, and an advance guard of heavy cavalry and some infantry was posted on the Orontes, which flows on the north side of the city. Aurelian gave instructions to

his Moorish and Dalmatian horsemen to retire when their
heavier-armed opponents attacked them and wait until they
were worn out by the heat and the weight of their armour
before taking the offensive. These tactics succeeded. The
Palmyrene cavalry was utterly defeated, and Aurelian, by
sending his infantry across the river on the left flank of the
enemy, effectively cut off their communications with Antioch.
This preliminary skirmish settled the fate of the city, and
Zenobia and Zabdas decided upon a retreat.[26] This decision
was influenced by the attitude of the population of Antioch.
The Christians were at open war with their heretic bishop,
Paul, and desired the overthrow of his protectress ; the Jews
were hardly less hostile ; while the Greek element with the
example of Tyana before them was not likely to exert itself
for the maintenance of the Palmyrene Empire. Fearing
that the retreat of his army might be hindered by local
opposition, Zabdas put it about that the Romans had been
defeated and dressed up a man in the guise of Aurelian who,
it was alleged, had been captured. The ruse so far succeeded
that the Palmyrenes were able to abandon the city during the
night and next day Aurelian entered Antioch. He hastened
to reassure the population by the declaration of a general
amnesty, and many citizens who had fled with Zabdas availed
themselves of this general pardon to return to the city.[27]
The Emperor was further called upon by the Christians to
arbitrate in their quarrel with Paul, who had refused to
obey the synod, which had ordered his deposition or to vacate
the episcopal residence for his substitute Domnus. Aurelian
decided that the bishop's house belonged legally to the representative of the Christian community at Antioch, and when
each bishop asserted his claim to be so regarded, defined the
true representative as the person recognized by the bishop of
Rome. Strictly speaking, Aurelian was only arbitrating upon
a civil dispute about the ownership of a house, but his judgement is further interesting in showing his determination to
make Rome the centre of the religious as well as the political
life of the Empire. Paul was subsequently expelled and the
Christians of the East were drawn in closer sympathy to
Rome.[28]

The Palmyrenes withdrew to Apamea, where Zabdas
decided to retire on Emesa in preference to falling back

straight on Palmyra across the desert, probably because he expected help to arrive from Persia. Aurelian, after settling the internal affairs of Antioch, set out in pursuit. He quickly disposed of a rearguard left at Daphne, one of the suburbs of the city, and passing through Apamea, Larissa and Arethusa, which opened their gates to him, found the enemy waiting for him at Emesa with an army estimated at 70,000. Aurelian employed the same tactics as at Antioch, but this time his light cavalry was almost overwhelmed till the Emperor launched his legions against the light-armed infantry of his opponents. The movement was immediately successful. The Palmyrene infantry were put to flight, and the legions, wheeling round, attacked the cavalry from the rear and inflicted enormous casualties in their ranks. The Roman victory was decisive. Zenobia and Zabdas had no option but to fall back upon Palmyra, prepare for a siege and await reinforcements from Persia.[29]

The Romans had now to face the hardest part of the campaign. Palmyra was eighty miles distant from Emesa and the route lay across a desert in which there were few oases.[30] The nomad tribes were devoted to Zenobia, and the Roman army, although in all probability reinforced by Probus' Egyptian campaigning force, had suffered severely in the battle at Emesa. During the crossing of the desert further casualties were inflicted by attacks from the natives, and when Aurelian reached Palmyra he found the city prepared for defence.[31] The situation was perilous. Not only were siege operations necessary, but a constant watch had to be kept on the movements of the Persians and the desert tribes, and a line of communication maintained with Emesa, the nearest base for supplies. For some days the siege dragged on. Aurelian was himself wounded and his troops were beginning to suffer from the climate and privation. With the approach of summer the Emperor attempted negotiations, but his overtures were peremptorily rejected.[32] His resolution, however, did not waver and soon success rewarded his patience. He succeeded in buying over the nomad tribes from their alliance with Zenobia. This relieved him of all anxiety for his commissariat and lines of communication, and correspondingly weakened the resources of Zenobia. Finally, with the defeat of a Persian contingent, the fate of Palmyra

was sealed.[33] Famine broke out in the city and its capitulation
was only a matter of time. Zenobia determined on flight and
succeeded in making good her escape, but was captured as she
was crossing the Euphrates by some Roman cavalry that had
been sent in pursuit. Aurelian received her with kindness,
being well satisfied that the capture of the queen meant the
end of Palmyrene independence. For a few days the city
continued to hold out until, reassured by promises of clemency,
it capitulated. Aurelian found immense booty within its
walls, but refrained from any retaliatory measures against its
inhabitants, being content to carry off with him Waballath
and the leaders of the party of independence.[34]

Soon after the capture of Palmyra, Aurelian, as his title
Parthicus Maximus suggests, was engaged in some fighting
with the Persians, but the hostilities were of short duration.[35]
No attempt was made to recover the parts of Mesopotamia
and Armenia that were under Persian domination. Aurelian
was confirmed in this decision by the war-weariness of his
troops, by news of an invasion of Carpi in Lower Moesia and
by his determination to restore Gaul and Britain to the
Empire. Before leaving for Europe he appointed Marcellinus
with the title of prefect of Mesopotamia commander-in-chief
of the East with orders to prevent any Persian assistance
reaching Palmyra and encouraging its inhabitants to rebellion.[36] At Emesa he held a court at which Zenobia and the
Palmyrene leaders were committed to trial. The queen, with
cowardly injustice, cast the blame for her actions on her
advisers and in particular singled out Longinus as the arch-
culprit. Aurelian put to death all the counsellors whom she
named, but despite the urgent demands of his troops for her
execution, reserved Zenobia and the Palmyrene chiefs for his
triumph. In crossing the Propontis, however, the ship
conveying the prisoners was shipwrecked, and only Zenobia
and her son survived to feast the eyes of the people of Rome.[37]

§ 3. SECOND EXPEDITION AGAINST PALMYRA AND THE END
OF THE GALLO-ROMAN EMPIRE

Aurelian reached Lower Moesia probably in the autumn of
A.D. 272, and, defeating the Carpi on the Danube, restored the
frontier to a state of defence. Numbers of the defeated

invaders were transplanted to people the depopulated provinces of Lower Moesia and Thrace.[38] Aurelian, who received the title *Carpicus Maximus*,[39] was about to proceed on his journey westwards when alarming news came from the East, which suggested that all the work of the recent campaign would have to be repeated. Rebellions had broken out in Palmyra and in Egypt.

In Palmyra a conspiracy was formed by a certain Apsaeus in which many prominent Palmyrenes were involved, who, if not previously members of the independent party, saw in the absence of the Emperor a chance to restore the fortunes of their city. The movement was national in character, but in order to mask their intention the conspirators approached Marcellinus in the hope of detaching him from his allegiance to Aurelian by a proposal to proclaim him Emperor. Marcellinus asked for time for reflection and meanwhile acquainted Aurelian with the designs of the Palmyrenes. After a time Apsaeus despaired of Marcellinus and proclaimed a certain Antiochus king of Palmyra. The nationalist movement was now undisguised, and as a proof of its intentions, Sandarian, the military governor left by Aurelian, was put to death, together with his garrison of 600 archers.[40]

The rebellion in Egypt was headed by a Greek merchant called Firmus who was living at Alexandria, and who probably belonged to the party which had assisted Zenobia in her conquest of the country. Whether he was privy to the plot in Palmyra or whether his rebellion was dictated by dislike of Roman rule in Egypt and alarm for the loss of commerce, which the defeat of Palmyra entailed, cannot be certainly decided. It is, however, significant that Firmus did not proclaim himself Emperor, but was content to act as though prefect of the province. This may indicate that he was awaiting developments in Palmyra, and that, if Marcellinus attempted usurpation, he would be prepared to acknowledge him.[41]

The plans of the conspirators were completely upset by the amazing rapidity with which Aurelian acted on receipt of the dispatch from Marcellinus. By a series of forced marches he reached Antioch and proceeded straight for Palmyra, which had not had time to reconstruct its fortifications. The city was taken without a battle and sacked as a reward for its treachery. Antiochus' life was saved by his insignificance.[42] From Palmyra Aurelian hastened on to Alexandria. The revolt had not spread all over Egypt, and the failure of the conspiracy at Palmyra probably deterred the undecided from rallying to the cause of the rebellion. Firmus with his confederates was shut up in Bruchium, and rather than fall into the hands of Aurelian he committed suicide. Aurelian meted out severe punishment to Alexandria. The walls were razed and most of Bruchium was separated from the city.[43]

With the East finally subdued, Aurelian returned to Europe, and finding no fresh trouble on the Danubian frontier, prepared for the completion of his scheme of imperial unity by an attack upon the Gallo-Roman Empire. The condition of the province of Gaul had steadily deteriorated since Aurelian's accession. The country was a prey to German invaders who attacked both by land and sea.[44] Tetricus himself had with difficulty maintained his position. For Faustinus, the governor of one of the provinces, had succeeded for a time in detaching some of the army, which disliked Tetricus' pacific tendencies, from loyalty to their local Emperor,[45] while the population of Gaul was dissatisfied with an Emperor who could not ward off foreign invaders nor suppress internal rebellions, and was ready to come back inside the Roman Empire. In such circumstances Aurelian's task was not likely to be difficult nor prolonged ; by the action of Tetricus a single battle sufficed to decide the issue. The two armies encountered each other near Châlons, and a bloody battle ensued in which the Gallic legions fought with much bravery. But in the midst of the fighting Tetricus deserted his troops and surrendered to Aurelian. His army, thrown into confusion by the treachery of its commander, was completely defeated. The Gallo-Roman Empire was ended ; the unity of the Roman Empire was restored.[46]

After some provision for the future administration of Gaul and Britain and leaving Probus in command of the troops on the Rhine,[47] Aurelian, early in A.D. 274, set out for Rome to celebrate his victories. The work which he had achieved might justifiably cause him satisfaction and pride. No Emperor since Septimius Severus had won such a sequence of successes ; not for half a century had the Roman world been free from foreign invasions and unmolested by internal rebellions. Justly was Aurelian proclaimed RESTITUTOR ORBIS.[48] The triumph which he celebrated surpassed all others in magnificence, and is described with many literary embellishments by the Emperor's biographer.[49] Pre-eminent amid the host of captive prisoners from all the conquered nations that marched in procession were Zenobia and Tetricus. The sight of a Roman senator in captivity cannot fail to have aroused the resentment of his peers, but after the triumph Aurelian restored to him his rank and his property and nominated him to the post of *corrector Lucaniae*. Towards Zenobia and her son the Emperor displayed a generosity that was almost cavalier. He presented the Queen with a villa near Tibur, where she lived in the style of a member of the Roman nobility.[50]

§ 4. AURELIAN'S ADMINISTRATION

(A) ROME AND ITALY

Aurelian spent the greater part of the year A.D. 274 in Rome, and during this period introduced a number of reforms which were designed to re-create the internal stability of the Empire. The chief problem was the restoration of the coinage, which had become so degraded that it had lost even its face value. In place of silver Gallienus had put into circulation a mass of worthless billon, and with the collapse of the silver the gold coinage had also become irregular and unstable. In consequence prices soared to an enormous height, trade was undermined and speculation flourished. Individual fortunes were lost, and in town and country alike the honest citizen was faced with untold hardships without any prospects of better days to come. There can be no doubt that Aurelian realized the urgency of the problem, and his assumption of personal responsibility for the imperial currency is indicative of the honesty of his intentions. In arriving at a solution of the question he was, however, handicapped by the lack of silver available for minting, and this is the most probable explanation of the makeshift character of his reforms. Instead of establishing a regular gold and silver coinage, which was the one genuine remedy for the national bankruptcy, Aurelian still retained a billon currency and attempted to give his new *Antoniniani* a value which, if far below that of Caracallus', was certainly superior to that of Gallienus' coins. The new coins were heavier and of finer quality and workmanship, and while containing only about 4 per cent of silver, were given a silver coating, which, if it did not increase their intrinsic value, gave them the appearance of true silver coins. Further, an attempt was made to fix a standard of value for the new billon in terms of gold. Aurelian issued two billon coins, which were based no longer on the *denarius*, which by its association with Gallienus' *Antoniniani* had lost its proper value, but on the *sestertius*. The larger of these two new coins was the equivalent of two *sestertii*, the smaller of one *sestertius*. The *sestertius* represented in value 1/5000th part of the gold pound and was further subdivided into ten *libellae*. Thus the scale of Aurelian's coinage was as follows. A pound of gold was the equivalent of 2500 double *sestertii* (=the larger *Antoniniani*, each of which contained 20 smaller units or *libellae*) and of 5000 single *sestertii* (=the smaller *Antoniniani* or " normal " coin, each of which contained 10 *libellae*). The gold coins which Aurelian struck were rather heavier than those of Gallienus, but were irregular in weight ; copper coins he issued in small numbers, but in his own name and without the co-operation of the Senate. The merit of Aurelian's reform lies in its recognition of the sharp decline in the value of money and in his utilization of a smaller unit, the *sestertius*, in place of the *denarius*. Although a currency based on a billon coinage could not be expected to restore commercial confidence nor retard the upward tendency of prices to any appreciable extent, yet Aurelian's system did at least provide a standard of relative values and that, given the impossibility of establishing a true silver coinage, was perhaps the best that the Roman world could expect.[51]

The overthrow of Palmyra and the recovery of the Eastern provinces brought a great increase of wealth and revenue to the imperial treasury, which had for years been unable to balance its budget. Aurelian made use of this influx of money in order to restore financial confidence in Rome and to alleviate the distress in the capital which had resulted from the sharp rise in the price of food. He cancelled all arrears to the treasury and caused the public records in which these debts were registered to be burned in the Forum of Trajan, and vigorously suppressed the *delatores* and *quadruplatores*.[52]

More significant were his measures for providing the populace with food and other necessities. In Rome the price of bread was controlled by the State, which sold corn to the association of bakers and fixed the price at which they should put it on the market. Aurelian increased the *vectigal* of corn coming from Egypt in such a way that the bakers should be able to sell for the same price a loaf weighing an ounce more than heretofore.[53] He also established in place of the old monthly distributions of corn, which had become irregular, a daily distribution of two pounds of bread free of charge to all registered citizens, and made the right to receive it hereditary.[54] This principle he also extended to pork, oil and salt, which were now issued free of charge and at regular intervals.[55] The story of Vopiscus that he intended also to distribute wine free of charge is almost certainly a fiction,[56] but it is not improbable that the price of it was lowered in connection with a scheme for the reclaiming of waste land in Italy.[57] This development of the alimentary system necessarily involved a great increase in the duties of the *praefectus annonae*. It is further probable, but not certain, that the guilds of bakers and butchers were at this time increased in size and transformed from voluntary into compulsory associations and made subject to military discipline.[58] The reforms of Aurelian thus represent a further stage in the supremacy of the State over the lives of its individual members. In connection with the food supply the Emperor caused the bed of the Tiber to be cleared and its banks reconstructed.[59] New barracks were built in the Campus Agrippae, which, from their vicinity to the *forum suariorum*, may have been intended to house the *collegia suariorum*, if, as seems probable, the latter were militarized and placed under the control of the urban prefect.[60] Lastly, his care for the health of the people may be illustrated by the winter-baths which were erected in Trastevere, where there was a deficiency of cold water,[61] and an inscription from Grumentum in Lucania speaks of a reconstruction of a bath according to the regulations laid down by the Emperor.[62]

In the sphere of politics the administration of Aurelian presents few novelties. Towards the Senate he showed a respectful courtesy and asked for its co-operation on important matters such as the building of the walls and the reform of the coinage, but his attitude was essentially that of the master, and the senators, embittered by the punishment meted out to some of their colleagues in consequence of the outbreak in A.D. 271 and by the inclusion of Tetricus in the procession of prisoners, feared rather than loved their ruler. The administrative reforms of Gallienus were left in force and were applied to an increasing number of provincial commands.[63] Prominent members of the equestrian order, such as Marcellinus, the prefect of Mesopotamia, and Placidianus, the praetorian prefect, were rewarded for their services by senatorial rank.[64] Two new posts for senators, on the other hand, deserve attention. Tetricus was appointed on the model of the *iuridici* of Marcus Aurelius *corrector* of Lucania, and although this is an isolated instance in the reign of Aurelian, the institution prepared the way for Diocletian's division of Italy into seven provinces.[65] Secondly, Aurelian appointed senators to fill the office of high priests of the Sun, whose worship he officially established in Rome by the building of a temple and the institution of games in his honour, and gave them the name of *pontifices dei Solis*, from whom the old *pontifices* were distinguished by the assumption of the title *pontifices maiores*.[66]

In its religious aspect the reintroduction of the worship of the Sun gave expression to the monotheistic tendencies, which, as we have seen in an earlier chapter, were active among the pagans of the third century A.D. It was another attempt to find and recognize the Universal Deity whose particular manifestations were revealed in the great variety of local and individual cults. But the new state religion was designed also to serve a political purpose. Like Decius before him Aurelian seems to have become convinced that, if the unity of the Empire which he had restored by conquest and strengthened by administrative reforms was to be permanent, its citizens must join in some common recognition of its majesty. The imperial cult, which in earlier centuries had served this purpose, had through the stormy period of anarchy lost much of its prestige and value. It was essential to find a religion which would both satisfy the emotional needs of the Empire and at the same time provide a means for the expression of imperial loyalty, and the widely diffused cult of the Sun offered the best chance of success. Whether Aurelian further intended to use this official worship for the consolidation of his own autocracy is more than doubtful. The theory that he wished to establish a divine right of Emperors rests largely upon a passage of Petrus Patricius, who records that during a revolt of his troops Aurelian stated that it was God and not the soldiers who had invested him with the purple.[67] But against this evidence of a sixth-century writer must be set the testimony of coins and inscriptions. The latter do not suggest any marked theocratic tendencies. With the exception of two coins emanating from the mint at Serdica, on which he is styled DEUS ET DOMINUS (NATUS) AURELIANUS,[68] the titles given to him on the legends are similar to those accorded to his predecessors. In a few inscriptions he is called *deus*,[69] but no *official* dedications assign godhead to him during his lifetime. It is true that he felt a personal devotion to Sol and regarded him as his protector, and that on a stone from Pisaurum Hercules is called " *consors domini nostri*,"[70] but such practices were common as far back as the days of the Antonines. It is further to be observed that, unlike Elagabalus, Aurelian made no attempt to identify himself with the god whom he worshipped. Autocrat he undoubtedly was and intended to remain, but his absolutism he was content to rest upon his personality and achievements without imposing the fiction that he was the Chosen of God.

(B) THE FRONTIERS

The measures which Aurelian took for the defence of the provinces from which he had driven the invaders are very imperfectly known. The shortness of his reign and the suddenness of his death make it probable that many of the problems were left unsolved, and this is confirmed by events which succeeded his murder. Particularly is this true of Germany. Although Probus, who was left in command when Aurelian went to celebrate his triumph, reoccupied the southern part of the German *limes*, his conquest had no lasting results, and the Alamanni in A.D. 275 once again established themselves in the *agri decumates*.[71] On the upper Danube there was a renewed invasion late in A.D. 274 which Aurelian repelled, and here it is probable that some effective measures

14

were taken to restore the Raetian *limes*. Further down the Danube an important change was made. Dacia had been overrun time and again by the Goths, its defences were in ruins and the legions had been moved by Gallienus out of Transsylvania into Little Wallachia.[72] Aurelian was faced with the alternative of attempting the reconquest of Dacia or of withdrawing to the right bank of the river. He chose the latter course and his decision was wise. The expense of an aggressive campaign would have been great and the chances of holding the province at all permanently remote. Further the provinces of Pannonia, Moesia and Thrace, which had been ravaged by invasion and plague, were now sparsely populated. A withdrawal from Dacia gave the means for establishing the evacuated population along the right bank of the river. Aurelian, therefore, created a new province of Dacia out of parts of the two Moesias, Thrace and Dardania. The two old Dacian legions were established at Ratiaria and Oescus, and Serdica was made the capital of the new province.[73]

The reorganization of the Eastern provinces was probably taken in hand after the second Palmyrene campaign. Two new legions (I *Illyricorum* and IV *Martia*) were raised by Aurelian, and the former was sent to Phoenice and the latter to Arabia, so that the army of occupation in each of those provinces was raised to two legions.[74] The new units were recruited, as the name of one of them shows, from Illyricum, and Aurelian's intention in sending them to the East was doubtless to strengthen his hold on the recovered provinces by garrisoning them with soldiers whose sympathies and interests were European. To establish the frontier of the Euphrates, however, the reconquest of Mesopotamia was essential, and this project was included in the Emperor's programme for A.D. 275, while Probus was appointed prefect of Egypt in order to restore the frontier, which, during the revolt of Firmus, had been forced by the Blemmyes.[75]

§ 5. DEATH OF AURELIAN

Aurelian left Rome late in A.D. 274, but before he could concentrate his army for his Eastern campaign he was obliged to spend some time in Gaul where disturbances had broken out at Lugdunum from some unknown cause.[76] After restoring peace in the province and repelling a barbarian invasion of Raetia he mobilized his troops, which were, as usual, drawn from the Danubian legions, and when his preparations were complete, set out in the summer of A.D. 275 for Asia. He had, however, got no further than Caenophrurium, which is situated between Perinthus and Byzantium, when he fell a victim to a military plot. Aurelian had a confidential secretary called Eros, in whose good faith he had complete trust, till one day he detected him in a lie and threatened to punish him. The secretary, imagining his career ruined, decided to save himself. Trading upon Aurelian's notoriety as a disciplinarian, he drew up a list in what purported to be the Emperor's handwriting of the names of the chief officers of the Guard, to which he astutely added his own. He then distributed the document to the people concerned, with the added information that they had been condemned to capital punishment. The officers, some of whom may have had reason to anticipate the Emperor's displeasure, did not stop to question the authenticity of the document, and in alarm for their own safety, murdered Aurelian. A piece of senseless intrigue robbed Rome of one of the greatest of her Emperors.[77]

CHAPTER III

TACITUS AND PROBUS

§ 1. THE REIGN OF TACITUS

THE murder of Aurelian created an unprecedented situation. The soldiers of the Illyrian army declined to put up any candidate as his successor and referred the choice of a new Emperor to the Senate.[1] Two main reasons may be given for their action. Aurelian, despite the rigorous discipline which he had enforced, was popular with the soldiers, and their refusal to name any successor was an indication of their desire to dissociate themselves from the conspirators. Secondly, Probus, the most distinguished of Aurelian's generals, was in Egypt. He was known to be devotedly loyal to the late Emperor, and the soldiers felt reluctant to take any precipitate step until his wishes were known, while at the same time they were unwilling, by abstaining from all action, to give the Eastern army the opportunity of proclaiming a new Emperor. In the circumstances they therefore decided to refer the issue to the Senate, which, however impotent as a body, was still the constitutional source of every Emperor's powers. The Senate on its side was equally reluctant to accept the invitation of the Illyrian army and negotiations proceeded. For about a month an *interregnum* ensued,[2] during which time no changes were made in the imperial administration, and the Senate, to maintain the goodwill of the army, decreed Aurelian's apotheosis.[3] At length, on news of unrest on the northern frontier, the Senate gave way and chose its leader, M. Claudius Tacitus, who was already seventy-five years of age, and had been nominated by Aurelian as consul in A.D. 273, to fill the vacancy.[4]

The reign of Tacitus has been described as a revival of senatorial authority and as a reaction against the domination of the army, which since the days of Septimius Severus had made and unmade the Emperors of Rome. Such a theory, which looks for its support to the highly-coloured phraseology of the Augustan biographers, can only be accepted in a very limited degree. Nominally it is true the Senate did select one of its own number to be the new Emperor, but the long negotiations which preceded its decision indicate its realization of its own inability to take the initiative without the support of the army. Further, many members of the Senate were now promoted officers, and when the soldiers referred the choice of Aurelian's successor to the Senate they were inviting the intervention not of a body that they regarded as antagonistic to their interests, but of a body in whose counsels the military element might be expected to prevail. But even if full weight is given to the part played by the Senate in the nomination of Tacitus, the government, during his six months' reign, gives no support to a theory of a senatorial revival. The Senate did not recover its ancient privileges and prerogatives. The copper coinage, for which Aurelian had assumed responsibility, continues to be struck without the co-operation of the Senate. The familiar S.C. is absent from the legends on the coins. Secondly, and even more important, the administrative reforms of Gallienus, which had aimed a fatal blow at senatorial control of the provinces, were not repealed. On this the testimony of Victor is decisive. After referring to the growth of military domination that followed on the death of Probus, he adds, " had the edict of Gallienus become a dead letter, the military service could have been reformed when the legions were making concessions in a spirit of moderation during Tacitus' reign. In that case Florianus would never have rashly seized imperial power ; the choice of an Emperor would not have rested with the rank and file, had there been senators permanently stationed in the camp."[5] The implication is clear ; the edict of Gallienus was, in fact, never abrogated. In such circumstances it seems impossible to talk of any real senatorial revival.[6] The reigns of Tacitus and his half-brother Florianus merely continued the interregnum that followed the death of Aurelian and lasted till the proclamation of Probus. The aged senator and his brother would never have ascended the throne of the Caesars but for a conspiracy which was repugnant to Aurelian's own soldiers, and for the jealousy of one army of another, which delayed for some six months the choice of the natural successor to Aurelian.

Considering his age, Tacitus displayed a commendable energy during his short reign. Asia Minor was overrun by the Goths who, according to one account, had been commissioned for service by Aurelian for his Eastern campaign, and when the murder of the Emperor put a stop to the expedition, found an outlet for their impatience by an invasion of Roman territory as far south as Cilicia. Tacitus appointed his half-brother, Florianus, prefect of the Guard, and with his help succeeded in driving back the barbarians to their home.[7] Perhaps with the intention of safeguarding his position he appointed another relation called Maximinus governor of Syria. This proved a disastrous step. Maximinus, by the harshness of his administration, aroused such bitter resentment that a conspiracy was formed to assassinate him. When the plot succeeded, the assassins followed Tacitus, who was making his way back to Europe, and murdered him (spring of A.D. 276[8]). The aged senator deserved a kindlier fate. Called to assume imperial responsibilty when he might have counted upon some years of quiet retirement, he had done his work honestly and creditably. An unusual obverse inscription on one of his latest coins, which seems to identify the Emperor with the goddess Virtus, testifies to the appreciation by his subjects of the bravery with which he had accepted the labours and dangers of war for the welfare of the Empire.[9]

The death of Tacitus led to a renewal of civil war. His half-brother Florianus, according to the most trustworthy account, assumed the purple as a hereditary right, without waiting for the proclamation of his soldiers or the ratification of the Senate.[10] This unconstitutional act does not, however, appear to have occasioned surprise or resentment, and Florianus was recognized as Emperor throughout the western provinces.[11] Some fifteen to twenty days, however, after his accession, the army of the East proclaimed Probus Emperor.[12] Florianus, on receipt of the intelligence, decided to march against his rival, trusting, no doubt, in the numerical superiority of his forces. The armies encountered each other near Tarsus, but Probus avoided a pitched battle. These Fabian tactics soon succeeded. Disease broke out among the European soldiers. Dispirited and averse from a prolongation of civil war, they chose the easiest solution and murdered Florianus (summer of A.D. 276[13]).

§ 2.   THE REIGN OF PROBUS

M. Aurelius Probus was like the other two soldier-Emperors of the third century, a native of Illyricum, having been born at Sirmium in August, A.D. 232.[14] His reign of six years and four months was largely devoted to the consolidation of Aurelian's successes and to the reconstruction of the frontiers of the Roman Empire. The surrender of Tetricus had restored Gaul to the central government, but the insecurity of the frontier had been illustrated by the campaigns which Probus had been obliged to wage against the German invaders during his tenure of the command of the province in A.D. 274. The murder of Aurelian was the signal for fresh incursions from across the Rhine, and the unfortified cities of Gaul fell a prey to the barbarian invaders.[15]

After a short visit to Rome for the ratification of his imperial powers by the Senate,[16] Probus led his army into Gaul. The invaders consisted of two separate bands. In the south the Longiones, supported by the Alamanni, had entered Gaul by way of the Neckar Valley, while further north the Franks had crossed the Rhine. Probus divided his troops into two corps. While his generals campaigned against the Franks, he himself attacked the Longiones. Victory attended both armies, and Probus, after capturing Semnon, the chief of the Longiones, with his son, and recovering the prisoners and booty which were in their hands, made a treaty with the invaders, who were permitted to return into their own country, while Semnon and his son were set at liberty. Meanwhile the Burgundians had come to the assistance of the Franks and a further campaign was necessary. Numerically Probus' forces were far inferior to those of the enemy, but by skilful tactics he was able to defeat them in detail. Terms similar to those granted to the Longiones were conceded, but when the barbarians violated the agreement and did not surrender all their prisoners of war, Probus again attacked and captured their commander, Igillus.[17] Having thus freed Gaul from its invaders, the Emperor proceeded to take measures to safeguard it from further dangers. Roman forts were again established on the right bank of the Rhine so as to command the river-crossings and thus provide protection for the Roman towns situated on the Gallic side.[18] German prisoners were enlisted in the Roman army and distributed in small numbers among the garrisons of different provinces so as to obviate the possibility of a mutiny.[19] The success of this scheme is illustrated by the loyalty of the German troops sent to Britain, which lent no support to the governor of the province when he attempted to rebel against the Emperor.[20] Further, Probus sought to restore the economic life of the western provinces by encouraging the plantation of new vineyards, a policy which he later developed elsewhere in the Empire.[21] In commemoration of his victories the Emperor received the title *Germanicus*,[22] and coins struck with the legends TEMPORUM FELICITAS and SECURITAS PERPETUA suggest the new hopes of peaceful prosperity that the liberation of Gaul had aroused (A.D. 277).[23]

The year A.D. 278 was spent by Probus in repelling an invasion of Vandals from Illyricum, and, as the legend RESTITUTOR ILLYRICI on coins attests, in the reorganization of the government of that district.[24] In the next year he set out for the East.

His first objective was the restoration of peace in the provinces of Lycia and Pamphylia, which were being plundered by bands of robbers under the command of a certain Lydius. On the approach of the Roman army the leader of the bandits took refuge in the mountain fortress of Cremne. The story of the defence of this stronghold is graphically described by Zosimus, and its capitulation was only secured through the perfidy of one of the robbers. The traitor, who was a skilled gunner, had fallen foul of Lydius, and in anger at the punishment meted out to him, secretly made his escape to the Roman camp. Here he put his expert skill and knowledge at the disposal of the besiegers. Lydius was in the habit of reconnoitring each day his enemy's movements through a small postern-gate. This secret the traitor revealed to Probus, and obtaining a small escort to cover his position shot down his old leader when next day he was in process of making his reconnaissance. The death of Lydius was followed by the immediate surrender of the town, whose defenders were in the last stages of exhaustion from privation.[25] For the

prevention of further unrest in the country, Probus established colonies of veterans, to whom he granted land in
private ownership on condition that their sons at the age of
eighteen joined the army.[26] Perhaps it is from this source
that the legions entitled I–III *Isaurae* were recruited.[27]

Meanwhile the Blemmyes had again broken through the
Egyptian frontier and captured the towns of Ptolemais and
Coptos, but Probus' generals were able to eject them from the
province without the Emperor's personal intervention.[28]
Probus had probably intended when he left Europe to provoke
a war with Persia for the purpose of recovering Mesopotamia,
but during his stay in the East no hostilities occurred and
probably some sort of a truce was agreed upon.[29] This
suited both sides ; for Persia since the death of the great
Sapor in A.D. 272 had gone through a series of dynastic changes,
and the new king, Bahram II, had not yet consolidated his
position, while Probus' presence was once again demanded
by unrest in Europe. In Gaul a revolt had broken out, and
on the frontiers the barbarians were restive.

Probus, therefore, returned from the East in A.D. 280.
A Scythian tribe, the Bastarnae, had been driven from their
homes by the Goths and had wandered into Roman territory
in search of fresh lands. Probus satisfied their needs by
establishing them in Thrace, and they continued subject
to Roman sovereignty.[30] This system of defending the
frontiers by transplanting large numbers of barbarians
inside the Roman Empire, although in most cases it secured
a temporary peace, spelled danger for the future. Combined
with the policy of drafting captive prisoners into the
Roman army it meant in effect the barbarization of the
frontier provinces and of the troops entrusted with their
defence, which had more sentimental bonds of union with the
tribes which it was their duty to ward off than with the
Romans whom they had stipulated to serve. Towards this
solution of her difficulties Rome was in large measure driven
by the depopulation of her provinces and the persistent
pressure of invaders driven by land-hunger to find new
homes. But the policy of employing barbarians to fight
barbarians was one of the most cogent factors in the decline
of the Roman Empire.

The people of Lugdunum had been severely punished by

Aurelian for their share in the disturbances that took place
in A.D. 275, and towards Probus their attitude was one of
fear and antipathy. Profiting by the latter's absence in the
East they induced, with what hopes of success it is impossible
to imagine, a certain Proculus, a native of Albingaunum, who
had acquired considerable wealth and reputation as a bandit,
to assume the purple. Probably he had excited their enthusiasm by holding out a prospect of help from the Franks.
But the arrival of Probus quickly put an end to his schemes,
and his supposed allies, so far from lending assistance, contributed, according to Vopiscus, to his downfall.[31] More
serious was the rebellion of Bonosus, one of Probus' generals,
who, fearing the consequences to himself of the loss of a
Roman squadron on the Rhine, which through his remissness
was burned by the Germans, had himself proclaimed Emperor.[32] This rising took longer to suppress, and possibly the
revolt may have had repercussions in Spain and Britain.
The evidence is slight, an inscription from Valentia on which
the name of Probus is erased, and the revolt of the governor
of Britain, which cannot be exactly dated and which was
put down by Victorinus, consul in A.D. 282, who had been
responsible for the appointment and was sent by the Emperor
to clear up the trouble which he had indirectly caused.[33]
However that may be, peace was once again restored in the
Western provinces by A.D. 281, and Probus was able to
celebrate a triumph in Rome, which, if it lacked the presence
of a Zenobia or a Tetricus, was not far inferior to that of
Aurelian in its splendour and extravagance.[34]

Probus introduced no changes in the administration of the
provinces. The story of Vopiscus that he allowed the Senate
to appoint proconsuls for the senatorial and to provide
governors of consular rank for the more important imperial
provinces is an invention of the biographer.[35] The Emperor's
interest lay rather in the resuscitation of the economic life
of the provinces and in the maintenance of military discipline.
Vineyards were planted on the hillsides in the Pannonias and
Moesias, and a scheme for reclaiming the marshy land around
Sirmium was assigned as peace-work to the soldiers.[36] Like
the best Emperors of the earlier Principate, Probus realized
that discipline could only be kept up by giving the troops
work when they were not occupied with war and in counter-

acting the idleness of barrack life. This salutary policy was, however, the indirect cause of his death.

Probus did not stay long in Rome, but in the summer of A.D. 282 set out for Illyricum with the intention of mobilizing an expeditionary force for a campaign against Persia, in order that the recovery of Mesopotamia might complete his plans of frontier reorganization. But while he was at Sirmium news came that the army in Raetia had proclaimed the praetorian prefect, M. Aurelius Carus, Emperor. The report fanned the discontent of the soldiers at Sirmium, who were already embittered by the hard work to which they had been subjected, into open mutiny and Probus fell a victim to their hate.[37] His rule was a fitting complement to that of Aurelian, and gave the Roman world a greater security from foreign attack than it had experienced for many years. Like Aurelian he recognized that Rome's misfortunes had their origin in the insubordination of her troops, but in endeavouring to maintain a disciplined obedience both Emperors met their death.

When news of Probus' death reached the army in Raetia, Carus sent a dispatch to the Senate announcing his elevation by his troops, and nominated first his elder son, M. Aurelius Carinus, and soon afterwards his younger son, M. Aurelius Numerianus, joint rulers with himself, and gave them the rank of Caesar.[38] Although his reign lasted less than a year it was not devoid of military successes. Leaving his elder son as governor of the West, Carus accompanied by Numerianus proceeded to the East in pursuance of the plans made by Probus for the recovery of Mesopotamia.[39] On his way he defeated the Sarmatae and Quadi, who had crossed the Danube and plundered Pannonia,[40] and on reaching the Euphrates had little difficulty in overcoming the resistance of the Persian King, Bahram II. Seleucia fell into his hands and Roman sovereignty was recognized in Mesopotamia. Crossing the Tigris, Carus captured Ctesiphon, a success which he signalized by the acceptance of the title *Parthicus Maximus*, and was proceeding further with his invasion of Persian territory when he died, killed as one report says by a stroke of lightning, but more probably the victim of a conspiracy among his troops.[41]

Numerianus, who, with his brother Carinus, had been promoted to the rank of Augustus before their father had crossed the Persian frontier, decided to lead the army back to Europe. Military renown held no attractions for him ; his ambition was a life of literary dilettantism. The story goes that on the return journey he was afflicted with ophthalmia and sought the shade of a closed litter to protect his eyes from the Eastern sun. This enforced privacy gave his father-in-law Arrius Aper, the praetorian prefect, the opportunity to make away with the weakling. For some days he succeeded in keeping his crime a secret until near Nicomedia the army guessed the truth.[42] But Aper did not profit by his guile. The officers were enraged at the murder of their Emperor, and in their dislike and mistrust of Carinus refused to wait until he should take constitutional action for the punishment of his brother's murderer. Instead they held a council of war and nominated as Emperor one of their own number, called Diocles, who was in command of the *protectores domestici* (November 17th, A.D. 284).[43] The elevation of Diocles thus followed the precedent of the previous half-century in which Emperors were made and unmade in quick succession by the soldiers ; but his rule transformed the structure of the Roman Empire.

PART V

ORIENTAL DESPOTISM

CHAPTER I

DIOCLETIAN AND HIS COLLEAGUES

§ 1. DIOCLETIAN AND CARINUS

C. AURELIUS VALERIUS DIOCLETIANUS, by which name the new Emperor was in future known, was, like so many of his predecessors, an Illyrian of low birth, who had risen from the ranks, and had at the time of his elevation already held the consulship.[1] But, although he owed his promotion to his military abilities, he was, unlike the average Illyrian Emperor, no mere soldier. Indeed, he seems to have had some misgivings about his own merits as a general, and frequently chose to leave the harder strategical tasks to his colleagues. His own interests lay rather in government and organization. No branch of the internal administration was left untouched by him, and, if his reforms sometimes were hasty and ill-judged, there can be no question of the disinterested honesty with which he devoted himself to the rehabilitation of the Empire. Diocletian was no self-seeking adventurer determined from motives of personal glory to retain supreme power in his own hands. His abdication after twenty years is sufficient to refute such a calumny. If under his direction the Roman government became an undisguised absolutism, that was but the culmination of a process which had been gradually developing during the third century. Its recognition was a necessary condition for the re-establishment of the peace of the Roman world, and the new ruler showed himself a statesman in his disregard of pampering sentiment and tradition.

Diocletian's first act upon assuming imperial power was to clear himself of complicity in the death of Numerianus. He called upon the Sun to witness his innocence and gave practical proof of his integrity by putting Aper to death.[2] But although the East was unanimous in its support of

Diocletian, it was idle to expect that Carinus, who probably held a different theory about the cause of his brother's death, would quietly accept the military coup at Nicomedia. The elder son of Carus is depicted by his biographer as the incarnation of vice, but whatever his moral failings may have been, he seems to have possessed some ability as a general. At any rate his conduct of the campaigns against his formidable opponents was efficient.[3] Carinus mobilized a strong army drawn from the German legions and auxiliaries, and leaving the Rhenish frontier insufficiently protected, as subsequent events were to show, moved into Illyricum, where an usurper called M. Aurelius Julianus, who held the post of *corrector Venetorum*, had risen in revolt.[4] This rebellion was quickly crushed, and with a reinforced army Carinus moved eastward along the Danube to meet his opponent. The rival armies confronted each other in the valley of the Margus. The battle was fierce and hotly contested, and it would seem as if victory might have rested with the army of the West, had not Carinus been assassinated by a tribune, whose wife he had seduced.[5] This ended the opposition of the troops and Diocletian became Emperor of the whole Roman Empire. Towards the officials who had held posts under his predecessor he adopted a conciliatory attitude, confirming them in their appointments, and Aristobulus, who had been nominated to the consulship of 285 by Carinus, held it conjointly with the new Emperor himself.[6]

§ 2. MAXIMIAN

Diocletian realized from the outset of his reign that the chief obstacle to the maintenance of imperial unity lay in the possibility of military revolts. If these were to be avoided, then he himself, it would seem, must assume command in all important campaigns. Generals must not be given the opportunity of winning victories which might induce their enthusiastic soldiers to invest them with the purple. The Emperor himself must move from province to province wherever his presence was most required. If he was to have an official residence, then it must be chosen with an eye to its proximity to the more important frontiers of the Empire. Rome was too far removed from the centre o activity to answer these requirements, and Diocletian only visited it once during his reign to celebrate his Jubilee. The place of the *palatium* with its resident court officials was now taken by the *comitatus*[7] or travelling staff, which accompanied the Emperor in his imperial peregrinations. But Diocletian was above all a practical statesman. The ideal of an omnipresent Emperor must, he saw, be translated into the world of action, and his first solution of the problem was the choice of a colleague to whom he could depute some of the duties of the Empire while retaining in his own hands the control of the government.

Diocletian had no son to fill this post and through whom he might further hope to establish a dynastic succession. His choice, therefore, fell upon one of his officer-friends, called Maximianus, who like himself was by birth an Illyrian and had risen from the ranks, and curiously enough, although younger, celebrated his birthday on the same day of the year. But there the resemblance between Diocletian and Maximian ceased. While the former was statesmanlike, shrewd and in some measure refined, the latter was a true product of his country, fierce, uncultured, and brutal, but yet endowed with marked strategical ability. Maximian, in fact, was the antithesis of Diocletian, and as such was a useful complement in the business of Empire. To him could be safely entrusted the command on frontiers where expert leadership was a necessity, while friendship for his elder colleague and a deep-rooted reverence and almost fear of his superior intellectual gifts might prove a safeguard against any attempted usurpation. In the summer of 285 Maximian was appointed Caesar and adopted the names of M. Aurelius Valerius Maximianus.[8] Probably at the same time and in order to emphasize the nature of the new relationship, Diocletian assumed the title of *Jovius* and gave to his colleague that of *Herculius*.[9] Just as Jupiter, the father of gods and men, is the supreme controller of the heavens and Hercules the pacifier of the earth,[10] so must *Jovius* and *Herculius* act in harmony under the protection of their patron gods, who symbolized the two essentials of Empire—command and action. Perhaps, too, Diocletian hoped that this fictitious adoption for himself and his colleague of a divine ancestry might veil the obscurity of their own origin.

15

The appointment of Maximian as Caesar was in large measure dictated by the unsettled condition of Gaul. The death of Probus and the withdrawal by Carinus of a large army from Gaul to meet the challenge of Diocletian had exposed the frontier once again to the attacks of German invaders. The seas were infested by pirates and, most serious of all, the internal peace of the country was disturbed by the revolt of the Bagaudae. These " fugitives " were probably so called because they had fled from their original occupations. Some, the majority no doubt, were peasants from the land, others artisans from the towns, while deserters from the army and barbarians who had wandered from their homes swelled their numbers. The purpose of their revolt is no less obscure than their identity. Historian and panegyrist give them but a scanty mention and seem almost ashamed to dwell upon their suppression. Under the leadership of two chiefs called Aelianus and Amandus they appear to have carried on for a number of months a successful guerilla warfare, with which the army of Maximian was unaccustomed to deal. Finally, in the spring of A.D. 286 the revolt was crushed,[11] the roads that led to the frontier were once again in Roman control, and Maximian was proclaimed Augustus on April 1st by his troops.[12] His elevation was confirmed probably with some reluctance by Diocletian. But in fact the latter lost little by the change in his colleague's status. Although edicts and rescripts were issued in their joint names, Diocletian as senior Augustus retained the initiation of legislation in his own hands.[13] No division of Empire was made between the two rulers, and although Diocletian normally resided at Nicomedia and Maximian at Milan, each of them during the next years is found campaigning in provinces far distant from their headquarters. The principle was retained that an Emperor went where he was required.

During the next two years Maximian restored order on the German frontier. His first task was to avert the danger to Gaul and Italy from a massed attack of Alamanni and Burgundi, who had swarmed across the Rhine between Mainz and the source of the river. But the devastated country could not supply the wants of these plundering raiders. Famine and plague decimated their numbers, and while some were captured by Maximian's advance-guard to grace his later triumphal entry into Trier, the remainder fled in confusion across the Rhine where the alliance was shattered by civil war.[14] The danger to Mainz was averted, but two years later the Alamanni again became restive. Diocletian had to come to the assistance of his colleague in a campaign which started in Raetia,[15] while in A.D. 291 or 292 Maximian led a second punitive expedition from Upper Germany across the Rhine.[16]

Lower down the Rhine the situation was more serious. The Franks had found allies in the Eruli and Chaibones, brave and daring warriors who came from the distant parts of Germany. Maximian met them in battle in the neighbourhood of Cologne and by the suddenness of his attack surrounded and destroyed them, fighting himself as a common soldier, sword in hand.[17] He was now free to engage with the Franks. After some fighting on the left bank of the river, he crossed the Rhine, and a great victory won by his praetorian prefect, Constantius, enabled him to advance towards the German Ocean.[18] Further hostilities were, however, avoided by a treaty made with one of the Frank chiefs, called Gennobaudes. In return for the recognition of his title as King of the Franks, he himself and his troops took the oath of loyalty to Rome. A Frankish king was thus established as a bulwark between Rome and Germany (A.D. 288).[19]

On sea Maximian was less fortunate. To protect the coasts of Gaul from the piracy of the Franks and Saxons, he established a naval base at Gesoriacum (Boulogne) and appointed Carausius commander-in-chief of the fleet.[20] The latter was a native of Menapia, the district which lies between the Rhine and the Scheldt, and like his countrymen, who had established trading colonies around the coasts of Britain and Ireland, he was an experienced and daring sailor. In a few weeks he cleared the Channel of pirates, but his success seems to have undermined his loyalty and aroused his ambitions. Instead of surrendering all the booty which he obtained to the provincial officials, he retained the richest prizes, and in this way greatly increased the size and efficiency of his fleet, which he manned with captured pirates. Maximian, suspecting a rival, sent orders for his execution, but Carausius, who had a gift for friendship, was warned in time and in self-defence proclaimed himself Augustus and transferred his fleet to Britain (A.D. 287).[21] Maximian accepted the challenge and fitted out a naval expedition against him, but through bad weather and inexperienced pilots it met with disaster.[22] Carausius was thus able to re-establish his position at Boulogne, and with the Channel and Britain in his power and the Franks of the Low Country as his allies, constituted a Franko-Roman Empire which was unique in character. Although it weakened the unity of the Roman Empire, yet it rendered an important service in the suppression of piracy. Maximian, with the approval of Diocletian, was forced to acknowledge for the present the power of Carausius, but his status as a third Augustus, which he proudly commemorated on his coins, was never officially recognized (A.D. 290).[23]

Meanwhile, Diocletian was beginning his reorganization of the other parts of the Empire. Although Nicomedia was his official residence, much of his time was spent on the Danubian frontier, as is indicated by the number of rescripts issued from Sirmium[24] and by two successful wars against the Sarmatae in A.D. 289 and 292. He also made at least two journeys to the East. The first in A.D. 290 was occasioned by a Saracen invasion of Syria,[25] the second in A.D. 291 by a rebellion in Upper Egypt, in which the Blemmyes were implicated. Coptos and Busiris rose in revolt and had to be stormed by Diocletian, whose campaigning army was composed of detachments from the Danubian legions.[26] Although quiet was restored and the Emperor was able to return to Europe, it was but a lull before the outbreak of a more serious rebellion. Besides his military activities, Diocletian profited by the internal troubles of Persia to place an Arsacid, Tiridates III, on the throne of Armenia. In this way the latter country passed once again into the sphere of Roman influence, and Bahram was not only compelled to acknowledge this change, but also agreed to give up all claim to Roman Mesopotamia (A.D. 288).[27]

Eight years of experience in the government of the Empire convinced Diocletian that his constitutional arrangements were inadequate for the prevention of revolts and for the maintenance of supreme authority by the imperial family. The tacit recognition of the usurper Carausius was an admission of failure, and Diocletian realized that he and

Maximian could not respond unassisted to all the demands that were made upon them. Accordingly he decided to appoint two Caesars to help the Augusti. Maximian's son, Maxentius, was considered too young for the work. On March 1st, A.D. 293, therefore, C. Galerius Valerius was nominated Caesar by Diocletian at Nicomedia and assumed the name Maximianus, and on the same day at Milan, C. Flavius Valerius Constantius, the praetorian prefect, was similarly elevated by Maximian.[28]

§ 3. THE TETRARCHY

A true estimate of the characters of the new Caesars who, like all Emperors of the period, were successful soldiers, is rendered difficult by the prejudices of the Christian writers. Galerius, a man of humble birth, is depicted as a monster of vice, because to him is attributed the origin and severity of the Christian persecution. Constantius, a Dardanian noble-man, by contrast is a ruler of wise judgement and philan-thropic disposition as became the father of the first Christian Emperor. But the truth has not been lost if it has been in part distorted. Constantius' achievements in Gaul and the popularity which he won among the provincials are a testimony to his statesmanship and, had he outlived his promotion to the rank of Augustus by more than a year, he might well have proved a worthy successor to Diocletian, whom in many respects he resembled. Galerius, on the other hand, as his later history shows, was essentially a man of action, direct, vigorous, cruel and unimaginative. The similarity of his outlook to that of Maximian may explain their mutual antipathy. Both Constantius and Galerius were good generals and that was the first essential at the time of their nomination. Each of the new Caesars was adopted by his Augustus, and in order to cement the family ties, Galerius was compelled to divorce his wife and marry Diocletian's daughter, Valeria. Constantius was already married to Theodora, Maximian's step-daughter, and had a five-year-old son, the future Emperor Constantine, by a concubine, Helena. Constantius was made the senior of the two Caesars and received, as the nominee of Maximian, the title of *Herculius*, while that of *Jovius* was conferred upon

Galerius.[29] Thus the Augusti and their Caesars formed a *collegium* or board of rulers, in which, when an Augustus abdicated, a Caesar automatically stepped into his place, while the choice of a new Caesar rested with the retiring Augustus. This system had the advantage that each Augustus must necessarily have first had experience of government as a Caesar. Later, when Diocletian decided to abdicate with Maximian, the constitutional principle was laid down that each ruler should retire twenty years after his nomination as Caesar.

The two new Caesars were not limited in their authority as Maximian had been in A.D. 285. They were given the tribunician power, were permitted to strike coins, and received the same honorific titles and imperial acclamations as the Augusti.[30] For in future a victory won by any member of the tetrarchy was commemorated in the nomenclature of them all. A division of the Empire was also made among the rulers. Maximian received Italy and the northern frontier provinces together with Africa and Spain ; Constantius, Gaul and Britain, which was at the time subject to Carausius. To Galerius were assigned the Balkans as far west as the river Inn, while Diocletian assumed responsibility for the East including Egypt.[31] This division was, however, not legally defined, but was based on expediency. When circumstances demanded, an Augustus might enter either of the two Caesars' territories.

The policy of increasing the number of imperial rulers was abundantly justified by the history of the succeeding five years. The Augusti and their Caesars were engaged almost continuously in either restoring the unity of the Empire or in defending it from external and internal forces of disintegration.

The first and most important work, the subjugation of Carausius, fell to Constantius, and from his headquarters at Trier he lost no time in making his plan of attack. As a preliminary to an expedition to Britain he began by driving Carausius' outlying fleet away from the shores of Gaul. Flotillas had been equipped on the rivers of the country, and from the different estuaries they attacked and drove the enemy's ships into the English Channel and in all probability succeeded in capturing a considerable number. Carausius'

main fleet, however, refused battle and lay in hiding at the
Isle of Wight in anticipation of Constantius' attempting a
disembarkation in Britain. But the latter realized that the
time was not yet ripe for this dangerous project. Instead, he
determined to consolidate his own position in Gaul.
Accordingly he marched upon Boulogne, which fell after a
memorable siege during which Constantius built a dam
across the harbour mouth to prevent any relief reaching the
port from Britain.[32] Having thus secured Carausius' main
stronghold on the Continent, Constantius proceeded to attack
his allies among the Franks. By the vigour of his assault
he drove them into their swamps and forests and
dispossessed them of the Island of the Batavians and the
neighbouring islands which they had occupied.[33] Carausius'
Empire was reduced to Britain and a partial command of the
Channel, and in the same year he fell a victim to a conspiracy
among his officers and was murdered by Allectus, his chief
minister, who assumed the status of Augustus in his place.[34]

Constantius delayed a further three years before making his
attack on Britain. Two fleets sailed from Gaul, one under
Constantius from Boulogne, the other under Asclepiodotus,
his praetorian prefect, from the mouth of the Seine. The
weather was foggy and Asclepiodotus succeeded in sailing
past Allectus' fleet, which was lying at anchor at the Isle of
Wight, and in effecting a landing at Bitterne (Clausentum).
Burning his ships, he marched on London. Allectus, who
was in the capital, hurried to meet him, but was defeated
and killed near Liss. Meanwhile, Constantius sailed up the
Thames and saved London, which was being plundered by
fugitives from Allectus' army. The capture of the city
resulted in the whole of Britain returning to the power of
Rome. The Empire was again united (A.D. 296).[35]

During Constantius' absence in Britain, Maximian watched
the German frontier, and his vigilance prevented any hostile
attacks. On his return, Constantius carried forward in
A.D. 297 the policy which Maximian had inaugurated with
Gennobaudes. On the island of the Batavians, from which
he had expelled Carausius' allies, some of whom he had
enslaved or converted into serfs, he established a Frankish
tribe called the Salii, whose home was in Frisia. These new
inhabitants settled down to a peaceful and orderly way of

life and, when required, served Rome loyally under the command of the military governor of Lower Germany.[36] In Upper Germany, however, peaceful relations could not be so easily effected. Whereas the Franks were on the whole ready for an alliance with Rome, the Alamanni regarded treaties as makeshift conveniences. Their disregard for the sanctity of oaths is illustrated by a sudden and unprovoked attack made by one of their bands upon Constantius near Langres, which was some forty miles from the frontier. Constantius was saved by the new fortifications of the town, and, after a sally in which he was wounded, not merely repelled the attackers, but pursued them to the Rhine (A.D. 298).[37] A combination of stern military reprisals and opportune gestures of friendship had re-established Roman authority in Gaul.

In the Danubian provinces during the years A.D. 293–6 Galerius was successful in maintaining peace and in developing the economic life of the country. In several wars with the Sarmatae and the Marcomanni he was victorious, and by cutting down forests and by skilful irrigation he greatly improved the agricultural properties of the country around Lake Balaton in Pannonia.[38] In A.D. 297 Maximian took Galerius' place upon the latter's appointment by Diocletian as commander of the army detailed for the Persian war, and his defeat of the Carpi was so complete that he was able to establish them as *dediticii* to swell the declining population of Pannonia.[39] In the next year he moved his headquarters once again, this time to Africa, where a Moorish tribe called the Quinquegetani had broken through the Numidian frontier.[40] On his return he visited Rome for the first time in his reign.[41]

Two events of importance occurred in Diocletian's part of the Empire, a revolt in Egypt and a war with Persia. Probably in the summer of A.D. 296 an usurper, called in the literary sources Achilleus, had himself proclaimed Augustus at Alexandria and for seven months held out in independence of Rome.[42] He is rightly identified with L. Domitius Domitianus, who issued coins from the Alexandrian mint inscribed *Imp. C. Lucius Domitius Domitianus Aug.* This coinage extends over two Alexandrian years corresponding to the twelfth and thirteenth years of Diocletian's reign. Therefore,

as the usurpation lasted seven months, Achilleus must have
been proclaimed Augustus about July, A.D. 296, and have
been put to death in the early spring of A.D. 297, shortly
before the outbreak of the Carpic War. The cause of the
rebellion is obscure. Perhaps it is a sequel to the earlier
unrest in Coptos and Busiris, but it may rather be connected
with Diocletian's ordinance that all the mints of the Empire
should in future issue only Imperial Roman coins, by which
an end was put to the emission of Greek coins from the mint
at Alexandria.[43] At any rate it would seem that Diocletian
regarded the rebellion as a dangerous nationalist rising, and
after its suppression he introduced administrative and economic reforms to which we shall return in a later chapter.[44]

In A.D. 293 Bahram II died, and the internal troubles of
Persia came to an end. He was succeeded by Narses, who
began to make plans for the recovery of Mesopotamia, which
his predecessor had ceded to Rome. Already as early as March,
A.D. 296, Diocletian speaks of " the hostile Persian nation,"[45]
and later in the same year Narses declared war. Diocletian,
as we have seen, appointed Galerius to the command in the
East, and the war opened disastrously for Rome. Galerius
with insufficient forces crossed the Euphrates at Callinicus,
and between that ford and Carrhae met the Persian army
and was completely defeated. Roman Mesopotamia fell
once again into the control of Persia.[46] The story of Diocletian's angry and humiliating reception of his Caesar, whom
he caused to run for a mile beside his chariot, may be pure
invention.[47] In any case Galerius hastened to retrieve the
disaster which his rashness had incurred. He sent for strong
reinforcements from the Danubian army, and in the following
year routed the Persians in Armenia, capturing a rich booty
which included the royal harem.[48] Following this defeat
the Persians evacuated Roman Mesopotamia, which was
occupied by Diocletian with an army from Syria. Anxiety
to recover his wives and personal possessions now prompted
Narses to sue for peace.[49] Contrary to the wishes of Galerius,
Diocletian made a treaty, by the terms of which the Roman
province of Mesopotamia was recognized as reaching to the
Upper Tigris, while the Roman sphere of influence extended
northwards through the client kingdom of Armenia so as to
include Caucasian Iberia. Merchants trading between the

Roman and Persian Empires were compelled to use the road that passed through the Roman garrison town of Nisibis, where the customs dues were levied.[50]

§ 4. THE RELIGIOUS POLICY OF DIOCLETIAN

During the third century A.D., the pagan world was moving gradually towards a monotheistic conception of God, and Aurelian's official recognition of the worship of the Sun was the culmination of this syncretizing tendency. Like Decius, too, he appreciated the value of an universally accepted religion as symbolizing and sustaining the unity of the Empire. Diocletian was no less convinced of the political advantages that might accrue from a living state religion, and the consecration of his dynasty to Jupiter and Hercules shows his determination to resuscitate the imperial cult. But whereas Aurelian was progressive in his religious ideas, Diocletian was conservative and almost reactionary in his re-creation of the polytheistic practices of the earlier Principate. Offerings were made by him to a great variety of gods. In Antioch he built a temple to Olympian Zeus and Nemesis and a shrine to Hecate, and restored a temple of Apollo.[51] In Aquileia he did honour to Sol and Apollo Belenus,[52] and consecrated a Mithraeum at Carnuntum.[53] At Rome, after the renovation of the water-supply, a dedication was made to " Father Tiber " and a statue was erected to the river god Vortumnus.[54] But while as a true polytheist he showed like reverence and respect for all the important cults in the Empire, it was Jupiter Capitolinus and the Capitoline Triad that Diocletian selected for the official religion of the State. This is illustrated by the number of inscriptions set up by the officials of the Empire which are dedicated to Jupiter Optimus Maximus with the not infrequent addition of the *Genius* and *Maiestas* of the Emperor and his colleagues.[55] Of further interest are coins with the legends JUPITER CONSERVATOR, FULGURATOR, TUTATOR, PROPUGNATOR,[56] HERCULES CONSERVATOR, PACIFER, VICTOR,[57] and GENIO POPULI ROMANI.[58] These epithets for the gods and the new and common legend GENIO POPULI ROMANI show the determination of Diocletian to base the state religion upon Graeco-Roman tradition, and it is significant that, with the exception of the panegyrists nd private inscriptions, no document or stone speaks of im or his colleagues as gods. The Augusti and their Caesars vere *Iovii* and *Herculii*, the earthly representatives but not he incarnations of their heavenly patrons.

How far this conservative polytheism was a matter of ersonal conviction it is difficult to say. Diocletian's belief n oracles and in the art of the *haruspices* is attested by both Lactantius and Victor, who call him " *scrutator rerum futur- rum*."[59] His " *pietas* " is a familiar theme with the pane- yrists.[60] But however sincere his personal religion may ave been, it is clear that a polytheistic and not a mono- heistic creed was better adapted to Diocletian's dynastic chemes. Each Augustus and Caesar would then have his wn particular protecting deity, and Diocletian's selection of upiter as his patron emphasized his controlling authority n the Tetrarchy.

Diocletian's conservative devotion to the " old religion " f Greece and Rome generated an antipathy for " new reeds," which might undermine the faith of his subjects nd weaken the unity of the Empire. This policy is first pparent in his edict against the Manichaeans, the adherents f a Persian creed, which was a blend of Zoroastrianism, Christianity and Neo-Platonism. This edict was most prob- bly issued in A.D. 296 when the Persian War was imminent, nd not in A.D. 302 when peace had been made between the wo Empires. Exception may perhaps be taken to the choice f this earlier date on the ground that it was politically short- ighted to persecute a sect which had already come under the an of the Persian government. But it is clear that Dio- letian's purpose was not limited to an attack upon the Manichaeans, but was an attempt to frustrate the infusion of Persian doctrines inside the Roman Empire. The edict was hus consonant with a foreign policy of hostility to Persia.[61]

It was from the Christian Church that Diocletian was to neet with the strongest opposition to the consummation of his religious policy. Despite the persecutions of Decius and Valerian the Church had not relaxed its proselytizing activities. Not only by its profession of a rigid monotheism, but also by its refusal to countenance any conformity by its members to the requirements of the imperial cult, it was constituting itself an organization in opposition to the State. In short, it presented its adherents with a choice between loyalty to Christ and loyalty to the Emperor. This dilemma told especially hardly upon the Christian soldiers, and while some were able to quieten their consciences, others like Maximilian preferred a martyr's death to even an outward conformity with paganism.[62]

For the greater part of Diocletian's reign there was no official persecution of the Christians, who were regarded as a chronic but not an active danger. Two explanations may be given of this tolerant attitude. First, the Church since the last persecution had suffered from schism and disaffection, and the Emperor perhaps underestimated its strength. Secondly, Christian influence was strong at the Court. Both Diocletian's wife and daughter had professed the faith, and probably they and their friends exerted considerable pressure on behalf of their co-religionists. In A.D. 302 or perhaps a year or two earlier a change took place in Diocletian's policy. A number of Christians were banished from the Court and soldiers who persisted in their faith were expelled from the army. Lactantius attributes this change to a complaint made by the *haruspices* against the Christians, and this accords well with the Emperor's notorious belief in portents. But it is difficult to understand why, if this proved so effective a manœuvre, the pagan priests had not tried it earlier. A more probable reason for Diocletian's action is to be found in the growing power of Galerius, an uncompromising opponent of Christianity.[63] Since his victory over the Persians his reputation as a general was high, and a suggestion coming from him that Christianity was prejudicial to the discipline of the army would be sufficient to impress upon Diocletian the need for action. Whether or no Diocletian acted on his own initiative in his expulsion of Christians from the army, there seems no sound reason for doubting the testimony of Lactantius that his first edict against the Christians, which was issued on February 23rd, A.D. 303, was the outcome of pressure from Galerius and his party at Court.[64]

The purpose of the first edict was to compel Christians to return to the worship of the pagan gods of the State, and to effect this end it enjoined the following penalties. Free-born Christians were deprived of the privileges which attached to Roman citizenship. Politically this meant that no Christian could hold office in the imperial and municipal services ; judicially that they lost the right of appeal and were no longer exempt from torture. Further the emancipation of Christian slaves was forbidden. Without precedent was a clause enjoining the demolition of churches and the burning of the sacred books. In this way Diocletian attempted to weaken the authority of the clergy by robbing them of the sources from which they instructed the laity and made fresh converts for the Faith.[65]

Shortly after the first edict two fires broke out in the palace at Nicomedia,[66] and reports were received of unrest at Melitene and in Syria.[67] This gave a fresh impetus to the anti-Christian party at Court, which found little difficulty in attributing both the conflagrations and the civil disturbances to the recalcitrancy of the Christians. Two fresh edicts were issued, each of which was directed solely against the clergy. While the first ordered their arrest and imprisonment, the second enjoined that they should be obliged to sacrifice to the gods of the State. If they complied, then they were set free that the example of their recantation might weaken the loyalty of the laity to their creed. If they refused, then they were kept longer in prison, subjected to various forms of compelling tortures, and were sometimes even put to death. Thus Diocletian hoped to render the laity leaderless and consequently more ready to abandon their religion.[68] Finally in A.D. 304 the Emperor extended the provision of his third edict to all Christians.[69] He was driven to this course, partly perhaps by disappointment at the results of his earlier measures and partly through an inability caused by increasing ill-health to make a stand against the callous insistency of Galerius. Under this persecution many Christians renounced their faith, and although later they were received back into communion, the terms upon which they should be readmitted were productive of much schismatic quarrelling. The persecution so far succeeded that it weakened the unity of the Church.

§ 5. THE ABDICATION OF DIOCLETIAN

In the late autumn of A.D. 303 Diocletian and Maximian came to Rome to celebrate the twentieth anniversary of the former's proclamation as Emperor. Festivities began on November 17th and continued for a month with the usual variety of games and spectacles.[70] Diocletian, who was now an old man and suffering from a prolonged illness, determined to utilize the occasion for the settlement of his dynastic schemes. He himself had now completed twenty years of government, the limit which he was anxious to impose upon his successors, but his immediate abdication, although consistent with the principle which he sought to establish, was not practical politics. Maximian, who had little aptitude for administration, would thereby become senior Augustus with Constantius as his colleague, while Galerius, now at the height of his military fame and eager for promotion, would be left unsatisfied to serve as Caesar to an Augustus for whom he felt the deepest detestation. Diocletian accordingly decided that the right solution was a simultaneous abdication by the two Augusti. After prolonged opposition he extracted a promise from Maximian, given on oath in the temple of Jupiter Capitolinus, that he would resign after the celebration of his *vicennalia* in the spring of A.D. 305.[71] The promotion of the two Caesars, Constantius and Galerius, was thus automatically secured ; the choice of their successors remained a problem.

When the Tetrarchy was established in A.D. 293 the principle of an hereditary succession inside the new dynasty was neither affirmed nor rejected by Diocletian. It seems, however, probable that at the time of the institution of the first Caesars he had regarded Maxentius, the son of Maximian, and Constantine, the bastard son of Constantius, as the probable successors to Galerius and Constantius when they were promoted to be Augusti. For Maxentius was married to Valeria Maximilla, the daughter of Galerius, and Constantine was in A.D. 298 betrothed to Maximian's infant daughter, Fausta.[72] But in the second ten years of his rule Diocletian seems to have changed his mind. While Constantine is given military preferment and as a *tribunus primi ordinis* distinguished himself in the service of Galerius,[73] Maxentius is passed over for military commands, and although obtaining senatorial rank is not permitted to hold the consulship.[74] This difference of treatment may have been in part due to Galerius, whose detestation of Maximian extended to his son, but is more essentially the result of Diocletian's own conviction that Maxentius lacked the talents and abilities that were essential for a Caesar.[75] The problem which thus confronted Diocletian in A.D. 305 was whether he could choose Constantine as Caesar, and at the same time pass over Maxentius in favour of some other candidate, in other words whether he could select a young man of seventeen who was but the bastard son of a Caesar, and reject an older man who was a son born in wedlock to his colleague. Fearing the consequences of such a slight upon the promise which he had wrested from Maximian in A.D. 303, Diocletian decided to pass over both Constantine and Maxentius, and made their youth the official grounds of his action. The principle of a hereditary succession was abandoned.

On May 1st, A.D. 305, Diocletian formally abdicated in the presence of his soldiers at Nicomedia, and at the same meeting announced his choice of the new Caesars to succeed Constantius and Galerius. In a highly coloured passage Lactantius describes the soldiers' enthusiasm for Constantine and their disappointed bewilderment when the names of Flavius Valerius Severus and Galerius' nephew Daia were read out. The latter, who assumed the names of Galerius Valerius Maximinus on his elevation, was then invested by Diocletian with the purple which he himself had worn. On the same day at Milan, Maximian resigned and instituted Severus in his office of Caesar. The two Augusti then retired into private life, Diocletian at Salona (Spalato), Maximian in Lucania, the former worn out by his long rule and content to watch from his retreat the fate of the dynastic scheme which he had evolved, the latter reluctantly submissive to his colleague's will, restless and dissatisfied, ready, should the opportunity come, to resume the work of an Augustus.[76]

CHAPTER II

MAXENTIUS AND THE RISE OF CONSTANTINE

§ 1. DEATH OF CONSTANTIUS

UPON the abdication of Diocletian and Maximian a new distribution of the Empire was made among the members of the Second Tetrarchy. Constantius administered Spain in addition to Britain and Gaul, which were already under his control. His Caesar, Severus, was given besides Africa and Italy the diocese of Pannonia, which was taken away from Galerius. The latter, however, more than compensated himself for the loss by receiving the whole of Asia Minor west of the Taurus mountains, while Maximinus was left with the rest of the Asiatic provinces and Egypt.[1] Although technically Constantius was the senior Augustus,[2] Galerius obtained, potentially at least, the greater power from this territorial distribution. Not only was he master of the East, but in Severus he had the means of exercising an effective control over the West. For the new Caesars were to a large extent his own nominees, and neither of them seemed to possess the strength of character necessary to combat his will. So long as Maximinus and Severus were prepared to play second fiddle, Galerius in effect controlled three-quarters of the Roman Empire. The presence of Constantine in his Court was of further advantage to Galerius.[3] Not only was he an useful hostage in any negotiations with Constantius, but his popularity with the soldiers might be used for pacifying their dissatisfaction at the nomination of new Caesars who were strangers to them. At the same time Galerius sought to minimize the chances of opposition from Maxentius by ensuring that he did not leave Rome.

Within a year, however, the political situation was completely changed. News of an invasion of the province of Britain by the Picts necessitated Constantius' presence in the island, and he made use of this opportunity to request the return of his son. Galerius complied with his senior colleague's demand, and Constantine after taking every precaution against pursuit joined his father at Boulogne in the early months of A.D. 306.[4] The expeditionary force sailed for Britain, but after a brilliant victory over the invaders Constantius died at York on July 25th. The army immediately proclaimed Constantine Augustus in place of his father.[5] Constantine had no alternative but to accept his soldiers' decision, and with the intention of avoiding civil war wrote to Galerius and requested his recognition of himself as his father's successor. Meanwhile he consolidated his position in the Western provinces. An invasion by the Franks presented him with the opportunity of withdrawing his main army from Britain, and after defeating the invaders he proceeded to the south of Gaul to await Galerius' answer.[6] The latter, realizing that a complete rejection of the army's action in Britain was likely to lead to civil war, decided upon a compromise. He raised Severus to the rank of an Augustus and granted Constantine the title and status of Caesar.[7] For the present Constantine accepted this inferior position, partly because he was not yet strong enough to dispute the senior Augustus' judgement, and partly out of respect for Diocletian's constitutional arrangements. Thus the Tetrarchy survived in its original form with two Augusti and two Caesars.

§ 2. THE PROCLAMATION OF MAXENTIUS

The report of Constantine's elevation gave a new incentive to Maxentius' ambitions. It was hardly to be expected that he, the legitimate son of Maximian, should quietly acquiesce in the preferment of Constantius' bastard offspring. It is, however, probable that the initiative was not taken by Maxentius himself, who lacked the necessary enterprise and personality. The promoters of the conspiracy in Rome were the praetorians and the common people; the cause of the rebellion was Galerius himself. Diocletian had greatly diminished the numbers of the praetorian guard and had limited its functions to garrison duties in Rome. Galerius now took a more decisive step in abolishing the praetorian camp. Some of the soldiers had already been drafted away;[8] the

few who still remained in Rome saw in Maxentius a means
of avenging themselves upon Galerius for the loss of their
traditional powers. A plot was formed by the praetorian
tribunes and the tribune of the *forum suarii,* who
commanded the urban cohorts, to proclaim Maxentius
Emperor.[9] This movement had the full support of the
people ; for Galerius had given orders that they in common
with the rest of the Empire should be made subject to
taxation, and officials had already been appointed to take
the census.[10] Further, the city prefect Annius Anullinus
was at least not opposed to the plan.[11] Finally on October
28th, A.D. 306, Maxentius was invested with the purple.[12] The
coup d'état was achieved almost without bloodshed ; the only
victim was the *vicarius* of the city prefect, Abellius, a staunch
partisan of Galerius.[13]

Maxentius was nevertheless not in a strong position. He
had few troops at his command and, although central and
south Italy with the neighbouring islands accepted him,
northern Italy (*pars annonaria*) remained loyal to Severus,
who was living at Milan. The early declaration of Africa in
his favour relieved him of anxiety for the food supply of the
city.[14] Maxentius, however, realized that he must still move
with caution. Although he had been proclaimed Emperor
by the praetorians and had been accepted by the Senate and
people, he refrained from employing the title of Augustus or
Caesar, and contented himself with the old title of *princeps.*[15]
This gesture, by which he intended to ingratiate himself with
Galerius, he supported by striking coins in honour of the
Augusti and Caesars, with the particular hope that his
recognition of Constantine might result in the latter's support
for his own claims.[16] But above all he realized the necessity
of invoking the help of his father, who had expressed his
disapproval of the conspiracy of the praetorians.[17] Not
only were his father's soldiers, many of whom were now
serving with Severus, indispensable to the maintenance of
his position, but also, if Maximian resumed office as senior
Augustus and recognized his son as co-regent, his usurpation
would be legitimatized. Accordingly he sent, with the
approval of the Senate, the purple insignia of office to his
father and nominated him Augustus for the second time.
Maximian accepted the invitation of his son without at first

resuming the official status of Augustus, and set out from his home in Lucania for Rome.[18] At the same time he wrote to Diocletian inviting him to re-enter public life in the interests of the peace of the Empire.[19]

Galerius' response to Maxentius' overtures was to order Severus, the Augustus of the West, to march upon Rome. His refusal to acknowledge Maxentius was not so much dictated by personal animosity or a reluctance to shatter the Diocletianic system as by fear of the consequences that would result from a recognition of the ancient privilege of the praetorians to make Emperors. Severus set out from Milan early in A.D. 307, but on reaching Rome his troops mutinied. Loyalty to their old commander Maximian made them refuse to fight against his son, and when a rich donative was distributed among them by Severus' praetorian prefect Anullinus, who had been drawn over to the side of Maxentius, they deserted their new leader.[20] Maximian had now reached Rome and resumed his position as Augustus.[21] No alternative was open to Severus but flight with such troops as still remained faithful to him. Maximian pursued him to Ravenna and here terms were arranged. Severus handed back the purple, which he had two years previously received from Maximian's hands, on condition that his life was spared. He was taken a prisoner to Rome, and, after being paraded through the streets, was imprisoned in a village on the Appian Way to serve as a hostage against Galerius.[22] Maxentius was proclaimed Augustus by his troops and now assumed the official title.[23]

The overthrow of Severus left Maxentius in control of the whole of the African and Italian dioceses with the exception of the province of Raetia, and he and his father, in anticipation of an attempted revenge by Galerius, determined to safeguard their position by an alliance with Constantine. Maximian left Rome for Gaul, and in the spring of A.D. 307 the marriage of his daughter Fausta with Constantine was celebrated.[24] At the same time he raised his son-in-law to the rank of Augustus, although the latter does not seem to have used the title officially till later in the year. In return for the recognition of the status which his army had previously conferred upon him, Constantine agreed to acknowledge Maxentius as Augustus. As a guarantee of good faith he

caused the name of Severus to be erased from monuments
set up in his honour in Gaul, and in the course of the year
issued coins on which Maxentius was styled Augustus.[25]

In the summer of A.D. 307 Galerius took the field. With
a stronger army than Severus had commanded, he marched
without opposition through Italy and pitched his camp at
Interamna.[26] Rome was, however, well provisioned to stand
a siege, and Galerius had neither sufficient troops to surround
the walls nor the necessary implements for an assault.
Dissatisfaction soon broke out in his ranks, which was fanned
into open mutiny by the timely largess of Maxentius.
Several legions deserted, and Galerius could only retain the
loyalty of the remainder by an undignified appeal to their
pity, combined with extravagant promises of reward. Even
so, he was obliged to beat a retreat after a futile attempt at
negotiations with Maxentius with the hope of inducing him
to renounce his status of Augustus in return for his personal
safety. On its northern march through Italy his army lost
all sense of discipline, plundering and ravaging the country-
side, but although it was thus an easy prey, Maxentius made
no attempt at pursuit. Whatever forces restrained him,
whether an innate lethargy, or a lingering reverence for his
wife's father, or the expectation that Constantine would cross
the Alps, his inactivity was both a political and military
blunder.[27]

Meanwhile, Maximian at the court of Constantine was
becoming estranged from his son and was laying his plans for
his overthrow. This change of attitude was by no means
solely the fruit of jealousy. Maximian realized the impossibility of any *rapprochement* between Maxentius and Galerius
and the consequent threat from their continual hostility to
the welfare of the whole Empire. Accordingly, he urged
Constantine, in whose rising power he saw the necessary
support for his own ambitions, to cross the Alps, crush
Galerius' retreating army and then join with himself in a
conspiracy to overthrow Maxentius.[28] Constantine, however,
refused these overtures. Although victory would almost
certainly have attended the projected attack upon Galerius,
the political consequences would not have been to his
advantage. For not only would he without justification have
upset the whole Diocletianic system, but an opportunity

would have been given to Maximinus to consolidate his power in the East. For the present, therefore, Constantine decided to play a passive part. But an open breach between him and Maxentius was not long delayed. News of the defeat of Galerius resulted in Spain declaring for Maxentius.[29] Constantine regarded this as an infringement of the powers which he had inherited from his father, to whose administrative sphere Spain had belonged, and broke off friendly relations with Maxentius. In the late autumn of A.D. 307 Maximian set out for Rome, determined to depose his son who had, in contravention of his father's promise, executed Severus soon after Galerius' retreat from the City.[30] After a few months of nominal joint-rule he decided to put his scheme to the test and summoned his old soldiers to a meeting, believing that they would rally to his side. A dramatic scene ensued. After expatiating on the current misfortunes, Maximian suddenly turned to his son and, denouncing him as the cause of all their troubles, tore the purple from off his shoulders. But the old Emperor had misjudged the temper of his audience. Maxentius leaped down from the platform and was rescued by the soldiers. Maximian was forced to flee from the City and once again made his way to Constantine. Maxentius reigned supreme in Rome. (Spring of A.D. 308.)[31]

§ 3. THE CONGRESS AT CARNUNTUM AND ITS CONSEQUENCES

After his disastrous experiences in Italy, Galerius decided to turn to the authority and experience of Diocletian as a remedy for the confusion in the Empire. Accordingly he nominated him as his colleague for the consulship of A.D. 308, and in the summer of that year invited him to a conference at Carnuntum, which Maximian came from Gaul to attend.[32] Although both Maximian and Galerius were at one in their eagerness that Diocletian should resume office, their mutual antipathy had not grown less with time, and Galerius was resolutely opposed to Maximian retaining the powers which he had resumed. The result of the conference was a victory for Galerius and a crushing defeat to Maximian's ambitions. Diocletian declined the invitation to re-enter public life and at the same time decided that Maximian must resign, and that all his imperial acts since his formal abdication in

A.D. 305 should be nullified. In consequence, Maxentius was declared an usurper and public enemy. In place of Severus, an old army friend of Galerius, Licinianus Licinius, who had distinguished himself in the Persian War, was made Augustus and was given the administration of Italy, Africa and Spain, which were actually under the control of Maxentius. Constantine was degraded to the rank of Caesar and the status of Maximinus was left untouched. (November, A.D. 308.)[33] Thus once again Diocletian had re-established his dynastic system of two Augusti and two Caesars, but in a manner which was both inconsistent with his principles and also could not fail to excite the indignation of the two junior members of the new Tetrarchy, who resented the promotion of Licinius over their heads, although he had never held the rank of a Caesar. Galerius attempted to placate them by bestowing upon them the title of *filii Augustorum*,[34] and possibly this empty honour might have satisfied Maximinus, if Constantine had shown a similar complacency. But when the latter refused to accept his degradation and news of his increasing power reached the East, Maximinus had himself proclaimed Augustus by his troops and Galerius was obliged to acknowledge his status (A.D. 310).[35]

The declaration by the congress at Carnuntum of Maxentius as an enemy of the State had no immediate effect upon the loyalty of his main army in Italy. So far, Galerius' hopes were disappointed. But in Africa a serious rebellion broke out, which resulted in the troops proclaiming the *vicarius* of the praetorian prefect, L. Domitius Alexander, Augustus.[36] The most probable cause of this revolt against the authority of Maxentius was the indignation of the soldiers of the province at the expulsion of Maximian from Rome and his subsequent degradation at Carnuntum, but there is also some reason to think that Constantine may have encouraged the rebellion as a useful preliminary step towards his projected attack upon Maxentius.[37] The economic effects of the loss of the African corn supply were naturally serious, but so long as Maxentius held Spain, famine could be averted, and no immediate steps were taken to end Alexander's usurpation. In the following year (A.D. 309), he suffered a great personal loss in the death of his son, Romulus, in whom he had rested his hopes for the future of the Herculian dynasty.[38]

After the failure of his negotiations at Carnuntum, Maximian had returned to Gaul, where he was kindly received by Constantine, who accorded him all the outward respect due to a senior Augustus, but was careful to prevent his assumption of actual powers. For a year the old man seems to have been content with his titular honours, but in A.D. 310 he saw an opportunity of re-establishing his authority. Constantine had taken the field against the Franks and, while he was campaigning near Cologne, Maximian won over some of the troops which he had left behind, and once again proclaimed himself Augustus at Arles. Despite the elaborate precautions which he had taken to delay his son-in-law's intervention, Constantine effected a speedy return from the Rhine. Maximian fled from Arles to Marseilles, where he was besieged and forced to capitulate by his own men.[39] His life was spared, but soon afterwards he was found dead. According to the official version he had committed suicide, but there is little doubt that exasperated by his indefatigable scheming Constantine had given the order for his death.[40] In Constantine's part of the Empire his memory was condemned.[41]

The nullification of Maximian's acts implied the final severance of Constantine from the Herculian dynasty and, because his position of Augustus had rested upon Maximian's recognition of his status, it was necessary for him to find a new constitutional basis for his authority. An official legend was put in circulation that his father, Constantius, was a natural son, or, as the later Christian version preferred to say, the nephew of Claudius Gothicus. Thus Constantine claimed descent from an earlier Roman Emperor and based his imperial position upon the principle of hereditary succession. In place of Hercules, the Unconquered Sun (who was worshipped in Gaul as Apollo) became his protecting deity. It is clear that this claim to be descended from Claudius could be used to establish a title to sole constitutional authority inside the Empire, and this may have been Constantine's ultimate intention. His immediate purpose was a political demonstration against Maxentius, whose claim to rule rested entirely upon his association with the Herculian dynasty which his father had founded.[42]

About the same time Constantine availed himself of an
attack by Frankish pirates to enter Spain, and after driving
off the invaders, annexed the province to his sphere of
administration.[43] This loss following upon the rebellion in
Africa had most serious consequences for Maxentius. Famine
broke out in Rome.[44] Street fighting occurred between the
favoured praetorians and the hungry people and the death-
roll rose as high as six thousand.[45] Finally, in the spring of
A.D. 311, Maxentius sent his praetorian prefect, C. Rufius
Volusianus, to Africa. The expedition was immediately
successful and Alexander was killed.[46] The food supply of
the city was once again secured, and a vigorous policy of
reprisals against the late usurper's adherents helped to fill
the depleted treasury.[47] Maxentius celebrated a triumph[48]
and, with his anxieties allayed, felt himself strong enough to
answer the challenge of Constantine. Forgetting his old
animosity for his father, he had caused him to be deified and
struck coins dedicated not only to his memory but also to
that of Constantius, as an indication of his claim to the whole
Western Empire.[49] War with Constantine was now inevitable,
but events which had taken place in other parts of the
Empire delayed its immediate outbreak.

§ 4.   CONSTANTINE'S INVASION OF ITALY

In the spring of A.D. 311, Galerius was stricken with a
wasting disease. Fearing, perhaps, that his sickness was a
judgement of an angry Christian God whose disciples he had
relentlessly persecuted, he issued an edict granting freedom
of worship under specified conditions to all Christians. A
few days later he died (beginning of May, A.D. 311).[50] The
Roman world was thus left in the hands of four Augusti,
but the unity of the Empire was threatened by their mutual
mistrust and antagonism. Maximinus Daia, who was
technically the senior Augustus, lost no time in strengthening
his hold over the East. He overran Asia Minor and Pontus
and forced Licinius to a settlement, by which the latter had
to content himself with the Danubian provinces. Thus the
Bosphorus became the boundary between what in effect
were two belligerent states.[51] Constantine was quick to
realize the necessity of a coalition with one of the Emperors

of the East, which would at least ensure their neutrality in his projected attack upon Maxentius. Possibly after an attempt at negotiations with Maximinus, he came to an understanding with Licinius, to whom he betrothed his sister Constantia.[52] Maximinus retaliated by forming a pact with Maxentius.[53] Having thus safeguarded himself from the possibility of a flank attack, Constantine declared war upon Maxentius[54] and in the early spring of A.D. 312 set out from Gaul.

The prospects of a victory for Constantine were not encouraging. The danger of a German invasion across the Rhine necessitated his leaving three-quarters of his army in Gaul, and his expeditionary force did not exceed 40,000. On the opposite side Maxentius had at his command a force which, if it did not reach the reputed figure of 188,000, was probably not less than four times as strong as that of his opponent.[55] The kernel of this army were the praetorians and Maximian's old soldiers who had deserted Severus and Galerius, and much was expected of a body of cavalry called *clibanarii*, whose riders and horses were protected by iron armour.[56] Against the numerical superiority of Maxentius' army, however, must be set the inferior quality and discipline of his soldiers, and above all the genius of Constantine as a general. Maxentius' policy was to retain the larger portion of his army under his own command in Rome, and in anticipation of a siege he provided the City with abundant stores of food. The wall of the City was strengthened and transformed on the model of the galleried sectors in Aurelian's wall. On the rampart walk a gallery was erected to make a covered passage, and it was provided with a number of loop-holes towards the country and open arcades towards the City. On the top of the gallery was an upper rampart-walk, which was open to the sky and defended by a frontal parapet. In many sectors the towers were rebuilt and heightened, while the gates were altered to suit the style of the wall. The new wall was probably larger than any other in the Roman world at the time of its erection, and behind this mighty bulwark Maxentius might have confidently defied a besieging army.[57] The remainder of his forces he established as outposts in northern Italy. A corps under the command of Ruricius Pompeianus garrisoned Verona with the probable purpose of defending the Brenner Pass, if Licinius should attempt a move from Noricum.[58] A smaller contingent was posted at Turin with an advance-guard at Segusio (Susa).[59]

Constantine crossed the Alps by Mont Genèvre and surprised the garrison at Segusio. Near Turin he met the main body of the enemy, and by a feigned retirement and subsequent enveloping manœuvre overcame the *clibanarii* who, encouraged to advance upon their retreating opponents, were frustrated by the weight of their armour. Turin was captured, and Milan and the other towns of Transpadane Gaul opened their gates to the victor.[60] Before, however Constantine could continue his advance upon Rome it was necessary for him to safeguard his lines of communication with Licinius. After fruitless negotiations from Milan with Ruricius he moved against Verona. His opponent was a skilled and experienced general, and it was only after a fierce battle lasting into the night, in which Ruricius was killed, that Constantine could claim the victory. Verona capitulated, and after a short siege of Modena, all northern Italy was in Constantine's hands. The road to Rome was open.[61]

The conquest of northern Italy had, however, weakened Constantine's army, and an advance upon Rome with a bare 25,000 men seemed to be inviting destruction. Nevertheless, Constantine, who had not in the past, despite his youth, shown signs of foolhardiness, decided to stake everything upon the cast. What, we may well ask, induced him to make this apparently hopeless venture ? The true answer, even if it seems no less astonishing than the enterprise itself, is to be found in the psychological effect upon Constantine's mind of the persecution of the Christians. Since the edicts of Diocletian in A.D. 303, the Christians had been persecuted with the utmost rigour in the eastern half of the Empire, which Galerius and Maximinus governed. In the west, on the other hand, Constantius and his son after him had refused to carry out the sterner injunctions of the edicts, and while their part of the Empire had enjoyed an almost unbroken prosperity, Galerius, the arch-instigator of the persecution, had just died a miserable death, and almost with his dying breath had been obliged to acknowledge his defeat by the issue of his Edict of Toleration. It is not surprising that this contrast should leave its mark upon an impressionable mind. The belief had gradually grown in Constantine that the Christian God was the greatest supernatural power in the world.[62] Whether or no we accept the familiar story of Constantine's vision, in which athwart the sun he saw the Cross inscribed with the legend, " By this conquer " ($\dot{\epsilon}\nu \tau o\acute{\nu}\tau\omega \nu\acute{\iota}\kappa a$),[63] it is certain that by the summer of A.D. 312, and perhaps even before he left Gaul, he had become convinced that under the banner of Christ he would be victorious over his enemy. In the strength of this belief he marched upon Rome, and in obedience to a further vision seen before the walls of Rome, caused the Christian monogram to be inscribed on his soldiers' shields.[64]

When the invading force had crossed the Apennines and was approaching Rome, Maxentius suddenly altered his policy and resolved to go out and meet the enemy in open battle. Although he was a superstitious man and an upholder of the old Roman cults and institutions, the story that he adopted this change of plan because the Sibylline books foretold that on the anniversary of his accession (October 28th) Rome's enemy would perish is a fabrication. It was a mistrust of the temper of the populace that impelled Maxentius to leave Rome.[65] After crossing the Tiber by the Milvian Bridge and a bridge of boats which had been constructed beside it, Maxentius' vanguard proceeded upstream till it reached the pass of the Saxa Rubra (Prima Porta). Here it found its way blocked by the enemy, and the whole column, whose rearguard was still fording the river, was brought to a standstill. Constantine saw his opportunity. Leaving a sufficiently large force to hold the defile, he led his troops across the hilly ridges, beneath which his enemy's army was massed, till he reached the Via Cassia, which coming from the north-west joins the Via Flaminia at the Milvian Bridge. Here he had room enough to deploy his soldiers on either side of the road with the bridge as their objective, while his flanks were protected by the rocky slopes on either side. Maxentius, hemmed between the hills and the river, had no alternative but to convert the left flank of his column of march into the centre of his order of battle, and await Constantine's attack. The victory was quick and decisive. The first onslaught broke the resistance of the front ranks and drove back the supporting troops in complete confusion towards the river. In its swollen waters Maxentius and thousands of his men were drowned, while the collapse of the pontoon bridge hurled others to their death.[66]

On the following day Constantine entered Rome, bearing the head of Maxentius, whose body had been recovered. Senate and people greeted him with enthusiastic rejoicings. The acts of Maxentius were nullified and his memory condemned; the praetorians were disbanded.[67] Christianity had won its first official victory, and a statue of Constantine was erected in Rome with the cross in his right hand as the symbol of his triumph.[68] On the Arch, which still to-day commemorates the liberation of the City from the tyrant, the inscription : "*Instinctu divinitatis, mentis magnitudine,*" acclaims the personal achievement of the Emperor, but at the same time attests the intervention of a divine power, to which, as pagan Rome was aware, Constantine would himself have attributed his success.[69]

CHAPTER III

CONSTANTINE AND LICINIUS

§ 1. THE END OF MAXIMINUS

IN the enthusiastic welcome which he had received in
Rome, Constantine saw an opportunity for strengthening
his constitutional position relatively to that of the two
remaining Augusti, Maximinus and Licinius. On the day
following his victory at the Milvian Bridge he permitted
the Senate, whose nominal powers he thus formally recognized,
to confer upon himself the status of senior Augustus, which
since the death of Galerius had belonged to Maximinus.[1]
In this way he was invested with the control of imperial
legislation and with the right to nominate to the consulship.
He immediately used his new authority to dispatch to
Maximinus, whom he named consul with himself for A.D. 313,
an order to stop the Christian persecution and to issue a
new decree of toleration, while shortly afterwards he
instructed Anullinus, the proconsul of Africa, to restore to
the Catholic Church all property which had formerly belonged
to it.[2] In the New Year he left Rome for Milan to celebrate
the marriage of Licinius and Constantia.[3]

At the conference, which was held after the wedding, an
attempt was made to come to an agreement on imperial
policy. The interests of the two negotiators were divergent,
and it was only after lengthy discussion that an understanding
was reached. Licinius offered no serious opposition to Constantine's proposal of complete religious toleration, and the
text of a rescript, similar to those which Constantine had
already sent to Anullinus and other Western provincial
governors, and commonly called the Edict of Milan, was
agreed upon, which Licinius was to carry with him as a
message of freedom to the Christians of the Eastern Empire.[4]
If Licinius consented to this measure as an useful weapon
against Maximinus, he was not so ready to accept the other

253

demands of Constantine and especially his claim to the status of senior Augustus. Eventually a compromise was reached. Licinius agreed to acknowledge the senior standing of his colleague on condition that he was permitted to retain the right of legislation in his own part of the Empire. In return Constantine authorized the adoption by Constantia of a bastard son of Licinius in order to legitimatize him as his father's potential successor. Finally, with regard to Maxentius' army and provinces, it was agreed to divide the military forces, but no settlement had been reached on the future administration of Italy and the adjoining provinces when the conference was adjourned.[5] Constantine was recalled to the Rhine by a Frankish rebellion, which he successfully crushed during the following months,[6] Licinius to the East by the threatening movements of Maximinus.

Maximinus is depicted by the Christian writers as surpassing all his contemporaries in lust, cruelty and drunkenness. This is clearly a reflection of the pertinacity with which he persecuted Christianity. Although he had at first complied with Galerius' Edict of Toleration, within six months he had revised his policy, making use of a memorial sent by the pagans at Nicomedia to reintroduce a suppression of the Christians. These oppressive measures, however, were less the fruit of cruelty than the product of a deliberate and, in a sense, statesmanlike policy. Indeed he seems to have been the only one of his pagan contemporaries who realized the importance of the Church as an organization. To counteract its influence he set up in the towns of his part of the Empire a pagan priesthood, which was graded like the Christian hierarchy, and by propaganda sought to invalidate the teaching of the Scriptures.[7] Although a man of low birth and little education he encouraged the promotion of literature and learning,[8] while against Lactantius' story of his lust for Valeria must be set the fact that the relatives of Galerius and Severus seem to have preferred—and wisely as the sequel shows—to live under his protection rather than that of Licinius.[9] Nor was Maximinus lacking in military capacity. In A.D. 312 he successfully warred against robber bands in Caria, whose plundering raids had occasioned a famine, and defeated the Armenians, who were challenging his sovereignty.[10]

Maximinus seems to have accepted his degradation from the position of senior Augustus with equanimity, and in accordance with Constantine's orders to have permitted Christian worship. Probably he hoped thereby to dissuade Constantine from interfering in his projected war with Licinius. Realizing that his chances of success lay in attacking Licinius in isolation he determined to strike while Constantine was engaged in Germany.

While it was still winter Maximinus moved from Syria with an army of 70,000 through snow-bound Asia Minor to Byzantium, which after a siege of eleven days was forced to capitulate. His next objective was Heraclea. Meanwhile Licinius had been summoned from Milan, and with an army numbering no more than 30,000 he reached Adrianople, while his opponent was engaged in the siege of Heraclea. The two armies then advanced to meet each other, and encamped some three miles apart at the post-stations of Tzirallum and Drizipara. On April 30 a battle was fought at Campus Serenus, in which Maximinus' army, whose numerical superiority was outweighed by the physical exhaustion of his soldiers, was completely defeated.[11] Maximinus made his escape disguised as a slave, and abandoning most of Asia Minor attempted in Cilicia behind the security of the Taurus range to concentrate an army with which to oppose Licinius and his pursuing force. From Nicomedia he issued an edict granting religious toleration, which was similar to that which had been drafted at Milan.[12] Whatever the purpose of this change of policy, whether it was to win the support of the Christian section of his subjects, or whether it was intended as a gesture to secure the intervention of Constantine, it was not destined to bear fruit. In the autumn of A.D. 313 Maximinus fell ill and died at Tarsus.[13] The whole of the Eastern Empire thus passed without bloodshed into the control of Licinius. With inhuman brutality he ordered the deaths not only of Maximinus' leading officials and his wife and children, but also of all the surviving relatives of Galerius and Severus.[14] The Jovian dynasty was thus overthrown, and with the death of Diocletian, three years later at Salona, its last representative was removed.[15] Constantine and Licinius were left as joint rulers of the Empire.

§ 2. TEN YEARS OF JOINT-RULERSHIP

After his victories in Germany Constantine attempted to give practical effect to the administrative scheme which he had outlined in his conversations with Licinius at Milan. It was his intention to appoint a Caesar with a sphere of control between those of the two Augusti which would comprise the territories of Maxentius and the Pannonian diocese, which Licinius had received on the death of Severus. Accordingly he nominated a certain Bassianus, who was married to his sister Anastasia.[16] The choice was, however, unacceptable to Licinius, who suspected that the new Caesar would be nothing less than a tool of Constantine. He therefore formed a conspiracy with Senecio to instigate his brother Bassianus to a military revolt against his brother-in-law. But the plot was detected. Bassianus was arrested and executed and, when Licinius refused to deliver up Senecio to punishment, his own complicity was revealed. An open rupture followed between Licinius and Constantine, and when the latter's statues were pulled down at Emona, war was imminent.[17]

Constantine's plan was to attempt to secure his position in the Danubian provinces before Licinius could concentrate his main army, which had not yet returned from its pursuit of Maximinus. Speed was essential, and with a small force numbering no more than 20,000 he marched from Gaul into Illyricum in the summer of A.D. 314. Licinius was, however, able to muster an army of 35,000, but despite its numerical superiority it suffered defeat with the loss of more than half of its strength at Cibalae in Pannonia on October 8.[18] Licinius retreated through Sirmium to the Balkans and at Adrianople prepared for further resistance. So little was his confidence weakened that he proclaimed the dethronement of Constantine and appointed one of his generals, Aurelius Valerius Valens, to be the new Augustus of the West.[19] A second battle was fought at Campus Mardiensis in Thrace with no decisive results. During the following night Licinius retreated north-west to Beroea, and placed himself between Constantine and the Danube.[20] The position was now dangerous to either side. For while Constantine was cut off from Gaul and might find himself between two fires when Licinius' army returned from the East, Licinius was faced with the possibility that his rival might occupy Byzantium and use his fleet to block the Bosphorus. A treaty was accordingly arranged. Licinius agreed to the deposition of Valens, whom he put to death, and to the cession of the whole of Illyricum with the exception of the Thracian diocese.[21] On the other side Constantine renounced, in confirmation of the previous agreement at Milan, the powers of legislation which had belonged by right to the senior Augustus. Each Emperor was now constitutionally entitled to issue edicts that were operative in his own part of the Empire.[22] Further it was decided that neither Emperor should enter his colleague's provinces except in the event of barbarian invasions.[23] Although constitutionally the government remained united and the coinage of both Emperors was valid throughout its length, in effect the result of the treaty was a division of the Empire into two halves in which each Emperor was independent of his colleague (December, A.D. 314).

To mark the apparent unity of the Empire, Constantine and Licinius together held the consulship of A.D. 315,[24] and co-operated after the repulse of a Gothic invasion in strengthening the fortifications upon the lower Danube.[25] In the same year Constantine's *decennalia* were celebrated in Rome, and the Arch, decorated with adornments taken from the monuments of Trajan and other Emperors, which stands to-day between the Colosseum and the Palatine, was dedicated.[26] On March 1, A.D. 317, three new Caesars were created. Two of them were Constantine's sons, Flavius Julius Crispus, the ten-year-old child of a concubine, and Flavius Claudius Constantinus, the eldest son of Fausta, who had been born a few weeks previously. The third Caesar was Licinius' bastard son, Valerius Licinianus Licinius.[27] But despite these outward signs of harmony, there was little real sympathy between the two Emperors, and, although civil war was averted for a decade, during the last four years of the period there were indications of a growing estrangement. The cause of the final rupture is most probably to be found in the implications of Constantine's religious policy.

By the Edict of Milan the same freedom of worship had been extended to the Christians as was enjoyed by the adherents of pagan cults, and in the same year the Christian

17

clergy like the pagan priests were exempted from personal *munera.*[28] But although it was not immediately possible to establish Christianity as the state-religion—for the army and most of the upper classes were convinced pagans—Constantine was determined to give an official recognition to the Christian Church with the intention that the moral and economic advantages which accrued to its organization might be utilized for the good of the State.[29] In furtherance of this idea of a union between Church and State, Constantine authorized two measures of outstanding importance. By a constitution published in A.D. 318 he recognized the jurisdiction of the episcopal courts and accorded to the verdicts of the bishops in cases which were by mutual agreement of the litigants brought for their decision the same validity as attached to the sentences of the civil judges.[30] In A.D. 321 a rescript addressed to the Roman people permitted any citizen to bequeath his property to the Church, which consequently was deemed to possess the status of a civic corporation.[31] But these favours involved responsibilities. If the Church was to be an effective partner for the State, it was essential that the State should guarantee that the authority of the Church's officials was universally recognized, and that they were not hampered in the execution of their duties. Schismatic disobedience was bound to be subversive of the visualized harmony between Church and State. Domestic troubles soon broke out within the Church, and as early as A.D. 313 Constantine was asked to arbitrate in what is known as the Donatist schism in Africa, a quarrel which had arisen over the validity of an appointment to the see of Carthage, as the consecrating bishop was alleged to have surrendered the sacred books of his Church to the inquisitors of the Diocletianic persecution. Constantine at first hoped that the Church would be able to settle its own differences, but when the schismatics refused to accept the episcopal verdict he decided to re-try the case himself. In A.D. 316, he gave a judgement confirming the findings of the bishops, and ordered the expulsion of the Donatists from their churches. The disturbances which ensued in Africa, however, forced the Emperor to admit defeat, and four years later in fear of incurring the name of a persecutor he extended to the heretics a complete toleration and left them to the Judgement of God.[32] Constantine had failed in his first attempt to restore unity in the Church.

So long as Licinius was prepared to uphold the religious policy to which he had given his assent at Milan, the unity of the Eastern Church was as essential to him as that of the Western was to Constantine. It was, therefore, necessary for him to interfere in the Arian dispute, which beginning at Alexandria was dividing the whole Eastern Church into two antagonistic sects. Whereas the orthodox under Alexander held that Christ was God, the followers of his presbyter, Arius, who included the theologian Eusebius of Caesarea, maintained that he was only His Creature. The influence of the Arians was strong at Court ; for Arius himself, who had been deprived of his office at Alexandria by Alexander, had made a profound impression upon the Empress Constantia, and Eusebius of Nicomedia, who was probably a relative of the praetorian prefect Julianus, was in high favour with Licinius. It was not, therefore, surprising that at two synods, held the one in Bithynia and the other in Palestine, the teaching of Arius was declared to be in accordance with the Christian Faith, and his reinstatement demanded. Alexander's response was the summoning of another synod of almost a hundred bishops, who a second time excommunicated Arius and his followers from the Catholic Church.[33] This open defiance led to a complete change in Licinius' religious policy. Although cruel and uncultured, Licinius, like Maximinus Daia, was not devoid of statesmanlike abilities. Profiting by his own and his colleague's experience, he came to the conclusion that the union of Church and State was a profitless pursuit, while to allow such a highly developed organization to exist outside the State was equally dangerous. Accordingly he decided to strike at the heart of the Church's power and in A.D. 320 forbade the holding of any further synods.[34] This initial step was followed by restrictions upon the philanthropic activities of the clergy and a ban against women attending the services of men.[35] Christians were expelled from the palace, and later from the army and the administrative services,[36] while imperial officials exceeded their mandate by condemning some of the faithful to death.[37]

That the religious recantation of Licinius hastened, if it

did not cause, the final rupture between him and Constantine is confirmed by other evidence. In A.D. 321 Constantine nominated his two sons Crispus and Constantine to the consulship, and in the following year held the office himself with his younger son as colleague. Licinius replied to this slight by assuming the consulship himself with his son.[38] This action was tantamount to a breach of friendly relationships, and both Emperors began to prepare for war. The withdrawal of troops from the Danubian frontier led in A.D. 322 to a Sarmatian invasion of eastern Pannonia, which Constantine successfully repelled with the capture of many prisoners and a rich booty.[39] In the next year the Goths made an incursion into the Thracian diocese. To avert the danger Constantine entered the territory of Licinius and, although the treaty made in A.D. 314 had authorized such an encroachment in the event of a barbarian invasion, Licinius chose to regard it as a contravention of the agreement. After embassies had been interchanged, war was declared in the spring of A.D. 324.[40]

Constantine had mustered an army of 120,000 infantry and 10,000 cavalry, and his fleet at Thessalonica under the nominal command of Crispus, who had previously won successes against the Franks and Alamanni, comprised 200 men-of-war and 2000 transports. Licinius' forces were even larger, and were drawn from practically all the Eastern provinces. His army numbered 150,000 infantry and 15,000 cavalry, his fleet 350 fighting-ships, which were mobilized in the Dardanelles.[41] On July 3rd, A.D. 324, Licinius suffered a severe defeat at Adrianople and fell back upon Byzantium.[42] In the hope of avoiding the necessity of a long siege Constantine decided to use his fleet to force the Dardanelles. A battle was fought at the entrance to the Straits, which resulted in the destruction of Licinius' fleet under their commander, Abantus. Byzantium was thus cut off from all provisions that might reach it by sea.[43] Before the arrival of Constantine's fleet Licinius, leaving a small garrison behind him, crossed to Chalcedon.[44] Just as ten years previously he had raised Valens to the status of Augustus, so now he conferred a similar honour upon his *magister officiorum*, Martinianus, and entrusted to him the duty of preventing Constantine from crossing into Asia Minor.[45] The latter, however, outwitted his vigilance and effected a landing at Riva near the northern end of the Bosphorus. On September 18th, the battle of Chrysopolis sealed the fate of Licinius, who escaped with 30,000 men to Nicomedia. Byzantium and Chalcedon capitulated.[46] Through the mediation of Constantia, Constantine at first consented to spare the lives of Licinius and Martinianus, and permitted the former to reside at Thessalonica and the latter in Cappadocia. Licinius, however, soon began to intrigue and, after referring the issue to the Senate, Constantine gave orders for his death. A similar fate befell Martinianus, but young Licinius, who was deprived of his rank of Caesar, was for the present spared.[47] For the first time for thirty-nine years the Roman Empire was united under the control of a single Augustus.

CHAPTER IV

THE REFORMS OF DIOCLETIAN AND CONSTANTINE

(A) ADMINISTRATIVE AND MILITARY

DURING the twenty years of Diocletian's rule radical changes were effected in practically every department of the imperial administration. As many of these reforms did not reach their full development till Constantine, it is convenient to review the work of the two Emperors together.

§ 1. THE COURT

The first essential for a programme of reform was the establishment and recognition by the army and the civil population of the supreme power of the Emperor. Without claiming identification for himself with God, Diocletian, by the adoption of Jupiter as the godfather of his new dynasty, had sought to emphasize the sacred and supernatural nature of his authority and to crown his own person with a halo of sanctity. To impress his subjects still further with a sense of his dignity, he introduced a court ceremonial and etiquette, which in its main features was based on the Persian model. The person of the Emperor was made much more unapproachable, and those who were granted an audience were obliged to prostrate themselves on coming into his presence (*adoratio*) and to kiss the hem of his garment.[1] He himself was seldom seen in public, and on all State occasions in place of the simple purple wore garments and shoes adorned with pearls and costly jewels. This Eastern practice was further developed by Constantine. At the celebration of his *vicennalia* in A.D. 325 his head was crowned with a diadem, the distinctive mark of an Oriental potentate, which was now to become the insignia of a Roman Emperor.[2] From this time, too, dates the establishment of the imperial *cubiculum* with an eunuch as its chief officer. This *praepositus sacri cubiculi*, as he was called, in course of time ranked with the highest officials of the State. He had control of the imperial wardrobe (*sacra vestis*), and under his command were both the *primicerius sacri cubiculi*, who was the Emperor's personal equerry, and the thirty *silentiarii*, who under the orders of three *decuriones* were responsible for maintaining quiet and decorum at Court.[3] Such were the outward signs that heralded the birth of the new despotism.

§ 2. PROVINCIAL ORGANIZATION

The two salient features of Diocletian's provincial reforms were the almost universal separation of military and civil power, and the division of the old provinces into smaller administrative units. The former principle had been applied by Gallienus to all provinces that were governed by senators, where the command of the garrison troops had been handed over to officers of equestrian rank, who from the time of Diocletian were called *duces*.[4] In the smaller provinces, on the other hand, which were under the control of knights, the military and civil functions of the governors had not been divided and, as the recently discovered inscription from Birdoswald shows,[5] this practice continued as late as A.D. 297. In the later years of Diocletian, however, the principle of divided authority became the rule, and only in such provinces as Mauretania and Isauria, where unsettled conditions prevailed, were the two functions combined, and here the wisdom of the expedient was proved by its permanency.[6]

The division of the old provinces into smaller units, which further weakened the power of their governors, was carried out in gradual stages and the completed scheme is reproduced in the provincial list of Verona.[7] Only such provinces as Sicily and the Maritime Alps, whose dimensions were already negligible, were left untouched. The remainder were either halved or divided into smaller fractions. For example Mauretania Caesariensis was, earlier than A.D. 293, partitioned into two;[8] Egypt, after the revolt of Achilleus had been crushed, was organized into three separate units,[9] while Asia was at first divided into three and subsequently

into seven smaller provinces.[10] Italy itself ceased to enjoy
an exclusive position and was brought under the general
provincial scheme. In short, the number of provinces was
doubled, and this preference for small administrative districts,
the military significance of which we shall consider later,
continued under the later Emperors till in the fifth century
A.D. their total exceeded 120.

Although some of the provincial administrators continued
to be drawn from the senatorial order, all the appointments
were now in the hands of the Emperor, and the nominal
control of the Senate completely disappeared. The governors
of Asia and Africa, who were responsible directly to the
Emperor and not to the praetorian prefect, together with the
governor of Achaea continued to be called proconsuls.[11] Of
the remainder the consular governors were styled *consulares*,
the praetorian *correctores*, while the generic title of *praeses*
was given to all governors of equestrian rank, who had the
rank of *perfectissimi*.[12] This continued separation of the
senatorial and equestrian orders was, however, abolished by
Constantine. From A.D. 321 onwards, knights as well as
senators were appointed *correctores*, and senators no less than
knights were given praesidial posts.[13] The senatorial ranks
were continually swelled by magistrates who had begun their
careers as knights and finished with senatorial status till by
the middle of the fourth century the most important State
officials all bore the title of *clarissimi*.

In order to facilitate the control of the provincial governors
by the central bureaucracy, Diocletian introduced a new and
more comprehensive scheme of internal organization. The
Empire was divided into twelve dioceses, and each diocese
was placed under the control of a *vicarius*. These *vicarii*
were the representatives of the praetorian prefects and were
all of equestrian rank, bearing the title of *perfectissimi*.[14]
They were thus of lower rank than the senatorial governors,
all of whom with the exception of the three proconsuls of
Asia, Africa and Achaea were made subject to the vicarial
authority. Thus an important principle, which was later
applied to other branches of the administration, was established by which men of higher standing were brought into
magisterial dependence upon officials of lower rank.[15] The
new divisions of the Empire corresponded in general with the

spheres of the *vicarii*, but two exceptions must be noted. The diocese of Italy, which stretched as far north as the upper Danube, was only superficially an unity. For while the *vicarius Italiae*, who resided at Milan, controlled the provinces north of the Apennines, Sicily, Corsica, Sardinia and the mainland south of the Apennines were under the jurisdiction of a special vicar residing at Rome, who was called *vicarius in urbe Roma*.[16] Secondly, although Egypt had lost its unity as a single province, prefects of Egypt still continued to be appointed, and served as intermediaries between the governors of the new provinces of the country and the *vicarius Orientis*.[17]

At the head of this complex system of administration stood the praetorian prefects, one of whom was attached to each Augustus and Caesar and thus lived with his master permanently away from Rome. Although they were deprived of the command of the praetorian guard, which was reduced by Diocletian to a garrison of Rome, they held under the Emperor supreme command of the forces of the Empire and retained the judicial powers which had accrued to their office during the third century.[18] The praetorian prefecture thus continued to combine both military and civil functions and fell outside the provisions of the principle which Diocletian had applied almost universally to the lower spheres of government. The establishment of vicars, however, did in effect weaken the powers of the prefecture; for their jurisdiction ran concurrently with that of the prefects, whose representatives they were, and appeals from their decisions were heard not by the prefects, but by the Emperor himself.[19] By this check upon the monopoly of power in the hands of his chief ministers, Diocletian sought to protect himself from a repetition of the military *pronunciamentos*, which in the past had so vitally sapped the strength of the Empire.

§ 3. BUREAUCRACY UNDER CONSTANTINE

Early in Constantine's reign the powers of the praetorian prefects were remodelled. When Crispus as a mere boy was sent to Gaul in A.D. 318, the prefect who accompanied him became in all but name the ruler of that part of the Empire. The danger of such an exceptional position was apparent, and the opportunity was taken of preventing its recurrence.

The prefects were accordingly deprived of all military command. Further, the Diocletianic principle of the close attachment of the prefect to the person of his Emperor was abandoned. In future the prefects were entrusted with the civil administration of specified territorial divisions of the Empire, and in the time of Constantine the Western Empire was divided into three parts, each under the control of a prefect, while the Eastern Empire was probably administered by two prefects acting collegially.[20] But although the possibility of usurpations was in this way lessened, the prefecture gained greatly in civil importance. The prefects became the vice-gerents of the Emperors and exercised a jurisdiction that was equipollent with that of their masters. This is expressly stated in an edict of Constantine addressed in A.D. 331 to all provincials, in which the judicial sentences of the prefects are made final without any further appeal to the Emperor.[21] The scope of their administration was also comprehensive. They controlled the imperial post[22] and the erection of public buildings.[23] The supervision of State-associations (*collegia*[24]) and the regulation of market prices were in their competence,[25] and the conduct of higher education was under their administration.[26] Most important of all was their responsibility for the corn-supply and the commissariat of the army,[27] which, combined with their control of recruiting,[28] gave them a most effective check over the military commanders, who had to indent for the rations of their soldiers to the vicars and render their accounts to the prefect's office.[29] Finally, in their capacity of vice-gerents they came to exercise an actual, if not a legal, authority over the vicars and the proconsuls, and, in contravention of the Diocletianic plan, the dioceses became divisions of the prefects' spheres of administration. The danger of this civil supremacy was, however, limited by one important condition. The appointment and the dismissal of the prefects were alike in the hands of the Emperor, and it was consequently in their own interest to exercise their powers to the satisfaction of their master.[30]

The limitation of the praetorian prefects to the position of vice-gerents of the Emperor necessitated new arrangements being made for the conduct of business which had previously belonged to them. An important change was made in the composition of the imperial *consilium*, which now received the name of *sacrum consistorium*, and became a standing committee for the transaction of both administrative and judicial business. Its members were permanent, and were given the title of *comites*, which had been previously conferred on the imperial *comitatus*, and were graded in three separate ranks. The praetorian prefect was no longer an ordinary member of this body, but might on occasions be called in to give his advice.[31] His place was taken by the *quaestor sacri Palatii*, who with the help of the imperial *scrinia* was further responsible for the issue of imperial edicts and rescripts and for keeping the register of the lesser state officials, which was called *laterculum minus*.[32] Secondly, Constantine established a *schola notariorum* independent of the praetorian prefect, which was a standing *officium*, composed of members with the rank of tribunes and *protectores domestici*. These *notarii* not only acted as secretaries to the *consistorium*, but might also be sent as imperial emissaries to the provinces. They were further assigned the task of drawing up letters patent for such military appointments as did not fall under the *laterculum minus* and for civil posts of the rank of *praeses provinciae* and upward, while their chief, the *primicerius*, was responsible for keeping the register containing the names of the higher state officials, called the *laterculum maius*.[33]

In addition to the *quaestor sacri Palatii* Constantine created in A.D. 320 a second important official, who was called the *magister officiorum*.[34] He was the chief of the government departments and was a permanent member of the *consistorium* with the rank of *comes primi ordinis*. A number of functions, which had previously been exercised by the praetorian prefect, were assigned to him. He held a general direction over the provision of arms, and as commander of the mounted body-guard (*scholae palatinae*) was responsible for the safety of the Emperor. He was also Minister for Foreign Affairs and master of ceremonies, exercising a judicial control over the Court servants without prejudice to that of the *praepositus sacri cubiculi*. Of no less importance was his command of the newly constituted *schola agentium in rebus*, which took the place of the *frumentarii*, who had been disbanded by Diocletian. These new officials acted as dispatch-bearers, supervised the transport of troops, and in their capacity of *curiosi* carried out an effective espionage into the conduct of magistrates and subjects alike. Entrusted with these diverse powers and responsibilities the *magister officiorum* exercised an authority which extended to every department of State, and which could be used by the Emperor to control the activities of the praetorian prefects.[35]

Next in seniority in the *consistorium* to the *magister officiorum* and the *quaestor* were the two Chancellors of the Exchequer, who controlled the *fiscus* and the *res privata*. After the death of Constantine they received the titles of *comes sacrarum largitionum* and *comes rerum privatarum*, and the title of *rationalis* was conferred upon the procurators who served under them.[36] The secretaries, who formed their *officium*, were also state officials of high standing and bore the generic name of *palatini*.[37] It is noteworthy that despite the separation by Diocletian of military and civil power, service in the *officia* still continued to be regarded as a *militia*, and in consequence the heads of departments had the same jurisdiction over their subordinates as the commanding officers had over their soldiers.[38]

Consistently with his policy of weakening the powers of the highest state officials Diocletian had appointed a vicar to the prefect of the city. This new office was abolished by Constantine, and its functions handed over to the *vicarius in urbe*, who was the representative of the praetorian prefect.[39] This change, however, weakened rather than strengthened the position of the city prefect, who had naturally less control over the *vicarius in urbe* than he had been able to exercise over his own vicar ; but for another reason the office still continued to be important. Constantine deprived the Senate of its judicial powers. As a consequence the court of the city prefect acquired an increasing distinction. All *clarissimi* brought their civil suits, and those resident in Rome their criminal suits, to his tribunal, so that, just as the praetorian prefect was the Emperor's vice-gerent, the prefect of the city became the representative of the Senate. In the later Roman Empire he was the only official who wore the *toga* and not the *cingulum*, and he symbolized the survival of Republican tradition.[40]

Constantine's resuscitation of the *patricii*,[41] like the conferment of the title of *censor* on his brother Delmatius and of *nobilissimus* on his nephew Hannibalianus,[42] has little significance except as an illustration of the Emperor's love of high-sounding appellations with perhaps an affected antiquarian interest. The new *patricii* had nothing but a name common with the past proud bearers of that distinction. The rank was not hereditary, but was only held for life and was a mere courtesy title bestowed on senators who had held the consulship. Apart from the consulship, the other Republican magistracies lost all their importance. It became, in consequence, difficult to find candidates for the quaestorship and praetorship, and as the provision of games was still one of the functions of these offices, they were converted into compulsory *munera* for men of senatorial status.[43] In A.D. 336, as he no longer lived in Rome, Constantine handed over the elections to the quaestorship and praetorship and nominations for the post of *consules suffecti* to the Senate.[44]

§ 4. THE ARMY REFORMS

During the first two centuries of the Principate the organization of the Roman Army had continued on the basis established by Augustus. There were two main types of troops, legions of a nominal strength of 6000 each recruited from Roman citizens, and *auxilia*, whose total man-power corresponded roughly to that of the legions, enlisted from provincials who had not yet received the full citizenship. This army was employed in the defence of the Empire and was stationed in the frontier provinces under the command of the provincial governors. Apart from the praetorians and the urban cohorts there was no system of reserves. When a punitive or aggressive war was declared, it was from the frontier armies that the contingents necessary for the expeditionary force were drawn. Herein lay one of the chief weaknesses of the Augustan system. The conduct of a foreign war involved the denuding of other parts of the Empire of their defensive garrisons. For a campaign against Parthia, for example, it was regularly the Danubian army that was called upon to strengthen the forces stationed in the East. Nor was the standing army, which on the accession of Septimius Severus numbered some 300,000 men, more than adequate for its primary duties of frontier defence. Consequently, if a foreign war was protracted, an opportunity was given to the barbarian tribes in other parts of the Empire to attack the weakened garrisons that lay between them and the adjoining province. It was this policy of denuding the frontiers to provide an expeditionary army that was in the main responsible for the chaos into which the Roman Empire fell in the third century A.D.

Two other notable weaknesses in the Augustan system must be observed. Both the provincial governors and the individual commanders of legions and auxiliary units were not uncommonly men of little military experience. Unlike their subordinates, the centurions, they had not chosen the army as their profession, but owed their appointments to their social and political status. Secondly, the Roman army was deficient in cavalry. Such as there was was provided almost exclusively by the auxiliary *alae*. Each legion had only 120 *equites*, whose function was probably to form a bodyguard for the legionary commander.

It was Gallienus who made the first important step to counteract these disadvantages. By his separation of military and civil power he took away from the provincial governors the command over the forces in their provinces and gave it to professional officers, while senators were replaced by knights in the subordinate posts. Secondly, realizing the disadvantages from which Rome suffered in her wars with Persia, he raised and organized mobile independent cavalry units, and in all probability increased the number of legionary cavalry. His example was followed by Aurelian, who placed the legionary cavalry in tactical, if not in administrative, independence of the infantry. These two principles, the organization of a campaigning army in separation from the garrison forces on the frontiers and the development of cavalry, are the basis of the reforms of Diocletian and Constantine, which are the culmination of a gradual process of evolution in the history of the Roman Army. The work of the two Emperors is most satisfactorily considered in conjunction. Even although Constantine must be credited with the consummation of the new system, there are clear indications that the plan which he elaborated was already inherent in the work of his predecessor. The reforms of Diocletian and Constantine are complementary and not antithetical.[45]

The first concern of Diocletian was the safety of the frontiers, and it was chiefly with this object in view that he decided upon an increase in the number of legions. On his accession he found some forty legions in existence and, although certainty is not attainable, it seems probable that he raised their total to about sixty. These new units were not raised simultaneously, but at intervals, to meet the requirements of the new provincial organization, which Diocletian gradually established throughout the Empire. As the smaller frontier provinces were created out of the old larger administrative units, each was given its own garrison troops. The principle of distribution was in accordance with the practice of the third century, namely, the assignment of a pair of legions to each province. Thus, while in a few cases a single legion might be deemed an adequate garrison, in no case did any province receive more than two. In addition to legions, each frontier province had its quota of auxiliaries, and it is probable that Diocletian's increase in the number of legions extended proportionately to the *auxilia*. Whether all the new legions were of the same effective strength as those already in existence is doubtful, but there is reason to think that, whereas the units created early in his reign conformed to the old numerical standard, those raised later, especially for Egypt and the Eastern provinces, were of much smaller dimensions and perhaps did not exceed the strength of a thousand. Strategically then the purpose of Diocletian's provincial and military reforms was to create a more effective system of frontier defence by a more detailed distribution of the available garrison troops.[46]

The scope of Diocletian's reform was not, however, limited to the problem of imperial defence. The increase in the size of the Danubian army at any rate, which was effected early in his reign, was to serve as a means for equipping such expeditionary forces as were required, without as heretofore depleting the garrison forces below the level of safety. This seems clear from the evidence of a papyrus, which shows that Diocletian's army with which he crushed the revolt of Achilleus in Egypt contained detachments drawn from pairs of legions in the Danubian provinces under the command of

separate *praepositi*,[47] while Galerius, after his initial defeat
by the Persians, reinforced his army with drafts taken from
the same area. So far, Diocletian was following the precedent
set by his predecessors, while at the same time attempting to
redress the disadvantages inherent in the system. Experience,
however, seems to have taught him that a more satisfactory
solution was to be found in the separation of mobile troops
from their parent bodies, the garrison legions.

The contingents of legionary cavalry, organized by
Aurelian in separation from the infantry with the title of
promoti, continued their independent existence under Diocletian. Earlier than A.D. 293 they came to be designated by
the title of *vexillationes*,[48] which had previously denoted
infantry detachments, but in Constantine's army became the
official nomenclature of the cavalry of the Field Army.
Further, the title *comites* is given to a detachment of horsemen
serving in Diocletian's army in Egypt,[49] and on an inscription
set up in Noricum in A.D. 312 some Dalmatian *equites* are
styled *comitatenses*.[50] This evidence shows that the separation
of cavalry from infantry, which was one of the salient features
of the Constantinian reforms, was in force under Diocletian,
and that the later title *comitatenses* had already been employed
to designate some, if not all, of the mobile cavalry units.
With the infantry the case is not so decisive. The fact that
two of the detachments in the Egyptian expeditionary force
remained to form the garrison of one of the new Egyptian
provinces,[51] and that a detachment of XI *Claudia* was
stationed permanently at Aquileia and provided soldiers for
Maximian's African campaign,[52] warrants the belief that
Diocletian retained a considerable number of detachments as
mobile units away from their parent legions. The clearest
evidence, however, comes from a body of troops called
lanciarii. They formed a *corps d'élite* drawn from the legions,
and took the place of the praetorians, who were reduced to
garrison duties in Rome, as the bodyguard of the Emperor.[53]
One of their soldiers is inscribed on an inscription as serving
in sacro comitatu,[54] from which it follows that the *lanciarii*, as
a whole, were given the title of *comitatenses*. Even if they
were the only infantry troops that enjoyed this privileged
status, there is still ample justification for maintaining
that it was Diocletian who began the organization of the

independent Field Army, which was permanently established by Constantine.

In the Field Army of Constantine there were two classes of troops, which differed from each other in status but not in function. They were called *palatini* and *comitatenses*, and correspond roughly to our Guards and Regiments of the Line. In each category there was both cavalry and infantry, the former taking precedence over the latter—a striking testimony to the newly recognized value of this arm. The cavalry contingents were called *vexillationes*, each of which numbered 500, and was under the command of a tribune. Some of these units were the legionary *promoti*, the majority, as their names show, were barbarian in origin, drawn for the most part from subject states of the Empire. The infantry consisted mainly of legions, each a thousand strong and commanded by a tribune. Some of these new legions were detachments drawn from the garrison legions on the frontiers; others, which bore names unfamiliar in the previous history of the legions, were probably formed out of auxiliary cohorts. In the *palatini* but not in the *comitatenses* there were also infantry contingents called *auxilia*. These have no connection with the old cohorts, but were picked German and Gallic troops, which subsequently, as in Julian's Persian War, became the mainstay of the army.[55] The Field Army was under the control of two *magistri*, one of whom, the *magister peditum*, held command over the infantry, the other, the *magister equitum*, over the cavalry. After the death of Constantine the number of *magistri* was increased and the previous limitation of their command to either cavalry or infantry disappeared. By the middle of the fourth century A.D. there were two *magistri militum praesentales* at each imperial headquarters, and others were given a regional command in Gaul, Illyricum and the East. The Field Army, numbering some 200,000 men, was divided into two main parts, roughly equal in size and corresponding to the Western and Eastern Empires, and its units were established away from the frontiers in towns which lay adjacent to the main routes of communication.[56]

For his personal bodyguard Constantine created a number of *scholae palatinae*, which were composed of cavalry recruited from Germany. Each *schola* numbered 500 and was under the general command of the *magister officiorum*; its soldiers were

18

both better equipped and higher paid than the cavalry of the Field Army.[57] In addition a change was made in the organization of the protectors. Two divisions were made, and while the ordinary protectors were at the disposal of the *magistri militum*, the more exclusive group, known as *protectores domestici*, attended under the command of the *comes domesticorum* upon the wishes of the Emperor.[58]

Standing in order of precedence between the Field and Garrison armies was a class of legions known as *pseudo-comitatenses*. In origin most of them were frontier-legions, and were now placed under the command of the *magister militum* of the district without receiving the full status and privileges of *comitatenses*. Perhaps the true explanation of this hybrid class of troops may be found in the hypothesis that they were intended primarily to act as a second line of defence for the frontiers, but could, if necessity arose, be used by the commander-in-chief as mobile units in the Field Army.[59]

The garrison armies on the frontiers, which were commanded by *duces*, some of whom had the rank of *comites*, were, like the Field Army, composed of cavalry and infantry, and the same order of seniority was maintained. In some provinces the *cunei equitum* headed the list,[60] in others, where there were no *cunei*, the place of honour was taken by the *equites*.[61] The former were barbarian formations recruited, in all probability, from Germany, the latter were the residuum of the cavalry units raised by Gallienus, the flower of which had been taken for the Field Army.[62] Next came the legions, detachments from which were stationed in *castella* along the frontier, while the *praefectus* remained with the remnant of the troops at headquarters.[63] Lowest in status were the *alae* and *cohortes*, some of which were recruited by Diocletian, while others dated back to the Principate.[64]

Constantine's reforms effected a radical change in the character of the Roman army. Not only were the frontier troops reduced in number,[65] but they were converted into a mere local militia. All the best soldiers were absorbed in the ranks of the new Field Army. Secondly, it was no longer the legions, which were still recruited from Roman citizens,[66] that had pride of place in the scale of honour ; their position was usurped by the *auxilia*, while the infantry as a whole was ranked below the cavalry. Germans and Illyrians were the flower of the new army, and it is no great exaggeration to say that the more barbarian the soldier the higher was his military value assessed. This transformation was not, however, an arbitrary preference for the foreigner ; it was the sequel to the history of the third century, during which civil war and plague had diminished the citizen population of the Empire, just as the distress attendant upon excessive taxation had sapped its vitality.

§ 5. FRONTIER FORTIFICATIONS

Consistently with his policy of increasing the size of the garrison army, Diocletian devoted much attention to the defences of the Empire. The eastern frontier south of the Euphrates was, by the nature of the country, ill adapted for artificial barriers such as had been erected in Upper Germany. There was no clearly defined *limes*, except in so far as the Syrian and Arabian deserts formed a natural limit to Roman expansion. Attempts had, however, been made, notably by Trajan, through the construction of his Via Nova, to link Mesopotamia with the Red Sea. It was in this district that Diocletian's most important work was carried out. As a means of connecting Osroene with Arabia and Palestine he built a paved road which ran northwards from Palmyra to Sura, and had Damascus for its southern terminus.[67] Upon the main frontier route, which ran from Petra, through Bostra and Palmyra, to Circesium on the Euphrates, he erected or reconstructed forts at points of strategic importance. Of these the most important were Kasr Bser, which is called *castra praetorii Mobeni*,[68] Deir-el-Kahf, some twenty-five miles south-east of Bostra,[69] and Circesium itself, which received new walls.[70] These forts were distinguished by their square towers and small posterns at the principal entrances, a new style which is also to be found in a Diocletianic fort at Oberwinterthur (Vitodurum) in Switzerland.[71] Besides these defensive works Diocletian also constructed armouries at Edessa, Antioch and Damascus, from which the needs both of a garrison and mobile army could be expeditiously supplied.[72]

Africa, which had suffered from the invasion of the Bavares, gives indications of similar frontier reorganization to that on the eastern frontier.[73] Not only was the *limes* strengthened, but the damage done to towns and outworks was repaired. Inscriptions tell of the reconstruction of Rapidum[74] which had been demolished by the invaders, and the building of a bridge at Auxia.[75]

Although the creation of a Field Army by Constantine reduced both the quality and quantity of troops on the frontiers, the material defences of the Empire were not neglected by him. The Danubian area was the scene of his most important activities. Epigraphical evidence makes it probable, if not certain, that the stone wall in the Dobrudja was built in A.D. 317. This wall, which replaced the great earth wall, ran from Cernavoda to Costanza, and at intervals along its course, forts, twenty-two in number, were constructed.[76] After the defeat of Licinius, Constantine carried out an extensive reorganization in Lower Moesia. A stone bridge was built across the Danube and a fortress, called Dafne Constantiniana, was erected on its northern bank at a site not far from the confluence of the Ardisch and the main river.[77] The strategic foresight of the Emperor was proved in his subsequent campaigns with the Goths.

CHAPTER V

THE REFORMS OF DIOCLETIAN AND CONSTANTINE

B. ECONOMIC AND SOCIAL

§ 1. INTRODUCTION

THE century which preceded the accession of Diocletian had witnessed the early stages in the gradual decline of local autonomy and personal liberty inside the Roman Empire. Frequent usurpations and foreign wars, an increasing bureaucracy and a wasteful public expenditure, plague and famine, had each contributed to the collapse of the imperial system of finance. To redress the deficiencies in revenue the government had resorted to a policy of compulsory state-service. Town and country dwellers alike were called upon to perform such pecuniary and personal services as the State might require. Local and individual interests were, wherever necessary, sacrificed to the superior claims of Empire. Citizenship was becoming a synonym for servitude. The situation was further aggravated by the absence of any regulated system of supply and demand. Requisitions were made as circumstances demanded ; their nature, no less than the times at which they might be claimed, were fluctuating and uncertain. Although so far from retarding these tendencies of the third century, Diocletian and his successors accelerated the predominance of the State over the individual ; under the stable centralized government which they established the obligations of their subjects were more clearly defined and stereotyped. The population were organized according to their professions in classes, membership of which was hereditary and compulsory, and particular duties were assigned to each. State-service, which had been demanded spasmodically and in irregular forms, became normal and prescribed. If this

277

system spelled the death of personal freedom, the subjects of the Empire had at least the negative consolation that the terms of their slavery were, in theory at least, specifically defined.

§ 2. REFORM OF THE COINAGE

To give an air of artificial prosperity, many of the Emperors of the third century had favoured a policy of currency inflation, which culminated in Gallienus' issue of billon in place of pure silver. In consequence prices soared to fabulous heights, and in default of a reliable basis of tariffs, trade and commerce were undermined. Aurelian's attempts to check the falling value of money had been only a partial success. A currency resting on a billon coinage could not be expected to restore confidence to the world of business, or appreciably to stem the upward tendency of prices. The great merit of Diocletian's reform, which set the model for his successors, was that he re-established a pure coinage of reliable denominations in both gold and silver. In place of the old *aureus* he struck a new gold coin equivalent to 1/60th of the gold pound, and a new silver coin, probably called *argenteus*, which corresponded in everything but name to the Neronian *denarius*. On the other hand, for the provision of small money he continued the practice of his predecessors and struck white-coated bronze coins in three denominations. The heaviest of these, commonly called the *follis*, was the well-known *Genio populi Romani* type with laureate head of the Emperor, weighing about 150 grains ; the second was a series with a radiate head of the Emperor, each of approximately 60 grains weight, whilst the smallest coins were stamped with the laureate head and weighed about a third of the middle type. These bronze coins were tariffed in terms of gold and silver in the following scale : One gold pound =60 *aurei* = 1200 *argentei* =2400 *folles* =9600 radiate coins =24,000 smallest bronze coins =48,000 *denarii*.[1] But although Diocletian reduced Aurelian's " twenty-piece " to one-fourth of its former value,[2] his bronze coins were tariffed too high for their intrinsic worth. The business world refused to accept the values assigned to them. In consequence, prices again rose, and in A.D. 301 the Emperor issued his famous edict, which attempted in the greatest detail to fix prices above which articles must not be sold, with the most severe penalties for infringements. It is hardly necessary to say that the legislation was a failure. But if Diocletian's methods are condemned as short-sighted folly, his attempt to suppress the profiteering that is made possible by a sudden change in money values deserves a sympathetic respect.[3]

After the abdication of Diocletian the value of the *denarius* in terms of gold steadily depreciated ; the *follis* was reduced by stages to less than one-third of its original weight and its value was readjusted at a lower scale, which was, perhaps, the equivalent of Diocletian's second bronze denomination.[4] In A.D. 312, when Licinius and Constantine divided the Empire, a temporary difference occurred between the coinage of East and West. Whereas Licinius continued to issue the Diocletianic gold and silver coins, Constantine instituted a new system, which after A.D. 324 was adopted throughout the Empire.[5] His new gold coin, the *solidus*, was lighter than the *aureus* and was rated at 1/72nd of the gold pound. The place of the *argenteus* was taken by the *siliqua* (1/1728th of the gold pound), which was equal to 1/24th of the *solidus*, and a larger coin called the *miliarense* (1/1000th of the gold pound), fourteen of which went to the *solidus*. The *follis*, which contained ten *denarii*, was now scaled at 1/10th of a *siliqua*, so that the new system of tariffs was as follows : One gold pound=72 *solidi*=1728 *siliquae*=17,280 *folles*= 172,800 *denarii*.[6] As compared with the Diocletianic scale perhaps the most noticeable feature is the substitution of one silver-bronze coin for three, and the attempt to stem its further depreciation with the consequential rise in prices by scaling down its value one fifth in terms of gold.

For the establishment of this pure coinage an ample supply of precious metals was clearly necessary. This was acquired mainly by calling in and re-striking at the new value the gold coins that were still in circulation, but additional supplies of ore were derived from the Armenian mines which Diocletian's Eastern campaigns had placed at the State's disposal, and from the melting down of gold ornaments, while later the closing of the pagan temples made further stocks available. Most noticeable in the fourth century is the rise in the value of gold, and with the exception of Britain, the comparative rarity of silver coins in the Western Empire.. The reason for this scarcity of silver is not certain ; but it was probably caused partly by the export of silver to countries outside the Empire, and partly by the substitution of silver for gold on articles of luxury, which reduced the amount available for coinage.[7]

The rigid control of the coinage by the Emperors is characteristic of their general policy. All mints throughout the Empire were now imperial, and issued coins of uniform types which were distinguished by letters indicating the city, the *officina* where they were struck, and the series to which they belonged.[8] Provincial and local systems entirely ceased. Although this unification by the spread of a monotonous culture destroyed local traditions and peculiarities and was detrimental to artistic development, its practical advantages were obvious. Difficulties of the money-exchange disappeared, and ample supplies of money were rendered available without the expense of transport. The allocation of the provincial mints did not, however, correspond entirely to the system of provinces and dioceses. Spain had no mint of its own and was dependent for its supplies upon south Gaul.[9] In Africa the mint at Carthage was closed after A.D. 311 and the province had to turn to Italy for its money.[10] The most probable explanation of these two cases is to be found in the military insignificance of the districts, but this cannot be applied to two other exceptions. In A.D. 326 the mint at London was shut, and, with the exception of a short period under Magnus Maximus, Britain had in future no coinage of its own.[11] Further, the silver found in hoards in this country, but rarely in other parts of the Western Empire, suggests that Britain was scantily supplied with gold and had to use silver for its instrument of commerce, while the fact that the silver is hoarded may perhaps indicate an attempt to protect the provincial interests against the imperial government rather than a foreign invader.[12] This indifference to the prosperity of the island, which was perhaps due to the comparatively small revenue which it provided, or may have been a punishment for the usurpations of Carausius and Allectus, is illustrative of the selfish and short-sighted policy of the Emperors. Where the government required money, there it was amply provided ; where these conditions did not exist, trade was left unsupplied with its necessary medium of exchange. In short, money was regarded as an imperial implement and not as an article of commerce. This theory receives further confirmation from the treatment of Egypt. After about A.D. 324 she had hardly any gold or silver of her own, but was obliged to use silver-bronze coins for her trade.[13] Prices in consequence rose and high values were attached to almost worthless coins. Widespread misery and poverty were the sequel, which were intensified by restrictions placed by the government upon the amount of money that foreign merchants might carry with them into the country.[14] The fact that these conditions did not affect the government immediately, as the Egyptian taxes were paid in kind, is a clear illustration of the ruthless and blind selfishness with which, when no imperial interests seemed to be jeopardised, it systematically crushed the life and liberty of its subjects.

In the foreign world the Constantinian gold coinage enjoyed a high reputation. Even Persia, with its strong national bias, struck gold but seldom ; the *solidus* circulated freely, and the Roman standard was gladly accepted. This was doubtless in part due to the victories by which Roman prestige had been restored, but it also speaks well for the intrinsic value of the gold coinage.[15] Nor was the government blind to the danger of forgeries. The Theodosian Code abounds in edicts threatening severe penalties to moneyers who clipped the edges of the *solidus*, or issued bronze coins without the standard alloy of silver.[16] The supreme supervision of the mints was placed in the hands of the *comes sacrarum largitionum*, while the control of the provincial mints was entrusted to *rationales*.[17] The mint-officials (*monetarii*) formed, like other servants of the State, an exclusive caste. Their profession was hereditary, and no moneyer was permitted to resign his office unless he could find a substitute.[18] The frequent attempts at evasion of their duties suggest that the emoluments were poor, and the severe penalties for forgery indicate the illicit means by which their wages were sometimes increased.

§ 3. REFORMS IN TAXATION

(a) *Causes.* The increase in the size of the army and in the number of government officials involved an additional expenditure which the imperial revenues, steadily declining in value through the progressive depreciation of the coinage,

were entirely unable to meet. The adverse balance was
further swelled by Diocletian's building policy. Apart from
the wise restoration of damaged public property, the Emperor
gave free rein to his love of the magnificent. At Nicomedia
he built palaces for his wife and daughter, basilicas, and a
circus which was begun in A.D. 304, while the baths of the
town were renovated.[19] At Milan, the chief residence of his
colleague, the palace mentioned by the panegyrist Mamertinus
most probably belongs to this period, and the naming of the
baths after Hercules betrays the same origin.[20] Carthage, too,
received its share of glory as the legend FELIX CARTHAGO on
coins suggests.[21] But it was in Rome, partly no doubt in
compensation for its loss of political importance, that the
greatest developments took place. A fire, which broke out
in the autumn of A.D. 284 in the theatre of Pompey, had spread
to the forum and damaged both the Senate-house and the
Basilica Julia. Diocletian repaired these losses on a grand
scale. The colonnade of Pompey's theatre was restored,
temples were renovated and a new *Curia*, which still stands
to-day, was built in the Forum. Most magnificent and
extensive of all were the baths, which were erected on a site
part of which is now occupied by the church of S. Maria degli
Angeli, and dedicated in A.D. 305-6. Here was not only
abundant accommodation provided for bathers, but a library,
to which the books from Ulpian's library were transferred, was
built and the court-yards and colonnades adorned with costly
works of art.[22] In other parts of the Empire arches commemorated the successes of the Emperor, of which the most
important, both artistically and historically, was set up at
Salonica in honour of Galerius' Persian victory.[23] Lastly
at Spalato (Salona) Diocletian built an enormous palace,
resembling rather a fortress than an imperial residence,
to which he retired on his abdication. In the grounds of the
palace were vestibules, porches and court-yards, a temple
to Jupiter and a mausoleum where the body of the Emperor
was later laid to rest. The buildings were adorned with
mosaics, which, both in style and in conception, were unfamiliar in Roman art and in all probability were of Eastern
origin.[24]

(b) *Character*. It was in order to redress the adverse
balance in the budget, which the sinking value of money

combined with a rising national expenditure had produced,
that Diocletian introduced his new scheme of taxation. Its
main principle was the substitution of a tax in kind, which was
called the *annona*, in place of a tax in money. This type of
taxation was not a novelty. In pre-Diocletianic days, when
the regular taxes were insufficient, special requisitions were
made by imperial decree (*indictio*), which were called *annonae*.[25]
The reform of Diocletian thus converted what was an exceptional burden into an ordinary tax, and the *indictio* became a
regular institution, which was soon employed as a basis of
chronology, since the taxable property of the Empire was
subject to reassessment at first in cycles of five and subsequently of fifteen years.[26]

For the purpose of assessment a system called *capitatio*
was devised. All the productive land of the Empire, together
with the labour employed upon it, was divided into a number
of theoretically equal units called *capita*. *Caput* may thus
signify either an area of land or the labour expended upon it,
but for purposes of convenience it became normal to confine
the term to living objects, and to make use of another term,
iugum, to denote the real property. The assessment was thus
based on *iuga* and *capita*, and a separate tax was levied on
either class of property. These taxes do not exactly correspond to a land tax and a personal tax ; for neither were the
land units of equal acreage nor does *caput* in its more
particular use mean an individual person. The principle
which determined the size of the *iugum* was the quality of the
land for purposes of production, while similarly the *caput*
was organised on the basis of the working capacity of the
different types of labour. Thus, although there were two
taxes, they were both assessed on the one common basis of
productive value, which was represented by the standard
units of *iuga* and *capita*.[27] A few examples will illustrate how
this theory worked in practice. The land was divided into
different categories, according as it was agricultural or used
for vineyards or olive yards, and the agricultural property was
further subdivided into three classes according to the quality
of the soil. The *iuga* thus varied in size with the nature of the
land, and in the eastern half of the Empire at any rate a scale
was introduced by which a *iugum* consisted of 5 *iugera* of
vine-land, which was the equivalent of 20 *iugera* of first- or 40

iugera of second- or 60 *iugera* of third-class agricultural land, while the olive yards were similarly graded.[28] Again the same principle was employed in assessing the *capita*. While one man's labour was rated as a single *caput*, a woman's was reckoned as half that value, and animals proportionately lower.[29] Thus although, as we shall see, abuses later crept in, the principle of assessment was intended to be equitable, and the two kinds of taxation were parts of one comprehensive scheme.

Italy in common with the rest of the Empire was brought under this scheme of taxation. In the time of Diocletian the northern part of the peninsula (*regio annonaria*) paid the *annona*, and although the southern area (*regio suburbicaria*) was not till later made liable for this tax, it had to provide Rome with meat, wine, wood and lime.[30] As the scheme applied exclusively to the land, it was only landowners whose names appeared on the census, which was taken by officials called *censitores*. The collection of the taxes was in the hands of *exactores* or *susceptores*, who were drawn from the municipal senators, and while the large proprietors paid to them the tax on the *capita* of their slaves, their *coloni*, in common with free small-holders, were responsible directly to the government officials.[31]

As compared with the irregular practices of the earlier third century, it might be supposed to have been an advantage to the taxpayer to have his liabilities defined. But in practice this worked under Diocletian's successors less satisfactorily than it promised. The control of the *annona* was in the hands of the praetorian prefect, and when the amount of the yearly contribution had been fixed by imperial decree, he and his subordinates apportioned the tax among the provinces, and appointed the centres to which delivery must be made.[32] This assignment was necessarily influenced by imperial requirements, such as the movement of troops, and the burden in consequence might fall with unfair heaviness upon different districts. Further, if the amount requisitioned was insufficient, a supplementary *indictio* (*superindicta*) could be issued.[33] More serious were the disadvantages that resulted from the five years' gap between the takings of the census. If a piece of land declined in productive value in the interval, no allowance was made. *Iuga* and *capita* remained as they had been registered at the preceding census;[34] for the visits of the *inspectores*, whose function was to revise the census, were rare occurrences.[35] This fell particularly hardly upon the small farmer who did not possess sufficient land to balance his losses. In the collection of taxes, too, corruption soon sprang up, and landowners bargained with the state-officials for the commutation of their contribution into money —a practice which was at a later date recognized by law (*adaeratio*).[36] But while the rich might successfully bribe the assessors and collectors to overlook some of their liabilities, the poor man had neither the means nor influence to escape from the noose of taxation.

Under Diocletian's scheme the town-dwellers who possessed no real property received preferential treatment. This Galerius tried to abolish by decreeing in A.D. 307–8 that the system of *capitatio* should be extended to the towns and by attacking the privileged position of the City of Rome. It is probable, however, that this measure was only partially carried out, even in his own part of the Empire, while the threat to Rome was, as we have seen, the cause of Maxentius' proclamation as Emperor.[37] In A.D. 313 the exemption of the towns from *capitatio* was again officially recognized.[38]

Constantine, however, considerably increased the taxation of the Empire. His imperial expenditure (*sacrae largitiones*), which comprised as one of its largest items donatives to the army, demanded a money revenue in addition to a taxation in kind, and the improved currency made the proposition practicable. The new taxes fell upon the senatorial class and the town-inhabitants. Senators were graded in three classes and made liable for a yearly payment of 2, 4 and 8 *folles*, which was called *follis senatorius*. Its commoner title, *collatio glebalis*, shows that it was really a supplement to the *annona*, for which the senatorial landed proprietors were liable. The same tax was later in the reign imposed on the senatorial order at Constantinople.[39] In the municipal towns the local senators were already heavily burdened. In imperial taxation they were either liable for the *annona* or for the *aurum coronarium*,[40] which had become in the third century a regular tax, while contributions to their local funds were a continual drain on their pockets. The only section of the civil community

which had so far escaped from the net was the trading
and commercial class. Upon it Constantine now imposed
a tax called *auri lustralis collatio*. As the name shows, this
payment was made in gold and regularly every five years at
the beginning of a *lustrum*, a date which corresponds to the
normal time for the distribution of a donative. Trading was
interpreted in a liberal sense, and the tax was payable by
prostitutes and by farmers who brought their produce to
market in the town.[41]

§ 4. COMPULSORY SERVICE

The system of taxation introduced by Diocletian and
developed by Constantine involved the grading of the population in classes, each of which was made responsible for the
performance of specified services and obligations. The
claims of the State were everywhere paramount. Senator no
less than *colonus* had public duties imposed upon him, which
took precedence over his own private work and interests.
The principle of voluntary service, which had been characteristic of the Principate, was converted into a compulsory
system, in which the individual had only a limited choice of
professions. Just as politically personal independence was
subjected to the absolute authority of the Emperor and his
bureaucrats, so economic freedom was sacrificed to the over-
riding claims of the State. Servitude superseded liberty as
the hall-mark of Roman citizenship.

A necessary basis for the success of the Diocletianic system
was the stabilization of the different classes of taxpayers. If
the land and personal taxes were to yield a reliable revenue,
it was essential that the number of taxable units should be
maintained at a constant figure ; if the necessary services of
the State were to be efficiently provided, the supply of workers
must be regulated. For the realization of these conditions
the Emperors determined upon a policy of rigid state-
control. They attempted to put into practice the principle
that every man should continue in his present employment,
and that sons should follow their fathers' vocations. Although
promotion to a higher grade of service was not made impossible, the privilege was jealously guarded. Drastic
punishments were the fate of those who attempted to evade

their present responsibilities by seeking refuge in some other walk of life. The effect of this policy was to create a caste-system in the Empire. Municipal senators and ship-owners, farm-labourers and firemen, each belonged to an exclusive group, membership of which was hereditary. This artificial classification was no less detrimental to trade and commerce, whose prosperity is dependent upon opportunities for private initiative, than it was damping to the hopes of ambition. Life became for many subjects of the Empire a monotonous drudgery, in which the best fruits of their labour were seized by the State. The fourth century presents a picture of economic stagnation and social discontent, with the freedom of the individual increasingly curtailed by state-restrictions and his activities subjected to the scrutiny of an ubiquitous officialdom.

The Theodosian Code provides abundant illustrations of the manner in which the system of compulsory service was enforced. During the third century the government had made use of what was in origin the voluntary association of ship-owners for the transport of the food supply of the City and of the rations for the army. With the substitution of the *annona* for a money-tax an additional burden was placed on the *navicularii*, and the necessity of carrying fiscal property gratis to the exclusion, if necessary, of private cargoes made the service unprofitable and unpopular.[42] A further deterrent was the fear, when the Empire was divided among mutually antagonistic rulers, of falling into the hands of the enemy, and Maxentius, to compensate this unwillingness to serve, had forced senators to undertake a share of the responsibility On his death this measure, together with his other acts, was annulled,[43] but as early as A.D. 314 Constantine made member-ship of the body of shipowners an hereditary obligation,[44] and later in his reign exempted it from the performance of all other imperial duties.[45] Similar treatment was applied to the other *collegia*, which were concerned with the food supply of the City. Bakers and butchers were forced to remain in their guilds or to provide a substitute in the event of their wishing to retire. Any attempted evasion by alienation of their property or by obtaining promotion to higher rank was, if detected, punished by returning the culprit to his original occupation.[46]

The fate of the municipal senators was perhaps the hardest

of all to bear. Not only were they themselves liable for a tax either in kind or in money, but they were further responsible for the collection and payment of the poll tax from members of their towns and for the upkeep of the municipal services. The difficulty of finding candidates for a post, which in the earlier days had been welcomed as an honour, is shown by the new regulations introduced by Diocletian. Previous disqualifications, such as illiteracy or the stigma of a judicial condemnation, were removed. Age and physical debility could no longer be used as a means for obtaining exemption, and a decurion's previous consent for the nomination of his son was now deemed unnecessary.[47] In the reign of Constantine further legislation was passed. In A.D. 325 decurionate service was made compulsory,[48] and six years later the age limit was lowered from twenty-five to eighteen, while at the same time a device of the local senators to alleviate their personal burdens by increasing their numbers through the co-option of boys under eighteen was expressly forbidden.[49] A decurion might legally escape from his local town by gaining admission to the Roman Senate or by receiving a post in one of the imperial *officia*. Illegitimate methods of evasion, on the other hand, were punished by relegation to the *curia*, and the frequent edicts issued show how prevalent were the attempts. These were of three main kinds. A decurion might through surreptitious means obtain a military appointment or the status of a knight, or he might join the army, or seek refuge in the Church by ordination. Against all these flights from curial duties legislative measures were enacted. A rescript of A.D. 317 orders the return to their *ordo* of all decurions who have bought for themselves equestrian rank with the intent of deserting their local Senate-house.[50] In A.D. 325 it was ruled that decurions or those already nominated for their *curia* who had enlisted in the army were to be sent back to their towns, and in the following year this provision was further extended to those whose property made them eligible for the decurionate.[51] In A.D. 320 a ban was placed on decurions becoming clergymen. The church was to recruit its priests from the ranks of the *humiliores*, on the stated principle that it is the duty of the rich to shoulder the secular burdens, as it is the privilege of the poor to be maintained by the riches of the Church.[52]

The hereditary principle was further applied to military service. Sons of serving soldiers might either follow their fathers' profession or, if they refused and were over twenty-five, they were sent to the *curiae*.[53] A similar choice was offered to the sons of veterans, and those who were unfit for military duties were made decurions.[54] Despite all these regulations of Constantine the *curiae* remained desolate, and secret evasions of duty continued, till in the later fourth century " hunt the decurion " became, as it were, the sport of the imperial bureaucracy.[55]

The plight of the small farmer was no less miserable, and, like the decurion, he sought to escape from the burden of the new taxation. The class that was principally affected was that of the *coloni*. In the earlier Principate it had been the custom of large landed proprietors like Pliny to let out part of their land in short term leases to free tenants. Although the latter were in no sense permanently attached either to the soil or to their landlord, in practice they had tended to remain on the same estates, not infrequently for the reason that they had fallen into arrears with their rent. Another type of *colonus* was to be found on the imperial estates, notably in Africa, where they constituted a free peasantry paying a fixed rent to the crown. The favourable terms granted at first to them by the government had led to an affection for their plots of land, and thriving village communities had grown up.[56] The complaints, however, of the tenants of the *saltus Burunitanus* to Commodus[57] show that the imperial officials were encroaching upon the rights of the *coloni*, and in the third century there was less inclination to continue working on the domains than there had been in the second. Diocletian's system of *capitatio* must have increased this spirit of restlessness, and to prevent a depopulation of the countryside, Constantine made a definite change in the status of the *coloni*. How or when this was enacted is unknown, but by A.D. 332 the *coloni* were permanently attached to the soil.[58] The effect of this measure was to reduce them to a virtual serfdom. The *coloni* might be moved from farm to farm by their landlord, but they could not leave his estate. If they broke this rule and sought out a new master, it was the duty of the latter to return them to their original master, and he was responsible for paying the tax due for them during

19

the period in which he had employed them.[59] A *colonus* was permitted to acquire personal property, but he might not alienate it without his master's consent, while his marriage was similarly subject to the same approval.[60] Children of *coloni* were obliged to stay on the land, so that here, as in other trades and professions, the principle of compulsory hereditary service was enforced.[61] It was this limitation upon the activities of Roman citizens that gave opportunity to barbarians from outside the Empire, who were not bound by such restrictions, to rise to the higher offices of State.

The reforms of Diocletian and Constantine systematized the tendencies that had been apparent in the history of the previous century. Beneath the despotism that absorbed the military monarchy the power of the army and bureaucracy was predominant. To the maintenance of this absolutism with its hierarchy of officials and privileged soldiers, among whom the barbarian element was the most highly esteemed, the civil population in town and country alike was forced to contribute pecuniary and personal services. The dying words of Septimius Severus, " enrich the soldiers and despise the rest of the world," had received their fullest consummation. But, if the Empire in the Constantinian era enjoyed a respite from invasion and civil disturbances, a great majority of its subjects had lost their personal freedom and with it their courage and their hopes.

CHAPTER VI

CONSTANTINE AND CHRISTIANITY

§ 1. A.D. 306–324

ANY attempt to treat history as a logical process of evolution in which each age develops as a necessary sequence to that which has preceded it is confronted with the appearance from time to time of personalities which seem to have diverted the stream of civilization from its natural course. Constantine is one of these personalities, which cannot be simply explained as the outcome of the past and which do not easily harmonize with their contemporary environment. However much his autocratic powers and administrative reforms may be represented as the culmination of the experience of the third century, no such rationalization will explain his belief in the power of Christianity as a stabilizing force for the future of the Empire. The Christians were but a small minority in the imperial population, who had been driven by persecution out of the public services of the State. The unity of the Empire, so thought many of Constantine's contemporaries, could only be safeguarded by the suppression and, if possible, the elimination of the noxious creed. Yet it is on this derided and detested faith that Constantine decided to build the future destiny of Rome, and his determination transformed the history of the world. The sincerity of his motives and the genuineness of his conversion have, as is natural with such an intractable personality, been upheld and condemned with almost equal sympathy and aversion. Prejudices have run so high that it is at times difficult to believe that it is the same historical figure who is the subject of the portrait. It will, therefore, be best to assemble the relevant facts, to some of which reference has already been made in the narrative chapters, and to use them as the basis of our interpretation.[1]

In A.D. 305 Constantius succeeded Maximian as the second holder of the rank of Augustus in the newly founded Herculian dynasty. After his death in the following year his soldiers proclaimed his son Constantine Emperor, and, although the choice of the army did not receive Galerius' official recognition, his status was recognized in 307 by Maximian, who gave him his daughter Fausta in marriage. For the first four years of his reign Constantine was thus the representative of the dynasty which was under the protective guardianship of Hercules. On the coins of the period it is Hercules who is honoured as CONSERVATOR and COMES, and in a panegyric delivered in A.D. 307 hopes are expressed for the perpetuity of the dynasty in the descendants of Maximian and Constantine, " *Imperatores semper Herculii.*"[2] This association of Constantine with the Herculian religion was, however, terminated in A.D. 310 by the death of Maximian, with the subsequent condemnation of his acts and memory. To substantiate his claims to Empire, Constantine caused the story to be circulated that he was the direct descendant, through his father, of Claudius Gothicus. Thus the second Flavian dynasty succeeded the Herculian, and the Unconquered Sun became the Emperor's tutelary deity. This Sun-worship, which was indigenous in Illyricum, the native country of Claudius, was also widespread in Gaul, where it took the form of the cult of Apollo, and there is some reason to think that Constantius despite his official connection with Hercules was in his private life a solar monotheist.[3] If so, it may be assumed that Constantine, notwithstanding his sojourn at the courts of Diocletian and Galerius, was familiar with the creed. His official adoption of it for dynastic purposes was doubtless consonant with his own personal belief, and it also met with widespread approval from the population of Gaul. At the birthday celebrations of the city of Trier in A.D. 310 Apollo is the panegyrist's theme. He represents Constantine as repairing to Apollo's temple to find his own God (" *Apollo tuus* ");[4] indeed the resemblance between Constantine and his patron so impresses the orator that he speaks of the temple as the abode of the Emperor's *numen* (" *numinis tui sedes* "[5]). Similarly on the coinage issued from Constantine's mints SOL INVICTUS COMES is the common legend, and this thought is echoed in a panegyric of A.D. 311, in which the speaker hails Apollo as the inseparable companion of the Emperor ("*Ille quasi maiestatis tuae comes et socius* "[6]).

While Constantine was thus openly proclaiming his belief in a solar religion, Galerius, the arch-instigator of the persecution of the Christians, died after a fruitless recantation of his policy of oppression. The fate of the enemy of the Christian religion cannot fail to have made a deep impression upon the mind of Constantine and to have served to accentuate the antithetical fortunes of the Eastern and Western Empire, in the former of which the edicts of Diocletian had been rigorously enforced, and in the latter greatly mitigated by the clemency of Constantius. These psychological experiences may well have led him to the opinion that the Christian God was the most powerful supernatural agent on the earth, especially as a belief in the intervention of the divine in mundane affairs was a current superstition of the age. At what time or at what place he finally became convinced that under the banner of Christ he would conquer Maxentius is unknown. The vision of the Cross in the sky, of which Eusebius states he had heard from Constantine himself, is not dated by the historian,[7] although a late legendary account places it at Arles. Lactantius, on the other hand, knows nothing of the vision, but records that when his army was before the walls of Rome, Constantine was warned in a dream to inscribe the Christian monogram on his soldiers' shields.[8] Whether we accept or reject either or both of these stories, practical considerations make it at least probable that the conviction that Christ would give him the victory must have been firmly rooted in Constantine's mind before he advanced from Northern Italy upon Rome, and perhaps even before he crossed the Alps. How else are we to explain his daring and apparently hopeless enterprise?

The victory at the Milvian Bridge confirmed Constantine's conversion, and Christians and pagans alike commemorated the part which he believed the supernatural had played in the battle. In Rome, according to Eusebius, a statue of the Emperor was erected bearing the cross in his hand,[9] and on the triumphal arch in the Forum the overthrow of Maxentius is stated to have been achieved partly by Constantine's own greatness of mind, partly *instinctu divinitatis*, words which might be interpreted in different senses by Christian and pagan readers.[10] At Trier coins were issued, on the obverse of which Constantine is portrayed wearing a helmet of the same type as that to which the Christian monogram was later added, while on the reverse in place of *Mars Conservator* is depicted a colourless scene with a commonplace expression of loyalty.[11] In a speech delivered at the same time and place the panegyrist speaks of the unknown " *deus* " who gave Constantine courage for the war, and the " *mens divina* " which promised him victory. The orator is a heathen, but a heathen, as Seeck has aptly said,[12] " who knew very well what Constantine liked to have said about him."

Constantine himself was not slow to shew his gratitude to the Christian God. In his capacity of senior Augustus he sent instructions to Maximinus to stop the Christian persecution,[13] wrote to Anullinus, the proconsul in Africa, to restore to the Catholic Church the property which had been confiscated from it,[14] and informed Caecilianus, the Catholic bishop of Carthage, that he had given orders for the provision of money to be distributed among African Catholics.[15] A little later he gave further instructions to Anullinus that Catholic clergy were to be exempted from public liturgies.[16] These measures indicate two things, first Constantine's belief that the maintenance and proper observance of Christian worship was closely bound up with the welfare of the Empire, and secondly his determination to secure an united Church by supporting the Orthodox party in Africa in their struggle with Donatism, which he condemns as " a vain and bastard delusion." In February, A.D. 313, Constantine met his colleague Licinius at Milan, and the text of a rescript, probably similar to those which had already been sent to the governors of the Western provinces, was drafted, which Licinius should put into effect on his return to the East. This rescript, which is commonly called the Edict of Milan, granted freedom of worship to all subjects of the Empire, and recognized the Christian churches as legal corporations. Thus a policy of religious toleration was proclaimed, by which Christians and pagans alike were permitted the unhampered enjoyment of their individual creeds.[17]

During the next few years Constantine was engaged in attempts to end the Donatist schism in Africa, which had arisen on the question of the validity of the ordination of Caecilian, bishop of Carthage, and his letters throw an interesting light upon his attitude towards the Church. The exclusion of the Donatists from the benefactions accorded to the Catholic Church led them to appeal to the Emperor to appoint judges from Gaul to settle the dispute. The latter complied with the request, chose three bishops from Gaul and wrote to the Pope and a certain Marcus, asking them in conjunction with their Gallic colleagues to hear the evidence of the ten Donatist and ten Orthodox representatives from Africa, and to pronounce judgement, adding that it pained him to think of schism among the bishops and of some of his subjects turning aside to vain superstitions, and assuring the Pope of his deep respect for the lawfully constituted authority of the Church. This tribunal, which Constantine had set up, was converted by the Pope into a council by the addition of fourteen Italian bishops, and judgement was given in favour of the Catholic bishop Caecilian.[18] The Donatists, however, refused to accept this verdict, and Constantine determined to refer the issue to a more representative assembly of bishops, who were to assemble at Arles. The motives which induced him to take this course are clearly set out in a letter to the vicar of Africa. Constantine is afraid of the effects that the schism will have upon the outside world, and also of the wrath that God may mete out upon himself, if he fails to remove dissensions inside His Holy Church.[19] In other words Constantine is already interested in the missionary activities of the Church among the pagans —later he used to call himself the bishop of those outside the Church—and secondly he believes that the unity of the Church is his own especial charge from God. The Council of Arles confirmed the findings of the Pope ; but the Donatists again protested and asked the Emperor to try the case himself. In a remarkable letter written to the bishops before they returned to their sees, Constantine not only congratulates them on their findings, but he refers to the blessings which God has bestowed upon himself, " his servant," in showing him the errors of his own past life and guiding him into the way of truth—a clear testimony to his own conversion. With regard to the Donatists, who have rejected the judgement of God as delivered by His appointed representatives, and have appealed to him " who himself awaits the judgement of Christ," Constantine says that he has given instructions that they shall be brought to his Court in order " that they may behold something worse than death," and may be prevented from disseminating doctrines that may call down the wrath of God. The motive is once again the fear of heavenly vengeance.[20]

After a variety of attempts to end the schism, including a proposed personal visit to Africa in which he promises to " destroy and scatter those that do not worship the Supreme God with fitting reverence," Constantine finally tried the case himself in November, A.D. 316, and pronounced a verdict in favour of Caecilian. Force was now employed to stamp out the schism. The Donatist churches were handed over to the imperial treasury, and a military repression of the schismatics was begun. These efforts were, however, unavailing, and four years later, perhaps in fear of acquiring the reputation of a persecutor, Constantine gave up the attempt to restore unity to the African Church. The Donatist exiles were recalled and their fate was left to the tribunal of God.[21]

The years A.D. 320–3 saw extensive legislation in favour of the Church. The bishops were granted judicial powers equipollent with those of civil judges in cases which were brought by the mutual consent of the litigants to their courts.[22] Citizens were permitted to bequeath their property to the Church, and manumissions of slaves in Church were legalized.[23] Penalties against celibacy were rescinded,[24] and Christians were exempted from taking part in sacrifices at the pagan festivals.[25] On the other hand, consistently with the policy enunciated at Milan, Constantine allowed the continuance of the old religious institutions with their priestly offices, and himself retained the title of *pontifex maximus*. While the private consultation of the *haruspices* was forbidden, their public activities were still permitted, and in the event of a thunderbolt striking the palace or any public building enquiry of the meaning of the portent from the *haruspices* is actually ordained—a notable indication of the Emperor's superstitious fears.[26] Lastly the coinage of the period provides apparently conflicting evidence with regard to Constantine's religious belief. Whereas a series of coins issued from Siscia with the helmeted head of the

Emperor inscribed with the Christian monogram is a clear testimony to his conversion, the persistence of the solar legend on others would seem to suggest that he had not yet discarded the tutelary deity of the Flavian dynasty.[27] This apparent inconsistency, however, is, as we shall see, not insoluble or necessarily incompatible with a profession of Christianity.

§ 2.   A.D. 324–37

After the death of Licinius and the abolition of his acts, Constantine issued two edicts which have been preserved by Eusebius and may be accepted as authentic. In the first, personal and property rights were restored to those Christians who had suffered under the persecution—a comprehensive measure of reparation : the second announces the Emperor's policy towards paganism. The same toleration is accorded to the old religions as had been promised at Milan ; " let no one molest another ; let each hold to that which his soul desires " writes Constantine, but he adds significantly that the wise will do well to be persuaded that purity and holiness can only be obtained by submission to the Holy Laws of God.[28] Religious freedom is still guaranteed, but the concession is coloured with a contempt for the continued resistance to the claims of the Church. Constantine had now no longer an imperial rival to fear, and he was beginning to prepare for a frontal attack upon paganism, but first he was faced with another schism inside the Church.

The Arian controversy, which arose over the nature of the divinity of Christ, had, as we saw in an earlier chapter, divided the Eastern Church into two parties. The Orthodox were led by Bishop Alexander of Alexandria, the heretics by Arius, who was supported by Eusebius of Caesarea and Eusebius of Nicomedia. The latter party had influence at Licinius' court and had attempted to secure the reinstatement of Arius. This move was countered by Alexander, and Licinius in disgust at the flouting of his authority had forbidden the summoning of any further synods. When Constantine became sole Emperor the Eastern Church was still torn by the schism. His first attempt to heal the dissension was a letter addressed to Alexander and Arius, his presbyter, which his counsellor Hosius, Bishop of Cordova, was

commissioned to deliver. In this document Constantine ex-
horts the disputants to put an end to their battle of words on
abstruse points of theology, which should have been reserved
for a philosophic discussion and not rashly communicated to
the ears of the masses, and to come to an agreement on the
fundamental beliefs of the Christian religion, and offers
himself as a mediator in the quarrel.[29] To the Emperor it is
the unity of the Church that is of primary importance, and
all else must be sacrificed to that end. He has no patience
for what he regards as philosophical quibblings, and completely fails to realize that what was dividing the Church of
the East was not an abstruse point of theology, but a fundamental article of faith. Hosius' mission was a failure, and a
meeting of bishops held at Antioch condemned Arius and
arranged for a more representative council to meet at Ancyra
to formulate the creed of the Eastern Church. Marcellus, the
bishop of Ancyra, was an extreme supporter of Alexander,
and the intention of the bishops in holding their council in
his see was doubtless to settle their differences without the
intervention of Constantine. This move was countered by
the Emperor, who in his passion for unity did not wish either
of the extreme factions to triumph, by a proposal to make
the council œcumenical in character, and then by transferring
its meeting to Nicaea, where its deliberations could be
controlled by his personal presidency.[30]

The bishops with their attendant priests and deacons
travelled at public expense to Nicaea, where they were
received and entertained at a state banquet by the Emperor.
The prelates were of widely different degrees of education;
the most learned was undoubtedly Eusebius of Caesarea, while
others like Alexander, who brought his deacon Athanasius
with him, and Marcellus were familiar with the main
subject that was to be discussed. But a great number,
including the confessors who had suffered for their faith, were
famed rather for their virtues than for their learning. For
many who had been accustomed to a long and severe
persecution, this meeting with the Head of the Roman
State must have been a solemn and awe-inspiring occasion.[31]
After a lengthy discussion the representatives of the two
parties in the Arian dispute agreed with two dissentients
to accept the solution that was probably suggested by

Constantine himself, the *homo-ousion* or consubstantiality of the Son and the Father which was inserted in the Creed.[32] The Emperor was deeply gratified by his successful efforts to restore unity to the Church, and it was not long (doubtless assisted by the ambiguity of the term *homo-ousios*) before Arius himself surrendered to his will. At the resumed session of the Council of Nicaea in A.D. 327, Constantine was able to announce the conversion of Arius, and the bishops who had been excommunicated were received back into the Orthodox Communion.[33] But the Emperor's troubles were not yet past. Alexander and his successor Athanasius showed no readiness to pardon Arius, and a bitter and degrading feud began between the Eusebian party, which championed the cause of compromise and unity, and Athanasius. In A.D. 335 Constantine decided to bring the dispute to an issue. He ordered the bishops to assemble at Tyre and commanded Athanasius, who had refused to attend an earlier council at Caesarea, to appear before it. The latter reluctantly obeyed, but in face of the Eusebian opposition fled to Constantinople and appealed to the Emperor. The bishops were summoned to explain their conduct to " the servant of God," but at the subsequent meeting Athanasius exasperated Constantine by his uncharitable obstinacy, and was banished to Gaul.[34] Yet no successor was appointed to the see of Alexandria. Constantine was ready to wait for the submission of Athanasius ; that alone was lacking to make his labours for Church unity a triumphant success. At the time of the Emperor's death Athanasius was still an exile.

Meanwhile, there were other indications of Constantine's propagandist zeal. In A.D. 325 the solar legend disappeared from the imperial coinage and the *labarum* or Christian monogram took its place, while a type represented the Emperor and his sons in an attitude of prayer with their eyes turned upwards to heaven.[35] In the imperial nomenclature " Victorious " was substituted for " Unconquered," the common attribute of the Sun-God.[36] Although there was no general suppression of pagan temples, the erection of the statues of idols in them was forbidden. The town of Hispellum, for example, was permitted to have a temple dedicated to the " gens Flavia," but the customary pagan ceremonials were rigorously curtailed.[37] In other parts of the Empire

certain temples were closed, the temple of Asclepius at Aegae
for instance, and the shrine of Aphrodite at Aphaca in
Phoenicia, but for moral rather than religious reasons.[38]
While no public money might be used for the restoration
of pagan altars and shrines, Christian churches on
a magnificent scale were erected in different parts of the
Empire. Soon after Constantine's conversion the episcopal
residence in Rome was transferred to the old house of the
Laterani on the Caelian Hill, and adjoining this *domus
ecclesiae* a basilica was built; another, whose massive ruins
still survive, was erected on a site adjacent to the Forum,
and others were built over the tombs of SS. Peter, Paul and
Laurence.[39] In 326 Helena set out on a visit to the Holy
Land, and churches were built at sites connected with the
life of Jesus, at Bethlehem, Golgotha and the Mount of
Olives. On her return she caused a basilica to be erected at
the Sessorium, where she placed, tradition says, the relics
of the Sacred Cross which she had found in Palestine.[40]
But most important of all was the founding of Constantinople,
which was to serve as the Christian capital of the Empire.
Work was begun as early as A.D. 324, and the new city was
dedicated on May 11th, A.D. 330. The choice of the site, if
dictated primarily by strategical considerations, served also
to emphasize the fact that it was from the East that
Christianity had begun its march of conquest and in the East
made its most numerous converts, for whom the new capital
now symbolised their triumphant emancipation from persecution. In the new city, which was four times as large as
old Byzantium, a new forum was constructed, the Hippodrome
begun by Septimius Severus was completed, an official
residence built for the Senate, and most magnificent of all,
a palace for the Emperor himself, over the chief entrance to
which Constantine and his four sons were depicted with the
serpent beneath their feet and the cross above their heads.
Churches were built in different parts of the capital, of which
the most notable were those dedicated to SS. Irene and Sophia,
and the Church of the Twelve Apostles, where, in the midst
of the representative tombs, the sarcophagus of Constantine
was later placed. But the adornment of the City was not
confined to Christian works of art. Pagan statues were
brought from different parts of the Empire. The Tripod

and the statue of Apollo were transported from Delphi, a special place of honour was reserved for the Dioscuri and a temple was built for the Roman Tyche. Constantinople thus presented a curious contrast of a dying pagan religion side by side with a rising Christianity.[41] The significance of this mixed testimony is difficult. The theory that the pagan temples were erected by the municipal authorities of old Byzantium, who had not sought or required the imperial sanction, is unconvincing.[42] More probably most, if not all, of the heathen works of art were intended as a mere beautification of the city, and this view acquires further probability, if Eusebius is right in saying that Constantine forbade all pagan ceremonials.[43] On the other hand, the temple to the Roman Tyche may be an illustration of Constantine's superstition, and symbolise his desire to make his new capital a second Rome, while the great statue of Helios transformed so as to represent Constantine raises once again the problem, to which we shall return, of the relation of the Emperor's Christianity to the solar religion of his dynasty.

Lastly, a word must be said about Constantine's self-appointed office of " bishop of those outside the Church." In this category he included both heretics and pagans, and two letters, whose authenticity has recently been rendered probable, if not certain, illustrate his attitude.[44] The first, which is addressed to all heretics, orders the confiscation of their churches and forbids any assembling of themselves. It is propaganda ; the threats are used in order to induce the heterodox to return to the Holy Catholic Church, and suit the lips of the bishop of those outside its fold. The second letter is the more interesting. It is addressed to Sapor, king of the Persians, and, after narrating the wonders which Christianity has wrought in the Roman Empire, entrusts the large body of Christians living within the Persian Empire to the care of its monarch, who is enjoined " to love them as befits his love of man." The tone of the letter is strange and perhaps improbable, but it is paralleled in other letters of the Emperor whose authenticity is not in question, and receives some further confirmation in the subsequent appeal of the Christians in Armenia to Constantine when Sapor invaded their country. It was while preparing for a campaign against Persia that Constantine died and on his death-bed

received the Sacrament of Baptism.[45] Thus at the very
end of his life he became a full member of the Church on
whose behalf he had spent so many years of labour.

§ 3. SUMMARY

An attempt may now be made to estimate the nature of
Constantine's religion and the goal towards which his policy
was directed. The battle of the Milvian Bridge was the
turning-point in his career. He had advanced upon Rome
with the convinced belief that the Christian God would give
him the victory, and the battle had proved the justification
of his confidence. Partly in gratitude for his success, but
more essentially with a sincere persuasion that the power of
Christ, which had been demonstrated in war, would be no
less predominant in peace, he proceeded to give effect to his
faith. The Church was the means by which the supernatural
force could be made of greatest avail in the Empire, and
Constantine determined, as his legislation shows, that Church
and State should work in close co-operation. A further
condition of success was that the Church should not be
weakened by schismatic dissensions, and, in his attempts to
end the Donatist and Arian disputes, this goal of unity,
although not always realized, was consistently pursued and
never lost sight of by the Emperor. Political circumstances,
however, made it impracticable for Constantine to favour
the Christian Church to the exclusion of all other creeds.
The aristocracy, the government officials and the army were
predominantly pagan, and Licinius did not share his
colleague's convictions. Consequently Constantine's policy is
gradual but at the same time progressive. At Milan a
programme of religious toleration for all creeds was agreed
upon, but taken in conjunction with other contemporary
measures it was a toleration with a marked bias in favour
of Christianity. After the death of Licinius this tolerant
attitude was still maintained, but Constantine now felt
himself free to employ a threatening propaganda against
those who withstood the claims of his religion. This was
the prelude to the further suppression of pagan ceremonies,
and Constantinople was the triumphant expression of the
Emperor's matured policy.

Constantine's belief in Christ was essentially a conviction of His power in the world. That, and not the ethical or the doctrinal teaching of Christianity, of which till his death he had no clear understanding, was the reason for his faith. But his conversion was none the less real. Attempts to paint Constantine as a calculating politician, who was resolved to exploit in his own interest the organization which gave the Church its corporate strength, and whose toleration for all creeds was but a means for the recognition of his own autocracy, find little or no support in the documents contemporary with his reign.[46] At the time of his conversion it was anything but political prudence to identify himself with a body of people which formed a small minority of the population of the Empire, which was disinterested in politics, and whose solid support for his cause was in any case questionable. Nor was Constantine " essentially unreligious." As Boissier and Lot have well said, free-thinkers were comparatively rare in the fourth century.[47] On the contrary, Constantine was a man who believed that he had a definite mission in the world. As the " servant of God," as he is so fond of calling himself, he was convinced that he had been entrusted with a charge by his God, and, even although the true meaning of Christianity remained for him a closed book, that was his misfortune, but in no way detracts from the sincerity with which he sought to realize his conception of the Christian religion.

But if Constantine was the Christian that we have represented, what is to be made of his apparent continued attachment to the religion of the Sun, which he had professed before his conversion, and in particular what explanation is to be given of the solar legend on coins of the years A.D. 312–24, and the colossal statue to the Emperor at Constantinople with the inscription : " Κωνσταντίνῳ λάμποντι Ἡλίου δίκην " ? The answer of one group of historians is to deny Constantine's Christianity and to attribute to him a profession of religious syncretism.[48] But if this is true, why did Constantine concern himself so closely with the promotion of unity inside the Christian Church ? If his ideal was an universal religion which should include particularist creeds, it must surely have been a matter of indifference to him whether there were one or several Christian churches. But, on the contrary, his whole policy was directed towards the establishment of a single Catholic Church. A more satisfactory solution is to be found along the lines recently advocated by Professor Baynes.[49] The retention of the solar legend on the coinage had a constitutional significance. It was to serve as evidence of the source from which Constantine claimed to derive his imperial authority, to establish in the face of any possible challenge his title to rule as the descendant of Claudius II. It is to be observed that this type of coin was struck *only* during Licinius' life-time and ceased after his death, when the immediate danger to Constantine's rule had been averted. But in addition to dynastic considerations there was probably another reason for Constantine's continued reverence for the religion of the Sun. His own conversion to Christianity had been hastened, if not accomplished, by the vision of the cross, which, as he affirmed to Eusebius and therefore believed himself, he had seen athwart the sun in the heavens. Reflecting on those matters he may have come to the conclusion that Christ was the true manifestation of God, whom in his unregenerate days he had worshipped as the Sun. Doubtless it was this revelation that he had in mind when in his letter to the bishops assembled at Arles he wrote that there were in him at the first things which appeared far removed from the truth. If so, then Constantine may have hoped that the religion of the Sun might serve for others besides himself as a bridge between paganism and Christianity. Further, the solar religion had many affinities with Christianity, and the forms of its worship were not calculated to give offence to the Christians. The Church had long thought of Christ as the Light of the World, as the Sun of Righteousness rising with healing in His wings. The day of the Sun was the day of the Resurrection when Christ, like the Unconquered Sun, had risen victorious over death and dissipated the clouds of darkness. The colossal statue of Constantine in Constantinople with its radiate crown facing the rising sun might thus be reverenced by both pagan and Christian. To the former the Emperor would appear shining in the splendour of the visible Sun, to the latter as reflecting the glory of the God whose servant he believed himself to be.[50]

CHAPTER VII

THE LAST YEARS OF CONSTANTINE

§ 1. COURT AFFAIRS

IN A.D. 326 Constantine went to Rome to be present at
the celebrations commemorating the twentieth year of
his reign, and the tenth anniversary of the elevation of
his sons Crispus and Constantine to the rank of Caesar.[1]
But the happy event was marred by a domestic tragedy.
Crispus, the elder of the two Caesars, since his naval victory
over Abantus, stood high in his father's esteem and enjoyed
a general popularity. This aroused the jealousy of the
Empress Fausta, who saw in her stepson an obstacle to her
own sons' future careers. Accordingly she determined upon
his removal, and chose for her method of encompassing his
ruin a charge of attempted adultery with herself, which was
tantamount to an indictment for high treason. The young
Caesar, who was on his way from the East to Gaul, was
arrested, imprisoned in the Adriatic fortress of Pola and put
to death.[2] But Fausta's enjoyment of her triumph was
brief. On the information, it is said, of Helena she was found
guilty of adultery with a slave and condemned, in accordance
with a law passed some three months earlier, to die in a bath
of boiling water.[3] Through the absence of trustworthy
evidence it is difficult to disentangle the truth from this web
of jealousy, passion and hatred. The punishment meted
out upon Fausta, if she was guilty, was, if taken in isolation,
legally no less admissible than the execution of Crispus.
But even if the latter was innocent, which the absence of any
attempt to reinstate his character makes by no means
certain, and Constantine was outwitted by the machinations
of a wife who inherited much of her father's meddlesome
ambition, it is difficult to believe that in permitting a capital
charge to be brought against his wife, the Emperor was

acting only from a strict regard for the laws of the State and the probity of its citizens and not rather using that profession as a means for vengeance. The pagan writers, of course, rejoiced over these domestic tragedies, and Zosimus narrates how Constantine after vainly seeking expiation for his guilt from the pagan priests was regenerated by Christian baptism.[4] This story and the dating of his conversion is unhistorical, but the testimony of the writer may be so far accepted as an indication of the moral stigma which Constantine felt hanging over himself. It was perhaps to quieten his conscience that he devoted the property of Fausta to the enrichment of the Church, and Helena's journey to the East may not unreasonably be regarded as a penitential pilgrimage.

In the spring of A.D. 330 Constantine established his *consistorium* at Constantinople, and proceeded in every way possible to make conditions in the new capital correspond to those at Rome. By the grant of *ius Italicum* the city was freed from paying the old provincial tribute, and grants of free corn, which was transported from Egypt, were made to the commons.[5] A Senate, composed mainly of decurions who to the detriment of their own towns had been encouraged by special privileges to settle at Constantinople, was set up on the model of that at Rome, with the exception that its members ranked lower in the scale of dignity than their Western counterparts.[6] The place of the city-prefect at Rome was taken by a proconsul,[7] and an obligation, which remained in force till A.D. 438, to build and own houses in the city, was placed upon the wealthier tenants of the crown lands in Asia Minor and Pontus, who received free bread in compensation.[8] The population was thus largely Greek-speaking, and the attempt of Constantine, which is discernible in the coinage, to give it a Latin character, made only a superficial impression.[9]

§ 2. FOREIGN AFFAIRS

In the late summer of A.D. 328 Constantine took up his residence at Trier for the purpose of supervising the military operations against the Alamanni. Under the nominal command of young Constantine the campaign resulted in a

decisive victory.[10] For three years peace prevailed on the
Rhenish and Danubian frontiers, but in A.D. 332 the Sarmatae
appealed for help against a threatening invasion of the
Goths. Their request was granted, and Constantine II was
sent from Gaul to assume command, while his brother
Constantius, who had been raised in A.D. 324 to the rank of
Caesar, succeeded him. The Roman army crossed the
Danube and inflicted such a crushing defeat upon the Goths
that they capitulated and gave hostages, which included
the son of their king Araric. A treaty was arranged by the
terms of which the Goths, in return for a Roman subsidy of
money and corn, undertook to defend the frontier and provide
auxiliaries for the Roman army.[11] Some two years later
the leading tribe of the Sarmatians, the Argaragantes, broke
faith with Rome, but the necessity of Roman intervention
was averted by internal trouble in Sarmatia. The dependants
of the Argaragantes, the Limogantes, who had been armed to
assist in repelling the Gothic danger, rose against their masters.
Their rebellion was a complete success and, while some of the
Argaragantes retreated northwards, as many as 300,000 with
their wives and children surrendered to Constantine. The
Emperor enlisted some of them in the army and gave land
to others to settle on in the depopulated areas of the Balkan
Peninsula and in Italy. These measures, if they accelerated
the barbarization of the Empire, gave security for a generation
from invasions across the Danubian frontier (A.D. 334).[12]

In A.D. 335 an attempted usurpation of imperial power
occurred in Cyprus. A certain Calocaerus, who commanded
the camel corps, had himself proclaimed Augustus. The
circumstances which encouraged this futile enterprise are
unknown, and the rebel was quickly overcome and put to
death under torture by Constantine's nephew Delmatius,
who held the post of *magister militum*.[13] As a reward for his
services the latter was raised to the rank of Caesar, an honour
which he shared with Constantine's three sons, the youngest of
whom, Constans, had been born in A.D. 323 and created Caesar
ten years later.[14] The usurpation seems, however, despite
its short duration, to have aroused in the Emperor an apprehension of further threats to his dynasty, and young Licinius,
who had been living in seclusion in Africa, was regarded as a
possible danger. Constantine determined to remove him and

chose a method which was unnecessarily cruel and vindictive. Licinius, who was the bastard son of a slave-woman, was reduced to his mother's servile status, and then arrested as a runaway slave, fettered and finally put to death at Carthage (A.D. 336).[15]

. Meanwhile the bonds of friendship between Rome and Persia were becoming weaker. After a period of internecine strife Sapor II had succeeded in A.D. 310 to the throne of the Sassanids. As soon as he felt himself securely established he began to lay his plans for the recovery of the provinces that had been ceded to Rome after the victory of Galerius. By A.D. 333 his ambitions had become known to Constantine, and Constantius was sent from Gaul to assume command in the East.[16] In the next year hostilities broke out. Through the intrigues of Waras, Persian satrap of Atrpatakan, Tiran, king of Armenia, was treacherously seized and carried off to the Persian Court where his eyes were put out. To avenge this crime the feudal nobility of Armenia called a national assembly and despatched two ambassadors to solicit Roman aid. In their absence Sapor marched into Armenia and took possession of the country, forcing the Armenian nobles to seek refuge inside the Roman Empire. The peace of A.D. 297 was thus formally broken, and Constantine, who was anxious, as we saw in the last chapter, not to sacrifice a stronghold of Christianity, decided to intervene. Rejecting as a possible solution the re-establishment of the Arsacid dynasty, he nominated his nephew Hannibalianus, who was married to his eldest daughter Constantia, king of Armenia. The latter on his appointment marched to Oscha in the canton of Basan, surprised and routed the Persians and took formal possession of the land belonging to the Armenian satraps (A.D. 336).[17] The Roman Empire was thus divided into five military spheres under the control of the Emperor's three sons and two nephews. Constantine II ruled Gaul, Spain and Britain, Constantius the Asiatic provinces and Egypt, and Constans Italy and Africa together with the Pannonian and Dacian dioceses. Delmatius received most of the Balkan Peninsula, while Armenia, Pontus and Cappadocia were assigned to Hannibalianus. But despite this system of territorial commands the administration remained under the supreme and sole control of Constantine himself.

In A.D. 337, while preparing to drive home the successes won by Hannibalianus against the Persians, who had sent a fruitless embassy demanding the evacuation of Armenia, Constantine fell ill and died at Nicomedia on the Feast of Pentecost, May 22nd.[18] On his death-bed he received the Sacrament of Baptism, and was thus at the last received into the Church, which he had enriched with his munificence and in which he had sought to realize his ideal of a united Catholic Christendom.[19]

During the twenty-one years of his reign Constantine enhanced the military glory of Rome and vindicated her prestige. The frontiers were secured and the provinces safeguarded from civil war and foreign invasion. Justly is he celebrated as one of the world's great generals. But although peace was maintained, most of the subjects of the Empire were neither prosperous nor happy. The evils of the third century were increased rather than diminished. The bureaucracy grew in power and also in corruption through the choice of imperial favourites for posts of responsibility.[20] The army, more than doubled in strength and predominantly barbarian in character, continued the privileged instrument of autocracy. Besides these legacies of the past there emerged a new society, the Church, upon which the Emperor lavished the wealth of the State and bestowed special concessions. To support this gigantic machine of Empire and the extravagances of its ruler, the civil population with few exceptions was ground down by oppressive taxation and a system of compulsory service. Local prosperity was undermined and personal liberty destroyed. Yet despite an improvident statesmanship, and a character in which the Christian virtues were blended with the current vices of the age, Constantine has left a permanent influence upon the history of the world. By his realization of the power in Christianity to become an instrument of civilization, and by the unrelaxing energy with which he sought to realize his ideal of a single and united Catholic Church that should work in harmonious co-operation with the State, the Emperor merits his familiar title of " The Great." It was not unfitting that " the servant of God " should be laid to rest in the Church of the Twelve Apostles.

ABBREVIATIONS

CIL	=*Corpus Inscriptionum Latinarum.*
CIG	=*Corpus Inscriptionum Graecarum.*
IG	=*Inscriptiones Graecae.*
IGRR	=*Inscriptiones Graecae ad res Romanas pertinentes.*
A.E.	=*Année Epigraphique.*
Eph. Ep.	=*Ephemeris Epigraphica.*
Dess. ILS	=Dessau, *Inscriptiones Latinae Selectae.*
FHG	=*Fragmenta Historicorum Graecorum* (Müller).
BGU	=*Aegyptische Urkunden aus den Museen zu Berlin.*
Pap. Ox.	=*The Oxyrhynchus Papyri.*
P. Giess.	=*Griechische Papyri im Museum des Oberhessischen Geschichtsvereins zu Giessen.*
P. Gen.	=*Les Papyrus de Genève.*
PSI	=*Publicazioni della Società Italiana per la ricerca dei Papyri greci e latini in Egitto.*
Wilcken	=Mitteis und Wilcken, *Grundzüge und Chrestomathie der Papyruskunde.*
Cohen	=*Médailles Impériales* (2nd edition).
CBM	=*Catalogue of coins in the British Museum.*
M and S	=Mattingly and Sydenham, *Roman Imperial Coinage.*
Cl. Q.	=*Classical Quarterly.*
EHR	=*English Historical Review.*
Hist. Zeit.	=*Historische Zeitschrift.*
JHS	=*Journal of Hellenic Studies.*
JRS	=*Journal of Roman Studies.*
Num. Chron.	=*Numismatic Chronicle.*
Num. Zeit.	=*Numismatische Zeitschrift.*
Rh. Mus.	=*Rheinisches Museum für Philologie.*
A and J	=Abbot and Johnson, *Municipal Administration in the Roman Empire.*
Diz. Epig.	=Ruggiero, *Dizionario epigrafico.*
Ges. Schrift.	=Mommsen, *Gesammelte Schriften.*
Migne Gr. ⎱ Lat. ⎰	=*Patrologiae Cursus completus, series Graeca* ⎱ ed. J. P. Migne. *Latina* ⎰
P-W	=Pauly-Wissowa-Kroll, *Real-Encyklopädie der klassischen Altertumwissenschaft.*
Seeck, Regesten	=Seeck, *Regesten der Kaiser und Päpste für die Jahre* 311 *bis* A.D. 470.
Seeck, Untergang	=Seeck, *Geschichte des Untergangs der antiken Welt.*
Cod. Just.	=*Codex Justinianus.*
Cod. Theo.	=*Codex Theodosianus.*

The lives of the Emperors in the *Historia Augusta* are referred to simply as *Vita* with the name of the individual Emperor.

NOTES

INTRODUCTION

[1] Toynbee, *The Hadrianic School*, p. xxi.

[2] *Vita Pii*, 25, 7. On Hadrian's Imperial Idea see further, H. Stuart Jones, *The Roman Empire*, pp. 178–95 ; Pelham, *Essays on Roman History*, p. 216 ; Toynbee, *op. cit.*, pp. 1–6 ; and in greater detail on his Principate, W. Weber, *Untersuchungen zur Geschichte des Kaisers Hadrians* ; B. W. Henderson, *The Life and Principate of the Emperor Hadrian*.

CHAPTER I

[1] Eutrop., VIII, 8.

[2] "παρὰ τοῦ πατρὸς τὸ ἥμερον καὶ μενετικὸν ἀσαλεύτως ἐπὶ τῶν ἐξητασμένως κριθέντων καὶ τὸ ἀκενόδοξον περὶ τὰς δοκούσας τιμάς καὶ τὸ φιλόπονον καὶ ἐνδελεχές " (εἰς ἑαυτόν, 1, 16).

[3] "*quaestor liberalis, praetor splendidus* " (*Vita Pii*, 2, 9).

[4] Dess. *ILS*, 1850.

[5] *Vita Pii*, 2, 11.

[6] *Equus publicus* given to him at the age of six ; made a member of the *collegium Saliorum* at eight (*Vita Marci*, 4, 2).

[7] Spartianus and Capitolinus contradict themselves and each other in ascribing the adoption of Lucius now to Marcus and now to Antoninus *Vita Hadr.*, 24, 1 ; *Vita Ael.*, 5, 12 ; *Vita Pii*, 4, 5 ; *Vita Veri*, 2, 2) ; but inscriptions make it clear that it was Antoninus who adopted both. (Dess. *ILS*, 356, 357, 359.)

[8] M and S, II, pp. 394–95, nos. 445–54.

[9] M and S, III, p. 27, nos. 13–14[b].

[10] M and S, III, pp. 104–7, nos. 574–596 ; Toynbee, *The Hadrianic School*, pp. 144–52.

[11] *Vita Pii*, 5, 2 ; Dio, LXX, 1.

[12] Capitolinus gives four different interpretations of the meaning of *Pius*, but it is best explained as a tribute to Antoninus' reverence for religion (Paus., VIII, 43, 5 ; C. H. Dodd, *The Cognomen of the Emperor Antoninus Pius*, in *Num. Chron.* XI (1911), Fourth Series, pp. 6 ff.) For the imperial title *Augusta*, M and S, III, pp. 66–8, nos. 327–342[a].

[13] *Vita Pii*, 6, 6 ; M and S, III, pp. 29–32, nos. 33–58 ; Mommsen, *Staatsrecht*, II[3], p. 779.

[14] Dess. *ILS*, 338, 2182.

[15] *Ibid.*, 272, 2183 ; M. and S, III, pp. 20–21.

[16] Toynbee, *op. cit.*, pp. 112–13.

[17] Possibly *procuratores ad silices* were instituted by him (*CIL*, VI, 1598). The characteristic trait of his policy is, however, 'μηδὲν καινοτόμον' (εἰς ἑαυτόν, 1, 16).

[18] Dess *ILS.*, 1325.

[19] *Vita Marci*, II, 6.

[20] *Vita Pii*, 8, 7–8.

[21] Dess. *ILS*, 6680.

[22] Lacour-Gayet, *Antonin le Pieux*, pp. 403–31.

[23] *Vita Pii*, 4, 10.

[24] Dess. *ILS*, 336.

[25] *Vita Pii*, 8, 3.

[26] *CIL*, X, 6891.

[27] Dess. *ILS*, 5824.

[28] *Ibid.*, 334.

[29] *CIL*, X, 3832.

[30] *Puellae Faustinianae*, M and S, III, p. 165, nos. 1149–1152 ; *Diva Faustina*, M and S, III, pp. 69–77, nos 343–410d.

[31] M and S, III, pp. 13–14 ; *Chron.* of A.D. 354 (Mommsen, *Chron. min.*, I, p. 146).

[32] Dio, LXX, 7.

[33] *Vita Pii*, 5, 4 ; Macdonald, *The Roman Wall in Scotland* (2nd edit.), p. 8.

[34] *CIL*, VII, 1125 ; *Eph. Ep.*, IX, 1390 ; Macdonald, *op cit.*, pp. 404–5. For the career of Lollius Urbicus, Dess. *ILS*, 1065 ; *P–W*, XIII, coll. 1392 ff.

[35] The year of the imperial salutation cannot be exactly determined. *Imp. II* appears on one inscription of A.D. 142 (Dess. *ILS*, 340), but not on others of that year, and is absent from some of A.D. 143, (e.g., *ibid.*, 341 ; *CIL*, III, 4641, 4649). Coins struck between A.D. 140 and 143 on which *Imp. II* first occurs, do not give the number of *trib. pot.*, but only *COS. III.* (M and S, III, pp. 39–40, nos. 107a–113). Probably the salutation was accepted towards the end of A.D. 142. For *Britannia* coins, M and S, III, p. 121, nos. 743–45 ; Toynbee, *op.cit.*, p. 60.

[36] Macdonald, *op. cit.*, pp. 81–95 and 466–82.

[37] *Ibid.*, pp. 359–400. Barr Hill is an illustration of the strength of the southern defences (*ibid.*, p. 276).

[38] *CIL*, VII, 1141.

[39] *CIL*, VII, 1107, 1104 (from Croy Hill); *Eph. Ep.*, IX, 1390 (from Balmuildy) ; Macdonald, *op. cit.*, pp. 401–6.

[40] " ἀπετέμετο δὲ καὶ τῶν ἐν Βριταννίᾳ Βριγάντων τὴν πόλλην, ὅτι ἐπεσβαίνειν καὶ οὗτοι σὺν ὅπλοις ἦρξαν ἐς τὴν Γενουνίαν μοῖραν ὑπηκόους Ῥωμαίων " (Paus., VIII, 43, 4), probably refers to this revolt and not the earlier trouble under Lollius (Macdonald, *op. cit.*, pp. 7–11).

For coins commemorating the crushing of the revolt, which were minted in A.D. 155., M and S, III, p. 142, nos. 930, 934.

For the reinforcements from Germany, Dess. *ILS*, 9116.

For the rebuilding of Birrens in A.D. 158, Haverfield, *The Roman Occupation of Britain*, pp. 120–22. The lapse of time between the issue of the coins and the rebuilding of the fort is indicative of the seriousness of the rising.

[41] Fabricius, *s.v. limes* in *P–W*, XIII, coll. 593–97 and 607–11 ; Pelham, *Essays on Roman History*, pp. 202–5 ; Cheesman, *Auxilia of the Roman Imperial Army*, pp. 85 ff.

[42] Dess. *ILS*, 2479 ; Fronto, Loeb, I, p. 236.

[43] Parker, *The Roman Legions*, p. 165, n. 5.

[44] Dess. *ILS*, 1362, 1362ª, 1362ᵇ.

[45] *Ibid.*, 9056.

[46] *BGU*, II, 372 ; A and J, p. 524, no. 175.

[47] Dess. *ILS*, 1092 ; *CIL*, III, 940, 1061, 1416 ; note also the establishment of *burgi* and *praesidia* for the protection of Thrace (*A.E.*, 1927, no. 49).

[48] *Vita Pii*, 9, 6–10.

[49] M and S, III, p. 110, no. 619 ; cf. " *rex Quadis datus* " (no. 620).

[50] Dess. *ILS*, 1076.

[51] *Vita Pii*, 9, 6.

[52] M and S, III, p. 247, nos. 429–42. The temple of Faustina in the *Via Sacra* was also dedicated to his memory (Dess. *ILS*, 348).

CHAPTER II

[1] Marcus did not take up the serious study of philosophy till he was twenty-five (Fronto, Loeb, I, p. 216).

[2] εἰς ἑαυτόν, I, 7.

[3] *Id.*, IV, 23.

[4] *Id.*, VI, 30.

[5] *Id.*, VII, 7.

[6] *Id.*, XII, 26.

[7] *Id.*, XII, 36.

[8] *Vita Marci*, 1, 2–4.

[9] Dess. *ILS*, 354.

[10] *Ibid.*, 356 ; M and S, III, pp. 173–90 (Aurelius Cæsar).

[11] *Vita Marci*, 6, 3.

[12] Dess, *ILS*, 353–6.

[13] Marcus' tribunician years began in December (perhaps on the tenth day of the month in accordance with the normal practice), A.D. 146. Antoninus' tribunician years dated from February 25th, A.D. 138., but when Marcus became his colleague, he appears to have transferred the date to December. Thus the tenth year of Antoninus' tribunician power corresponds with the first year of Marcus' (M and S, III, p. 2).

[14] Probably this is a mistake of the biographer (*Vita Marci*, 6, 6). Antoninus had only the *ius quartae relationis* (*Eph. Ep.*, III, p. 156), and this is normal for the period (cf. *Vita Pert.*, 5, 6).

[15] *Vita Marci*, 7, 6. Marcus retained for himself the title of *pontifex maximus*. The joint-rulership is commemorated by coins with the legend CONCORDIA AUGUSTORUM (M and S, III, pp. 214–15, nos. 1–11).

[16] *CIL*, II, 2552 ; III, 117, 199.

[17] Dess. *ILS*, 359.

[18] Coins of 161 with *Liberalitas* (M and S, III, p. 215, nos. 15–17). For the extension of alimentation, *Vita Marci*, 7, 8. The title borne by the children is doubtful, but probably they were called after Verus and Lucilla (cf. the later institution in honour of Faustina, *Vita Marci*, 26, 6).

[19] Fronto, Loeb, II, p. 40.

[20] Ramsay, *Studies in the History and Art of the Eastern Provinces*, p. 128.

[21] *Vita Marci*, 8, 9.

[22] *Ibid.*, 8, 7–8 ; *CIL*, VII, 225, 758, 773 ; Macdonald, *op. cit.*, pp. 11–12.

[23] Fronto, *Principia Historiae*, 16 (Loeb, II, p. 214).

[24] *Vita Marci*, 8, 6 ; cf. Dess. *ILS*, 9057.

[25] Dess. *ILS*, 1098.

[26] *Ibid.*, 2311.

[27] *Ibid.*, 1098.

[28] *Ibid.*, 8977, 1091.

[29] His safe voyage is commemorated on a group of coins with the type of a galley and the legend FELIC. AUG. TR, P. III COS. II (M and S, III, pp. 319–20, nos. 1325–1340).

[30] Title ARMENIACUS on Verus' coins of A.D. 163 (M and S, III, p. 321, nos. 1360–1363) ; on Marcus' coins of A.D. 164 (*ibid.*, pp. 281–3, nos. 861–868, 888–892). For the Armenian victory, *ibid.*, III, p. 254, nos. 498–506 ; for the installation of Sohaemus, Fronto, Loeb, II, p. 144 ; M and S, III, p. 255, nos. 511–13.

On the chronology, C. H. Dodd, *Chronology of the Eastern Campaigns of the Emperor Lucius Verus* in *Num. Chron.*, XI (1911), Fourth Series, pp. 209–67.

[31] Dess. *ILS*, 8910.

[32] Fronto, Loeb, II, p. 148.

[33] The literary evidence is fragmentary and confused (Dio, LXXI, 2 ; *Vita Marci*, 8, 6–9, 2 ; *Vita Veri*, 6, 9–8, 3 ; *Frag. Dion. apud Suidam, s.v.* Ζεῦγμα, printed at end of book LXXI in Tauchnitz text).

The title PARTHICUS MAXIMUS is found on coins of Verus struck between August and December, A.D. 165 (M and S, III, p. 326, nos. 1429–1436), and on Marcus' coins of A.D. 166 (*ibid.*, pp. 285–6, nos. 915, 926).

See further Schwendemann, *Der Historische Wert der Vita Marci*, p. 157, and C. H. Dodd, *op. cit.*

[34] The victory is commemorated by a fourth imperial salutation (M and S, III, pp. 225–6, nos. 159, 165; pp. 287–8, nos. 928–944 ; p. 328, nos. 1455–1460).

The title MEDICUS was assumed only for the triumph in Rome and then dropped because of its empty significance (M and S, III, p. 288, no. 940 ; p. 328, no. 1455 ; cf. Dess. *ILS*, 365–366). For the terms of the peace, *Vita Veri*, 7, 8 ; Schwendemann, *op. cit.*, p. 161.

[35] Possibly on October 12 (Schwendemann, *op. cit.*, pp. 163–5).

[36] *Vita Veri*, 8, 2–3. An oracle of Klarian Apollo to the people of Troketta probably refers to the effects of this plague (Keil u. Premerstein, *Berichte über eine Reise in Lydien*, no. 16).

[37] Ritterling, *s.v.*, *Legio* in *P–W*, XII, coll. 1300–1 ; Dess. *ILS*, 8977.

[38] *Vita Marci*, 12, 13–14 ; Ammianus, XXIX, 6, 1 ; Lucian, *Alex. Pseudomant.*, 48. The chronology is obscure and cannot be precisely determined from the meagre literary sources, nor from coins. See further C. H. Dodd, *The Danubian Wars of Marcus Antoninus* in *Num. Chron.*, XIII (1913), Fourth Series, pp. 162–79.

[39] Pompeianus (*CIL*, III, p. 888, D, XLVI) ; Fronto (Dess. *ILS*, 1098) ; Pertinax (Dio, LXXI, 3,2).

[40] *CIL*, III, p. 888, D, XLVI, dated to May 5th A.D. 167. On this *diploma* the Emperors are given a fifth salutation. This is not found on coins till the next year, either because of the dislocation at the mint caused by the economic crisis, or, more likely, because Marcus felt it was untimely and asked the Senate not to confer it officially (Dodd, *op. cit.*, p. 167).

[41] Dess. *ILS*, 1098 ; for V *Macedonica*, Parker. *op. cit.*, pp. 167–68 ; the attack on Alburnum was not earlier than June, A.D. 167 (*CIL*, III, p. 949, *Cautio depositi* XII, dated May 29th, A.D. 167).

[42] For the date of the Emperors' departure from Rome, Dodd, *op. cit.*, p. 165.

[43] *Vita Marci*, 14, 5. The death of the praetorian prefect, Furius Victorinus, probably occurred in A.D. 168, after, and not before, the crossing of the Alps (Dodd, *op. cit.*, p. 178).

[44] M and S, III, p. 333, nos. 1507–1512.

[45] *Sestertius* with the legend PROFECTIO AUG. with Marcus in military dress on horseback, dated to end of A.D. 169 (M and S, III, p. 290, no. 963).

[46] *Vita Marci*, 21, 9.

[47] Possibly he paid a short visit to Rome in A.D. 174 (M and S, III, p. 207).

[48] Eutrop., VIII, 13.

[49] *Vita Marci*, 21, 10 ; IMP. VI on coins of A.D. 171 (M and S, III, p. 231, nos. 236–242 ; VIC. GER. on no. 240) ; IMP. VI VIC. GER. (*ibid.*, p. 293, nos 1000–1002).

[50] Coins of A.D. 172 with the legend GERMANIA SUBACTA (*ibid.*, pp. 294–5, nos. 1021–1027). Marcus received the title *Germanicus* (Dess. *ILS*, 370).

[51] Dess. *ILS*, 1098. He is said to have fallen fighting " *adversum Germanos et Iazyges*."

[52] Dio, LXXI, 8–10 ; Domaszewski, *Das Regenwunder der Marcus-Saüle* in *Rh. Mus.*, XLIX, pp. 612–19 ; Petersen in *Rh. Mus.*, L, pp. 453–74 ; Mommsen in *Ges. Schrift.*, IV, pp. 498–513.

[53] A seventh imperial salutation was accepted in the summer of A.D. 174. (M and S, III, pp. 301–2, nos. 1109–1121 ; the last numbered coin has also the legend MARTI VICTORI). On the problem of the chronology, see further, C. H. Dodd, *op. cit.*, pp. 179–99 and pp. 276 ff.

[54] Dess. *ILS*, 373; M and S, III, pp. 238–9, nos. 326–334, and on Commodus' coins, *ibid.*, pp. 335–6, nos. 1532–1545.

[55] *Vita Marci*, 24, 5.

[56] Dio, LXXI, 11–16; on the establishment of barbarian settlements inside the Empire, which have no connection with the later development of the system known as the *colonate*, see further Clausing, *The Roman Colonate*, pp. 84–91.

[57] Ptolem., III, 8, 3: *Vita Marci*, 22, 1; Paus., X, 34, 5; Aelius Aristides, *Or.*, XXII K; cf. Boulanger, *Aelius Aristide*, pp. 329–32 and 488–9; Dess. *ILS*, 8501, 9118. That the raiders went by sea is maintained by Premerstein in *Klio*, XII, pp. 139–78, but neither Dess. *ILS*, 9118 nor 1327 prove his contentions.

[58] Dess. *ILS*, 1327.

[59] Dio, LXXI, 12.

[60] *Ibid.*, 4.

[61] Dess. *ILS*, 6147, although both the date and identity of the *Bellum navale* are controversial (Premerstein, *op. cit.*; Mommsen in *Eph. Ep.*, III, pp. 322 ff.)

[62] *Ibid.*, 1119; Premerstein, *op. cit*; Schwendemann, *op. cit.*, p. 90, n. 2.

[63] *Vita Severi*, 2, 3–4.

[64] Dess. *ILS*, 1327.

[65] *CIL*, III, p. 2328[72], D. CXII.

[66] *Vita Marci*, 21, 6–7.

[67] Brigands were particularly troublesome on the road between Viminacium and Naissus. *Stationes* were established to keep them in check, and it seems that captured *latrones* were incorporated in them. (*CIL*, III, 8242, 8266; Rostovtzeff, *Social and Economic History*, p. 523; cf. above, Chapter I, n. 47).

[68] Premerstein in *Klio*, XIII, p. 84.

[69] *Id.* in *Klio*, XI, pp. 355–66.

[70] Dio, LXXI, 22, 3.

[71] At the same time he was made *princeps iuventutis* (M and S, III, p. 336, nos. 1534–1536).

[72] Schwendemann, *op cit.*, pp. 181–4.

[73] It was given the name of *colonia Faustiniana*.

[74] Dio, LXXI, 28, 2–4: *Vita Marci*, 26, 11–13; Coins of A.D. 176 with the legend CLEMENTIA AUG. (M and S, III, pp. 304–5, nos. 1158–1161.)

[75] Dio. LXXI, 31, 3.

[76] *Vita Commodi*, 2, 4: *Vita Marci*, 16, 1; Dess. *ILS*, 374. Heer *Der historische Wert der Vita Commodi*, pp. 23–5.

[77] That the *tribunicia potestas* was not conferred upon Commodus at the same date as he received the *praenomen Imperator* (November 27th, A.D. 176), nor till after his entry on the consulship on January 1st, A.D. 177, is attested by the following coins, M and S, III, pp. 336–7, nos. 1546–1549. Secondly, coins of A.D. 177 give him two years of *trib. pot.*, those minted after April styling him *trib. pot. II* (M and S, III, pp. 337–40, nos. 1550–1553 for *trib. pot.*, nos. 1554–1587 for *trib. pot. II*).

The best solution of the problem is that of Mommsen, who supposes that Capitolinus (*Vita Commodi*, 2, 4) is right in dating the beginning of the *imperium* only on November 27th, A.D. 176, and that of the tribunician power early in A.D. 177. Consequently the first tribunician period should have extended from *circa* February–December 9th, A.D. 177. But soon November 27th, A.D. 176, came to be identified as Commodus' *dies imperii*, and consequently the first year of *trib. pot.* was made to end on December 9th, A.D. 176, and the second to begin on December 10th, A.D. 176, and end on December 9th, A.D. 177. After that the dating becomes normal. (Mommsen, *Staatsrecht*, II³, p. 801, n. 2 ; Schwendemann, *op. cit.*, pp. 190–1 ; Heer, *op. cit.*, pp. 27–9 ; C. H. Dodd, *Coinage of Commodus during the Reign of Marcus*, in *Num. Chron.*, XlV (1914), Fourth Series, pp. 34–59.)

⁷⁸ The ninth *salutatio* of Marcus (M and S, III, pp. 242–3, nos. 380–383 ; pp. 309–10, nos. 1214–1226), the second of Commodus (*ibid.*, p. 266, nos. 645–647 ; p. 340, nos. 1578–1587).

⁷⁹ Dio, LXXl, 33, 1.

⁸⁰ M and S, III, p. 209.

⁸¹ Dio, LXXI, 33, 3 ; LXXII, 2, 1.

⁸² The tenth *salutatio* of Marcus (M and S, p. 244, nos. 401–408 ; p. 312, nos. 1239–1243): the third *salutatio* of Commodus (*ibid.*, pp. 267–8, nos. 659–666 ; pp. 342–3, nos. 1607–1614).

⁸³ Dio, LXXI, 20, 2.

⁸⁴ *Ibid.*, 33, 4 ; *Vita Marci*, 27, 10–11.

⁸⁵ Dess. *ILS*, 1118 ; *Vita Marci*, 11, 6.

⁸⁶ *CIL*, X, 3865 ; III, 249 ; Dess. *ILS*, 1420.

⁸⁷ *Procurator summarum rerum*, Dess. *ILS*, 1452 ; *CIL*, X, 1785 ; *Subpraefectus annonae*, Dess. *ILS*, 1412, 1421. Hirschfeld, *Die Kaiserlichen Verwaltungsbeamten*, (2nd edition), pp. 33, 246.

⁸⁸ Dess. *ILS*, 1118 ; *Digest*, XL, 12, 27.

⁸⁹ Dio, LXXI, 28.

⁹⁰ *Vita Marci*, 10, 10 ; *Digest*, II, 12, 1 ; Schwendemann, *op cit.*, p. 33.

⁹¹ Hänel, *Corpus Legum*, p. 130 ; *Vita Marci*, 11, 8, for further legislation.

⁹² Dio, LXXII, 1, 1.

⁹³ *Vita Marci*, 28, 1.

⁹⁴ *Caesares*, p. 429 (*Juliani Imp. Opera I*, ed. Hertlein).

⁹⁵ *Vita Marci*, 18, 3 ; M and S, III, pp. 397–8, nos. 264–275 ; p. 441, nos. 654–664 ; Schwendemann, *op. cit.*, p. 204.

CHAPTER III

¹ Dio, LXXII, 2–3 ; LXXIII, 6, 1.

² M and S, III, pp. 366–7, nos. 4–10ᵇ ; possibly the reason for the acclamation may have been a victory won by Marcus' generals before that Emperor's death. (Heer, *op. cit.*, p. 40.)

[3] Dess. *ILS*, 1420, records T. Flavius Germanus as *curator triumphi felicissimi Germanici secundi* ; *Vita Comm.* 3, 6 ; M and S, III, p. 403, no. 306.

[4] *Vita Comm.*, 12, 7 ; M and S, III, p. 368, no. 22 (= the second *liberalitas* of his sole rule, the first having been given on his accession, *ibid.*, p. 367, nos 10–10[b]).

[5] The new name is first found on coins of A.D. 180 (M and S, III, pp. 366–7, nos. 4–8[a]).

[6] *CIL*, VI, 2099, 1 (*Acta Arvalium*).

[7] *Vita Comm.*, 4, 1–4.

[8] Quintianus was not the son of the famous general Ti. Claudius Pompeianus, Lucilla's second husband, but of a senator of the same name, who married L.'s daughter and was put to death by Commodus (*Vita Comm.*, 5, 12 ; Dio, LXXII, 4, 4 ; Heer, *op. cit.*, p. 62).

[9] Probably the conspirators intended to make Lucilla's husband the new Emperor (Heer, *op. cit.*, pp. 44–6).

[10] *Vita Comm.*, 4, 5 ; Heer, *op. cit.*, pp. 46–7.

[11] *Vita Comm.*, 4, 6–8 ; *Vita Did. Iul.*, 2, 1 ; Dio, LXXII, 5. 1.

[12] *Vita Comm.*, 5, 1.

[13] Dio, LXXII, 10, 1 ; Heer, *op. cit.*, p. 56.

[14] Her death probably did not occur till after A.D. 185, if the titles given to Commodus (*pius felix*) on an African dedication to him and Crispina are correct ; for Commodus did not assume the title *felix* till late in A.D. 185 (*CIL*, VIII, 16530).

[15] M and S, III, p. 363 ; for the suspension of *alimenta*, *Vita Pert.*, 9, 3.

[16] Dio, LXXII, 9 ; the improbability of the story is suggested by the continuance of the mutiny of the soldiers in Britain after Perennis death. The embassy from Britain consisted, it may be conjectured, not of a detachment of 1500 soldiers, but of the superseded *legati legionum* (*prodita re per legatos exercitus* in *Vita Comm.*, 6, 2), who complained not of Perennis' treachery—for how could the army in Britain know or suspect that Perennis intended to make his son, who was in Illyricum, Emperor ?—but of his appointment of equestrian commanders.

[17] Herod., I, 9, 7–8, and see further, Heer, *op cit.*, pp. 65–70.

[18] *Vita Comm.*, 6, 2 ; Dio, LXXII, 9, 4 ; Herod., I, 13, 4.

[19] Coins with PIUS FELIX on obverse, and CONCORDIA MILITUM, JUPITER (CUSTOS) and SALUS on reverse (M and S, III, p. 380, nos. 126–27 ; p. 379, no. 117 ; p. 418, nos. 450, 457).

[20] *Vita Comm.*, 8, 1 ; *CIL*, VI, 2099, 12 (*Acta Arvalium*).

[21] Herod., I, 9, 10.

[22] *Vita Comm.*, 6, 13.

[23] *Ibid.*, 6, 9 ; Dio LXXII, 12, 4.

[24] Heer (*op. cit.*, pp. 76–9) dates the fall of Cleander to A.D. 190 on the grounds that (1) the consulships of his twenty-five nominees fall in that year, and (2) the institution of an African corn-fleet was in the same year. This he connects with the scarcity of food in Rome, which was made the occasion for the attack upon Cleander. But the creation of the corn-fleet should probably be ante-dated to A.D. 186, as coins of

that year with the type of a ship and the legend PROVIDENTIA AUGUSTI seem to refer to that event (M and S, III, p. 422, nos. 486–487). Secondly, although A. D.190 is the year of the twenty-five consuls, their nominations must have been made in A.D. 189. Thirdly, it is difficult, if Cleander lived till A.D. 190, to get round (as Heer attempts to do) the statement of Lampridius (*Vita Comm.*, 14, 8), that no praetorian prefect held office for more than three years.

²⁵ *Vita Comm.*, 7, 8, cf. Dess. *ILS*, 1421, *proc(urator) Aug(usti) ad bona cogenda in Africa*, which may refer to a confiscation of property in Africa, which had belonged to senators condemned to death by the Emperor.

²⁶ M and S, III, pp. 433–5, nos. 595–607.

²⁷ Dio, LXXII, 15, 2. This title may have been bestowed a year earlier. On two coins of A.D. 190 Commodus is represented as a priest ploughing (i.e. the founder of the new Rome), and the legend reads COLONIA L(UCIA) AN(NIA) COM(MODIANA), (M and S, III, pp. 430–1, nos. 560, 570).

²⁸ Dio, l.c. ; *Vita Comm.*, 17, 7–8. The only certain instance of a legion with the surname is III *Augusta* (*CIL*, VIII, 3163), but the paucity of examples is not surprising, as the honour was conferred so shortly before Commodus' death.

²⁹ Dio, LXXII, 15, 3–5 ; cf. Dess. *ILS*, 400.

³⁰ HERCULES ROMANUS AUGUSTUS (M and S, III, pp. 395–6, nos. 249–254ᶜ ; p. 439, nos. 637–640, 643–644) ; Rostovtzeff, *Commodus-Hercules in Britain*, in *JRS*, XIII (1923), pp. 91–105.

³¹ Dio, LXXII, 20–21.

³² *Ibid.*, 22, 2.

³³ *Vita Comm.*, 9. 3.

³⁴ *Ibid.*, 17, 2.

³⁵ *Ibid.*, 17, 4 ; Herod. II, 1, 2 ; Heer *op. cit.*, pp. 118–19.

³⁶ Dio, LXXII, 8, 1.

³⁷ Dess. *ILS*, 395 ; " *eo tempore in Sarmatia res bene gestas per alios duces in filium suum Perennis referebat* " (*Vita Comm.*, 6, 1).

³⁸ *Vita Comm.*, 12, 8.

³⁹ Dess. *ILS*, 396.

⁴⁰ Dio, LXXII, 8 ; coins of A.D. 184–5 celebrate British victories, and Commodus accepts the title BRITANNICUS and three salutations (M and S, III, p. 416, nos. 437, 440 ; p. 418, nos. 451–452 ; p. 419, no. 459ᵉ).

⁴¹ For the view that the Antonine Wall was not abandoned till the rebellion of A.D. 196 when the Hadrianic Wall was breached, E. Birley in *Archæologia Aeliana*, 4th series, vol. VII, pp. 166–8, and Collingwood, *Roman Britain* (2nd ed.), p. 26. The opposite opinion is maintained by Macdonald, *op. cit.*, pp. 479–82.

⁴² *Vita Pert.*, 3, 5–6 ; M and S, III, p. 420, nos. 465, 468ᵃ⁻ᵈ.

⁴³ Rostovtzeff, *op. cit.*, p. 99.

⁴⁴ *CIL*, III, 1092 ; Domaszewski, *Die Religion des röm. Heeres*, p. 54.

⁴⁵ For Maternus, Herod., I, 10 ; coins with types of HILARITAS and

SALUS (M and S, III, p. 382, nos. 150–151 ; p. 424, nos. 497–498, 504 ; p. 425, nos. 514–515).

⁴⁶ *CIL*, XI, 6053 ; Ritterling, *s.v. Legio* in *P–W*, XII col. 1307.

CHAPTER IV

¹ *Vita Pii*, 4, 10 ; M and S, III, pp. 104–7, nos. 574–596 ; Toynbee, *op. cit.*, pp. 144–52.

² *Vita Pii*, 9, 1 ; Pausanias, VIII, 43, 4 ; *CIG*, II, 2721.

³ *Vita Pii*, 9, 2, and for Narbo, *CIL*, XII, 4342.

⁴ Dess. *ILS*, 337, and *CIL*, III, 836.

⁵ Bryant, *The Reign of Antoninus Pius*, pp. 54–5.

⁶ Boulanger, *Aelius Aristide*, pp. 482–5.

⁷ Thisbe and Coronea, *IG*, VII, 2870 ; A and J, p. 424, no. 104 ; Pagus Lucretius, Dess. *ILS*, 6988.

⁸ Boulanger, *op. cit.*, pp. 347–62 ; Rostovtzeff, *Social and Economic History of the Roman Empire*, pp. 127–30.

⁹ W. Hüttl, *Antoninus Pius*, II, pp. 199–372, has collected the epigraphical evidence for the Principate of Antoninus in which municipal dedications figure in large proportions.

¹⁰ e.g. Dess. *ILS*, 6147, and cf. the speech of a Gallic senator in fulsome gratitude to the Emperor for reducing the cost of gladiatorial shows (*s.c. Italicense de sumptibus ludorum gladiatoriorum minuendis* of A.D. 176–7, on which see further, Mommsen, *Ges. Schrift*, VIII, pp. 499–531, and cf. Keil u. Premerstein, *Bericht über eine Reise in Lydien*, no. 26).

¹¹ Liebenam, *Philologus*, LVI (1897), pp. 290–325 ; *s.v. Curator reipublicae* in *Diz. Epig.*, II, pp. 1345–77.

¹² Dio, LXXI, 4, and for the distress caused by *munera*, *P. Gen.*, 37 ; A and J, p. 529, no. 180.

¹³ Dess. *ILS*, 6870 ; A and J, p. 435, no. 111.

¹⁴ M and S, III, p. 48, nos. 177–185 ; p. 134, nos. 859–863 ; for Pallantium, Pausanias, VIII, 43, 1.

¹⁵ For further details about the Eastern cults and their dissemination in the West, Cumont, *Les Religions Orientales dans le Paganisme Romain*, especially pp. 17–124 ; Wissowa, *Religion und Kultus der Römer*, especially, pp. 348–79.

¹⁶ On Mithraism, Cumont, *Les Mystères de Mithra*, and the same author's *Textes et Monuments figurés relatifs aux mystères de Mithra* ; cf. *Les Religions Orientales*, pp. 125–49.

¹⁷ *Epistle to Diognetus*, 5–7. For a translation, B. J. Kidd, *Documents illustrative of the History of the Church*, I, no. 29.

¹⁸ Lucian, *de morte Peregrini*, 12–13 (=Kidd, I, no. 51); Athenagoras, *Legatio pro Christianis*, 1–3 (=Kidd, I, no. 58).

¹⁹ Origen, *contra Celsum*, II, 55, and III, 49 (=Kidd, I, nos. 60 and 128).

²⁰ *De morte Peregrini*.

²¹ Aristides, *The History of Barlaam and Josaphat*, 15–16 (*Texts and*

Studies, I, i, pp. 100 ff.) (=Kidd, I, no. 26). Justin, *Apology*, in *Cambridge Patristic Texts* (ed. Blunt).

²² Eusebius, *Hist. Eccles.*, IV, 26, 10.

²³ Justin, *Apology*, 11, 2, 9 ; Euseb., *H.E.*, IV, 15 ; *Martyrium Polycarpi* (Kidd, I, no. 36).

²⁴ For the attitude of Marcus to the Christians, εἰς ἑαυτόν, XI, 3 ; for the martyrdom of Justin and his companions under Rusticus the prefect, *Acta Justini et Sociorum*, 1, *Ante-Nicene Christian Library*, II, pp. 367–70 (Kidd, I, no. 49).

²⁵ For the persecution at Lyons, Eusebius, *H.E.*, V, 1 ; for the Scyllium Martyrs, *Texts and Studies*, I, 2, pp. 112 ff. See further on Christianity in the Antonine Age, B. J. Kidd, *A History of the Church to A.D.* 461, I, pp. 242–56, and Duchesne, *The Early History of the Church*, I, pp. 163–95.

²⁶ Philostratus, *Vit. Soph.*, II, pp. 142–50 (ed. Loeb).

²⁷ See further on the Art of the period, Toynbee, *The Hadrianic School*, especially pp. XXIII–XXXI ; 144–59 ; 164–201 ; Strong, *Art in Rome*, II, pp. 112–36 ; *id.*, *Roman Sculpture*, pp. 268–98 ; cf. Wickhoff, *Wiener Genesis*, translated by Mrs. Strong under the title *Roman Art*.

PART II

CHAPTER I

¹ Dio, LXXIII, 1 ; Herod., II, 2–3 ; *Vita Pert.*, 4, 5–5, 6.

² Dio, LXXIII, 5, 1 ; Dess. *ILS*, 408.

³ *Vita Pert.*, 6, 9.

⁴ *Ibid.*, 6, 10–11.

⁵ *Ibid.*, 9, 6.

⁶ *Ibid.*, 10, 1–10.

⁷ Dio, LXXIII, 10, 3 ; *Vita Pert.*, 11, 6–9.

⁸ Dio's estimate of his character in LXXIII, 10, 3.

⁹ The story of the auction seems to be authentic, even if the picturesque details given by Herodian are imaginative rather than historical (Herod., II, 6, 3–13 ; Dio, LXXIII, 11 ; *Vita Did. Iul.*, 3, 1–3).

¹⁰ Dio, LXXIII, 13, 5 ; Zon., XII, 7, III, p. 96 (ed. Dindorf).

¹¹ *Vita Sev.*, 5, 1, reading " *Idibus Aprilibus.*"

¹² Gold coins were struck by XIV *Gemina* and I *Minervia* alone among the Danubian and German legions. This may indicate that they took the lead in the proclamation of the Emperor (Cohen IV, p. 31, S. Severus, nos. 258, 271, 273). Coins exist with the names of all the Danubian legions except X *Gemina*. This exception is probably not accidental, but indicates some temporary opposition to Severus. (Hasebroek, *Untersuchungen zur Geschichte des Kaisers Septimius Severus*, p. 17 ; Ritterling, *s.v. Legio* in *P-W*, XII, col. 1310.)

21

[13] Sixteen days is insufficient for (a) news of the murder of Pertinax to reach Niger ; (b) Niger's proclamation as Emperor by his troops ; (c) news of the latter event to reach Severus at Carnuntum. Probably the proclamations in Syria and at Carnuntum roughly synchronized.

[14] Dio, LXXIII, 15, 1 ; Herod., II, 15, 2–3 ; *Vita Sev.*, 6, 9.

[15] *Vita Did. Iul.*, 6, 3 ; Dio, LXXIII, 17, 1.

[16] Dio, LXXIII, 16 ; Julianus also put to death Laetus (a namesake of the Laetus referred to below in n. 48), and Marcia, who had plotted Commodus' death, in the hope of gratifying the praetorians.

[17] Dio, LXXIII, 17, 1–2 ; *Vita Sev.*, 5, 5.

[18] *Vita Did. Iul.*, 6, 5–6.

[19] *Ibid.*, 6, 9 ; *Vita Sev.*, 5, 7 ; Dio, LXXIII, 17, 2.

[20] *Vita Did. Iul.*, 7, 5.

[21] *Ibid.*, 8, 7–9 ; Dio, LXXIII, 17, 3–5 ; Zon, XII, 7, III, p. 98.

[22] He offered Pompeianus a share of the Empire, which the old man discreetly refused (*Vita Did. Iul.*, 8, 3).

[23] *Vita Sev.*, 6, 1–4.

[24] Domaszewski, *Die Religion des röm. Heeres*, p. 37.

[25] Herod., II, 13.

[26] *Ibid.*, 14, 3.

[27] He had assumed the title in Pannonia (Herod., II, 10, 9, supported by coin evidence, Cohen, IV, p. 31, nos. 255–272), and it was now officially recognized by the Senate (Hasebroek, *op. cit.*, pp. 42–3).

[28] Dio, LXXIV, 4–5.

[29] *Liberalitas prima* (Cohen, IV, pp. 32–3, S. Severus, nos. 279–287) Herod., II, 14, 5 ; *Vita Sev.*, 8, 5.

[30] The date is thirty days after his entry into Rome (*Vita Sev.*, 8, 8).

[31] For further details of his early career, Platnauer, *The Life and Reign of Septimius Severus*, pp. 74–8.

[32] Herod., III, 1, 2–3.

[33] Dio, LXXIV, 6, 2 ; Herod., III, 2, 2. The earliest reference to him in Egypt is June 14th, A.D. 193 (*BGU*, IV, 719). Byzantium was probably won over by Claudius Attalus, governor of Thrace, who was later expelled from the Senate for assistance given to Niger (Dio, LXXIX, 3, 5).

[34] Herod., III, 1, 4.

[35] *Vita Sev.*, 8, 9 ; FIDES LEGIONUM on coins (Cohen, IV, pp. 19–20, nos. 145–149).

[36] For P. Septimius Geta, *CIL*, III, 905 ; *Vita Sev.*, 8, 10. For Cilo, Dess. *ILS*, 1141–1142.

[37] *CIL*, VI, 1450. The early fighting at Perinthus took place before Septimius arrived (Hasebroek, *op. cit.*, p. 56).

[38] Dess. *ILS*, 1140 ; Herod., III, 2, 1 ; Dio, LXXIV, 6, 4–5.

[39] Dio, *l.c.* ; for the rivalry of Nicomedia and Nicaea, Dio Chrysost. *Or.*, 38.

[40] The battle of Nicaea was fought not later than January, A.D. 194, as on a *diploma* dated January 31st, A.D. 194, the Emperor has three imperial salutations. (*A.E.*, 1908. no. 146).

[41] *BGU*, II, 362.

⁴² Herod., III, 3, 1–2.

⁴³ Dio, LXXIV, 7–8, 3 ; Herod., III, 4, 2–3 ; *CBM, Lycaonia,*
p. XCIV ; Hasebroek, *op. cit.*, p. 61.

⁴⁴ *Vita Sev.*, 9, 4 ; Herod., III, 6, 9 ; Cohen, IV, p. 99, nos. 5–7 ;
Digest, L, 15, 1, 3.

⁴⁵ Dio, LXXIV, 8, 4–5.

⁴⁶ The earliest known governor of Syria Phoenice is Venidius Rufus
in A.D. 198 (*CIL*, III, 205), but most probably the change was made
three years earlier (Hasebroek, *op. cit.*, p. 70 ; Brünnow und Domaszewski, *Provinz Arabia*, III, pp. 250–1).

⁴⁷ Dio, LXXIV, 8, 4.

⁴⁸ The literary evidence is confused and tends to treat the so-called
First and Second Parthian Wars as one campaign (Herod., III, 5, 1 ;
Vita Sev., 9, 9–10 ; Dio, LXXV, 1, 1–3 ; Victor *de Caes.*, 20, 14–17 ;
Eutrop., VIII, 18 ; Syncellus, I, p. 671, (Bonn)) ; for Nisibis,
'ἀξίωμα τῇ Νισίβει δοὺς, ἱππεῖ ταύτην ἐπέτρεψεν' (Dio, LXXV, 3, 2),
cf. LXXV, 9, 1, where the Second Parthian War is shown to
have been begun by a Parthian attack on the city, which was
defended by Laetus, who, I take it, was acting as governor of
Osroene. (This Laetus, who is of equestrian rank, must be clearly
distinguished from Septimius' senatorial general of that name, who
fought in the First Parthian War and at Lugdunum, and was put to death
during the Second Parthian War by the Emperor (Hasebroek, *op. cit.*,
p. 34, n. 5, and p. 116). Abgarus was later reinstated at the time of
the Second Parthian War. The date at which C. Julius Pacatianus
was procurator of Osroene (Dess. *ILS*, 1353) is uncertain. Tentatively
I would suggest that he was the first governor of the province and was
succeeded by Laetus.

⁴⁹ Dio, LXXV, 2, 3–3, 2, accepting the emendation ᾿Αδιαβηνὴν
for the corrupt ῎Αρχην.

⁵⁰ Acclamations V–VII are found on coins of A.D. 195. The titles
PARTHICUS ARABICUS, PARTHICUS ADIABENICUS appear on coins with
IMP. V (Cohen, IV, pp. 40–41, nos. 362–363, 365–368), but were then
given up by Septimius after the Senate had officially decreed them.
(Dess. *ILS*, 417–418 ; *Vita Sev.*, 9, 11, where the motive is said to be
" *ne Parthos lacesseret.*")

⁵¹ For this dating of the fall of Byzantium and the return of
Septimius to Viminacium, Hasebroek, *op. cit.*, pp. 79–80.

⁵² Dio, LXXIV, 14, 3 ; Herod., III, 6, 9 ; Platnauer, *op. cit.*, p. 98.

⁵³ *Cod. Just.*, IV, 9, 1. Caracallus (which seems to be the correct
form of his name) has the title Caesar on Alexandrian coins before
August 28th, A.D. 196. (Dattari, *Num. Augg. Alexandrini*, 4042 ;
CBM, Alexandria, 1473.)

⁵⁴ DIVI M(ARCI) PII F(ILIUS) with *trib. pot. III imp. V.* (Cohen, IV,
p. 16, no. 126) and with *imp. VII* (*ibid.*, nos. 123–125, 127–128). The
earliest inscription with a complete list of Antonine ancestors is *CIL*,
VIII, 9317, " *t.p.* III *imp.* VI " cf. V, 4868 ; VIII, 24004).

⁵⁵ Dess. *ILS*, 442–444, 2438 ; Domaszewski, *Die Religion des röm.
Heeres*, pp. 71–3.

[56] Herod., III, 5, 2, and III, 6, 8. On the early career of Albinus, Hirschfeld, *Kleine Schriften*, pp. 411 ff. ; Platnauer, *op. cit.*, pp. 100–2.

[57] *CIL*, II, 4125.

[58] Dio, LXXV, 6, 2 ; cf. the defence of *civitas Trevirorum* by *leg.* XXII *Primig.*, which probably refers to an attempt by Albinus to capture the town (Dess. *ILS*, 419).

[59] Perhaps to be identified with the mission of P. Porcius Optatus (Dess. *ILS*, 1143). The army probably marched by way of Poetovio, as is suggested by an inscription set up by a tribune of the tenth praetorian cohort, " *proficiscens ad opprimendam factionem Gallicam iussu principis sui* " (*CIL*, III, 4037).

[60] For Cilo, Dess. *ILS*, 1141 ; for Cassius Clemens, Dio, LXXIV, 9 (rightly assigned to this occasion by Hasebroek, *op. cit.*, p. 94) ; for *liberalitas secunda*, Cohen, IV, p. 33, nos. 288–290 ; for the detachment sent in advance, Herod., III, 6, 10, and possibly, but not certainly, Dess. *ILS*, 1353.

[61] Herod., III, 7, 2–3 ; Dio, LXXV, 6, 6–8.

[62] Dess. *ILS*, 1140, 9493 ; Domaszweski, *Die Rangordnung des röm. Heeres*, p. 65.

[63] *Vita Sev.*, 13 ; Dio, LXXV, 8, 3.

[64] Dio, LXXV, 9, 1–2 ; Herod., III, 9, 2 ; on Abgarus' coins are his own head and Septimius' (Hunterian Collection, III, p. 306, nos. 10–23 ; Eckhel, *Doctrina num. vet.*, III, p. 514) ; cf. Dio, LXXVII, 12, 1 ; LXXIX, 16, 2 ; and see above n. 48.

[65] This was his probable route ; for Rhesaena is *colonia Septimia* and was later garrisoned by III *Parthica* (Hill in *JRS*, VI (1916), p. 166).

[66] For the chronology, including the visit to Egypt, Hasebroek, *op. cit.*, pp. 118–24 ; for the campaign, Platnauer, *op. cit.*, pp. 116–17. As Armenia was neutral, it is unlikely that he contemplated an invasion of that country (Herod., III, 9, 2).

[67] Dio, LXXV, 10–11, 1.

[68] That the war was over before the end of the year is attested by an inscription from Rome dated January 1st, A.D. 200 (*A.E.*, 1916, no. 46). It seems most improbable that Mesopotamia, whose garrison consisted of I and III *Parthicae*, was made into a province after the First Parthian War, as Septimius was clearly anxious to avoid Parthian enmity till he had removed his rivals at home (Domaszewski, *Geschichte der röm. Kaiserzeit*, II, p. 253 ; for the opposite view, Mommsen, *The Provinces of the Roman Empire*, II, pp. 78–9).

[69] *Digest*, L, 15, 1, 5 ; *CBM, Galatia*, p. lvi ; Février, *Essai sur l'histoire politique et économique de Palmyre*, pp. 64–9.

[70] Malalas, XII, p. 293.

[71] Dio, LXXV, 13, 2.

[72] *Vita Sev.*, 17, 2 ; A and J, p. 83 ; Rostovtzeff, *Social and Economic History*, p. 361 ; Wilcken, I (i), pp. 34–43, 214–19 ; see also below, Chapter V, n. 21.

[73] *Vita Sev.*, 17, 4. The last of the " *audi Memnonem* " graffiti which is dated is of February 24th, A.D. 196 (*CIL*, III, 51).

[74] *Vita Sev.*, 16, 8.

⁷⁵ For the visit to the camps on the Danube and extensive making and restoration of roads, Herod., III, 10, 1 ; Hasebroek, *op. cit.*, pp. 127–8. For the festival, games and *congiarium = liberalitas tertia*, Dio, LXXVI, 1, 1 ; Cohen, IV, p. 33, nos. 291–292. For the inscription on the Arch, Dess. *ILS*, 425.

⁷⁶ For Castinus, Dess. *ILS*, 1153 ; on κολλητίωνες, Hasebroek, *op. cit.*, pp. 102–3 ; for Bulla, Dio, LXXVI, 10.

⁷⁷ For disturbances in Tripolis, *Vita Sev.*, 18, 3. For a list of towns granted privileges, Hasebroek, *op. cit.*, p. 134. For the *via Septimiana*, *CIL*, VIII, 2705.

⁷⁸ Marquardt, *Staatsverwaltung*, 1³, p. 310.

⁷⁹ Herod., III, 8, 10.

⁸⁰ For equestrian *comites*, e.g. Dess. *ILS*, 1353 : the earliest dateable inscription with *vir perfectissimus* is *CIL*, VI, 1603, although the titles *vir egregius* and *vir perfectissimus* probably date from the principate of Marcus (*Cod. Just.*, IX, 41, 11), and that of *vir eminentissimus* from the Principate of Hadrian (*Corp. Glossarum*, III, 388, 5) ; Hirschfeld, *Die kaiserl. Verwaltungsbeamten* (2nd edition), pp. 451–2.

⁸¹ *Vita Pes. Nig.*, 7, 4 ; for the functions of the prefect, H. Stuart Jones, *The Roman Empire*, p. 246 ; Platnauer, *op. cit.*, pp. 175–7 ; for his control of the food supply, Hirschfeld, *op. cit.*, pp. 244–5.

⁸² Herod., III, 10, 6 ; for his career, Dio, LXXV, 14–16.

⁸³ The quarrel between Septimius and Plautianus seems to belong to the year A.D. 203. Dio says (LXXV, 16, 4) that Pl. only survived the trial of Racius Constans by one year ; therefore, as Pl. died in A.D. 205, the trial must have taken place in A.D. 204 or late A.D. 203, and it is reasonable to suppose that it followed fairly quickly on the Emperor's order to pull down some of the statues of Pl., which the governor of Sardinia interpreted to his cost in too sweeping terms. Others place the rupture in A.D. 198, and Hasebroek (*op. cit.*, pp. 108–9, 129–32) supposes two quarrels and two reconciliations by what appears to me a very forced interpretation of Dio, LXXV, 14–16, and *Vita Sev.*, 14, 7. For the marriage of Caracallus and Plautilla, Cohen, IV, p. 103, no. 1 ; p. 144, nos. 22–23.

⁸⁴ Dio, LXXVI, 2–4 ; Herod., III, 11, 4–12, 12 ; *Chron. Paschale* (Mommsen, *Chron. Min.*, I, p. 226).

⁸⁵ Dio, LXXVI, 6–9.

⁸⁶ *Digest*, XLVII, 11, 4.

⁸⁷ *Digest*, XXVII, 9.

⁸⁸ Paul, *Sententiae*, V, 29, 2.

⁸⁹ *Digest*, XLIX, 14, 2, 6 ; XLVIII, 18, 16.

⁹⁰ *Vita Sev.*, 12, 4 ; Herod., III, 8, 2 ; Dio, LXXIV, 8, 4.

⁹¹ He is first called *procurator patrimonii privati* (*CIL*, X, 6657), and then *procurator rei privatae* or simply *procurator privatae*. He received a salary of 300,000 HS per annum (X, 6569) and ranked with the *rationalis* (*Digest*, XLIX, 14, 6, 1).

⁹² Cohen, IV, pp. 32–4, nos. 279–300 ; *Chron.* of A.D. 354 (*Chron. Min.*, 1, p. 147).

⁹³ *de Antidot.*, 1, 3 ; *de Theriaca*, 1, 2 ; Platnauer, *op. cit.*, p. 187.

[94] *Vita Sev.*, 14, 2.

[95] Pelham, *Essays on Roman History*, p. 261 ; Strong, *Art in Rome*, II, pp. 139–48.

[96] H. Stuart Jones, *Companion to Roman History*, pp. 37–8.

[97] Dio, LXXVI, 11, 1 ; Herod., III, 14, 2 ; PROFECTIO coins (Cohen, IV, p. 61, nos. 573–575).

[98] For Virius Lupus, *CIL*, VII, 210, 273 ; for Alfenius Senecio, inscription from Birdoswald published in *Trans. of C. and W. Antiq. and Arch. Soc.*, XXX, p. 199 ; for the dating of the restoration of Hadrian's Wall, E. Birley in *Arch. Aeliana*, Fourth Series, VII, pp. 166–8 ; Collingwood, *Roman Britain* (2nd ed.), pp. 36–9.

[99] Dio, LXXVI, 13, 2.

[100] Dio, LXXVI, 13, 4, and 15, 2 ; Herod., III, 15, 3.

[101] Dio, LXXVI, 13, 1.

[102] Cohen, IV, pp. 75–6, S. Severus, nos. 722–731 ; p. 195, Caracallus, nos. 493–494 ; p. 267, Geta, nos. 138–139.

[103] Collingwood, *op. cit.*, p. 39.

CHAPTER II

[1] *CIL*, XII, 1856 (and Mommsen's notes)=Dess. *ILS*, 1353 ; C. W. Keyes, *The Rise of the Equites in the third century of the R.E.*, pp. 32–3 ; Ritterling, *s.v. Legio* in *P-W*, XII, col. 1308. I cannot agree with Keyes' statement that Dio, LV, 24, 4, implies that II *Parthica* was formed after I and before III *Parthicae*.

[2] Ritterling, *op. cit.*, coll. 1482–1483, in criticism of Domaszewski, *Die Rangordnung*, p. 165.

[3] Domaszewski, *Geschichte des röm. Reiches*, II, p. 262.

[4] Platnauer, *op. cit.*, p. 162.

[5] Dess. *ILS*, 2103 ; *CIL*, X, 532 ; Ritterling, *op. cit.*, col. 1313 ; for the *bellum Judaicum*, Hasebroek, *op. cit.*, pp. 70–2.

[6] Domaszewski, *Die Rangordnung*, pp. 16 and 75.

[7] Dio, LV, 26, 6 ; Baillie Reynolds, *The Vigiles of Imperial Rome*, pp. 64–8.

[8] Domaszewski, *op. cit.*, pp. 133–4 and 90 ; Rostovtzeff, *Social and Economic History*, p. 598.

[9] Dessau, *Die Herkunft der Offiziere und Beamten des röm. Kaiserreichs*, in *Hermes*, 1910, pp. 1–26.

[10] Examples from the legions, Dess. *ILS*, 1180, 1332, 9014 ; from the *auxilia*, *CIL*, VIII, 9359, *A.E.*, 1908, no. 206, cf. Cheesman, *Auxilia of the Imperial Roman Army*, pp. 94–100.

[11] *CIL*, III, 14507, cf. a list of soldiers discharged from II *Traiana* in Egypt in A.D. 194 (Dess. *ILS*, 2304).

[12] Dess. *ILS*, 2771 (I *Parthica*) ; Dio, LXXVIII, 13, 4, with *Vita Car.*, 6, 7 (II *Parthica*), cf. Dess. *ILS*, 1356 ; *CIL*, VIII, 20996.

[13] C. W. Keyes, *op. cit.*, pp. 30–1.

[14] Dess. *ILS*, 1331 ; Domaszewski, *Die Verwaltung der Provinz Mesopotamien*, in *Wien. Stud.*, IX, pp. 297–9.

[15] Keyes, *op. cit.*, pp. 3 ff.

[16] Domaszewski, *Die Rangordnung*, pp. 43, 34 ; *CIL*, III, 12659 ; Dess. *ILS*, 8847.

[17] *CIL*, III, 8571 ; Domaszewski, *op. cit.*, p. 172.

[18] Dess. *ILS*, 484, *CIL*, III, 14479, 3306 ; Domaszewski, *op. cit.*, pp. 32–3.

[19] After passing through the three or four equestrian *militiae*, he received the title *a militiis* (*CIL*, III, 6757 ; Domaszewski, *op. cit.*, p. 131).

[20] "*a muneribus quae non patrimoniis indicuntur, veterani perpetuo excusantur*" (*Digest*, L, 5. 7, cf, XLIX, 18, 1).

[21] *Id.*, XXVII, 1, 9.

[22] Dess. *ILS*, 2354, 2438, 2445, 9096–9100.

[23] Aquincum (*ibid.*, 2375) ; Potaissa (*CIL*, III, 876).

[24] Parker, *The Roman Legions*, pp. 237–8.

[25] Herod., III, 8, 5.

[26] H. Stuart Jones, *Companion to Roman History*, p. 240 ; Platnauer, *op. cit.*, p. 168.

[27] *Vita Sev.*, 7, 6 ; Herod., II, 14, 5.

[28] Domaszewski in *Neue Heidelb. Jahrb.*, X, pp. 231, 236 ; *Die Rangordnung*, p. 111.

[29] Fabricius, *s.v. Limes* in *P-W*, XIII, col. 665 ; *CIL*, VIII, 10992 ; Dess. *ILS*, 9177.

[30] Pelham, *Essays on Roman History*, p. 207.

[31] *CIL*, III, 128.

[32] Ems (*CIL*, XIII, 7734) ; Roomburg (Dess. *ILS*, 9178) ; Daci (*ILS*, 9179).

CHAPTER III

[1] Dio, LXXVI, 15, 2.

[2] Dio. LXXVII, 1, 1.   Herod., III, 15, 6.

[3] Herod., III, 15, 4.   Dio, LXXVII, 1, 1.

[4] Dio, LXXVII, 1, 3.   Possibly in other parts of the Empire sympathy was also shown to Geta, if the right restoration of the cognomen in an inscription of XIII *Gemina* and VII *Gemina* is *Getica* (Dess. *ILS*, 1370 and Ritterling, *s.v. Legio*, *P-W*, XII, col. 1317) ; cf. CONCORDIA MILITUM on Geta's coins (Cohen, IV, p. 255, nos. 18–21).

[5] Herod., IV, 1, 1–2.

[6] *Ibid.*, 1, 5.   *Consecratio* coins (Cohen, IV, pp. 12–13, nos. 80–91).

[7] Herod., IV, 3, 5–9.

[8] Dio, LXXVII, 2, 2–6 ; Herod., IV, 4, 3 ; *Vita Car.*, 2, 4 ; Eutrop., VIII, 19 ; Victor *de Caes.*, 20, 32.

[9] Dio, LXXVII, 3, 1–2 ; Herod., IV, 4, 5–8.

[10] *Vita Car.*, 2, 7–8.

[11] Dio, LXXVII, 4, 1 ; cf. Ritterling, *op. cit.*, col. 1317.

[12] *Ibid.*, 3, 3.

[13] *Ibid.*, 4, 1 ; Herod., IV, 6, 1–2.

[14] Dio, LXXVII, 12, 6.

[15] Herod., IV, 6, 3 ; Dio, LXXVII, 4.

[16] e.g. Dess. *ILS*, 458–460 ; Dio, LXXVII, 12, 6.

[17] Herod., IV, 7, 1–2 ; PROFECTIO AUG. (Cohen, IV, p. 196, nos. 508–509).

[18] Dio, LXXVII, 9.

[19] *Vita Car.*, 5, 1.

[20] For *vexillationes* under Suetrius Sabinus, Dess. *ILS*, 1159 ; for *vexillationes* under Alexianus, an inscription found at Salona in 1911 and published by Egger in *Jahresh. Österreich Beiblatt* (1919), pp. 294–322. On the question of the posts held by these two officers at the time of the campaign see, as against Egger, *op. cit.*, Ritterling, *s.v. Legio, P-W*, XII, col. 1317.

[21] Dess. *ILS*, 2319, 2345.

[22] On Faimingen see Drexel, *ORL. B*, no. 66, *Kastell Faimingen*, p. 30 ; cf. Dio, LXXVII, 13, 4, and Pelham, *Essays on Roman History*, p. 207.

[23] Dio, LXXVII, 13, 5.

[24] Dess. *ILS*, 451 ; *Vita Car.*, 5, 4, and on the probable site of the battle, Ritterling, *op. cit.*, col. 1319 ; VICTORIA GERMANICA (Cohen, IV, p. 210, nos. 645–646).

[25] Dio, LXXVII, 14, 1–2.

[26] *Ibid.*, 14, 3 ; Herod., IV, 7, 3.

[27] For consultation of *Apollo Grannus*, Dio, LXXVII, 15, 6 ; for Baden-Baden = *Aurelia Aquensis*, Nisle, *De bellis ab Antonio Caracallo in Germania et Sarmatia gestis*, p. 14.

[28] Dio, LXXVIII, 3, 3 ; Vict. *epit.*, 21, 2 ; *Vita Car.*, 9, 7.

[29] See Part II, Chap. V, pp. 115–6 ; Herod., IV, 8, 1.

[30] Dio, LXXVIII, 27, 5 ; *Vita Car.*, 5, 4.

[31] Dio, LXXVII, 16, 7 ; Herod., IV, 8, 1 ; *CIL*, III, 14416.

[32] Dio, LXXVII, 7 ; Herod., IV, 8, 1–2.

[33] Dio, LXXVII, 7, 1–2.

[34] Herod., IV, 8, 3–5.

[35] Dio, LXXVIII, 8, 4.

[36] Dio, LXXVII, 18, 1.

[37] *Ibid.*, 19, 3 ; cf. *ibid*, 20, 1 ; Herod., IV, 8, 6 ; for the African *vexillatio*, Dess.. *ILS*, 470.

[38] Dio, LXXVII, 21, 1 ; cf. *ibid.*, 12, 2.

[39] *Ibid.*, 19, 1.

[40] *Ibid.*, 22, 1–23, 4 ; Herod., IV, 8, 6–9, 8 ; *Vita Car.*, 6, 2–3.

[41] Herod., IV, 9, 8. Probably at this time a dispute between Thyatira and Hierokaisareia was settled by the Emperor " *praesens* " (Keil u. Premerstein, *Zweite Reise*, no. 18).

[42] Dio, LXXVIII, 1, 1 ; Herod., IV, 10, 1–11, 1.

[43] Dio, LXXVII, 12, 1. This seems the most probable chronology.

[44] *Id.*, LXXVIII, 1, 2 ; Herod., IV, 11, 2–9 ; VICTORIA PARTHICA on coins (Cohen, IV, pp. 211–12, nos. 647–662).

[45] Dio, LXXVIII, 4, 1.

[46] Herod., IV, 12, 3–13, 8 ; Dio's version of the story differs in detail (LXXVIII, 4–5).

47 Dio, LXXVIII, 30, 2–3 ; for Marcellus, Dess. *ILS*, 478.

48 *Id.*, LXXVII, 17, 1 ; Herod., IV, 7, 2.

49 Dio, LXXVII, 17, 1–4.

50 Mommsen, *Staatsrecht*, II³, p. 270.

51 Dio, LXXVII, 9, 4 ; reduced again by Macrinus (LXXVIII, 12, 2) ; Hirschfeld, *Die Kaiserl. Verwaltungsbeamten*, (2nd ed.), pp. 97–8.

52 Dio, LXXVII, 9. 2.

53 *Ibid.*, 14, 4.

54 Mattingly, *Roman Coins*, pp. 125, 191 ; Mickwitz, *Geld u. Wirtschaft im röm. Reich*, pp. 18–37.

55 Dio, LXXVII, 3, 1–2 ; 9, 1 ; 10–11, 1 ; Strong, *Art in Rome*, II, pp. 145–7 ; *Vita Car.*, 9, 4–5 ; Victor *de Caes*, 21, 4.

56 Herod., V, 1, 5.

57 *Ibid.*, 2, 1 ; *Vita Macr.*, 7, 1–4. FELICITAS TEMPORUM, FIDES PUBLICA, SALUS PUBLICA on coins (Cohen, IV, pp. 291–2, nos. 14–21 ; p. 293, no. 31 ; p. 301, nos. 113–120).

58 *Vita Macr.*, 5, 7 ; *Vita Car.*, 11, 5 ; Dess. *ILS*, 469–472, 1168. *Consecratio* coins, Cohen, IV, pp. 145–6, nos. 32–35 ; for the titles of his son Diadumenianus, *ibid.*, pp. 311–16.

59 Dio, LXXVIII, 12.

60 *Ibid.*, 14 ; cf. Herod., IV, 12, 1.

61 *Ibid.*, 26–27 ; Herod., IV, 15, 1–8.

62 Dio, LXXVIII, 28.

63 *Ibid.*, 29 ; Herod., V, 2, 6.

64 Dio, LXXVIII, 23, 1.

65 Herod., V, 3, 2.

66 *Ibid.*, 3, 3 ; Dio, LXXVIII, 30–31.

67 Herod., V, 3, 4–12.

68 *Ibid.*, 4, 3–4.

69 Dio, LXXVIII, 34, 5.

70 *Ibid.*, 35, 1.

71 *Ibid.*, 37–9 ; Ritterling, *s.v. Legio*, *P-W*, XII, coll. 1322–1323.

CHAPTER IV

1 Dio, LXXIX, 1, 3 ; 2, 2.

2 Herod., V, 5, 1 ; *Vita Hel.*, 5, 1.

3 Herod., V, 5, 6–7.

4 *Vita Hel.*, 6, 7.

5 Dio, LXXIX, 7, 1 ; Dess. *ILS*, 2657, in which the name of the legion is erased. Perhaps some of its soldiers were transferred into III *Augusta* (Dess. *ILS*, 2314–2317), but this may have occurred earlier under Caracallus (Ritterling, *s.v. Legio*, *P-W*, XII, col. 1527).

6 Herod., V, 5, 8 ; Dio, LXXIX, 11 (for the ritual) ; *Vita Hel.*, 3, 4–5.

7 Herod., V, 6, 3–4 ; Dio, LXXIX, 12, 1.

8 Herod., V, 6, 7–10.

9 e.g. Dess. *ILS*, 473, 475 ; Cohen, IV, pp. 347–8, nos. 246–253 ; cf. p. 350, nos. 276–277.

[10] Herod., V, 6, 1–2 ; Dio, LXXIX, 9 ; for her coinage, Cohen, IV, pp. 380–3.

[11] Dio, LXXIX, 13–15.

[12] *Ibid.*, 6, 1–3.

[13] *Ibid.*, 4, 1–2.

[14] *Vita Hel.*, 12, 1 ; cf. *ibid.*, 6, 1.

[15] Dio, LXXIX, 17 ; Herod., V, 7, 1–3 ; for the date, Thiele, *De Severo Alexandro Imperatore*, pp. 57–60 ; Hönn, *Quellenuntersuch. zu den Viten des Heliogabalus und des Severus Alexander*, p. 48 ; Jardé, *Sévère Alexandre*, p. 11, n. 1. On July 10th Alexander was co-opted into the *sodales Antoniniani* (*CIL*, VI, 2001 p. 448), and this may be the date of his adoption by E. But *CIL*, VI, 3069 dated June 1st, A.D. 221, shows E. and A. associated in supreme power. Is this an error or did the adoption take place late in May ? (For Julia Maesa's coinage, Cohen, IV, pp. 391–8.)

[16] Herod., V, 7, 4 ; *Vita Hel.*, 15, 5.

[17] Herod., V, 7, 5.

[18] Dio, LXXIX, 19 ; *Vita Hel.*, 13, 1–4 ; Herod., V, 8, 3.

[19] Dio, LXXIX, 20 ; *Vita Hel.*, 17, 1–6 ; Herod., V, 8, 5–8 ; for March 6th in preference to March 11th, Thiele, *op. cit.*, pp. 61–7.

[20] "τὸ σχῆμα τῆς βασιλείας ἐκ τυραννιδος ἐφυβρίστου ἐς ἀριστοκρατίας τύπον μεταχθείσης" (Herod., VI, 1, 2).

[21] Herod., *loc. cit.* On the problem of the date and authorship of the *Historia Augusta*, N. H. Baynes, *The Historia Augusta*, where the most important theories of earlier writers are summarised and a new opinion advanced.

[22] Dio, LII, 14–40.

[23] For his views on monarchy, *id.*, XLVI, 34 ; LIII, 17.

[24] "τὸ πρόσχημα τῆς πολιτείας" (XXXVII, 26, 3) ; "σεμνὸν καὶ ἀξιολογὸν ἐστι τό τε τὴν βούλην πάντων κυρίαν δοκεῖν εἶναι" (LII, 31).

[25] P. Meyer, *De Maecenatis oratione a Dione ficta*, pp. 87 ff.

[26] Jardé, *op. cit.*, pp. 26–32.

[27] *Vita Alex.*, 16, 1.

[28] Jardé, *op. cit.*, pp. 22–6, especially in criticism of the rejection of the number 70 on the basis of *Cod. Theo.*, VI, 4, 9, by Thiele and Hönn (Thiele, *op. cit.*, p. 11 ; Hönn, *op. cit.*, p. 91).

[29] *Vita Alex.*, 21, 3.

[30] The only praetorian prefects in the reign of Alexander that may have been senators are those mentioned with the title λαμπρότατοι in a papyrus of A.D. 232 (Wilcken, I (2), p. 62, no. 41, col. III ; Jardé, *op. cit.*, pp. 34–44).

[31] *Vita Alex.*, 43, 3 ; Mommsen, *Staatsrecht*, I³, p. 559 ; Jardé, *op. cit.*, pp. 44–53.

[32] *Vita Alex.*, 33, 1.

[33] *CIL*, VI, 1450.

[34] Suetrius Sabinus (Dess. *ILS*, 1159) ; Annius Honoratus (*ibid.*, 1174) ; Comazon (Dio, LXXIX, 21, 1) ; he retained office only till A.D. 223.

[35] Dio, LXXX, 1 and 5.

[36] Dio, LXXX, 2, 2. Epagathos, who was responsible for the murder, was appointed prefect of Egypt, and was subsequently brought to Crete and tried there to avoid any further disturbance in Rome.

[37] " La Cyropédie d'écrivains sénatoriaux " (Lécrivain, *Études sur l'histoire Auguste*, p. 233).

[38] Dio, LXXX, 2, 1; Dess. *ILS*, 482, 484–485; for Mammaea's coinage, Cohen, IV, pp. 490–501; for the deification of Maesa (*ibid.*, pp. 391–2, nos. 1–7).

[39] Dio, LXXX, 2, 2.

[40] *Vita Alex.*, 20, 3; 49, 3–4; on the question of the name or names of Alexander's wife or wives, Jardé, *op. cit.*, pp. 67–73, with his convincing restoration of *CIL*, VIII, 1492. In opposition to Thiele he holds, it seems rightly, that Alexander was married only once and that his wife's name in full was Gneia Seia Herennia Sallustia Barbia Orbiana (Dess. *ILS*, 486; Cohen, IV, pp. 478–9; 486–8).

[41] *Vita Alex.*, 40, 6; *CIL*, III, 536; cf. regulations about the rate of interest (*Vita Alex.*, 26, 3); for Mammaea, Herod., VI, 1, 8.

[42] Five *liberalitates* on coins (Cohen, IV, pp. 412–17, nos. 107–145); *Vita Alex.*, 26, 1, wrongly says three; cf. increase in alimentation (*Vita Alex.*, 57, 7).

[43] *Vita Alex.*, 25, 3 and 6; Eutrop., VII, 15; *Chron.* of A.D. 354 (*Chron. Min.*, I, p. 147); Hönn, *op. cit.*, p. 52; Cohen, IV, pp. 411–12, nos. 102–104; pp. 449–50, nos. 479–480, commemorate his building activities.

[44] *Vita Alex.*, 21, 1.

[45] Details have been collected by Thiele, *op. cit.*, p. 115, and by Groebe in *P-W*, II, col. 2532; cf. growth of *castella* in Africa (Carcopino in *Revue Africaine*, 1918, pp. 5–22).

[46] Dio, LXXX, 3, 2; Agathias, IV, 24; Mommsen, *The Provinces of the Roman Empire* II, pp. 81–9.

[47] Artaxerxes' plans and projects in Dio, LXXX, 4, 1; Herod., VI, 2, 2.

[48] Herod., VI, 3, 1; 4, 3; Dess. *ILS*, 1173; Ritterling, *s.v. Legio*, *P-W*, XII, col. 1326.

[49] Assumption of title *proconsul* (*CIL*, VI, 2108). PROFECTIO coins (Cohen, IV, pp. 450–2, nos. 486–494).

[50] Herod., VI, 4, 5.

[51] Heracleo (Dio, LXXX, 4, 2); for pretenders, Herod., VI, 4, 7; Zos., 1, 12, who mentions two, Antoninus and Uranius; Syncellus, I, pp. 674–5, who speaks only of Uranius and places the scene of the revolt at Edessa at the time of the Persian War. See further on the number and identity of the usurpers, Jardé, *op. cit.*, pp. 65–7. For the troops from Egypt, Herod., VI, 4, 7, who is confirmed by a papyrus which records only one instead of the normal three cohorts at Syene (Wilcken, I (2), p. 62, no. 41, col. III).

[52] Herod., VI, 5, 1–2; 5, 5–6, 3.

[53] *Ibid.*, 6, 6; *Vita Alex.*, 56, 1; Cohen, IV, p. 445, no. 446.

[54] Herod., VI, 7, 2; Cohen, IV, p. 484, no. 19; Thiele, *op. cit.*, p. 105.

[55] Herod. (VI, 7, 5) makes Alexander move direct from the East to Germany and is silent about the triumph.

[56] *Vita Alex.*, 58, 4.

[57] Herod., VI, 7, 8.

[58] Cohen, IV, p. 483, no. 16.

[59] Herod., VI, 7, 9.

[60] *Vita Alex.*, 63, 5.

[61] Herod., VI, 8, 1–2.

[62] *Ibid.*, 8, 3–9, 8 ; cf. Zos., 1, 13, 1–2 ; *Vita Alex.*, 59, 7–8, and Jardé, *op. cit.*, pp. 88–94.

CHAPTER V

[1] Dess. *ILS*, 2382, before the move, and *ibid.*, 2375, after the move of I *Adiutrix* from Upper to Lower Pannonia. For the consular governor, *ibid.*, 1159 ; Ritterling, *op. cit.*, *P-W*, XII, col. 1393.

[2] See Part II, Chapter I, pp. 64, 68–9.

[3] II *Parthica* is not included as it was stationed in Italy.

[4] Ritterling, *op. cit.*, col. 1320.

[5] My article, *The Legions of Diocletian and Constantine*, in *JRS*, XXIII, 1933, pp. 173–89.

[6] *Proc. et praes. Sardiniae* (*CIL*, VI, 1636); *praes. Mauretaniae* (VIII, 9002) ; *proc. Augg. nn. agens vices praesidis* (*Dacia Apulensis*, III, 1625, 7901) ; C. W. Keyes, *op. cit.*, p. 5.

[7] *Digest*, I, 18, 1.

[8] See Part II, Chapter II, p. 84.

[9] *CIL*, VIII, 2705.

[10] *Ibid.*, 8470, 10351, 10353, 10364.

[11] For the epigraphical evidence, Hasebroek, *op. cit.*, pp. 127–8.

[12] *CIL*, III, 6904, 6907, 6911, 6922.

[13] *Ibid.*, 205, 6723, 6725.

[14] Dess. *ILS*, 454.

[15] *Ibid.*, 422 ; *IGRR*, III, 967.

[16] Dio, LXXV, 3, 2 ; Head, *Hist. Num.*, p. 689.

[17] *Digest*, L, 15, 1–4.

[18] Vaga (*CIL*, VIII, 1217, 1222, 14394–14395) ; Thugga (VIII, 1487) ; Cuicul (VIII, 8318).

[19] *Digest*, L, 15, 8, 11.

[20] *Ibid.*, 15, 1, 9.

[21] See Part II, Chapter I, p. 71.

[22] A and J, pp. 456–7, no. 130 ; Dess. *ILS*, 423.

[23] For Sitifis, Carcopino in *Revue Africaine*, 1918, pp. 5–22. This policy was developed notably by Severus Alexander. For Pizus, A and J, pp. 458–9, no. 131 ; Rostovtzeff, *Social and Economic History*, pp. 376–8.

[24] *Pap. Ox.*, VIII, 1100 ; Hasebroek, *op. cit.*, pp. 102–3.

[25] *CIL*, VIII, 9360 ; II, 1085.

[26] Dess. *ILS*, 429, 430.

[27] Keil u. Premerstein, *Zweite Reise*, no. 222 ; *Dritte Reise*,

nos. 9, 28, 55 ; A and J, pp. 478–82, nos. 142–144 ; Rostovtzeff, *op. cit.*, pp. 357, 364, 603. For a similar protest to Philip from the Aragueni in Phrygia (Dittenberger *Inscr. Or. Gr.*, II, no. 519).

²⁸ *BGU*, II, 484 ; Keil u. Premerstein, *Dritte Reise*, pp. 38–47 ; Wilcken, I (2), p. 235, no. 202.

²⁹ A and J, pp. 544–5, no. 190 ; cf. a similar protest presented to a centurion Julius Julianus (Wilcken, I (2), p. 416, no. 354).

³⁰ *BGU*, II, 372 = A and J, p. 524, no. 175 of A.D. 154. For the harshness of liturgies, *P. Gen.* 37 = Wilcken, I (2), p. 477, no. 400 = A and J, p. 529, no. 180.

³¹ *PSI*, 683, published in *Arch. f. Papyri* 7 (1923), pp. 84 ff. ; Rostovtzeff, *op. cit.*, p. 599.

³² *P. Giess.*, 40, II, 16 ff. ; Wilcken, I (2), p. 38, no. 22.

³³ Herod., IV, 9, 6–8 ; Dio, LXXVII, 22 ; Rostovtzeff, *op. cit.*, p. 368 ; Ritterling, *op. cit.*, *P-W*, XII, col. 1318.

³⁴ Ammaedara (Dess. *ILS*, 417) ; Cuicul (*ibid.*, 435) ; Gigtha (*ibid.* 436).

³⁵ Comana (*IGRR*, III, 325) ; Mulassa (*ibid.*, 384) ; Milyas (*ibid.*, 389) ; Osiena (*ibid.*, 418) ; Salagassum (*ibid.*, 352) ; cf. dedications to Septimius by Magnesia and Hierokaisareia and to Caracallus by Metropolis in Lydia (Keil u. Premerstein, *Eine reise*, no. 4 ; *Zweite reise*, no. 34 ; *Dritte reise*, no. 162).

³⁶ Sparta (*CIG*, I, 1320) ; Thespiae (*ibid.*, 1618) ; Thebes (*ibid.*, 1619) ; Troezen (*ibid.*, 1185) ; Megara (*ibid.*, 1075). Have these perhaps some connection with Caracallus' pose as Alexander ?

³⁷ A and J, pp. 113 ; 409, no. 89 = *IGRR*, III, no. 1056 ; 553, no. 197 = *Pap. Ox.* 62.

³⁸ *Digest*, L, 4, 18, 1.

³⁹ *Ibid.*, 4, 1, 3.

⁴⁰ *Ibid.*, 4, 18, 26.

⁴¹ *Ibid.*, 4, 1, 2 ; cf. 4, 18, 1–17.

⁴² *Ibid.*, 4, 1, 1 ; cf. 4, 18, 18–23.

⁴³ *Ibid.*, 4, 3, 15.

⁴⁴ For the number and character of liturgies in Egypt, Oertel, *Die Liturgie* ; Wilcken, I (1), pp. 339–51.

⁴⁵ *Digest*, L, 5, 2, 1–3 and 7 ; L, 6, 4 (3).

⁴⁶ *Ibid.*, 5, 2, 4 ; 5, 11.

⁴⁷ *Ibid.*, 6, 6 (5) ; 5, 12, 1 ; 5, 8, 1.

⁴⁸ *Ibid.*, 5, 7.

⁴⁹ *Ibid.*, 5, 13, 1 and cf. 6, 7 (6).

⁵⁰ *Ibid.*, 4, 18, 30.

⁵¹ *Ibid.*, 5, 8, 4.

⁵² *Ibid.*, 6, 6 (5), 12.

⁵³ Dess. *ILS*, 6987 ; Rostovtzeff, *op. cit.*, pp. 359–61.

⁵⁴ *Digest*, L, 5, 3 ; L, 6 (5), 9.

⁵⁵ Dio, LXXVII, 9, 5 ; *Digest*, L, 5, 17 ; A and J, p. 547, no. 192.

⁵⁶ The text of the papyrus (*P. Giess.* 40, col. 1) is defective, and many attempts have been made to restore it. The most recent, and on the whole most satisfactory, version is that of A. Wilhelm (*Amer.*

Journal of Archœology, N.S., 38 (1934), pp. 178–80) based upon those of E. Schönbauer (*Zeitschrift der Savigny-Stiftung für Rechtsgeschichte,* LI Band (1931), pp. 277 ff.) and J. Stroux (*Philologus,* LXXXVIII (1933), pp. 272–95), which I have followed. His text is as follows :

1. [Αὐτοκράτωρ Καῖσαρ Μᾶ]ρκος Αὐρήλι[ος Σεουῆρος] 'Αντωνῖνο[ς] λέγει·

2. [πάντως εἰς τὸ θεῖον χρ]ὴ μᾶλλον ἀν[αφέρειν καὶ τὰ]ς αἰτίας κ[α]ὶ το[ὺς] λ[ογι]σμοὺ[ς]

3. [δικαίως δ'ἂν κἀγὼ τοῖς θε]οῖς τ[οῖ]ς ἀθ[αν]άτοις εὐχαριστήσαιμι ὅτι τῆ[ς] τοιαύτη[ς]

4. [ἐπιβουλῆς γενομένης σῷο]ν ἐμὲ συν[ετήρ]ησαν. Τοιγαροῦν νομίζω [ο]ὕτω με-

5. [γαλομερῶς καὶ θεοπρεπ]ῶς δύ[να[σθαι τῇ μεγαλει[ό]τητι αὐτῶν ἱκανόν ποι-

6. [εῖν, εἰ τοσάκις μυρίους ὁσ]άκις ἐὰν ὑ[π]εισέλθ[ωσ]ιν εἰς τοὺς ἐμοὺς ἀν[θρ]ώπους

7. [ὡς 'Ρωμαίους εἰς τὰ ἱερὰ τῶ]ν θεῶν συνει[σ]ενέγ[κοι]μι. Δίδωμι τοίνυν ἅπα-

8. [σιν τοῖς κατοικοῦσιν τὴ]ν οἰκουμένην π[ολιτ]είαν 'Ρωμαίων, [μ]ένοντος

9. [οὐδενὸς ἐκτὸς τῶν πολιτευμ]άτων χωρὶς τῶν [δε]δειτικίων. 'Ο[φ]είλει [γ]ὰρ τὸ

10. [πλῆθος οὐ μόνον τἆλλα συνυπομέ]νειν πάντα, ἀ[λλ]ὰ ἤδη κ[α]ὶ τῃ νίκῃ ἐνπεριει-

11. [λῆφθαι. Τοῦτο δὲ τὸ ἐμὸν διάτ]αγμα ἐ[ξαπ]λώσει [τὴν] μεγαλειότητα [το]ῦ Ρωμαί-

12. [ων δήμου· συμβαίνει γὰρ τὴν αὐτὴ]ν περὶ τοὺς [ἄλλο]υς γεγενῆσθαι ἥπερ δ[ι]α-

13. [πρέπουσιν ἀνέκαθεν 'Ρωμαῖοι τιμῇ κα]ταλειφ[θεντων . . . . .] ων τῶ[ν ἐ]κίστης.

The identification of the new recipients of the franchise depends upon the restoration of ll. 8–9. Earlier editors read μένοντος πάντος γένους πολιτευμάτων χωρὶς τῶν δεδειτικίων, and interpret the words in varying senses. Of chief interest is the theory of Segré (*Atti della Soc. It. per il progresso delle Scienze,* Settima Riunione Siena, 1913, pp. 1013 ff. ; cf. Capocci, *Constitutio Antoniniana,* 1925), who translates δεδειτίκιοι as *civitates stipendiariae,* and by taking χωρὶς τῶν δεδειτικίων closely with the genitive absolute explains the edict as meaning that (a) the privileged position of *civitates foederatae* and Latin communities was to be maintained, and (b) Roman citizenship conferred upon the members of tribute-paying communities (*stipendiariae*). But the identification of δεδειτίκιοι with *civitates stipendiariae* is unsatisfactory, nor is it clear why, if Caracallus wanted, in gratitude for his escape from Geta, to increase the number of worshippers of the state-gods, he should exclude any urban communities from the franchise. For other theories, P. M. Meyer, *Jurist. Pap.,* I ; Wilcken, I (i), pp. 55–65 ; Rostovtzeff, *op. cit.,* p. 369 ; Bickermann, *Das Edikt des K. Caracalla,* who considers that the papyrus is not the edict, but a further amplification of it ; but in criticism of this theory, see Vogt in *Gnomon* 3 (1927), pp. 328–34.

[57] *BGU*, III, 747 ; A and J, p. 521, no. 173.

[58] *Digest*, L, 4, 3, which reflects, it may be taken, conditions that were in force after the issue of the edict.

[59] Rostovtzeff, *op. cit.*, Chapter IX *passim.*

CHAPTER VI

[1] " *ubique nostra regio tam praesentibus plena est numinibus, ut facilius possis deum quam hominem invenire.*" Petron. *Satyricon*, 17.

[2] Lucian, *Deorum Conc.* 14–18 (vol. III, ed. Jacobitz, pp. 390–92).

[3] e.g. Dess. *ILS*, 4354, 4365, 4362 ; Plut., *de Is. et Os.*, 32, 38, 52 (*Moralia* II, ed. Bernardakis, pp. 503, 509, 526) ; Apul., *Metamorph.*, XI, 5.

[4] e.g. *Serapi conservatori* (Dess. *ILS*, 4383).

[5] *Ibid.*, 4391.

[6] *Ibid.*, 4393, 4395–4398.

[7] Serapis and Mithras have commonly the title *Sol* with the epithets *magnus* and *invictus.*

[8] Dess. *ILS*, 4325–4326.

[9] *Ibid.*, 4286–4293.

[10] *Ibid.*, 4300–4324.

[11] e.g. *Mater deorum* and *Attis* (*ibid.*, 4171) ; *Isis* and *Sol* (*ibid.*, 4413), *Isis* of Ostia and *Mater deorum Transtiberina* (*ibid.*, 4406) ; *Minerva* and *Magna Mater* (*ibid.*, 4185) ; *Magna Mater, Syria Dea* and *Isis* (*ibid.*, 4178).

[12] For *Silvanus*, e.g., *ibid.*, 3528, 3543, 3470 (*Hercules et Silvanus*) ; for *Minerva*, e.g. *ibid.*, 3131, and for the temple, Eckhel, *d.n.v.*, VII, p. 187.

[13] *de Deo Socratis* 16, p. 156.

[14] Origen, *contra Celsum*, 8, 35.

[15] *Enneades*, III, 5, 6 ; IV, 4, 43.

[16] Eckhel, *op. cit.*, VII, p. 183 ; *mater deorum*, Cohen, IV, pp. 115–16, nos. 128–129, 137–139 ; *mater castrorum*, p. 116, nos. 130–136 ; *Juno Regina*, p. 113, nos. 96–99.

[17] Dess. *ILS*, 429, 439, 485.

[18] Herod., I, 10, 5 ; *vita Alex.*, 37, 6.

[19] *Vita Car.*, 9, 10 ; cf. Alexander's devotion to *Serapis* (*vita Alex.*, 26, 8).

[20] Domaszewski, *Die Religion des röm. Heeres*, pp. 59–60.

[21] *de Syria dea* (Lucian III, ed. Jacobitz, pp. 341–63).

[22] See further, Cumont, *Les Mystères de Mithra ; id., Textes et Monuments Figurés relatifs aux Mystères de Mithra ; id., Les Religions Orientales dans le Paganisme Romain*, pp. 125–49 ; cf. Part I, Chapter IV, pp. 45–6.

[23] On religious syncretism see further, Réville, *La Religion à Rome sous les Sévères ;* Platnauer, *op.cit.*, pp. 141–57. On Neo–Pythagorean- ism and Neo-Platonism, Whittaker, *Apollonius of Tyana*, pp. 1–53 (1909) ; *id., The Neo-Platonists* (2nd ed., 1928) ; C. Bigg, *The Christian*

Platonists of Alexandria (re-edited by F. E. Brightman 1913); *id.*, *Neo-Platonism* (1895); W. R. Inge, *Christian Mysticism* (1899); *id.*, *The Philosophy of Plotinus* (1932); A. D. Nock, *Conversion* (1933).

²⁴ Philostratus, *Vit. Soph.*, II, p. 121 (ed. Kayser).

²⁵ Whittaker, *Apollonius of Tyana*; Bigg, *Christian Platonists*, pp. 288–294.

²⁶ Réville, *op. cit.*, p. 257.

²⁷ *Vita Alex.*, 29, 2.

²⁸ Whittaker, *Celsus and Origen* in *Apollonius of Tyana*, pp. 54–122.

²⁹ *Id., The Neo-Platonists*, p. 34.

³⁰ *Ibid.*, pp. 27–34; Inge, *Christian Mysticism*, pp. 91–7; Bigg, *Christian Platonists*, pp. 296–316.

³¹ Tertull., *ad Scap.*, 4.

³² *Vita Sev.*, 17, 1.

³³ *Passio S. Perpetuae* in *Texts and Studies*, I, 2, p. 62.

³⁴ Euseb., *H.E.*, VI, 21, 3–4, and VI, 28; *Lib. Pontif.*, I, pp. 145–7 (ed. Duchesne).

³⁵ On the origin of Montanism, Euseb., *H.E.*, V., 16–18; for its asceticism, Tertull., *de Jejunio* and *de Pudicitia*; see furthur Duchesne, *The Early History of the Church*, I, pp. 196–206; B. J. Kidd, *A History of the Church to A.D. 461*, I, pp. 280–96.

On Monarchianism, Tertull., *adv. Praxean*; Duchesne, *op. cit.*, I, pp. 224–6; Kidd, *op. cit.*, I, pp. 359–71.

³⁶ For the works of Clement and Origen see Duchesne, *op. cit.*, I, pp. 243–60; Kidd, *op. cit.*, I, pp. 387–428.

PART III

CHAPTER I

¹ *Vita Max.*, 1, 5; 2, 3–7; 4, 4.

² Herod., VI, 8, 1; *Pap. Par.* 69=Wilcken, I (2), p. 62, no. 41, col. III, accepting his restoration (*Philologus*, LIII, p. 95).

³ Suggested by Herod., VII, 8, 4.

⁴ Herod., VI, 8, 3; Zos., I, 13, 1.

⁵ *Vita Max.*, 8, 1; Victor *de Caes.*, 25, 1; Eutrop., IX, 1.

⁶ Schulz, *Vom Principat zum Dominat*, pp. 51 ff., holds that Maximinus was the first, and perhaps the only, instance of a military despot in the history of the Roman Principate (which terminated according to him with Carus). He maintains that whereas other " usurpers " asked the Senate to condone the unconstitutional action of their soldiers and received their imperial powers from that body, Maximinus merely announced his election to the Senate as though the acclamation of his troops made his elevation constitutionally valid. But the evidence of the Latin authors cited by Schulz is quite indecisive. It is also to be observed that the Senate *did* ratify (doubtless from fear) the soldiers'

choice of Maximinus, who became consul in the following year (Vict. *de Caes.*, 25, 2 ; Liebenam, *Fasti Consulares imp. Rom.*, 29) in very much the same way as it had accepted the elevation of Macrinus.

[7] Herod., VII, 1, 4–8.

[8] *Ibid.*, 1, 9–11.

[9] *Ibid.*, 1, 3.

[10] *Ibid.*, 3, 1–4.

[11] Domaszewski in *Rh. Mus.*, LVIII, p. 383.

[12] Herod., VI, 7, 8 ; VII, 2, 1, and for *damnatio memoriae, CIL.*, XIII, 6677a, and *Rh. Mus.*, LVIII, p. 543. Possibly the Osroenian revolt occurred during, and not before, the German campaign, or (accepting Herodian's chronology) Maximinus gave the Osroenians a chance to retrieve their reputation, but on finding them inefficient fighters disbanded them in disgrace.

[13] Herod., VII, 2, 6–8 ; and for the suggested site of the battle, *Rh. Mus.*, LVIII, p. 545.

[14] Herod., VII, 2, 9.

[15] *CIL*, VI, 2009[23]. Cf. Dess. *ILS*, 491 ; Cohen, IV, pp. 515–16, nos. 105–116 ; pp. 521–2, nos. 1–4.

[16] Dess. *ILS*, 2308, 2309 ; *CIL*, III, 3336.

[17] Dess. *ILS*, 488–490.

[18] *Vita Max.*, 13, 3.

[19] Herod., VII, 4, 2–6 ; *Vita Gord.*, 7, 2–3.

[20] Herod., VII, 5, 1–7 ; *Vita Gord.*, 2, 2, and 8, 1–9, 8. His full title was *imp. Caes. M. Antonius Gordianus Sempronianus Romanus Africanus* (Dess. *ILS*, 493 ; cf. Herod., VII, 5, 8).

[21] Herod., VII, 6, 1–5.

[22] *Ibid.*, 6, 6–7, 2 ; *Vita Gord.*, 10, 5–11 ; Cohen, V, pp. 1–7. In a riot in Rome the prefect of the city, Sabinus, a partisan of Maximinus, was also killed. (*Vita Gord.*, 13, 9 ; Herod., VII, 7, 4.)

[23] *Vita Gord.*, 10, 1–2 ; Zos., 1, 14, 2 ; Dess. *ILS*, 1186, 8979, for two examples of the work of the *XX-viri*.

[24] Herod., VII, 7, 5.

[25] For Dacia, Domaszewski in *Rh. Mus.*, LVIII, p. 228, on Dess. *ILS*, 1371. On Spain and Pannonia, Stein in *P-W*, X, col. 863.

[26] Herod., VII, 9, 1–9.

[27] Zonaras, XII, 17, III, p. 127, ed. Dind. On the chronology of the year A.D. 238, v. Rohden in *P-W*, I, coll. 2623–2624, and Lehmann, *Kaiser Gordian III*, pp. 24–30.

[28] Herod., VII, 10, 1–5 ; Dess. *ILS*, 496.

[29] *Vita Max. et Balb.*, 8, 4 ; Lehmann, *op. cit.*, p. 50 ; Cohen, V, pp. 8–19.

[30] Herod., VII, 10, 5–9 ; *Vita Max. et Balb.*, 8, 3 ; *Vita Gord.*, 22, 2 ; Dess. *ILS*, 496.

[31] Herod., VII, 8, 9–11 ; the Pannonian legions were sent on in advance and suffered a defeat near Aquileia before the arrival of Maximinus (Herod., VIII, 2, 2).

[32] Herod., VIII, 1, 4–5.

[33] *Ibid.*, 2, 3–6.

22

[34] *Ibid.*, 4, 1–6.

[35] *Ibid.*, 3, 7–8 ; *Vita Maxim.*, 22, 1.

[36] Herod., VIII, 5, 8–9 ; *Vita Maxim.*, 23, 6–7.

[37] Herod., VIII, 6, 1–4 ; *Vita Maxim.*, 24, 2–3. The siege probably lasted only three weeks (Eckhel, *d.n.v.*, VII, p. 295 ; Lehmann, *op. cit.*, p. 28), and Maximinus' death is to be dated about May 20th.

[38] Herod., VIII, 6, 5–7.

[39] *Ibid.*, 7, 2–8.

[40] *Ibid.*, 8, 1–4. The Victory of Maximus is commemorated on both his and his colleague's coins (Cohen, V, p. 12, nos. 27–30 ; p. 18, nos. 37–41).

[41] Herod., VII, 11.

[42] Herod., VIII, 8, 5–7. The German troops wisely went home.

[43] *Vita Max. et Balb.*, 16, 3.,

[44] Salisbury and Mattingly in *JRS*, XIV (1924), p. 18 ; Cohen, V, p. 68, nos. 412–14.

[45] Ritterling, *P-W*, XII, col. 1336 ; Cagnat, *L'armée R. d'Afrique*, I, pp. 155 ff.

[46] Dess. *ILS*, 531.

[47] *Vita Gord.*, 23, 4. Against Mommsen's view (*CIL*, VIII, p. xxi) that Mauretania was given a legionary garrison, and von Rohden's (*P-W*, I, col. 2624) that detachments of the German legions I *Minervia* and XXII *Primigenia* were sent to the province, see Ritterling, *op. cit.*, *P-W*, XII, col. 1336.

[48] *Vita Gord.*, 24, 2–25, 5. The letters of Gordian and Timesitheus are almost certainly forgeries, but some of the statements contained in them may be authentic.

[49] *Vita Gord.*, 23, 6 ; Zos., I, 17, 2 ; Zon., XII, 18, III, p. 129. The marriage was earlier than August 29th, A.D. 241, as Tranquillina's name appears first on Alexandrian coins of Gordian's fourth year (i.e. August 29th, A.D. 241–August 28th, A.D. 242), and perhaps as early as May (*CIL*, VI, 2114). The lady's full name was *Furia Sabinia Tranquillina* (Dess. *ILS*, 502–504 ; Cohen, V, pp. 88–92).

[50] *CIL*, VI, 1611, and Domaszewski in *Rh. Mus.*, LVIII, pp. 218 ff. This humble origin is passed over in the Lyons Inscription, which describes his later career in detail (Dess. *ILS*, 1330, and Domaszewski, *op. cit.*).

[51] See further S. Krauss, *Neue Aufschlüsse über Timesitheus und die Perserkriege* in *Rh. Mus.*, LVIII, pp. 627–33, who considers the evidence of the Jewish *Elias-Apokalypse* (cf. the same author's *Der römisch-persische Krieg in der Jüd. Elia-Apok.* in *Jewish Quarterly Review*, XIV, pp. 359–72).

[52] Lehmann, *op. cit.*, pp. 66–7 ; Domaszewski, *Rh. Mus.*, LVIII, p. 230.

[53] *Vita Gord.*, 26, 3 ; Zos., I, 18, 1 ; Eutrop., IX, 2 ; Cohen, V, p. 54, no. 294.

[54] *Vita Gord.*, 26, 5–6 ; Zon., XII, 18, III, p. 129.

[55] *Vita Gord.*, 26, 4 ; cf. the title *victor Gothorum* on Gordian's tombstone. Im erial acclamations are only exceptionally found on Gordian's

inscriptions. On two stones dated A.D. 240 he is called *imp. II* and *III* (*CIL*, VI, 1091, and Dess. *ILS*, 500), and on one stone dated A.D. 242 *imp. VI*, which may have reference to the Gothic War (*CIL*, VIII, 5701).

⁵⁶ Petrus Patricius frg. 8 in *FHG*, IV, pp. 186–7, and on the chronology and interpretation of this passage Lehmann, *op. cit.*, pp. 72–6, following Wietersheim-Dahn, *Geschichte der Völkerwanderung*, I², pp. 194–7. That Menophilus' three years' governorship was from A.D. 242–5, and not earlier, is supported by the fact that the Carpi were inactive till A.D. 245 or 246.

⁵⁷ Dess. *ILS*, 9221, and for a similar use of the fleet in Severus Alexander's Persian Campaign, Dess. *ILS*, 2764, and Domaszewski in *Rh. Mus.*, LVIII, p. 387. TRAIECTUS AUG. (Cohen, V, pp. 58–9, nos. 342–344).

⁵⁸ *Vita Gord.*, 26, 6–27, 3 ; Zon., XII, 18, III, p. 129 ; Ammianus XXIII, 5, 17. Victory coins (Cohen, V, pp. 59–64, nos. 348–380).

⁵⁹ Eckhel, *op. cit.*, III, p. 516.

⁶⁰ *Vita Gord.*, 27, 6 and 28, 1.

⁶¹ *Ibid.*, 29, 1 ; Zos., 1, 18, 2 ; Zon., XII, 18, III, p. 130.

⁶² *Vita Gord.*, 29, 6–30, 9 ; Lehmann, *op. cit.*, pp. 79–81. The date of Gordian's death falls between February 13th and March 14th, the latter being the date of Philip's first edict (*Cod. Just*, III, 42, 6 and Clinton, *Fasti Romani ad ann.* 244). In favour of February 25th, see Lehmann, *op. cit.*, pp. 24–30.

⁶³ *Vita Gord.*, 31, 2–3 ; 32, 4 ; Zosimus, I, 19, 1 ; Zon., XII, 19, III, p. 130.

⁶⁴ Ammianus, XXIII, 5, 17 ; *Vita Gord.*, 34, 3. For an interesting interpretation of this inscription, Lehmann, *op. cit.*, pp. 82–3. If " *non victori Philipporum* " can mean " not victor over Philip's men," then the inscription becomes less an epitaph to the dead Emperor than a memorial of the power of the soldiers themselves to make and unmake their rulers.

CHAPTER II

¹ Zos., I, 19, 1 ; III, 32, 4 ; Zon., XII, 19, III, p. 130. The latter states that Philip first ceded Mesopotamia and Armenia and, when the Romans objected to the terms of the treaty, ignored the peace and reoccupied the countries. This is certainly wrong. There is no record of further fighting in Philip's reign between Rome and Persia, and Priscus' appointment (Dess. *ILS*, 1331 ; *IGRR*, III, 1202) and Philip's title *Persicus Maximus* (Dess. *ILS*, 506 ; *Parthicus Maximus* in *ibid.*, 507), although subsequently dropped, militate further against the theory.

² For Neapolis and Philippopolis, Assmann, *De coloniis oppidisque Romanis quibus imperatoria nomina vel cognomina imposita sunt*, pp. 144–5 (cf. Cohen, V, p. 131, no. 366) ; for Bostra, Cohen, V, p. 132, nos. 372–374.

³ For Philippopolis, Assmann, *op. cit.*, p. 144, no. 162 ; for Beroea,

Num. Zeit., XXIV, pp. 312 ff. ; the *terminus ad quem* for the arrival in Rome is a discharge of soldiers of II *Parthica* on July 23, A.D. 244 (Dess. *ILS*, 505).

⁴ For Marinus, Cohen, V, p. 180, Marinus, nos. 1–2 ; *IGRR*, III, 1199–1200 ; for Severianus, Zos., I, 19, 2.

⁵ Salisbury and Mattingly in *JRS*, XIV (1924), pp. 21–3.

⁶ *IGRR*, IV, 635 of A.D. 246 where the title is *Germanicus* ; but GERMANICUS MAXIMUS is found on coins of A.D. 248 (Cohen, V, p. 135, no. 3) and in a papyrus of A.D. 249 (*Pap. Lond.*, III, p. 321, no. 951).

⁷ Zos., I, 20, 1–2.

⁸ Cohen, V, p. 110, nos. 158–160 ; VICTORIA CARPICA (*ibid.*, p. 117, no. 238).

⁹ Philip was consul for the first time in A.D. 245 and for the second in A.D. 247 when his son first held the consulship. (For *Cos. II*, Cohen, V, p. 110, no. 158.)

¹⁰ Eutrop., IX, 3 ; Victor *de Caes.*, 28, 1 ; *Vita Gord.*, 33, 3.

¹¹ Zos., I, 20, 2 ; Zon., XII, 19, III, p. 131. The chronology is obscure, but the rebellion may be dated from three pieces of evidence :

1. Pacatianus struck a coin with the legend ROMAE AETER. AN. MILL. ET PRIMO (Cohen, V, p. 182, no. 7). Therefore he was in revolt against Philip after April 21st, A.D. 248.

2. There are no coins of Philip belonging to the tenth year of the Viminacian era, which began in August. If the revolt of Pacatianus is the reason, then it lasted later than August, A.D. 248 (Cohen, V, p. 172).

3. If the Goths profited by his revolt to invade Moesia, it is probable that they would choose the best season for campaigning.

Therefore the revolt probably began in the summer of A.D. 248 and lasted, as Zosimus and Zonaras suggest, some five or six months. For other views, E. Stein in *P-W*, X, coll. 762–763 ; Wittig, *id.*, XV, coll. 1265–1266.

¹² Jordanes, *Getica*, 91–92 ; Dexippus frag. 18 (*FHG*, III, p. 675) ; Rappaport, *Die Einfälle der Goten*, p. 35.

¹³ Zos., I, 20, 2 ; Dess. *ILS*, 9005; Domaszewski in *Rh. Mus.*, LIV, p. 159.

¹⁴ Polemius Silvius (*Chron. Min.*, I, p. 521). Victor (*de Caes.* 29, 2) with less probability places the revolt in Syria.

¹⁵ Zos., I, 38, 1 ; on his identification and the chronology, Schulz, *op. cit.*, pp. 99–102 ; Jardé, *op. cit.*, pp. 65–7.

¹⁶ Zos., I, 21, 2 ; Zon., XII, 19, III, p. 131.

¹⁷ Dess. *ILS*, 510.

¹⁸ Salisbury and Mattingly, *op. cit.*, pp. 3–4.

¹⁹ Zon., XII, 19, III, p. 132.

²⁰ For the date, Salisbury and Mattingly, *op. cit.*, pp. 3–4.

²¹ Vict. *de Caes.*, 28, 10.

²² They are not called *divi* on any inscriptions, and their names are frequently erased. Hence Eutrop., IX, 3, is wrong.

²³ J. G. C. Anderson in *JHS*, XVII (1897), pp. 417–22, and XVIII (1898), pp. 340 ff.

[24] *Cod. Just.*, IX, 51, 7 ; cf. AEQUITAS AUG. (Cohen, V, pp. 95–6, nos. 7–15) ; LAETITIA FUNDATA (*ibid.*, pp. 101–2, nos. 71–82).

[25] Petra Pertusa, Dess. *ILS*, 509 ; Concordia, Domaszewski, *Die Rangordnung*, pp. 185–7 (inscription of Traianus Mucianus = Dess. *ILS*, 9479) ; Aquileia, *CIL*, V, 808. The whole legion was not moved (as Domaszewski, *op. cit.*, p. 187, and Stein in *P-W*, X, col. 766 hold), but only a *vexillatio* (Ritterling in *P-W*, XII, coll. 1337–1338).

[26] List of milestones in Stein, *op. cit.*, col. 766 ; for dedications from Africa, Dess. *ILS*, 508, 513 ; *CIL*, VIII, 8809.

[27] *Congiaria, Chron.* of A.D. 354 (*Chron. Min.*, I, p. 147) ; Cohen, V, pp. 102–3 ; reservoir, Vict. *de Caes.*, 28, 1.

[28] *Die Kaiserrede des Pseudo-Aristides* (Aelius Aristides 35 B, Keil) ; Groag in *Wien. Studien* XL (1918), pp. 20–45, who rejects Keil's identification of the βασιλεύς with Macrinus (*Phil. Hist. Klasse*, 1905, pp. 381–428) ; Rostovtzeff, *Social and Economic History*, pp. 403–5.

[29] Euseb., *H.E.*, VI, 34 (κατέχει λόγος) ; Orosius, VII, 20, 2.

[30] Euseb., *H.E.*, VI, 36, 3 ; cf. VI, 41, 9, " ἡ τῆς βασιλείας ἐκείνης τῆς εὐμενεστέρας ἡμῖν μεταβολὴ διήγγελται " (words used by Bishop Dionysius of Alexandria, a contemporary of Philip).

[31] *Gesta Pontific. Rom.*, I, p. 25 (ed. Mommsen).

[32] Vict. *de Caes.*, 29, 1.

[33] Dess. *ILS*, 521 ; Wittig in *P-W*, XV, coll. 1248–1249.

[34] *CIL*, III, 12519, 13724, 13758 ; Stout, *Governors of Moesia*, pp. 71–2, no. 115.

[35] Joh. Antiochenus, frag. 148 (*FHG*, IV, pp. 597–8).

[36] *Cod. Just.*, X, 16, 3 ; *Pap. Ox.*, XIV, 1636 ; *Adventus* coins (Cohen, V, p. 186, nos. 3–7).

[37] Dess. *ILS*, 514–518.

[38] Discharge of veterans, *CIL*, III, p. 898, D, LVI A ; *congiarium, Chron.* of A.D. 354 (*Chron. Min.*, I, p. 147) ; Cohen, V, pp. 192–3, nos. 71–76 ; AEQUITAS, *ibid.*, p. 187, nos. 9–10 ; p. 208, no. 3 ; ABUNDANTIA, *ibid.*, p. 186, nos. 1–2 ; p. 208, no. 1.

[39] *CIL*, III, 4651, 12515, 3723, 10641 ; Dess. *ILS*, 515–516.

[40] Dess. *ILS*, 8922.

[41] From Spain, *CIL*, II, 4809, 4812–3, 4833, 4835, inscribed *trib. pot. procons. IIII cos II*, and so (whatever the explanation of *procons. IIII*) to be dated to the year A.D. 250 (cf. II, 6219), and, as the sons of Decius are not mentioned, earlier than September of that year. From Britain, *CIL*, VII, 1163, 1171, 1174, 1180, undated, but with the name of Decius only ; from Africa, *CIL*, VIII, 10457, 10313–10314, with *trib. pot. cos. II*.

[42] From Galatia, *CIL*, III, 14184[40 and 25], 13644 ; from Philadelphia, III, 14155.

[43] Zon., XII, 20, III, p. 132.

[44] Salisbury and Mattingly, *op. cit.*, pp. 12–16.

[45] Euseb., *H. E.*, VI, 41.

[46] For the Decian persecution, P. M. Meyer, *Abhandl. d. Berl. Akad*, 1910 ; *Pap. Ox.*, IV, 658 ; XII, 1464 ; Seeck, *Untergang*, III²

pp. 301–5 ; Duchesne, *The Early History of the Church*, I, pp., 267–70 ;
Wittig in *P-W*, XV, coll. 1279–1284.

[47] Zon., XII, 20, III, p. 132 ; Duchesne, *l.c.*

[48] Dess. *ILS*, 514.

[49] *CIL*, XIII, 9102, 9110.

[50] *CIL*, III, pp. 898–9, D, LVI B.

[51] The date of the Gothic invasion was probably A.D. 251 (Salisbury
and Mattingly, *op. cit.*, pp. 17–18), and not the spring of A.D. 250
(Wittig, *op. cit.*, coll. 1269–1273).

[52] Syncellus, I, p. 705, ed. Bonn ; Jordanes, *Getica*, 101–102.

[53] Victor *de Caes.*, 29, 1. Herennius is not Augustus till later than
January 1st, A.D. 251 (Salisbury and Mattingly, *op. cit.*, pp. 12–16), and
his elevation may well have coincided with his commission in Illyricum.

[54] *Ibid.*, 29, 3 ; in his absence Julius Valens for a few days assumed
the purple. This probably occurred in March and coincided with the
election of the Pope Cornelius (Cyprian *Ep.*, 55, 9 ; *Gesta Pontif. Rom.*,
I, pp. 28–31 (ed. Mommsen) ; Wittig, *op. cit.*, col. 1272 ; Seeck, *Untergang*, III[2], p. 501).

[55] The surrender of the town was expedited by the revolt of L.
Priscus against Decius (Vict. *de Caes.*, 29, 3 ; Ammianus, XXXI, 5, 17).

[56] Zos., I, 23 ; Zon., XII, 21, III, p. 136.

[57] Zos., I, 24 ; Zon., *l.c.*

[58] Zos., I, 25, 1 ; Vict. *de Caes.*, 30, 1 ; for the career of Hostilianus,
Salisbury and Mattingly, *op. cit.*, pp. 15–16.

[59] Vict. *de Caes.*, 30, 2 ; Zosimus (I, 25, 2) says that Gallus murdered
Hostilianus. Despite the erasure of their names on some stones there
was no official *damnatio memoriae* of the Decii (Wittig, *op. cit.*, coll.
1274–1276).

[60] *Pap. Ox.*, XII, 1554.

CHAPTER III

[1] Zos., I, 37, 3.

[2] Eutrop., IX, 7–8 ; Vict. *de Caes.*, 33, 6 ; Ammianus, XIV, I, 9 ;
Vita Gall., *passim.*

[3] Zos. (I, 27, 2) states that Antioch was captured, but Dexippus
(Syncellus, I, p. 716) and Zonaras (XII, 23, III, p. 141) rightly place
this event after the capture of Valerian.

[4] Zos., I, 28, 1 ; Zon., XII, 21, III, p. 137.

[5] Zon., *l.c.* ; Eutrop., IX, 5 ; Vict. *de Caes.*, 30, 2.

[6] Zon., XII, 21, III, pp. 136–7 ; Euseb., *H. E.*, VII, 1 ; Cyprian
Ep., LIX, 6.

[7] Zos., I, 28, 1–2 ; Zon., XII, 21, III, p. 138 ; Eutrop., IX, 5 ;
Vict. *de Caes.*, 31, 1–2.

[8] Aemilianus' reign probably lasted from May till early August.
He has coins belonging to two Dacian years (VII and VIII), but only
one year at Viminacium (XIV). As Valerian has also coins of year
XIV at Viminacium, Aemilianus' reign cannot have lasted till the end
of the Viminacian year (*circa* August 31st), but must have extended

beyond July 20th, the conjectural day at which the Dacian year began. (Salisbury and Mattingly, *op. cit.*, p. 21).

[9] Eutrop., IX, 7 ; Vict. *de Caes.*, 32, 1.

[10] Dess. *ILS*, 531, 2296.

[11] According to Victor (*de Caes.* 32, 3), Eutrop. (IX, 7), Orosius (VII, 22, 1).

[12] Zos., I, 30, 1 ; that Gallienus received the title Augustus and the normal imperial powers in A.D. 253 is attested by inscriptions (e.g. Dess. *ILS*, 531) and coins (M and S, V (1), p. 79, nos. 115–116 ; " CONCORDIA AUGG." p. 85, nos. 207–208).

[13] For the British detachments *CIL*, XIII, 6780 of 255 A.D. ; on coins VICTORIA GERMANICA appears in A.D. 256 (M and S, V (1), p. 71, no. 39 ; p. 72, no. 50) ; VICTORIA AUGG. IT. GERM. and GERMANICUS MAX. TER in A.D. 257 (*ibid.*, p. 48, nos. 129–130 ; p. 83, nos, 178–179 ; p. 81, no. 141) ; cf. RESTITUTOR GALLIARUM (*ibid.*, pp. 70–71, nos. 27–35).

[14] Zos., I, 30, 3.

[15] Cologne, Schultze in *Bonner Jahrb.*, XCVIII (1895), pp. 1, ff., esp. p. 42.

Neuss, Lehner, *id.*, CXI–CXII (1904), pp. 246–252.

Andernach, *ibid.*, CVII (1901), pp. 25–36.

Trier, Lehner, *Westd. Zeitschr.*, XV (1896), pp. 260–266. There is some doubt whether these works should be attributed to Gallienus or Postumus.

For a review of Gallienus' policy, Homo, *Rev. Hist.*, CXIII (1913), pp. 1–22, 225–67 ; Alföldi in *Fünf-und-zwanzig Jahre Röm-Germ. Kommiss.*, 1930, pp. 11 ff.

[16] GALLIENUS CUM EXERCITU SUO (M and S, V (1), p. 39, nos. 7–8).

[17] Eutrop., IX, 8 ; Zon., XII, 24, III, p. 143 ; Vict. *de Caes.*, 33, 3., The date is uncertain, but the invasion probably took place in A.D. 257. Africa was also disturbed by raids made by the Bavares under Faraxen, which were checked by A.D. 260 (Dess. *ILS*, 2767, 9006).

[18] Niederbieber was stormed in A.D. 259, and probably it was the last of the *castella* to hold out against the Germans (Ritterling, *Zwei Münzfunden aus Niederbieber* in *Bonn. Jahrb.*, CVII (1901), pp. 95 ff).

[19] Zon., XII, 24, III, p. 143 ; Vict. *de Caes.*, 33, 3 ; Eutrop., IX, 8 ; Zos., I, 37, 1. GERMANICUS MAX. V (M and S, V (1), pp. 69–70, nos. 17–19). For the identification of the acclamation with the victory at Milan, Alföldi, *Victories of the Emperor Gallienus*, in *Num. Chron.*, 1929, pp. 252–5.

[20] Vict. *de Caes.*, 33, 1–2 ; *Trig. Tyr.*, 9, 1 ; Zon., *l.c.*

[21] Gallienus had probably three sons. The eldest, P. Cornelius Licinius Valerianus, seems to have died *circa* A.D. 255 (*CIL*, VIII, 8473 ; M and S, V (1) pp. 28–9 ; pp. 116–27 ; Alföldi, *op. cit.*, pp. 262–7).

[22] Inscriptions found in the Mithraeum at Poetovio record a certain Aper as *praepositus leg. V. Maced. et XIII. Gem. Gallienarum* (Ritterling in *P-W*, XII, col. 1340). Aper's title shows that it was *vexillationes* of the legions that were at Poetovio. Despite the contrary statements of

Festus, Orosius and Jordanes, Dacia was not denuded of its garrisons till the reign of Aurelian, but under Gallienus the plateau of Transsylvania was given up and the legions were established in Little Wallachia. (Eutrop., IX, 15 ; *Vita Aurel.*, 39, 7 ; Filow, *Die Teilung des Aurelianischen Dakiens* in *Klio*, XII, pp. 234–9 ; Saria, *Zur Geschichte der Prov. Dakien* in *Strena Buliciana*, 1924, pp. 249 ff. ; Vulić, *Les deux Dacies* in *Musée Belge*, XXVII (1923), pp. 253 ff.)

²³ Vict. *Epit.*, 32, 3 ; *Trig. Tyr.*, 10, 1.

²⁴ For his coinage and that of Dryantilla, M and S, V (2), pp. 586–8.

²⁵ Vict. *de Caes.*, 33, 6 ; *Epit.*, 33, 1 ; *Vita Gall.*, 21, 3. The story is probably not merely a variant on that mentioned in n. 14, but a further authentic illustration of Gallienus' policy.

²⁶ Zos., I, 38, 2 ; *Vita Gall.*, 4, 3 ; Eutrop., IX, 9 ; Zon., XII, 24, III, p. 144. The chronology is doubtful, but A.D. 259 seems the most probable date for the beginning of Postumus' reign. On the coinage of the Gallic Empire there are recorded sixteen years of tribunician power, ten of which are given to Postumus and three each to Victorinus and Tetricus. It is agreed that Tetricus abdicated in A.D. 273. Therefore Postumus' reign probably began in A.D. 259 or at any rate not later than early A.D. 260 (M and S, V (2), pp. 322–6). Alföldi (*op. cit.*, p. 262) places it as late as between December 10th and 31st, A.D. 260. This theory is dependent upon his dating of the capture of Valerian, which on not altogether sufficient grounds he holds could not have been known in the West before October, A.D. 260, and his assignment of the revolts of Ingenuus and Regalian to late in A.D. 260. The problem cannot be certainly solved, but a date a year earlier than that given by Alföldi would seem to fit the evidence most satisfactorily.

²⁷ The legionary coins struck by Gallienus with the legends v PIA v FIDELIS, VI PIA VI FIDELIS, VII PIA VII FIDELIS have been rightly explained by Alföldi (*op. cit.*, pp. 252–8) as referring respectively to Gallienus' victories over the Alamanni at Milan, Ingenuus and Regalian. With the exception of II *Parthica* the units so honoured were stationed on the Rhenish and Danubian frontiers, and clearly this distinction could not have been conferred on the German legions after they had declared for Postumus. Therefore the crushing of Regalian is a *terminus a quo* for the recognition of Postumus on the Rhine.

For the legionary coins M and S, V (1), pp. 92–7, nos. 314–369.

(For other interpretations, Oman in *Num. Chron.*, 1918, pp. 80 ff., who connects the legends with the years of Gallienus' reign (i.e. A.D. 257–259) ; Ritterling in *P-W*, XII, coll. 1341–1343, who emphasizes the absence of the British and Spanish legions from the series and concludes that the coins must have been struck later than the revolt of Ingenuus in which British troops took part ; Dessau in *Eph. Ep.*, VII, pp. 432 ff., who examines the significance of imperial salutations ; Domaszewski in *Rh. Mus.*, LVII, pp. 514–6, who connects the series with Gallienus' *Decennalia.*)

For Spain and Britain, *CIL*, II, 4919, 4943 ; VII, 820, 823, 1150, 1160–1161.

²⁸ Zon., XII, 24, III, p. 143 ; *Vita Gall.*, 4, 4 ; 7, 1.

[29] VICTORIA PARTHICA (M and S, V (1), p. 104, no. 453). RESTITUTOR ORIENTIS (*ibid.*, p. 60, nos. 286–287).

[30] Zos., I, 31–33.

[31] *Ibid.*, I, 34–5.

[32] VICTORIA PARTHICA of A.D. 259 (M and S, V (1), p. 58, no. 262 ; p. 60, no. 291).

[33] Zos., I, 36 ; Zon., XII, 23, III, p. 140 ; Eutrop., VIII, 7 ; Vict. *de Caes.*, 32, 5.

[34] Letters of Dionysius of Alexandria in Euseb., *H. E.*, VII, 10–11 ; Cyprian, *Ep.* LXXVI–LXXIX ; Duchesne, *op. cit.*, I, pp. 272–6.

CHAPTER IV

[1] Zon., XII, 23, III,, p. 141.

[2] *Anon. Contin. Dionis* (*FHG*, IV, p. 193, fr. 3).

[3] Zon., XII, 24, III, p. 145 ; *Trig. Tyr.*, 12 ; M and S, V (2), pp. 580–3.

[4] *Pap. Ox.*, XII, 1476 of September 29th, A.D. 260.

[5] Zon., XII, 23, III, p. 141 ; Syncellus, I, p. 716 (Bonn).

[6] Zon., XII, 24, III, p. 145 ; *Trig. Tyr.*, 12, 12–14. Alföldi, *op. cit.*, p. 257.

[7] *Trig. Tyr.*, 19 and 21 ; *Vita Gall.*, 2, 2–4.

[8] Homo, *Le Règne de l'Empereur Aurélien*, pp. 45–8, and Février, *Essai sur l'Histoire Politique et Economique de Palmyre*, pp. 64–79.

[9] *FHG*, IV, p. 195, fr. 7, a story told by the Continuator of Dio, on which see Février, *op. cit.*, pp. 77–8.

[10] Waddington, *Inscriptions grecques et latines de la Syrie*, no. 2602.

[11] Petrus Patricius, fr. 10 (*FHG*, IV, p. 187).

[12] *Vita Gall.*, 10, 1 ; *Trig. Tyr.*, 15, 2 " *adsumpto nomine primum regali.*" Zon., XII, 23, III, p. 142 ; Syncellus, I, p. 716 (Bonn).

[13] Zon., *l.c.*, and XII, 24, III, p. 146.

[14] Zon., XII, 24, III, p. 146 ; *Vita Gall.*, 3, 1–5 ; *Trig. Tyr.*, 14, 1–2 ; 15, 4 ; 18, 3.

[15] Zos., I, 39, 1 ; *Vita Gall.* 10, 2–8 ; *Trig. Tyr.*, 15, 3–4 ; Eutrop., IX, 10.

[16] Waddington, *op. cit.*, no. 2583 ; Février, *op. cit.*, p. 88.

[17] *Vita Gall.*, 10, 1 ; *Trig. Tyr.*, 15, 5.

[18] Zos., I, 39, 2 ; Syncellus, I, pp. 716–17.

[19] For Aemilianus, *Vita Gall.*, 4, 2 ; for Heraclianus, *ibid.*, 13, 4–5.

[20] Details in Homo, *Le Règne de l'Empereur Aurélien*, p. 43, n. 2.

[21] M and S, V. (2), p. 337, nos. 14–15 ; p. 345, no. 97 (VICT. GERM. TR. P. V COS III) ; p. 363, no. 324 (RESTITUTOR ORBIS) ; p. 344, no. 87 (SALUS PROVINCIARUM). The mint was moved from Lyons to Cologne *circa* A.D. 265.

[22] Coins with a galley and the reverse inscriptions FELICITAS, LAE-TITIA (M and S, V (2), p. 338, no. 26 ; p. 343, no. 73 ; pp. 349–50, nos. 142–148 ; p. 357, no. 249 ; p. 359, no. 269 ; p. 361, no. 301 ; p. 364,

no. 339); cf. the legends NEPT. COMITI (p. 339, no. 30); NEPTUNO REDUCI (p. 343, no. 76 ; p. 354, nos. 214–17).

[23] On the chronology and sequence of the Gallic Emperors, M and S V (2), pp. 310–17, 325–6 ; Bolim, *Die Chronologie der Gall. Kaiser* (Lund 1932). For Victorinus, Dess. *ILS*, 563 ; *CIL*, XIII, 3679 ; for his legionary coinage, M and S, V (2), pp. 388–9, nos. 11–25 ; Oman in *Num. Chron.*, 1924, pp. 58 ff.

[24] *Vita Gall.*, 5, 6.

[25] For the invasion of the Goths, *ibid.*, 5, 6–6, 2 ; Zos., I, 39, 1. The details given by Zos. (I, 29, 2–3) by their similarity to those of the *Vita* (*l.c.*) seem to belong to this invasion, which is dated in the *Vita* by the consuls' names for A.D. 262.

For the revolt in Byzantium, *Vita Gall.*, 6, 8 ; 7, 4. If the sequence of events is correctly given, then the revolt shortly preceded the Decennalian celebrations in Rome.

[26] *Vita Gall.*, 8, 1–7 ; M and S, V (1), p. 138, nos. 92–96 ; Domaszewski, *Geschichte der röm. Kaiserzeit*, II, pp. 304–5. The legend FIDES MILITUM is common on the coins of Gallienus (e.g. M and S, V (1) pp. 133–4, nos. 38–41 ; p. 173, nos. 480–1).

[27] *Vita Gall.*, 11, 3–5.

[28] Euseb., *H. E.*, VII, 13.

[29] Porphyry, *Vita Plot.*, 12.

[30] Zos., I, 40, 1 ; *Vita Gall.*, 13, 6–8.

[31] *Vita Gall.*, 13, 9 ; Syncellus, I, p. 717.

[32] Zos., I, 40, 1 ; Zon., XII, 25, III, p. 147 ; Vict. *de Caes.*, 33, 17–18.

[33] Zos., I, 40, 2 ; Zon., *l.c.* ; Vict. *de Caes.*, 33, 21 ; *Epit.*, 33, 2 ; Damarau, *Kaiser Claudius II Goticus* (*Klio Beiheft* XXXIII), pp. 44–8.

[34] Vict. *de Caes.*, 33, 34.

[35] *Vir egregius*, Dess. *ILS*, 584 ; *CIL*, VIII, 2572 ; (the only known example before the reign of Gallienus is Dess. *ILS*, 2771) ; *a.v.l.*, Dess. *ILS*, 545 ; *CIL*, III, 4289, 3469, 3426.

[36] C. W. Keyes, *op. cit.*, pp. 36–41, as against Wilmanns, *de praefectis castrorum* in *Eph. Ep.*, I, pp. 95 ff., and Domaszewski, *Die Rangordnung*, pp. 119–20 ; cf. further, inscription of Traianus Mucianus (Dess. *ILS*, 9479) and Keyes' reply (*op. cit.*, pp. 41–3) to Domaszewski (*op. cit.*, pp. 185–92).

[37] Syria Coele, Dess. *ILS*, 1210–1211 ; Keyes, *op. cit.*, pp. 14–15 ; Tarraconensis, Dess. *ILS*, 599 ; *CIL*, II, 4103.

[38] Baynes (*JRS*, XV, pp. 195–201) in criticism of Homo (*Rev. Hist.*, CXXXVII, pp. 162–203 ; CXXXVIII, pp. 1–52) ; Keyes, *op. cit.*, pp. 49–54.

[39] The title *dux* does not occur certainly till A.D. 289 (*Panegyr. Incert.* X, 3, 3, ed. W. Baehrens) ; for the title *praepositus*, inscriptions from the Mithraeum at Poetovio (*P-W*, XII, col. 1340) ; Baynes, *op. cit.*, p. 200 ; Keyes, *op. cit.*, p. 51.

[40] Keyes, *op. cit.*, pp. 8–15.

[41] The earliest instance (earlier than A.D. 261) is Dess. *ILS*, 1332 ;

cf. *ibid.*, 545 (of A.D. 267). The full title *protector lateris divini* is found on an inscription belonging to the reign of Gallienus (*Orelli*, 1869).

⁴² For different theories about the *protectores*, Mommsen in *Eph. Ep.*, V, pp. 122 ff.; Babut, *Rev. Hist.*, CXIV (1913), pp. 225 ff.; Jullian, *Annales de la Faculté des Lettres de Bordeaux*, I (1884), pp. 59 ff.; Grosse, *Röm. Militärgeschichte*, pp. 13–15; Seeck, *Die Zeit des Vegetius* in *Hermes*, XI (1876), pp. 61 ff.; Domaszewski, *Die Rangordnung*, pp. 185–92; E. Stein, *Gesch. d. spatröm. Reiches*, I, pp. 82–4.

⁴³ Cedrenus. I, p. 454 (ed. Bonn).

⁴⁴ Zos., I, 43, 2; I, 40, 1–2; cf. I, 52, 3–4; Ritterling, *Festschr. f. O. Hirschfeld*, pp. 345–9.

⁴⁵ Dess. *ILS*, 569.

⁴⁶ Grosse, *op. cit.*, pp. 15–20; Stein, *op. cit.*, I, p. 92, n.1.; my article, *The Antiqua Legio of Vegetius* in *Cl. Q.*, XXVI (1932), pp. 137–49.

PART IV

CHAPTER I

¹ Zos., I, 41; *Vita Gall.*, 14, 2.

² *Vita Gall.*, 15, 1–2.

³ Various accounts are given about the murder of Aureolus, viz. " at the instigation of Aurelian " (*Vita Aurel.*, 16, 2); " by Claudius' soldiers " (Zos., I, 41); " by his own soldiers " (Vict. *Epit.*, 34, 2; *Vita Claud.*, 5, 3); " because he attempted a second tyranny " (Zon., XII, 26, III, p. 149).

⁴ Vict. *de Caes.*, 33, 31–2; 33, 27–8. But his account of the Senate's retaliatory measures bears signs of exaggeration, if not of invention (Damarau, *op. cit.*, pp. 46–7).

⁵ *Vita Aurel.*, 18, 1.

⁶ Vict. *Epit.*, 34, 2.

⁷ Dess. *ILS*, 569; M and S, V (1), p. 219, no. 108; p. 232, nos. 247–250; Markl, *Die Reichmünzstätten unter des Regierung Claudius II* in *Num. Zeit.*, XVI (1884). pp. 387, 417–18.

⁸ Dess. *ILS*, 568; *CIL*, II, 3833, 3834, 3737, 3619; Markl, *op. cit.*, pp. 410–16, but doubted by Webb in M and S, V (2), pp. 316–17.

⁹ *Pan. Incert.*, IX, 4, 1; V, 2, 5; V, 4, 2–4, ed. W. Baehrens (1911); Damarau, *op. cit.*, pp. 76–80.

¹⁰ Dess. *ILS*, 569.

¹¹ Auson., *Parental.*, IV, 9–10 (I, p. 64, ed. Loeb).

¹² *Trig. Tyr.*, 6, 3; Vict. *de Caes.*, 33, 12–13; Eutrop., IX, 9.

¹³ *Trig. Tyr.*, 24, 1; Vict. *de Caes.*, 33, 14; Eutrop., IX, 10.

¹⁴ *Vita Claud.*, 6, 2 and 5–6; Ammianus, XXXI, 5, 15; Zos., 1, 42, 1, who, probably wrongly, puts the size of the fleet at 6000 ships.

¹⁵ Zos., 1, 42, 2; 43, 1; *Vita Claud.*, 9, 3; 9, 7–8.

[16] Not before May, A.D. 269 (*Constitutio* dated April 25th, *Cod. Just.*, III, 34, 6).

[17] Zos., I, 43, 1–2 ; Vict. *de Caes.*, 34, 5 ; Eutrop., IX, 11.

[18] Zos., I, 45, 1–2 ; 46, 2 ; *Vita Claud.*, 11, 3 ; 9, 4.

[19] Zos., I, 46, 2 ; *Vita Claud.*, 11, 3 ; 12, 4 ; cf. n. 34.

[20] Zos., I, 46, 1 ; *Vita Claud.*, 12, 1 ; *FHG*, IV, p. 196, frag. 9, 2 ; for Probus' command, Zos., 1, 44, 2. See further on the Gothic War, Damarau, *op. cit.*, pp. 62–75.

[21] Dess. *ILS*, 571 ; M and S, V (1), pp. 232–3, nos. 251–252.

[22] Homo, *De Claudio Gothico*, pp. 60–4 ; Markl, *op. cit.*, pp. 455, 499 ff. ; cf. Voetter, *Die Münzen des Kaisers Gallienus* in *Num. Zeit.*, XXXIII (1901), pp. 81–92 ; Damarau, *op. cit.*, pp. 60–1.

[23] Zos., I, 44 ; *Vita Claud.*, 11, 1–2 ; A. von Sallet, *Fürsten von Palmyra*, p. 45 ; Damarau, *op. cit.*, pp. 54–61.

[24] Zos., I, 50, 1.

[25] *CIG*, II, 3747–3748.

[26] Dexippus frag. 24 (*FHG*, III, pp. 682–3, 685–6).

[27] *Vita Aurel.*, 17, 3–5 (the letter is fictitious) ; *Chron.* of A.D. 354. (*Chron. Min.*, I, p. 148.)

[28] Zos., 1, 46, 2 ; Zon., XII, 26, III, p. 151 ; for the chronology of his reign, Homo, *De Claudio Gothico*, pp. 34–8 ; Damarau, *op. cit.*, pp. 24–31 ; A. Stein in *Klio*, XXI (1927), pp. 78–82.

[29] For his apotheosis, *Vita Claud.*, 12, 3 ; Vict. *Epit.*, 34, 4 ; Dess. *ILS*, 572 ; M and S, V (1), pp. 233–7, nos. 256–299 ; for the statues, *Vita Claud.*, 3, 3 ; Vict. *Epit.*, 34, 4.

[30] M and S, V (1), p. 8 ; pp. 19–25 ; Homo, *op. cit.*, pp. 76–80.

[31] Homo, *op. cit.*, p. 82 ; for a restoration of the legionary baths at Aquincum, Dess. *ILS*, 570.

[32] *Vita Aurel.*, 37, 5.

[33] Zos., 1, 47, 1 ; Zon., XII, 26, III, p. 151 ; *Vita Claud.*, 12, 3 ; for his coinage M and S, V (1), pp. 239–47 ; Markl in *Num. Zeit.*, XXII (1890), pp. 11–24.

[34] *Vita Claud.*, 12, 4–5 ; Jordanes, *Getica*, 20 ; Amm., XXXI, 5, 16.

[35] Zos. and Zon., *l.c.*, in note 33 ; *Vita Aurel.*, 37, 6 ; Quintillus' reign probably lasted three months (Homo, *op. cit.*, pp. 35–8).

CHAPTER II

[1] Dexippus, *FHG*, III, p. 682.

[2] Th. Rohde, *Die Münzen des Kaisers Aurelianus, seiner Frau Severina und der Fürsten von Palmyra*, pp. 260–5, coins of Waballath, nos. 1, and 10–19.

[3] *CIL*, XII, 1551 ; Placidianus had now been appointed *praefectus praetorio*, and bears the title *vir clarissimus* ; cf. Dess. *ILS*, 569.

[4] For the date of the closing of the mint, Rohde, *op. cit.*, pp. 298–9, and pp. 344–5 ; Homo, *Essai sur le règne de l'Empereur Aurélien*, p. 70, n. 1, and p. 162, n. 1 ; Webb (M and S, V (1), p. 256) regards it as a consequence of the revolt of Felicissimus.

⁵ Dexippus, *FHG*, III, p. 685, and with some differences and much less detail Zos., I, 48.

⁶ Dexippus, *FHG*, III, p. 686 ; Zos., I, 49, 1 ; Vict. *de Caes.*, 35, 2.

⁷ Petrus Patricius, fr. 10, 3 (*FHG*, IV, p. 197) ; *Vita Aurel.*, 18, 3 ; 21, 1 ; Vict. *Epit.*, 35, 2.

⁸ Vict. *de Caes.*, 35, 6 ; *Epit.*, 35, 4 ; Eutrop., IX, 14. On the chronology, Homo, *op. cit.*, pp. 158–64 ; Groag, *s.v.*, *Domitius* in *P-W*, V, coll. 1372–1374.

⁹ Zos., I, 49, 2 ; *Vita Aurel.*, 21, 6.

¹⁰ *Vita Aurel.*, 18, 5 ; 20, 3 ; 21, 4.

¹¹ Vict. *Epit.*, 35, 2 ; cf. *CIL*, XI, 6308 = Dess. *ILS*, 583 and XI, 6309, for dedications to Aurelian in the name of the town of Pisaurum by C. Julius Priscianus, who has the titles " *Curator Rerum Publicarum Pisaurensis et Fanestris* " and " *praepositus muris* " (Bormann in *Corpus*, *l.c.*). The latter title was probably temporarily held in the crisis following the defeat at Placentia, when emergency measures had to be taken for the defence of the Italian towns. VICTORIA AUG. on early coins of the reign (M and S, V (1), p. 269, nos. 39–40).

¹² Zos., I, 49, 2 ; *Vita Aurel.*, 21, 6 ; Vict. *de Caes.*, 35, 6 ; Eutrop., IX, 14.

¹³ *Vita Aurel.*, 21, 9.

¹⁴ The year A.D. 271 for the beginning of the work is stated or implied in the following passages : *Chron.* of A.D. 354 (*Chron. Min.*, I, p. 148) ; Zos., I, 49, 2 ; *Vita Aurel.*, 21, 9 ; Vict. *Epit.*, 35, 6 ; Eutrop., IX, 15.

¹⁵ This statement has only the authority of Malalas (XII, pp. 299–300, ed. Bonn) to support it, but is probable enough in view of the policy of the Emperors of the third century in converting the *collegia* into compulsory state organisations (Rostovtzeff, *Social and Economic History of the Roman Empire*, p. 409 ; Groag, *op. cit.*, *P-W*, V, col. 1376 ; I. A. Richmond, *The City Wall of Imperial Rome*, p. 29).

¹⁶ For a detailed account of the Walls of Rome, Richmond, *op. cit.*, especially pp. 241–50 ; cf. Homo, *op. cit.*, pp. 214–306.

¹⁷ Zos., I, 49, 2 ; Vict. *Epit.*, 35, 3.

¹⁸ The date is between March 11th (*BGU*, III, 946) and August 29th, A.D. 271 (the beginning of the new Alexandrian year). For the coins of Waballath, Rohde, *op. cit.*, pp. 260–5, Waballath, nos. 2–9, 21–22 ; Zenobia, nos. 25–30.

¹⁹ Zos., I, 56, 2 ; *Vita Aurel.*, 30, 3.

²⁰ A. Réville, *Le Christianisme unitaire au III' siècle ; Paul de Samosate et Zénobie*, in *Revue des Deux Mondes*, LXXV (1868), pp. 86–106 ; Duchesne, *op. cit.*, I, pp. 340–44.

²¹ *Vita Prob.*, 9, 5. Alexandria was again in Roman control by August 29th, A.D. 271, or a little later, for there are no Alexandrian coins of Waballath's sixth year = Aurelian's second year, but coins are struck in the name of Aurelian alone.

²² Zosimus gives the details in his account of the battle at Emesa (I, 52, 3–4).

²³ *Vita Aurel.*, 22, 2 ; Ammianus, XXXI, 5, 17. The title *Gothicus*

Maximus appears first on inscriptions dated to the third year of Aurelian's *trib. pot.* (i.e. from December 10th, A.D. 271–December 9th, A.D. 272). (Dess. *ILS*, 8925 ; *CIL*, VIII, 10017 ; Dess. *ILS*, 576), also on a pre-Reform coin from Cyzicus (M and S, V (1), p. 303, no. 339).

²⁴ Zos., I, 50, 2 mentions simply the capture of Tyana. The details are given in *Vita Aurel.*, 22, 5–24, 1, and in Petrus Patricius, fr. 10, 4 (*FHG*, IV, p. 197).

²⁵ Zos., 1, 50, 2.

²⁶ The most trustworthy account of the first Palmyrene campaign is given by Zosimus, who mentions three battles : (*a*) on the Orontes before A. entered Antioch (I, 50, 3–4) ; (*b*) at Daphne when A. had resumed his march south (I, 52, 1–2) ; and (*c*) at Emesa (I, 53). *Vita Aurel.* records only two battles : (*a*) at Daphne (25, 1) and (*b*) at Emesa (25, 3), and wrongly places the former before A.'s entry into Antioch. Other authors only mention one battle at a place called Immae, which is probably a confusion with Emesa, as this battle is represented as the decisive issue in the campaign. (Rufus Festus, 24 ; Jordanes *Rom.*, 291 ; "*apud Hymnas*," Syncellus, I, p. 721 ; Homo, *op. cit.*, p. 93, n. 1.)

²⁷ Zos., I, 51.

²⁸ Euseb., *H.E.*, VII, 30, 19 ; Réville, *op. cit.*, pp. 103–4 ; Duchesne, *op. cit.*, I, p. 343.

²⁹ Zos., I, 52–54, 2. The strength of Zenobia's army lay in its heavy-armed cavalry=*clibanarii* (Ruf. Festus, 24, and for an account of their armour, *Pan. Incert.*, IV, 22, 4, ed. W. Baehrens).

³⁰ Homo, *op. cit.*, p. 101.

³¹ Zos., I, 54.

³² Petrus Patricius fr. 10, 5 (*FHG*, IV, p. 197) ; *Vita Aurel.*, 26, 6–27, 6, although the letters are fabrications ; Homo, *op. cit.*, p. 102, n. 4.

³³ *Vita Aurel.*, 28, 2.

³⁴ Zos., I, 55–56 ; *Vita Aurel.*, 28, 3.

³⁵ Victor *de Caes.*, 35, 1 ; *Vita Aurel.*, 35, 4. The title *Parthicus Maximus* appears on inscriptions belonging to the third year of A.'s *trib. pot.* (*CIL*, VIII, 9040 ; cf. with *t. p. IV*, Dess. *ILS*, 577). The titles *Palmyrenicus* and *Arabicus*, which are found on inscriptions, were not officially conferred on A., doubtless because the war against Palmyra was a civil war and not a campaign against an enemy outside the Empire. (*Palmyrenicus* in Dess. *ILS*, 579 ; *Arabicus* in Dess. *ILS*, 576.) VICTORIA PARTICA on a pre-Reform coin from Siscia (M and S, V (1), p. 291, no. 240).

³⁶ Zos., I, 60, 1. Perhaps he is to be identified with the Marcellinus who walled Verona in the reign of Gallienus (Dess. *ILS*, 544). Although he is called "prefect of Mesopotamia," the province was not completely recovered till the reign of Carus.

³⁷ Zos., I, 56, 2–3 ; I, 59 ; *Vita Aurel.*, 30, 2–3.

³⁸ *Vita Aurel.*, 30, 4 ; *CIL*, III, 12456 ; Vict. *de Caes.*, 39, 43–4 (for the settlements in Thrace).

³⁹ Dess. *ILS*, 8925 ; cf. *ibid.*, 576, 581, 582.

[40] Zos., I, 60 ; *Vita Aurel.*, 31, 1–2, where Antiochus is wrongly called Achilleus.

[41] *Vita Aurel.*, 32, 2 ; Homo, *op. cit.*, pp. 110–13.

[42] Zos., I, 61, 1.

[43] *Quad. Tyr.*, 5, 2 ; for Bruchium, Ammianus, XXII, 16, 15.

[44] Vict. *de Caes*, 35, 3 ; Homo, *op. cit.*, pp. 116–18.

[45] Vict. *de Caes.*, 35, 4.

[46] For the battle and its site, Eutrop., IX, 13 ; for the surrender of Tetricus, *Vita Aurel.*, 32, 3 ; *Trig. Tyr.*, 24, 2 ; Vict. *de Caes*, 35, 4–5.

[47] Zon., XII, 27, III, p. 153, for Probus' victories over the Alamanni, *Vita Prob.*, 12, 3.

[48] M and S, V (1), pp. 297–9, nos. 287–306.

[49] *Vita Aurel.*, 33–34.

[50] For the post of *corrector*, *Vita Aurel.*, 39, 1 ; Vict. *de Caes.*, 35, 5 ; Eutrop., IX, 13 ; for Tetricus' house *Trig. Tyr.*, 25, 4. According to Eutropius, *l.c.*, "*privatus diutissime vixit.*" For Zenobia, *Trig. Tyr.*, 30, 27.

[51] The larger Aurelian billon coins are marked xx, xx.I, xxI, KA, K.A., which Mattingly, whom I have followed, (*Sestertius and Denarius in Num. Chron.*, 1927, pp. 219–31, and in his *Roman Coins*, pp. 128–31, 191–3) interprets as coins containing 20 smaller units = 20 *libellae*. The smaller coins have sometimes the letters VSV = *Usualis* or normal coin, i.e. a *sestertius* containing 10 *libellae*, or (according to Rohde, *op. cit.*, p. 291) V + V = 10 with S = *semis*. (For other theories, Webb in *Num. Chron.*, 1919, pp. 234–43, and in M and S, V (1) pp. 8–14 ; Missong in *Num. Zeit.*, I (1869), pp. 105 ff. ; Rohde, *op. cit.*, pp. 287–93 ; Homo, *op. cit.*, pp. 155–75 ; Groag, *op. cit.*, in *P-W*, V, coll. 1394–1396 ; Mickwitz, *Geld u. Wirtschaft im röm. Reich*, pp. 57–70.)

[52] Vict. *de Caes.*, 35, 7 ; *Vita Aurel.*, 39, 3.

[53] "*panibus urbis Romae unciam de Aegyptio vectigali auxit*" (*Vita Aurel.*, 47, 1) Cf. PROVIDENTIA AUG. on coins from Rome (M and S, V, (1), p. 273, nos. 68–9).

[54] *Vita Aurel.*, 35, 1 ; Zos., I, 61, 3.

[55] *Vita Aurel.*, 48, 1 ; *Chron.* of A.D. 354 (*Chron. Min.*, I, p. 148) ; Vict. *de Caes.*, 35, 7.

[56] *Vita Aurel.*, 48, 1.

[57] *Cod. Just.*, XI, 58, 1 ; cf. proposal to plant vineyards in Etruria and Liguria (*Vita Aurel.*, 48, 2).

[58] See note 15 ; Waltzing, *Etude hist. sur les Corporations professionelles*, II, pp. 270–1.

[59] *Vita Aurel.*, 47, 3.

[60] *Chron.* of A.D. 354 ; Waltzing, *op. cit.*, II, p. 90.

[61] *Vita Aurel.*, 45, 2.

[62] Dess. *ILS*, 586.

[63] C. W. Keyes, *op. cit.*, pp. 8–15.

[64] Marcellinus was consul with Aurelian in A.D. 275 ; for Placidianus, *CIL*, XII, 1551.

[65] *Vita Aurel.*, 39, 1 ; Vict. *de Caes.*, 35, 5 ; *Epit.*, 35, 7 ; Eutrop., IX, 13 ; for the history of *correctores*, Premerstein in *P-W*, IV,

coll. 1651–1656 ; Homo, *op. cit.*, pp. 144–5 ; Jullian in *Rev. Hist.*, XIX, pp. 339–43, who ascribes the division of Italy into provinces to Aurelian.

[66] For the temple, *Vita Aurel.*, 25, 6 ; 28, 5 ; 35, 3 ; Vict. *de Caes.*, 35, 7 ; *Chron.* of A.D. 354. For the priests, Dess. *ILS*, 1210 (Virius Lupus, who is the earliest known instance) ; *CIL*, VI, 1397.

[67] Petrus Patricius frag. 10, 6 (*FHG*, IV, p. 198) ; Homo, *op. cit.*, pp. 184–95.

[68] M and S, V (1), p. 299, nos. 305–6 ; Groag (*op. cit.*, col. 1406) suggests that this attribution of divinity to Aurelian on the coins from Serdica may have some reference to his organization of the new province Dacia with its capital at Serdica. Cf. SOLI INVICTO on the reverse of coins from the same mint (M and S, V (1), pp. 299–300, nos. 307–315) ; Homo, *op. cit.*, pp. 366–72.

[69] Dess. *ILS*, 585 ; *CIL*, II, 3832.

[70] Dess. *ILS*, 583.

[71] Coins unearthed in the neighbourhood of Würtemberg are not later in date than the reign of Aurelian (Homo, *op. cit.*, p. 207, note 4) ; *Vita Tac.*, 3, 4.

[72] See Part III, Chap. III, note 22.

[73] V. *Maced.* was at Oescus, XIII *Gemina* at Ratiaria (Ritterling in *P-W*, XII, col. 1346).

[74] Ritterling, *Festschrift für O. Hirschfeld*, pp. 345–9.

[75] *Vita Prob.*, 17, 2 and 6.

[76] Zon., XII, 27, III, p. 153 ; *Vita Aurel.*, 35, 4.

[77] Zos., I, 62 ; Zon., *l.c.* ; *Vita Aurel.*, 35, 5–36 (where the secretary is called Mnesteus, perhaps a translation of μηνύτης) ; Vict. *de Caes.*, 35, 8 ; *Epit.*, 35, 8 ; Eutrop., IX, 15.

CHAPTER III

[1] *Vita Aurel.*, 40, 2 ; *Vita Tac.*, 2, 5 ; Vict. *de Caes.*, 35, 9.

[2] According to Vopiscus (*Vita Aurel.*, 40, 4 ; *Vita Tac.*, 2, 6) and Victor (*de Caes.*, 36, 1) the *interregnum* lasted six, or according to the *Epitomator* (35, 10), seven months. This is certainly wrong, and the error probably arises from a confusion of the *pseudo-interregnum* represented by the reigns of Tacitus and Florianus (*Vita Tac.*, 14, 5), with the actual *interregnum* which lasted only a few weeks. The chronology of this period can best be established by working backwards from Carinus and Numerianus. Carinus has 3 years of *trib. pot.* and 3 years of Alexandrian coins. Numerianus has 2 years of *trib. pot.* and 3 years. of Alexandrian coins (A. v. Sallet, *Die Daten der Alex. Kaisermünzen*, p. 89). Numerianus, therefore, died between August 29th, A.D. 284, and December 10th, A.D. 284, and Carinus early in A.D. 285. Their accession was previous to August 28th, A.D. 283. Carus is said to have ruled ten months and five days (*Chron. Min.*, I, p. 148) and has only one year of Alexandrian coins (i.e. from his accession to August 29th,

A.D. 283). Probus has eight years of Alexandrian coins, the first from his accession to August 29th, A.D. 276, the last from August 29th, A.D. 282, till his death. Therefore Probus must have been murdered and Carus proclaimed Emperor in September or October, A.D. 282.

Now Probus is said to have reigned six years and four months (*Chron. Euseb.*, p. 184, ed. Schöne). This would put his accession in May, A.D. 276, and this occurred some 15–20 days after Florianus' seizure of imperial power (implied by Zon., XII, 29, III, p. 154). Tacitus reigned six or seven months (Zon., XII, 28, III, p. 154 ; Eutrop., IX, 16 ; Vict. *de Caes.*, 36, 2), i.e. his accession was in October, A.D. 275, and, as Aurelian's murder may be placed in late August, A.D. 275, that leaves only little more than a month for the *interregnum* (cf. Homo, *op. cit.*, pp. 335–40).

³ *Vita Aurel.*, 37, 3–4 ; Eutrop., IX, 15.

⁴ *Vita Aurel.*, 41, 15 ; *Vita Tac.*, 3, 2–8, 2 ; Vict. *de Caes.*, 36, 1 ; Eutrop., IX, 16.

⁵ Vict. *de Caes.*, 37, 6.

⁶ N. H. Baynes in *JRS*, XV (2), 1925, pp. 195–201, in answer to Homo in *Rev. Hist.*, CXXXVII, pp. 162–203, and CXXXVIII, pp. 1–52 ; cf. Rostovtzeff, *op. cit.*, pp. 394 and 410.

⁷ Zos., I, 63, 1 ; Zon., XII, 28, III, p. 154 ; *Vita Tac.*, 13, 3 ; coins commemorating the victory (M and S, V (1), p. 343, nos. 171–173 ; p. 346, nos. 199–204).

⁸ Zos., I, 63, 2 ; Zon., *l.c.* ; Vict. *de Caes.*, 36, 2 ; *Epit.*, 36, 1 (the last two say nothing of the plot, but ascribe his death to natural causes).

⁹ IMP. C.M. CL. TACITUS P. F. AUG. VIRTUS (M and S, V (1), p. 343, no. 173).

¹⁰ " *non senatus auctoritate sed suo motu* " (*Vita Tac.*, 14, 1) ; " *nullo senatus seu militum consulto* " (Vict. *de Caes.*, 36, 2).

¹¹ Zon., XII, 29, III, p. 154 ; coins are comparatively numerous from the mints of Rome, Ticinum, Lugdunum and Siscia, but rare from Serdica and Cyzicus, while Antioch struck none, at it was in the control of Probus. (M and S, V. (1), pp. 350–60.)

¹² Zos., I, 64, 1.

¹³ *Ibid.*, I, 64, 2–4 ; *Vita Tac.*, 14, 2 ; Vict. *de Caes.*, 37, 1.

¹⁴ Clinton, *Fasti Rom. ad ann.* A.D. 282 ; *CIL*, I, p. 270.

¹⁵ *Vita Prob.*, 13, 5.

¹⁶ *Adventus* coins belonging to his early reign (M and S, V (2) p. 22, nos. 19–20).

¹⁷ Zos., I, 67–68. There is considerable duplication in his account, the events described in 67, 1 being repeated in more detail in 67, 3–68, 3.

¹⁸ *Vita Prob.*, 13, 8–14, 1.

¹⁹ *Ibid.*, 14, 7.

²⁰ Zos., I, 68, 3.

²¹ *Vita Prob.*, 18, 8 ; cf. n. 36.

²² Dess. *ILS*, 597 ; VICTORIA GERM. (M and S, V (2), p. 32, nos. 141–142 ; pp. 45–6, nos. 268–278.)

23

[23] *Ibid.*, pp. 26–7, nos. 73–77 ; p. 29, nos. 102–109 ; p. 69, nos. 476–477.

[24] *Ibid.*, p. 95, no. 730 ; cf. *Vita Prob.*, 16, 1–2.

[25] Zos., 1, 69–70 ; *Vita Prob.*, 16, 4–5, where the chief's name is given as Palfuerius.

[26] *Vita Prob.*, 16, 6.

[27] Ritterling, *P-W*, XII, col. 1348.

[28] Zos., I, 71, 1 ; *Vita Prob.*, 17, 2–3.

[29] *Vita Prob.*, 17, 4 ; 17, 6 ; 18, 1.

[30] *Ibid.*, 18, 1 ; Zos., I, 71, 1. This incident may have taken place on Probus' journey to the East and not during his return.

[31] *Vita Prob.*, 18, 5 ; *Quad. Tyr.*, 13, 4 ; Eutrop., IX, 17.

[32] *Quad. Tyr.*, 15, 1–2 ; Vict. *de Caes.*, 37, 3 ; M and S, V (2), p. 592.

[33] Dess. *ILS*, 597, but it is also erased on an inscription from Campania (*CIL*, X, 3728) and two from Africa (VIII, 100, 1353), so the reason for the Spanish erasure may have no connection with Bonosus. For the rebellion in Britain, Zos., I, 66, 2 ; Zon., XII, 29, III, p. 155.

[34] *Vita Prob.*, 19.

[35] *Ibid.*, 13, 1 ; N. H. Baynes, *op. cit.*, p. 198.

[36] Vict. *de Caes.*, 37, 3 ; Eutrop., IX, 17 ; *Vita Prob.*, 18, 8 ; cf. 21, 2.

[37] Zon., XII, 29, III, pp. 155–6, referring to Carus' revolt, says that Probus sent an army against him which went over to Carus, and that Probus was murdered by his guards. *Vita Prob.*, 20, 1–2 ; 21, 3 ; Eutrop., IX, 17 ; Vict. *de Caes.*, 37, 4, say nothing of Carus' usurpation and attribute Probus' death to the soldiers' discontent at his rigorous discipline. Probably the two versions should be combined.

[38] *Vita Prob.*, 24, 4 ; Eutrop., IX, 18, 1 ; Zon., XII, 29, III, p. 155, who suggests that Carus' hand was forced by his troops.

For the names and titles of Carus and his sons, Dess. *ILS*, 601, 606. For the coinage of the sons while *Caesares*, M and S, V (2), pp. 156–65, 187–91.

[39] *Vita Cari*, 7, 1 ; Vict. *de Caes.*, 38, 2 ; Zon., XII, 30, III, p. 156.

[40] *Vita Cari*, 8, 1 ; 9, 4 ; Eutrop., IX, 18 ; Jord., *Rom.*, 294.

[41] *Vita Car.*, 8, 1–3 ; Eutrop., IX, 18 ; Vict. *de Caes.*, 38, 3–4 ; *Epit.*, 38, 3 ; Dess. *ILS*, 600 (*Persicus Maximus*) ; M and S, V (2), p. 137, nos. 18–26 ; p. 145, nos. 95–98.

[42] *Vit. Car.*, 11–12 ; Vict. *de Caes.*, 38, 6–8 ; *Epit.*, 38, 4–5 ; Eutrop., IX, 18 ; Zon., XII, 30, III, p. 157.

[43] Vict. *de Caes.*, 39, 1 ; *Epit.*, 39, 1 ; Eutrop., IX, 19 ; Zon., XII, 31, III, p. 159. For the date, Seeck, *Untergang*, I⁴ (*Anhang*), p. 438, 22. Diocletian celebrated his *Vicennalia* on November 17th, A.D. 303 (Euseb., *Mart. Pal.*, II, 4, cf. Lact., *de mortibus pers.*, 17, 1, where *a. d. XV Kal. Dec.* should be read in emendation of *a. d. XII*, etc.).

PART V

CHAPTER I

¹ For his full name Dess. *ILS*, 613, 617, 620. For his first consulship Dess. *ILS*, 615 of A.D. 285 on which he is styled *cos. II*, and *Chron. Paschale* for A.D. 285 (Mommsen, *Chron. Min.*, I, p. 229).

² Vict. *de Caes.*, 39, 13 ; Eutrop., IX, 20 ; Zon., XII, 31, III, p. 159.

³ For the biographer's opinion of his character, *Vita Carini*, 16, 1 ; cf. Victor *Epit.*, 38, 7.

⁴ Vict. *de Caes.*, 39, 9–10 ; *Epit.*, 38, 6 ; Syncellus, I, p. 725. For the post of *corrector Venetorum*, Mommsen in *Eph. Ep.*, I, p. 140 ; for Julianus' coins, M and S, V (2), pp. 593–4.

⁵ *Vita Carini*, 18, 2 ; Vict. *de Caes.*, 39, 11–12 ; *Epit.*, 38, 8 ; Jord., *Rom.*, 295 ; *Chron.* of A.D. 354 (*Chron. Min.*, I, p. 148). Hydatius (= *Consularia Constantinopolitana*) for A.D. 285 (*Chron. Min.*, I, p. 229). [Cited in subsequent notes as Hydatius.]

⁶ Hydatius for A.D. 285 and *Chron. Pasch.* for same year (*Chron. Min.*, I, p. 229).

⁷ See further Seeck, *s.v. Comitatus* in *P-W*, IV, coll. 622 ff.

⁸ Eutrop., IX, 20 ; Amm. XXVII, 6, 16 ; *CIL*, VIII, 10227, although there is no confirmatory numismatic evidence. Maximian was not given the *tribunicia potestas* until he was made Augustus ; but after A.D. 293, when Galerius and Constantius were appointed *Caesares* and given the *tribunicia potestas*, Maximian's *tribunicia potestas* was made to date from his appointment as Caesar in A.D. 285. Thus in inscriptions that are earlier than A.D. 293 Maximian has two years fewer of *trib. pot.* than Diocletian, but in those after A.D. 293 only one year less (cf. Dess. *ILS*, 617 of A.D. 288 and 630 of A.D. 293 with Dess. *ILS*, 640 of A.D. 294 and 642 of A.D. 301, and see further Seeck, *Untergang*, 1⁴ (*Anhang*), p. 447, 26, 1). For the birthday of Diocletian and Maximian, *Pan. Incert.*, XI, 19, 1, ed. W. Baehrens.

⁹ *Pan. Incert.*, X, 1–2 ; X, 4, 2 ; XI, 2, 2 ; XI, 14 ; Lact. *de mort. pers.* 8 ; *Anon. Val.*, 1, 1 (Momm. *Chron. Min.*, I, p. 7) ; Vict. *de Caes.*, 39, 18 ; Dess. *ILS*, 621–623.

¹⁰ *Pan. Incert.* X, 11, 6.

¹¹ Eutrop., IX, 20 ; Vict. *de Caes.*, 39, 17 ; Zon., XII, 31, III, p. 160 ; *Pan. Incert.*, X, 4, 2–3 ; VII, 8, 3 ; Jullian, *Histoire de la Gaule*, VII, pp. 51–6.

¹² Hydatius for A.D. 286 (*Chron. Min,*, I, p. 229).

¹³ See further Seeck, *op. cit.*, 1⁴, pp. 26–8, and pp. 449–50 ; E. Stein, *Gesch. d. spät-römischen Reiches*, I, p. 96. Seeck's contention, based on the difference of tone in *Panegyrici* X and XI (ed. W. Baehrens), that relations between Diocletian and Maximian continued strained till their meeting at Milan in the winter of A.D. 288–9, deserves attention, but the evidence upon which he relies hardly bears out his hypothesis.

¹⁴ *Pan. Incert.*, X, 5, 1–2 ; Jullian, *op. cit.*, VII, pp. 60–61.

[15] *Id.*, X, 9, 1 ; XI, 5, 4 ; XI, 7, 1.

[16] *Id.*, VIII, 2, 1.

[17] *Id.*, X, 5 ; XI, 7, 2.

[18] *Id.*, XI, 7, 2 ; X, 11, 7 ; as this victory was won by the praetorian prefect, no imperial acclamation was received, cf. the parallel case of Asclepiodotus, who defeated and killed Allectus (see below).

[19] *Id.*, X, 10, 3 ; for the title "*reges Franciae*" ; *id.*, VI, 10, 2 ; and Jullian, *op. cit.*, VII, pp. 61–3.

[20] Eutrop., IX, 21 ; Victor, *de Caes.*, 39, 20 ; Jullian (*op. cit.*, VII, p. 63, n. 3) thinks that the post of *dux tractus Armoricani et Nervicani* may date from the time of Carausius' appointment.

[21] Victor, *de Caes.*, 39, 21 ; Eutrop., IX, 21 ; Dess., *ILS*, 8928.

[22] *Pan. Incert.*, X, 12, 1–2.

[23] Among the coins of Carausius (on which, including his propagandist issue of legionary coins, see M and S, V (2), pp. 435–48), those stamped with the heads of Diocletian, Maximian and Carausius and with the legend CARAUSIUS ET FRATRES SUI on the obverse and PAX AUGGG. on the reverse are of particular interest. They celebrate "the peace" made between Carausius and the two Augusti in A.D. 290, and indicate Carausius' desire to be acknowledged as Augustus while he concedes the first and second places in the "triarchy" to Diocletian and Maximian (M and S, V (2), p. 550 ; Webb, *The Coins of Carausius*, p. 242, nos. 1226–1228, cf. pp. 81–3).

[24] Mommsen, *Zeitfolge der Verordnungen Diocletians u. seiner Mitregenten* in *Ges. Schrift.*, II, pp. 195 ff., and especially pp. 270–3.

[25] *Pan. Incert.*, XI, 5, 4 ; cf. Dess. *ILS*, 642.

[26] *Hieron. Chron.*, p. 308, 7, Fotheringham, "*Busiris et Coptus contra Romanos rebellantes ad solum usque subversae sunt*" ; Cedrenus, I, 467, 19, "τῷ ζ ἔτει αὐτῶν (=7th Alexandrian year of Diocletian, i.e. between August 29th, A.D. 290 and August 28th, A.D. 291) τὴν Βούσιριν καὶ τὴν Κοπτὸν πόλεις ἐν Θήβαις τῆς Αἰγύπτου ἀποστατησάσας τῆς τῶν Ῥωμαίων ἀρχῆς εἰς ἔδαφος κατέσκαψαν"; *Pap. Ox.*, I, no. 43 shows that detachments from XI *Claudia*, IV *Flavia* and VII *Claudia* were in Egypt on January 28th, A.D. 295. As the rebellion of Achilleus did not take place till the summer of that year, it seems probable that the *vexillationes* must have been brought to Egypt for the earlier campaign against Busiris and Coptos. (See further Kubitschek, *Zur Geschichte des Usurpators Achilleus* (*Akd. der Wiss. in Wien, Phil.-hist. Klasse Sitzungber.* 208 Band 1 Abhandlung), especially pp. 7–10.)

[27] *Pan. Incert.*, XI, 5, 4 ; X, 10, 6.

[28] *Id.*, VIII, 3, 1 ; Lact. *de mort. pers.*, 35 ; *Chron. Paschale* for A.D. 293 (*Chron. Min.*, I, p. 230) ; Vict. *de Caes.*, 40, 11 ; Dess. *ILS*, 642.

[29] Lact. *de mort pers.*, 9 ; Vict. *de Caes.*, 39, 24 ; *Epit.*, 39, 2 ; *Anon Val.*, 1, 1 (*Chron. Min.*, I, p. 7) ; Maurice, *Numismatique Constantinienne*, I, p. 343.

For the date of Constantine's birth, Seeck, *Untergang*, I⁴ (*Anhang*), pp. 434–6.

[30] e.g. Dess. *ILS*, 642. For the coins of Constantius as Caesar,

M and S, V (2), pp. 297–302 ; for the coins of Galerius as Caesar, *ibid.*, pp. 304–9.

Probably a praetorian prefect was assigned to each Caesar (E. Stein, *op. cit.*, I, p. 105 ; cf. Seeck, *op. cit.*, II², pp. 64 and 505).

³¹ According to Lact. *de mort. pers.*, 8, 3, Spain belonged to Maximian ; according to Vict. *de Caes.*, 39, 30, and Julian (*Or.* 2, p. 65, Hertlein) to Constantius. For reasons for accepting Lactantius, see Stein, *op. cit.*, I, p. 99, n. 6 ; *contra*, Seeck, *op. cit.*, I⁴, p. 455.

³² *Pan. Incert.*, VIII, 6 ; cf. for the earlier operations " *innumerabili hostium classe ferventem exclusit Oceanum* " (*Pan. Incert.*, VI, 5, 2) ; cf. Jullian, *op. cit.*, VII, pp. 80–81.

³³ *Pan. Incert.*, VII, 4, 2 ; VI, 5, 3.

³⁴ Vict. *de Caes.*, 39, 40 ; Eutrop., IX, 22 ; *Pan. Incert.*, VIII, 12, 2.

³⁵ *Pan. Incert.*, VIII, 14–17 ; Vict. *de Caes.*, 39, 42 ; Eutrop., IX, 22 ; Dess. *ILS*, 8929. For Allectus' coinage, M and S, V (2), pp. 558–70.

³⁶ *Pan. Incert.*, VI, 6, 2, of A.D. 310, but referring to events after the British campaign and before the Langres incident. (Jullian, *op. cit.*, VII, p. 86, n. 1.)

³⁷ *Ibid.*, 4, 2 ; 6, 3 ; Eutrop., IX, 23.

³⁸ Vict. *de Caes.*, 39, 43 ; Eutrop., IX, 25 ; Hydatius for the year A.D. 294 (*Chron. Min.*, I, p. 230). For work at Lake Balaton, Vict. *de Caes.*, 40, 9.

³⁹ The date is later than the rebellion of Achilleus and earlier than Maximian's African campaign. Because Diocletian was in Egypt and Galerius fighting the Persians, Maximian took the command (*Pan. Incert.*, VIII, 5, 2 ; Vict. *de Caes.*, 39, 43 ; Eutrop., IX, 25 ; cf. Seeck, *op. cit.*, 1⁴ (*Anhang*), pp. 450–51).

⁴⁰ *Pan. Incert.*, VII, 8, 6 ; VIII, 5, 3 ; Vict. *de Caes.*, 39, 22 ; Eutrop., IX, 23 ; Dess. *ILS*, 645.

⁴¹ Dess. *ILS*, 646.

⁴² Eutrop., IX, 23 ; Vict. *de Caes.*, 39, 23 ; *Epit.*, 39, 3 ; *Pan. Incert.*, VIII, 5, 2 ; Zon., XII, 31, III, p. 160.

⁴³ Kubitschek, *op. cit.*, especially pp. 24–32 in criticism of J. Vogt, *Die Alexandrin. Münzen*, I, p. 226 ; cf. Seeck, *op. cit.*, 1⁴ (*Anhang*), p. 450.

⁴⁴ Eutrop., IX, 23, and see Part V, Chapter V, pp. 278–281.

⁴⁵ *Mosaicarum et Romanarum legum collatio*, 15, 3, 4 (rec. Mommsen, p. 187) ; cf. K. Stade, *Der Politiker Diokletian u. die letze grosse Christenverfolgung*, p. 84.

⁴⁶ Eutrop., IX, 24 ; Vict. *de Caes.*, 39, 33.

⁴⁷ Eutrop., *l.c.* ; Amm., XIV, 11, 10 ; Rufus Festus, 25. It is not recorded by Lactantius (cf. Stade, *op. cit.*, p. 46).

⁴⁸ Eutrop., IX, 25 ; Vict. *de Caes.*, 39, 34 ; Costa, *s.v. Diocletianus* in *Diz. Epig.*, II, p. 1814.

⁴⁹ Petrus Patricus fr. 13 (*FHG*, IV, p. 188).

⁵⁰ Vict. *de Caes.*, 39, 36–37 ; Petrus Patricius, fr. 14 (*FHG*, IV, p. 189) is the most important text :

"ἦν δὲ τὰ κεφάλαια τῆς πρεσβείας ταῦτα, ὥστε κατὰ τὸ ἀνατολικὸν κλίμα τὴν Ἰντηληνὴν μετὰ Σοφηνῆς καὶ Ἀρζανηνὴν μετὰ Καρδουηνῶν καὶ

Ζαβδικηνῆς ʽΡωμαίους ἔχειν, καὶ τὸν Τίγριν ποταμὸν ἑκατέρας πολιτείας ὁροθέσιον εἶναι, ʼΑρμενίαν δὲ Ζίνθα τὸ κάστρον ἐν μεθορίῳ τῆς Μηδικῆς κείμενον ὁρίζειν, τὸν δὲ ʼΙβηρίας βασιλέα τῆς οἰκείας βασιλείας τὰ σύμβολα ʽΡωμαίοις ὀφείλειν, εἶναι δὲ τόπον τῶν συναλλαγμάτων Νίσιβιν τὴν πόλιν παρακειμένην τῷ Τίγριδι."

⁵¹ Malalas, p. 306, 20 ; p. 307, 14.

⁵² Dess. *ILS*, 624–625.

⁵³ *Ibid.*, 659, on which see Stade, *op. cit.*, p. 106.

⁵⁴ *Ibid.*, 626, 3588 ; cf. *Chron.* of A.D. 354 (*Chron. Min.*, I, p. 148).

⁵⁵ e.g. *ibid.*, 3091, 628, 635, 623 ; *CIL*, VIII, 8924, 9988 ; Stade, *op. cit.*, pp. 94–102.

⁵⁶ *Conservator*, e.g. M and S, V (2), pp. 224–5, nos. 35–49 ; pp. 233–4, nos. 131–143 ; *Fulgurator*, *ibid.*, pp. 234–5, nos. 144–146 ; p. 237, nos. 167–168 ; *Tutator*, *ibid.*, p. 226, nos. 50–57 ; *Propugnator*, *ibid.*, p. 244, nos. 236–238.

⁵⁷ *Conservator*, *ibid.*, pp. 282–4, nos. 543–552 ; *Pacifer*, *ibid.*, p. 284, nos. 553–556 ; *Victor*, p. 275, no. 489 ; p. 293, no. 619.

⁵⁸ e.g. Cohen, VI Diocletian, nos. 83–132 ; Maximian Herculius, nos. 138–225.

⁵⁹ Lact. *de mort. pers.*, 10, 1 ; Vict. *de Caes.*, 39, 48.

⁶⁰ " *Felicitatem istam, optimi imperatores, pietate meruistis* " (*Pan. Incert.*, XI, 18, 5).

⁶¹ *Mos. et Rom. legum collatio* (rec. Mommsen, p. 187), 15, 3, 1 ; Stade, *op. cit.*, pp. 83–86.

⁶² *Acta Maximiliani*, Ruinart, *Acta Mart.*, pp. 340 ff.

⁶³ Euseb., *H. E.*, VIII, 4, 2 ; VIII, 1, 7 ; Lact. *de mort. pers.*, 10 ; Stein, *op. cit.*, I, p. 121 ; Stade, *op. cit.*, pp. 157–61 ; Seeck, *Untergang*, III², pp. 309–14, 503 ; Costa in *Diz. Epig.*, II, pp. 1858–61.

⁶⁴ Lact. *de mort pers.*, 13.

⁶⁵ Lact., *l.c.* ; Euseb., *H. E.*, VIII, 2, 4 ; Stade, *op. cit.*, pp. 162–7. Baynes in *Cl. Q.*, XVIII (1924), pp. 189–93.

⁶⁶ Lact. *de mort. pers.*, 14 ; Euseb., *H. E.*, VIII, 6, 6.

⁶⁷ Euseb., *H.E.*, VIII, 6, 8.

⁶⁸ Euseb. *Mart. Pal.*, 2, 5 ; *H. E.*, VIII, 6, 10.

⁶⁹ Lact. *de mort pers.*, 15 ; Stade, *op. cit.*, pp. 174–6.

⁷⁰ Lact. *de mort. pers.*, 17, 2.

⁷¹ *Pan. Incert.*, VII, 8, 8 ; VII, 10, 5 ; Vict. *de Caes.*, 39, 48 ; Eutrop., IX, 27.

⁷² Lact. *de mort. pers.*, 18, 9 ; Victor, *Epit.*, 40, 14 ; *Anon. Val.*, 3, 7. The date of Maxentius' marriage is not much later than A.D. 293 as his son Romulus is *nobilissimus vir* in A.D. 309 (Dess. *ILS*, 672–673).

⁷³ Lact. *de mort. pers.*, 18.

⁷⁴ Dess. ILS, 666.

⁷⁵ On the whole question see Stein, *op. cit.*, I, pp. 100–1 ; Seeck, *Untergang*, I⁴ (*Anhang*), pp. 456 ff., and especially Groag, *s.v. Maxentius* in *P-W*, XIV, coll. 2420–2421.

⁷⁶ Lact. *de mort. pers.*, 17–19 ; Vict. *de Caes.*, 40, 1 ; *Epit.*, 39, 5 ; Eutrop., IX, 27 ; Zos., II, 8, 1 ; Zon., XII, 32, III, p. 163.

CHAPTER II

[1] Eutrop., X, 1 and 2 ; Zos., II, 8, 1 ; Vict. *de Caes.*, 40, 1 ; *Anon. Val.*, 3, 5 ; E. Stein, *Geschichte*, I, p. 96, n. 6.

[2] Dess. *ILS*, 646, 656.

[3] *Anon. Val.*, 2, 2 ; Vict. *de Caes.*, 40, 2.

[4] *Anon. Val.*, 2, 4 ; Vict. *de Caes.*, 40, 2 ; *Epit.*, 41, 2 ; Zos., II, 8, 3.

[5] *Anon. Val.*, 2, 4 ; Eutrop., X, 1, 3 ; Vict. *de Caes.*, 40, 4 ; Hydatius for A.D. 306 (*Chron. Min.*, I, p. 231).

[6] *Pan. Incert.*, VII, 4, 3 ; VI, 10, 2.

[7] For Licinius' elevation, Lact. *de mort. pers.*, 20 ; Zos., II, 11 ; Vict. *de Caes.*, 40, 8 ; for rank of Constantine, Lact., *op. cit.*, 25 ; Maurice, *Num. Const.*, I, p. LIII ; Seeck, *Untergang*, I[4] (*Anhang*), p. 482.

[8] Lact. *de mort. pers.*, 26, 3 ; Vict. *de Caes.*, 39, 47.

[9] Zos., II, 9, 3 ; for the functions of the *tribunus fori suarii*, Dess. *ILS*, 722.

[10] Lact. *de mort. pers.*, 26, 2.

[11] For Maxentius retains him in his post, *Chron.* of A.D. 354 (*Chron. Min.*, I, p. 66).

[12] *Pan. Incert.*, XII, 16, 2, shows that the battle of the Milvian Bridge took place on the sixth anniversary of M.'s *dies imperii* (i.e. October 28th, A.D. 306) ; Groag, *s.v. Maxentius* in *P-W*, XIV, coll. 2423–2424.

[13] Zos., II, 9, 3.

[14] Maurice, *Num. Const.*, I, p. 348, and 351, no. 1 ; Cohen, VII, p. 173, Maxentius, no. 66. On these coins from the mint at Carthage Maxentius is called *nobilissimus Caesar*, and not *princeps invictus* as he at first styled himself. The discrepancy may be explained by the assumption that they were issued as soon as the news of the *coup d'état* at Rome reached Carthage and before Maxentius' choice of the title *princeps* was known. M. is thus given on them the same status as Constantine.

[15] Maurice, *op. cit.*, I, p. 172, nos. I and II.

[16] Maurice, *op. cit.*, I, p. 351, and for coins struck at Rome in honour of Constantine, *ibid.*, I, pp. 172, 174.

[17] Vict. *de Caes.*, 40, 5.

[18] Lact. *de mort. pers.*, 26, 6–7 ; *Anon. Val.*, 4, 10 ; *Pan. Incert.*, VII, 10.

[19] Eutrop., X, 2, 3. Perhaps the letter was not sent till after Maximian had reached Rome. (Groag, *op. cit.*, col. 2427.)

[20] Zos., II, 10, 1 ; Eutrop., X, 2, 4 ; Vict. *de Caes.*, 40, 7 ; *Anon. Val.*, 4, 9.

[21] Maurice, *op. cit.*, I, p. 174.

[22] Lact. *de mort. pers.*, 26, 9 ; *Anon. Val.*, 4, 10.

[23] Maurice, *op. cit.*, I, pp. 175 ff. (from Rome) ; pp. 303 ff. (from Aquileia) : pp. 351 ff. (from Carthage).

[24] *Pan. Incert.*, VII, 1, 1–2 ; Lact. *de mort. pers.*, 27, 1 ; Zos., II, 10, 5.

[25] For the erasing of Severus' name from monuments, *CIL*, XII, 5504a, 5525. For the coinage, Maurice, *op. cit.*, I, pp. 175–6 ; II, p. 89, on the dating of which see Sydenham, *The Vicissitudes of Maximian after his Abdication*, in *Num. Chron.*, Fifth Series, 55 (1934), pp. 141–67 at pp. 158–9.

[26] *Anon. Val.*, 3, 6.

[27] Vict. *de Caes.*, 40, 8–9 ; *Anon. Val.*, 3, 7 ; Lact. *de mort. pers.*, 27 ; Zos., II, 10, 3 ; Zon., XII, 34, III, p. 168. For the order of the events, Groag, *op. cit.*, coll. 2431–2432.

[28] Zos., II, 10, 6–7.

[29] Maurice, *op. cit.*, II, p. 227, and for the history of Spain, *ibid.*, II, pp. 201–10, on which see E. Stein, *op. cit.*, I, p. 99, n. 6.

[30] *Anon. Val.*, 4, 10 ; Hydatius for A.D. 307 (*Chron. Min.*, I, p. 231) ; Sydenham, *op. cit.*

[31] Lact. *de mort. pers.*, 28 ; Zos., II, 11 ; Eutrop., X, 3, 1. The estrangement of Maximian and Maxentius is shown by the fact that the consulship which the former had assumed with Constantine in Gaul in A.D. 307 was not published in Rome (Mommsen, *Ges. Schrift.*, VI, p. 326). The open breach between them is probably to be dated to April, A.D. 308 (*Chron. of* A.D. 354, p. 67, and Groag, *op. cit.*, col. 2437).

[32] Mommsen, *Ges. Schrift.*, VI, p. 328 ; Zos., II, 10, 4 ; Vict. *Epit.*, 39, 6 ; Lact. *de mort. pers.*, 29, 1 ; for the chronology, Groag, *op. cit.*, coll. 2437–2438.

[33] Lact., *op. cit.*, 29, 2 ; Eutrop., X, 4, 1 ; Vict. *de Caes.*, 40, 8 ; *Anon. Val.*, 3, 8 ; 5, 13 ; for the date (November 11th, A.D. 308) Hydatius (*Chron. Min.*, I, p. 231) ; Seeck, *Untergang*, I⁴ (*Anhang*), p. 489.

[34] Dess. *ILS*, 683.

[35] Victor *Epit.*, 40, 18 ; Seeck, *op. cit.*, I⁴ (*Anhang*), p. 490.

[36] Zos., II, 12 ; Vict. *de Caes.*, 40, 17 ; *Epit.*, 40, 2 ; Polem. Silv. (Momm., *Chron. Min.*, I, p. 522).

[37] Suggested by Dess. *ILS*, 8936, "*impp. dd. nn. L. Domitio Alexandro et Fl. Constantino Augg.*" (from Africa *proconsularis*) ; cf. Dess. *ILS*, 674.

The account given by Zosimus of the causes of the rebellion is full of improbabilities (cf. Groag, *op. cit.*, coll. 2441–2442).

[38] The date is fixed by the fact that Romulus is *consul II* with Maxentius in A.D. 309, but in the following year his father is sole consul. (Hydatius, *Chron. Min.*, I, p. 231.) Romulus was canonized, and a heroon was dedicated to him, which used to be identified with the small round temple which forms to-day the vestibule to the Church of SS. Cosmas and Damian in the Forum. Now its site is thought to have been in the Circus of Maxentius (Whitehead, *N. Bull. di arch. crist.*, XIX (1913), pp. 149 ff. ; Ashby, *Roman Campagna*, p. 182). For Maxentius' building activities, Vict. *de Caes.*, 40, 26, and *Chron. of* A.D. 354 (*Chron. Min.*, I, p. 148) ; cf. Groag, *op. cit.*, coll. 2459–2462).

[39] *Pan. Incert.*, VI, 16–20 ; Lact. *de mort. pers.*, 29, 4 ; Eutrop., X, 3, 2 ; Vict. *Epit.*, 40, 5.

[40] Lact. *de mort. pers.*, 30, 5 ; Eutrop., *H. E.*, VIII, 13, 15 ; Vict. *Epit.*, 40, 5 ; " *iustissimo exitu* " (Eutrop., X, 3, 2) ; " *iure interierat* " (Vict. *de Caes.*, 40, 22).

[41] Lact. *de mort. pers.*, 42, 1 ; Euseb., *Vita Const.*, 1, 47.

[42] *Pan. Incert.*, VI, 2, 2 ; V, 2, 5 ; *Anon. Val.*, 1, 1 ; Eutrop., IX, 22 ; Dess. *ILS*, 699, 702, 723, 725.

[43] *Pan. Incert.*, IV, 17, 1 ; Stein, *op. cit.*, I, p. 133 ; Maurice, *op. cit.*, II, p. 236.

[44] *Pan. Incert.*, XII, 4, 4 ; Euseb., *H. E.*, VIII, 14, 6 ; *Vita Const.*, I, 36.

[45] *Chron.* of A.D. 354 (*Chron. Min.*, I, p. 148) ; Groag, *op. cit.*, coll. 2465–2466.

[46] Zos., II, 14, 2 ; Vict. *de Caes.*, 40, 18 ; Dess. *ILS*, 1213.

[47] Zos., II, 14, 4 ; Vict. *de Caes.*, 40, 19 ; Dess. *ILS*, 5570.

[48] Zos., *l.c.* ; Maurice, *op. cit.*, I, p. 188, no VII ; p. 198, no. VIII ; p. 200, no. XVIII = coins with VICTORIA AUG. or VICTORIA AETERNA.

[49] Dess. *ILS*, 647, 671 ; Maurice, *op. cit.*, I, pp. 191 ff. ; I, pp. 267 ff. = coins with legends DIVO MAXIMIANO PATRI and DIVO CONSTANTIO COGNATO.

[50] Lact. *de mort. pers.*, 33–35 ; *Anon. Val.*, 3, 8 ; Euseb., *H. E.*, VIII, 16, 4 ; *Vita Const.*, I, 57 ; Hydatius (*Chron. Min.*, I, p. 231).

[51] Lact. *de mort. pers.*, 36, 1 ; Euseb., *H. E.*, IX, 10, 2.

[52] Zos., II, 17, 2 ; Lact. *de mort. pers.*, 43, 2.

[53] Lact. *de mort pers.*, 43, 3 ; 44, 10 ; Maurice, *op. cit.*, I, p. lxxx, and I, p. 196.

[54] For a discussion of the different accounts given by literary authorities of the responsibility for the declaration of war, see Groag, *op. cit.*, coll. 2470–2472.

[55] *Pan. Incert.*, XII, 5, 1 ; Zosimus' figures (II, 15, 1) for both sides are clearly exaggerated.

[56] *Pan. Incert.*, IV, 22, 4.

[57] *Chron.* of A.D. 354 (*Chron. Min.*, I, p. 148) merely states "*Fossatum aperuit, sed non perfecit* (*sc. Maxentius*)," but see Richmond, *The City Wall of Imperial Rome*, pp. 251–6 ; cf. *Pan. Incert.*, XII, 16.

[58] *Pan. Incert.*, XII, 8 ; IV, 25.

[59] *Id.*, XII, 5, 4.

[60] *Id.*, XII, 6 ; IV, 21–24.

[61] For Verona, *Pan. Incert.*, XII, 8–10 ; IV, 25–6 ; for Modena, IV, 27, 1.

[62] For the persecution of the Christians between A.D. 303 and 311, Stade, *op. cit.*, pp. 176–83. The presence of Hosius, Bishop of Cordova, in Constantine's army is also significant (Seeck, *op. cit.*, 1⁴, p. 496).

[63] Euseb., *Vita Const.*, I, 28. The vision is not recorded in the author's *Ecclesiastical History*.

[64] Lact. *de mort. pers.*, 44. It is probable that the *labarum* or standard with the Christian monogram *XP* was adopted by

Constantine as early as A.D. 312, and not in A.D. 317 as Maurice (*Num. Const.*, I, pp. cv–cvii, cxxvii) contends; (see Franchi de' Cavalieri in *Studi Romani, Rivista di Archeologia e Storia*, 1913, pp. 161–88; Allard in *Rev. des Questions Historiques*, N.S. 51 (1914), pp. 89–101). On the controversy whether the Christian monogram described by Lactantius is the same as or different from that described by Eusebius in his account of the *labarum*, see in addition to the above-cited articles, Baynes, *Constantine and the Christian Church* (Raleigh Lecture before the British Academy), pp. 61–5.

⁶⁵ Zos., 11, 16, 1 ; Lact. *de mort. pers.*, 44, 8 ; *Pan. Incert.*, XII, 16 ; Groag, *op. cit.*, col. 2476 ; Piganiol (*L'Empereur Constantin*, p. 62) suggests that Constantine's fleet may have succeeded in occupying Ostia.

⁶⁶ For attempts to reconstruct the battle, Seeck, *Untergang*, I⁴, pp. 127–9, 496 ; Maurice, *Constantin le Grand*, pp. 41–7 ; Costa, *La Battaglia di Costantino a Ponte Milvio*, Bilychnis, 2 (1913), pp. 197–208 ; cf. also Delbrück, *Geschichte d. Kriegskunst*, II, p. 269.

⁶⁷ Zos., II, 17, 2 ; Vict. *de Caes.*, 40, 25.

⁶⁸ Euseb., *H. E.*, IX, 9, 10 ; *Vita Const.*, I, 40.

⁶⁹ Dess. *ILS*, 694 ; Platner and Ashby, *A Topographical Dictionary of Ancient Rome*, pp. 36–8 ; on the interpretation of the quoted words of the inscription, Baynes, *op. cit.*, pp. 66–8.

CHAPTER III

¹ Lact. *de mort. pers.*, 44, 11, supported by *CIL*, V, 8021, 8060, 8963. For Maximinus' exercise of the powers of a senior Augustus, Dess. *ILS*, 663–664.

² For the consulship, *CIL*, VI, 507. At the end of April Licinius was substituted in place of Maximinus (Seeck, *Untergang*, I⁴ (*Anhang*), p. 500). For the letters, Euseb., *H. E.*, IX, 9, 12 ; X, 5, 15–17 ; Baynes in *Cl. Q.*, XVIII (1924), pp. 193–4 ; XIX (1925), pp. 94–100.

³ Lact. *de mort. pers.*, 45, 1 ; *Anon. Val.*, 5, 13.

⁴ Lact. *de mort. pers.*, 48, 2 ; Euseb., *H. E.*, X, 5, 1–14. On the Edict of Milan, its meaning and authenticity, Baynes, *Constantine and the Christian Church*, pp. 69–74, where there is a full bibliography and discussion ; Stein, *op. cit.*, I, p. 141, n. 3.

⁵ Seeck, *op. cit.*, I,⁴ pp. 140–42. Constantine was ready to appoint a Cæsar to administer Maxentius' territories, if Licinius also agreed to hand over Rætia, Noricum and the Pannonian diocese, which had previously belonged to Severus, to this new Cæsar.

⁶ *Anon. Val.*, 5, 13 ; *Pan. Incert.*, XII, 21–2.

⁷ Lact. *de mort. pers.*, 36, 4 ; Euseb., *H. E.*, VIII, 14, 9 ; IX, 4, 2 ; Baynes in *Cl. Q.*, XVIII (1924), pp. 193–4 ; XIX (1925), pp. 95–6.

⁸ Vict. *Epit.*, 40, 18.

⁹ Lact. *de mort. pers.*, 39–41, and see further E. Stein, *op. cit.*, I, pp. 135–8. For an unfavourable verdict on Maximinus, Seeck, *op. cit.*, I⁴, pp. 145–8.

[10] Euseb., *H. E.*, IX, 8, 1–2 ; Lact. *de mort. pers.*, 37, 4 ; Seeck, *op. cit.*, I⁴, pp. 148 and 503.

[11] Lact. *de mort. pers.*, 45–47 ; Zos., II, 17, 3.

[12] Euseb., *H. E.*, IX, 10, 6 ; Baynes, *Cl. Q.*, XVIII (1924), p. 194.

[13] Lact. *de mort. pers.*, 49 ; Eutrop., X, 4, 4 ; Vict. *de Caes.*, 41, 1 ; *Epit.*, 40, 8.

[14] Euseb., *H. E.*, IX, 11, 3–7 ; Lact. *de mort. pers.*, 50–51.

[15] Hydatius for A.D. 316 (*Chron. Min.*, I, p. 231) ; Zos., II, 8, 1 ; Seeck, *op. cit.*, I⁴, p. 501.

[16] *Anon. Val.*, 5, 14.

[17] *Id.*, 5, 15 ; Euseb., *Vita Const.*, I, 50, 2.

[18] *Anon. Val.*, 5, 16 ; Zos., II, 18 ; Eutrop., X, 5 ; Hydatius for A.D. 314 (*Chron. Min.*, I, p. 231).

[19] *Anon. Val.*, 5, 17 ; Zos., II, 19, 2 (both of whom wrongly call him Cæsar) ; Vict. *Epit.*, 40, 2 ; Maurice, *op. cit.*, III, pp. 114–15.

[20] *Anon. Val.*, 5, 17–18.

[21] *Id.*, 5, 18 ; Zos., II, 20, 1.

[22] Euseb., *H. E.*, X, 5, 18–7, 2. In the Theodosian Code there are no edicts in Licinius' name alone, because his acts were annulled in A.D. 324 (*Cod. Theo.*, XV, 14, 1), but cf. Dess. *ILS*, 8940.

[23] *Anon. Val.*, 5, 21.

[24] *Id.*, 5, 19 ; Hydatius for A.D. 315 (*Chron. Min.*, I, p. 231).

[25] Dess. *ILS*, 8938.

[26] The Decennalian celebrations began a year in advance of the actual anniversary. For coin evidence, Maurice, *op. cit.*, I, pp. 216, 412–15 ; for the arch, Dess. *ILS*, 694.

[27] *Anon. Val.*, 5, 19 ; Zos., II, 20, 2 ; Vict. *de Caes.*, 41, 6 ; *Epit.*, 41, 4 ; Hydatius for A.D. 317 (*Chron. Min.*, I, p. 232) ; Maurice, *op. cit.*, I, p. cv.

[28] *Cod. Theo.*, XVI, 2, 1.

[29] E. Stein, *op. cit.*, I, pp. 146–7.

[30] *Cod. Theo.*, I, 27, 1. Later in A.D. 333 according to the *Constitutio Sirmondiana* I (*Cod. Theo.*, I (2), p. 907, ed. Mommsen and Meyer) the jurisdiction of the bishops was recognized in all civil suits, if one of the litigants against the will of the other appealed to their court. This privilege is so remarkable that it may well raise doubts as to the authenticity of the Constitution.

[31] *Cod. Theo.*, XVI, 2, 4.

[32] For the Donatist Schism, the collection of documents by Soden, *Urkunden zur Enstehungsgeschichte des Donatismus* in Lietzmann, *Kleine Texte*, 122 ; Seeck, *Untergang*, III², pp. 318–41, 505–24 ; Stein, *op. cit.*, I, pp. 152–4 ; Baynes, *Constantine and the Christian Church*, pp. 11–16 ; and for further details see Chap. VI, pp. 294–6.

[33] Seeck, *Untergang*, III², pp. 385–404 ; Stein, *op. cit.*, I, p. 156, n. 1.

[34] Euseb., *Vita Const.*, I, 51 ; II, 66. For the date, Seeck, *op. cit.*, I⁴, p. 509, based on *Hieron. Chron.*, p. 312, Fotheringham, and Cedrenus, I, p. 495 B.

[35] Euseb., *H. E.*, X, 8, 11 ; *Vita Const.*, I, 53.

[36] *H. E.*, X, 8, 10.

³⁷ *Ibid.*, X, 8, 14–18 ; *Vita Const.*, I, 52 and 54.

³⁸ Seeck in *Rh. Mus.* LXII (1907), pp. 533 ff.

³⁹ Zos., II, 21 ; Maurice, *op. cit.*, I, pp. cxxi–cxxii ; II, pp. 393–394.

⁴⁰ *Anon. Val.*, 5, 21–22 ; *CIL*, I, p. 336 ; Euseb., *Vita Const.*, I, 50.

⁴¹ *Anon. Val.*, 5, 23 ; Zos., II, 22, 1–2.

⁴² *Anon. Val.*, 5, 24–25 ; Hydatius for A.D. 324 (*Chron. Min.*, I, p. 232) ; for the reconstruction of the whole war, Pears, *The Campaign against Paganism*, in *EHR*, XXIV (1909), pp. 1–17.

⁴³ *Anon. Val.*, 5, 25–6 ; Zos., II, 23, 2–24, 3.

⁴⁴ *Anon. Val.*, 5, 27 ; Zos., II, 25, 1.

⁴⁵ *Anon. Val.*, 5, 25 ; Zos., II, 25, 2 ; Maurice, *op. cit.*, III, pp. 45, 123 ; Stein, *op. cit.*, I, p. 159, n. 3.

⁴⁶ *Anon. Val.*, 5, 27–28 ; Zos., II, 26 ; Hydatius for A.D. 324 (*Chron. Min.*, I, p. 232).

⁴⁷ *Anon. Val.*, 5, 28–9 ; Zos., II, 28 ; Eutrop., X, 6 ; Zon., XIII, 1, III, pp. 174–5 ; Vict. *de Caes.*, 41, 9–10 ; *Epit.*, 41, 7.

CHAPTER IV

¹ For the Persian influence, Lact. *de mort. pers.*, 21, 2 ; Seeck, *Untergang*, II², pp. 7 and (*Anhang*) 469. For the early introduction of *adoratio*, Pan. *Incert.*, XI, 11, 1, referring to the winter of A.D. 288–9. Cf. Vict. *de Caes.*, 39, 4 ; Eutrop., IX, 26 ; Zon., XII, 31, III, p. 162.

² Vict. *Epit.*, 41, 14 ; Maurice, *Num. Const.*, I, p. cxxix.

³ Stein, *op. cit.*, I, p. 169, n. 1, and p. 205 ; Dunlap, *Univ. of Michigan Stud.*, *Hum. Series*, XIV (1924), pp. 180–222 ; for the *silentiarii*, *Cod. Theo.*, VIII, 7, 5, as dated by Seeck, *Regesten*, p. 42.

⁴ Pan. *Incert.*, X, 3, 3, and Part III, Chap. IV, pp. 179–180.

⁵ *JRS*, XXI (1931), p. 60, and pl. V, 2 ; cf. for other examples, *CIL*, VIII, 2572, and Dess. *ILS*, 627–628.

⁶ Anderson, *The Genesis of Diocletian's Provincial Reorganization* in *JRS*, XXII (1932), pp. 24–32 at p. 30.

⁷ *Laterculus Veronensis* in Seeck, *Notitia Dignitatum*, pp. 247–53 ; Mommsen, *Verzeichniss der römischen Provinzen*, in *Ges. Schrift.*, V, pp. 561 ff. ; Bury, *The Provincial List of Verona*, in *JRS*, XIII (1923), pp. 127–51 ; Anderson, *op. cit.*

⁸ Dess. *ILS*, 6886 ; *CIL*, VIII, 8924.

⁹ Eutrop., IX, 23.

¹⁰ Anderson, *op. cit.*, p. 31.

¹¹ e.g. Anicius Julianus, *proconsul* of Africa under Diocletian (Dess. *ILS*, 1220) and Rufius Volusianus (Dess. *ILS*, 1213) ; Fabius Titianus, *proconsul* of Asia under Constantine (Dess. *ILS*, 1227) ; Vettius Rufinus, *proconsul* of Achaea under Diocletian (Dess. *ILS*, 1217), and the following references to *proconsul Africae* in *Cod. Theo.* dated to the reign of Constantine, I, 12, 1 ; VI, 35, 2 ; VIII, 10, 1 ; IX, 10, 1 ; IX, 34, 2 ; X, 15, 1 ; XI, 16, 1 ; XII, 1, 9 ; XV, 3, 1.

¹² For *consulares*, e.g. Dess. *ILS*, 1216, 1219, 1223 ; *Cod. Theo.*, I, 2, 6 ; XI, 16, 2.

For *correctores* (senatorial), e.g. Dess. *ILS*, 677, 708, 1212, 1227, 1231 ; *Cod. Theo.*, I, 16, 1 ; IX, 19, 1 ; XII, 1, 3 ; XVI, 2, 2.

For *praesides*, e.g. Dess. *ILS*, 627, 628, 631, 635, 638 ; *Cod. Theo.*, I, 16, 3 ; II, 6, 1 ; II, 19, 2 ; VII, 20, 1 ; IX, 40, 3 ; XI, 3, 1 ; XIII, 10, 2.

[13] For equestrian *correctores*, Dess. *ILS*, 1218, and under Constantius II, *ibid.*, 734, 749.

For senatorial *praesides*, Dess. *ILS*, 6111–6111[b], 740, 5699.

[14] For the division into dioceses, see *Laterculus Veronensis* (Seeck, *op. cit.*, pp. 247 ff.).

For the *vicarii*, Dess. *ILS*, 1214, 1218 ; *Cod. Theo.*, I, 15, 2 ; II, 15, 1 ; III, 5, 6 ; VIII, 15, 2 ; IX, 8, 1 ; IX, 15, 1 ; IX, 18, 1 ; IX, 34, 1 and 3 ; X, 4, 1 ; XI, 7, 2 ; XII, 1, 12.

[15] E. Stein, *op. cit.*, I, p. 104.

[16] Dess. *ILS*, 1214 ; Seeck, *Untergang*, II[2], p. 506.

[17] Gelzer, *Studien zur byzant. Verwaltung Ägyptens* (Leipzig, 1909), pp. 5 ff.

[18] It seems probable that each Caesar as well as each Augustus had his own prefect : see as against Mommsen (*Ges. Schrift.*, VI, p. 287), Seeck, *op. cit.*, II[2], pp. 505–6.

For the praetorian guard, Vict. *de Caes.*, 39, 47 ; Lact. *de mort. pers.*, 26, 3.

[19] E. Stein, *op. cit.*, I, pp. 55 and 103.

[20] Seeck, *Untergang*, II[2] (*Anhang*), p. 508, and *Regesten*, pp. 142–5 ; Baynes in *JRS*, XV (1925), pp. 204–8, on which see E. Stein, *op. cit.*, p. 179, n. 1.

[21] *Cod. Theo.*, XI, 30, 16 ; cf. for the jurisdiction of the praetorian prefects, *Cod. Theo.*, I, 5, 1 ; I, 5, 2 ; I, 5, 3 ; I, 16, 3 ; I, 16, 6.

[22] *Id.*, VIII, 5, 4.

[23] *Id.*, XV, 1, 3.

[24] *Id.*, XIV, 8, 1 ; XIII, 5, 5.

[25] *Id.*, XIV, 4, 1–2.

[26] *Id.*, XIII, 3, 1–2.

[27] *Id.*, XI, 1, 3 and 9 ; I, 5, 5–7 ; Zos., II, 33, 4 ; Lydus, *de mag.*, II, 7.

[28] *Cod. Theo.*, VII, 13.

[29] *Id.*, VII, 4, 3 ; XI, 25, 1 ; Grosse, *Römische Militärgeschichte*, pp. 158–9.

[30] See further on the praetorian prefecture, Mommsen, *Ges. Schrift.*, VI, pp. 284–99 ; E. Stein, *Untersuchungen über das Officium der Prätorianerpräfectur seit Diokletian*, and the same author's *Geschichte*, I, pp. 178–81.

[31] Seeck, *s.v. Consistorium* in *P-W*, IV, coll. 926 ff., and *s.v. Comites*, *ibid.*, IV, coll. 626 ff.

[32] Mommsen, *Ges. Schrift.*, VI, pp. 387–94 ; Seeck, *Notit. Dignit.*, p. 34.

[33] Mommsen, *op. cit.*, pp. 392–3 ; Seeck, *Untergang*, II[2], pp. 93–4 ; Stein, *Geschichte*, I, pp. 170–71.

[34] *Cod. Theo.*, XVI, 10, 1.

³⁵ For the *magister officiorum*, Seeck, *Untergang*, II², pp. 92–5 ;
Mommsen, *Ges. Schrift.*, VI, pp. 405–6 ; Seeck, *Notitia Dignit.*, pp. 31–3.
For the *agentes in rebus*, Grosse, *op. cit.*, pp. 104–6 ; Hirschfeld, *Kleine
Schriften*, pp. 624–45.

³⁶ Hirschfeld, *Die Kaiserlichen Verwaltungsbeamten* (2nd ed.),
pp. 35–7, 46–7 ; Seeck, *Notit. Dignit.*, pp. 35–8.

³⁷ *Cod. Theo.*, VI, 30 ; VI, 35, 1.

³⁸ Stein, *Geschichte*, I, p. 106.

³⁹ Dess. *ILS*, 1214 ; Seeck, *Untergang*, I⁴ (*Anhang*), p. 506.

⁴⁰ Stein, *Geschichte*, I, pp. 183–4.

⁴¹ Zos., II, 40, 2, and Hirschfeld, *Kleine Schriften*, pp. 662–3.

⁴² For title *censor*, Migne Gr., 25, 365 ; for *nobilissimus*, Zos., II,
39, 2.

⁴³ *Cod. Theo.*, VI, 4, 2.

⁴⁴ Seeck, *Untergang*, II², p. 312.

⁴⁵ On the army reforms of Diocletian and Constantine, see Mommsen,
Das röm. Militärwesen seit Diokletian in *Ges. Schrift.*, VI, pp. 206–83 ;
Seeck, *Untergang*, II², pp. 33–51 ; Grosse, *Römische Militärgeschichte*,
pp. 25–106 ; Nischer in Kromayer and Veith, *Heerwesen und Krieg-
führung*, pp. 482–3 and pp. 568–88 ; *id.*, *The Army Reforms of Diocletian
and Constantine* in *JRS*, XIII (1923), pp. 1–55, on which see further
Baynes in *JRS*, XV (1925), pp. 201–4, and my article *The Legions of
Diocletian and Constantine* in *JRS*, XXIII (1933), pp. 175–89 ; Ritterling, *s.v. Legio* in *P-W*, XII, coll. 1348–1362.

⁴⁶ *The Legions of Diocletian and Constantine*, pp. 175–82.

⁴⁷ *Pap. Ox.*, I, 43 ; Ritterling, *op. cit.*, coll. 1359–1360.

⁴⁸ *Cod. Just.*, X, 55, 3 ; cf. *id.*, VII, 64, 9 ; E. Stein, *Geschichte*, I,
p. 92, n. 1.

⁴⁹ *Pap. Ox.*, I, 43, col. II, 24–8, and col. I, 15.

⁵⁰ Dess. *ILS*, 664.

⁵¹ V *Macedonica* and XIII *Gemina* (Seeck, *Notit. Dignit.*, p. 59).

⁵² *CIL*, V, 895, 896 =Dess. *ILS*, 2332 ; " *obitus in Mauretania* "
(*CIL*, V, 893).

⁵³ Dess. *ILS*, 2045, 2782 ; *The Legions of Diocletian and Constantine*,
pp. 185–6.

⁵⁴ Dess. *ILS*, 2781.

⁵⁵ Seeck, *Notit. Dignit.*, pp. 13–18 ; Grosse, *op. cit.*, pp. 29–42 and
49–51.

⁵⁶ Kromayer and Veith, *op. cit.*, pp. 581–3.

⁵⁷ Seeck, *Notit. Dignit.*, pp. 31–2 ; Grosse, *op. cit.*, pp. 93–6.

⁵⁸ For the vexed problem of the *protectores* see the literature cited
in Part III, Chap. IV, n. 42.

⁵⁹ *The Army Reforms of Diocletian and Constantine*, pp. 30–31
(I have modified Nischer's theory in a point of detail) ; cf. Mommsen,
op. cit., *Ges. Schrift.*, VI, p. 219.

⁶⁰ Seeck, *Notit. Dignit.*, pp. 64, 86–97 (Thebais and the Danubian
provinces).

⁶¹ *Ibid.*, pp. 67–85 (the Eastern provinces).

⁶² Grosse, *op. cit.*, pp. 51–4.

[63] e.g. *Notit. Dignit.*, pp. 87, 90–1, 93, 96–7.

[64] Grosse, *op. cit.*, pp. 42–7.

[65] Their total strength was approximately 300,000 (Grosse, *op. cit.*, pp. 251 ff.) ; for a higher estimate Kromayer und Veith, *op. cit.*, p. 581. Cf. Zos., II, 34, 2 for Constantine's frontier policy.

[66] For the recruiting of the army, Mommsen, *op. cit.*, *Ges. Schrift.*, VI, pp. 246–60 ; Grosse, *op. cit.*, pp. 198–220. The system was partly voluntary and partly compulsory, and was unrestricted by the qualifications that had previously been in force for the legions and *auxilia*. Citizen, subject and foreigner were equally eligible, but no recruit was accepted who was attempting to escape other obligations (e.g. service in the *curiae* or *collegia*) by joining the army. Volunteers fall under three main categories : (1) free peasants ; (2) barbarians outside the Empire ; (3) prisoners of war. Service on the other hand was compulsory for (1) sons of soldiers who were physically fit ; (2) *vagi* (*Cod. Theo.*, VII, 18, 10), i.e. men who were neither landowners nor bound to the soil as the *coloni* ; (3) *vacantes* (*Cod. Theo.*, XII, 1, 137), i.e. men not belonging to any *collegium* or other state-organization ; (4) the provision of a recruit was a tax on the landed proprietors. (On the methods by which this obligation was fulfilled (known as *Protostasia* and *Prototypia*), see Seeck, *Untergang*, II², pp. 47–51).

[67] " *Strata Diocletiana* " (Dess. *ILS*, 5846).

[68] *CIL*, III, 14149, and von Domaszewski in *Kiepert-Festschrift*, p. 69.

[69] *CIL*, III, 14380.

[70] Amm., XXIII, 5, 2, and on the *limes Orientalis*, Fabricius in *P-W*, XIII, coll. 654–9 ; Brünnow und Domaszewski, *Die Provinz Arabia*, especially II *Abschn.* 5 ; Chapot, *La Frontière de l'Euphrate*, pp. 245–51 and 328–34 ; von Domaszewski in *Kiepert-Festschrift*, pp. 65 ff. For a survey of Diocletian's work on the frontiers, Costa, *Diz. Epig.*, II, pp. 1836–45.

[71] Dess. *ILS*, 640, dated to A.D. 294 ; cf. new walls and gates for Grenoble (Cularo) in Dess. *ILS*, 620–620a.

[72] Malalas, p. 307.

[73] Dess. *ILS*, 628.

[74] *Ibid.*, 638.

[75] *Ibid.*, 627, and on the African *Limes*, Cagnat, *L'armée R. d'Afrique*, II, pp. 523 ff.

[76] Dess. *ILS*, 8938 ; Fabricius, *op. cit.*, coll. 647–50.

[77] Vict. *de Caes.*, 41, 18 ; Maurice, *op. cit.*, II, pp. 513–15.

CHAPTER V

[1] Mattingly, *Roman Coins*, pp. 222–6 ; Maurice, *Num. Const.*, I, pp. xxxviii–xl and III, pp. xxix–xlviii ; Seeck, *Untergang*, II², pp. 230–7. The reform was instituted early in D.'s reign and certainly before A.D. 296 (Stein, *Geschichte*, I, p. 112, n. 2).

[2] Mattingly, *op. cit.*, p. 225, who holds that Diocletian's system is based like Aurelian's on the *sestertius*, with this difference, that D.

identified its tenth part (*libella*) with the " *denarius communis* " (cf. above Part IV, Ch. II, n. 51).

[3] Dess. *ILS*, 642 ; Lact. *de mort. pers.*, 7 ; Mattingly, *op. cit.*, pp. 263–4 ; Mickwitz, *op. cit.*, pp. 70–75.

[4] Maurice, *op. cit.*, I, pp. xxxix–xli ; Mattingly, *op. cit.*, pp. 227–8.

[5] Maurice, *op. cit.*, I, pp. xli–xliii ; for Licinius' continuance of Diocletian's system, *ibid.*, II, p. 581 ; III, pp. 125, 206.

[6] Mattingly, *op. cit.*, pp. 227–8.

[7] *Ibid.*, pp. 259–60 ; Mickwitz, *op. cit.*, pp. 65–6.

[8] The following is a list of the imperial mints with their distinguishing letters : L = Londinium ; TR = Trier ; LD = Lugdunum ; Ar. or Const. = Arelate ; R = Rome ; T = Ticinum ; AQ = Aquileia ; K = Carthage ; Sisc = Siscia ; SD or SERD = Serdica ; Sirm. = Sirmium ; TS = Thessalonica ; Cons. = Constantinople ; HT = Heraclea in Thrace ; K = Cyzicus ; N = Nicomedia ; A or ANT = Antioch ; ALE = Alexandria. (See further, Maurice, *op. cit.*, under the different *ateliers*.)

[9] Mattingly, *op. cit.*, p. 256. Hoards of coins later in date than A.D. 308, which are assigned by e.g. Maurice (*op. cit.*, II, p. 209) to Tarraco, were issued not from Tarraco but from Ticinum in Italy (Letter T).

[10] Maurice, *op. cit.*, I, pp. 339–69.

[11] Maurice, *op. cit.*, II, p. 51.

[12] Mattingly, *op. cit.*, p. 267.

[13] *Ibid.*, p. 257, and Maurice, *op. cit.*, III, pp. 270–82.

[14] *Cod. Theo.*, IX, 23, 1 of A.D. 356 (? 352).

[15] Mattingly, *op. cit.*, p. 254.

[16] *Cod. Theo.*, IX, 21 and 22.

[17] Seeck in *P-W*, IV, col. 674.

[18] *Cod. Theo.*, X, 20, 1.

[19] Lact. *de mort. pers.*, 7, 9–10 and 17, 4 ; Dess. *ILS*, 613.

[20] *Pan. Incert.*, XI, 11, 1 ; Victor, *de Caes.*, 39, 45 ; Costa, *op. cit.*, *Diz. Epig.*, II, pp. 1862–5.

[21] Cohen, VI, p. 464, Diocletian, no. 438 ; cf. "SALVIS AUGG. ET CAESS., AUCTA KART." (*ibid.*, no. 437).

[22] *Chron.* of A.D. 354 (*Chron. Min.*, I, p. 148) ; Dess. *ILS*, 646, 621–622, 626, 1211 ; *Vita Probi*, 2, 1 ; *FHG*, IV, p. 167 ; Strong, *Art in Rome*, II, pp. 170–2.

[23] Dess. *ILS*, 634 ; Kinch, *L'Arc de Triomphe de Salonique* (Paris, 1890).

[24] Diehl, *Man. d'art Byz.*, pp. 105–8 ; *Id.*, *En Méditerranée*, pp. 32–62 ; Zeiller in *Comptes rend. de l'Acad. d'inscrip. et bell. lett.*, 1908, pp. 423 ff.

[25] *Cod. Just.*, X, 16, 2 (A.D. 260) ; *ibid.*, 16, 3 (A.D. 249).

[26] Seeck, *s.v. Indiktionenzyclus* in *P-W*, IX, coll. 1327 ff. ; *id.*, *Untergang*, II[2], p. 266.

[27] H. Bott, *Die Grundzüge der Diokletianischen Steuerverfassung*, especially pp. 18–37, which is a recent and important analysis of Diocletian's Reform. For other interpretations of *capitatio*, Seeck, *Untergang*, II[2], pp. 268–79 ; *id.*, *s.v. Caput* in *P-W*, III, coll. 1546 ff. ; *s.v. Capitatio* in *P-W*, III, coll. 1516 ff. ; Piganiol, *L'impôt de*

capitation sous le bas-Empire Romain (Chambéry, 1916); Thibault, *Les impôts directs sous le bas-Empire Romain* in *Revue générale du droit* (1899), pp. 289 ff. and 418 ff. ; XXIV (1900), pp. 32 and 112 ff.

[28] *Syrische Rechtsbücher*, I, Band K, III, p. 135.

[29] *Cod. Theo.*, XIII, 11, 2 ; children under a certain age were not included in the census, and soldiers in the field army received total, and in the garrison army, partial exemption (*Cod. Theo.*, VII, 20, 4). Most important is the evidence of the " Register-inscriptions " from the eastern half of the Empire, e.g. from Thera (*I.G.*, XII, 3, nos. 343–349) ; from Mytilene (*ibid.*, nos. 76–80 ; *IGRR*, IV, nos. 109–114) ; cf. Keil u. Premerstein, *Dritte Reise in Lydien*, pp. 68 ff., and Bott, *op. cit.*, pp. 40–44. For the papyrus evidence on the working of the system in Egypt, Wilcken, I (1), pp. 219 ff., and Bott, *op. cit.*, pp. 45–7.

[30] Seeck, *Untergang*, II[2], p. 264.

[31] Stein, *Geschichte*, I, p. 111.

[32] *Cod. Theo.*, VII, 4, " *De erogatione militaris annonae.*"

[33] *Cod. Theo.*, XI, 16, 5 (of A.D. 343) ; *ibid.*, 1, 10 (A.D. 365).

[34] Bruns, *Fontes Iuris Romani*, pp. 270–71, no. 97 A (A.D. 370–71) ;

[35] *Cod. Theo.*, XIII, 11. Euseb., *Vita Const.*, IV, 3.

[36] *Cod. Theo.*, VII, 4, 28 (A.D. 406).

[37] Lact. *de mort. pers.*, 23 ; for the policy of Maximinus Daia, Stein, *Geschichte*, I, p. 137,

[38] *Cod. Theo.*, XIII, 10, 2.

[39] Seeck in *P-W*, IV, coll. 365–7 ; Zos., II, 38, 4.

[40] *Cod. Theo.*, XII, 13, 2–3.

[41] *Id.*, XIII, 1. Zos., II, 38, 2.

[42] *Cod. Theo.*, XIII, 5, 4 ; XIII, 8, 1.

[43] *Id.*, XV, 14, 4 ; Euseb., *H. E.*, VIII, 15, 1.

[44] *Id.*, XIII, 5, 1–3.

[45] *Ibid.*, 5, 5–7.

[46] *Id.*, XIV, 3, 1 (*pistores*) ; XIV, 4, 1 (*suarii*). The number of *centonarii* and *fabri* was also increased by the addition of *dendrophori* to their *collegium* (XIV, 8, 1).

[47] Illiteracy (*Cod. Just.*, X, 32, 6) ; *infamia* (X, 32, 12) ; age or physical unfitness (X, 32, 13) ; father's consent (X, 32, 5).

[48] Seeck, *Regesten*, p. 134, 12, and *Untergang*, II[2], pp. 567–8.

[49] *Cod. Theo.*, XII, 1, 19 (A.D. 331).

[50] *Ibid.*, 1, 5, " *si vero decurio suffragio comparato perfectissimatus vel ducenae vel centenae vel egregiatus meruerit dignitatem, declinare suam curiam cupiens, codicillis amissis suae conditioni reddatur* " ; cf. Lact. *de mort. pers.*, 21, 3.

[51] *Ibid.*, 1, 10 ; 1, 13, " *quoniam curias desolari cognovimus.*"

[52] *Id.*, XVI, 2, 3 ; cf. XVI, 2, 6, " *opulentos enim saeculi subire necessitates oportet, pauperes ecclesiarum divitiis sustentari.*"

[53] *Id.*, XII, 1, 18 (reading XXV in line 4).

[54] *Id.*, VII, 22, 2 ; XII, 1, 15.

[55] For later legislation against evasion, (*a*) by obtaining posts in the army, *id.*, XII, 1, 37 (A.D. 344) ; XII, 1, 38 (A.D. 346) ; XII, 1, 40 (A.D. 353) ; and (*b*) through ordination, XII, 1, 49 and 50 (A.D. 361–2) ;

24

VIII, 4, 7 (A.D. 361); and IX, 45, 3 (A.D. 398); cf. Amm., XXII, 9, 12.

⁵⁶ Of the voluminous literature on the history of the *colonate* see especially Rostovtzeff, *Studien zur Geschichte des röm. Kolonates* (Leipzig, 1910); Vinogradoff, *The Growth of the Manor*, pp. 45–83, 106–13 (London, 1905); Seeck, *s.v. Colonatus* in *P-W*, IV, coll. 483–510; Clausing, *The Roman Colonate* (New York, 1925).

⁵⁷ A and J, p. 435, no. 111.

⁵⁸ *Cod. Theo.*, V, 17, 1 (A.D. 332).

⁵⁹ See n. 58.

⁶⁰ *Cod. Theo.*, V, 19, 1 (*peculium* of *colonus*); *Cod. Just.*, XI, 48, 24; XI, 69, 1 (marriage of *colonus*).

⁶¹ *Cod. Just.*, XI, 48, 23, 1, " *terrae inhaereant quam semel colendam patres eorum susceperunt* "; see further on the legal status of the *coloni*, Clausing, *op. cit.*, pp. 18–30.

CHAPTER VI

¹ In this chapter I am much indebted to Professor Baynes' *Constantine and the Christian Church*, particularly for the valuable discussion of the authenticity of some of Constantine's letters, and for his comprehensive bibliography.

² *Pan. Incert.*, VII, 2, 5; Maurice, *Num. Const.*, II, pp. 81–91, 217, 230.

³ Euseb., *Vita Const.*, I, 17; II, 49.

⁴ *Pan. Incert.*, VI, 21, 4.

⁵ *Ibid.*, 22, 2.

⁶ *Id.*, V, 14, 4, and on the solar Dynasty of the second Flavians, Maurice, *op. cit.*, II, pp. xx–xlviii; Batifoll, *Les Étapes de la conversion de Constantin* in *Bull. d'ancienne littérature et d'archéologie Chrétiennes*, III (1913), pp. 179–83.

⁷ *Vita Const.*, I, 28–9.

⁸ *De mort. pers.*, 44.

⁹ *Vita Const.*, I, 40.

¹⁰ Dess. *ILS*, 694.

¹¹ Alföldi, *The Helmet of Constantine with the Christian Monogram*, in *JRS*, XXII (1932), pp. 12–14.

¹² *Pan. Incert.*, XII, 2, 4–5; Seeck, *Untergang*, I⁴, p. 473.

¹³ Baynes in *Cl. Q.*, XVIII (1924), pp. 193–4; XIX (1925), pp. 94–100.

¹⁴ Euseb., *H. E.*, X, 5, 15–17; Soden, *Urkunden zur Enstehungs geschichte des Donatismus* (in Lietzmann, *Kleine Texte*, no. 122), p. 10, no. 7.

¹⁵ *H. E.*, X, 6, 1–5; Soden, *op. cit.*, pp. 10–11, no. 8.

¹⁶ *H. E.*, X, 7, 1; Soden, *op. cit.*, pp. 11–12, no. 9; Baynes, *op. cit.*, pp. 68–9.

¹⁷ Seeck, *Das sogenannte Edikt von Mailand*, in *Zeitschrift für Kirchengeschichte*, XII (1891), pp. 381–6; Baynes, *op. cit.*, pp. 70–74.

[18] Soden, *op. cit.*, pp. 12–16, nos. 10–13.

[19] *Ibid.*, pp. 16–18, no. 14 ; on the authenticity of the documents in the " dossier " of Optatus, Baynes, *op. cit.*, pp. 75–8.

[20] Soden, *op. cit.*, pp. 23–4, no. 18.

[21] Soden, *op. cit.*, pp. 25–52, especially nos. 21–23, 26–27, 29–31.

[22] *Cod. Theo.*, I, 27, 1.

[23] *Id.*, XVI, 2, 4 ; *id.*, IV, 7.

[24] *Id.*, VIII, 16.

[25] *Id.*, XVI, 2, 5.

[26] *Id.*, IX, 16, 1–2 ; XVI, 10, 1.

[27] For the Christian monogram type, Alföldi, *op. cit.*, pp. 9–23 ; for the *Sol Invictus* type, Maurice, *Num. Const.*, II, pp. 400–1. For a series struck in A.D. 314 with a small cross side by side with the figures of *Sol Invictus* and *Mars Conservator, ibid.*, II, pp. 249–50.

[28] *Vita Const.*, II, 24–42 ; II, 46–60.

[29] *Ibid.*, II, 64–72.

[30] On the Council of Antioch, Schwartz, *Nachrichten von der Kgl. Gesellschaft der Wissenschaften zu Göttingen*, VI (1905), pp. 272 ff. ; Seeberg, *Die Synode von Antiochien im Jahre 324–325 (Neue Studien zur Geschichte der Theologie und der Kirche*, edd. Bonwetsch und Seeberg, Heft 16) ; A. E. Burn, *The Council of Nicaea*, pp. 12–19.

[31] *Vita Const.*, III, 7–16.

[32] Burn, *op. cit.*, pp. 20–43 ; Duchesne, *op. cit.*, II, pp. 111–18 ; Baynes, *op. cit.*, pp. 85–9.

[33] *Vita Const.*, III, 23 ; Schwartz, *Nachrichten*, 1911, pp. 367–426 ; Baynes in *Journal of Egyptian Archaeology*, XI (1925), pp. 58–61.

[34] Baynes, *op. cit.*, in n. 33, pp. 61–5 ; XII (1926), pp. 145–56, especially at p. 149. The explanation of Athanasius' refusal to go to Caesarea and his appearance, although reluctant, at Tyre is probably to be found in the suggestion that after the Caesarean Council Arius recanted and signed the orthodox creed.

[35] *Vita Const.*, IV, 15–16 ; Maurice, *Num. Const.*, II, pp. 354–5, 507–13.

[36] *Vita Const.*, II, 24, 46, 64.

[37] *Ibid.*, IV, 16 ; Dess. *ILS*, 705.

[38] *Vita Const.*, III, 54–58.

[39] Duchesne, *op. cit.*, II, pp. 51–2.

[40] For Helena's pilgrimage, *Vita Const.*, III, 42–44 ; for other Christian buildings, Duchesne, *op. cit.*, II, pp. 61–6.

[41] *Vita Const.*, III, 48 ; IV, 58–60 ; *Chron. Paschale* for A.D. 328 (*Chron. Min.*, I, p. 233) ; Themistius, *Or.*, I, p. 69 (ed. Dindorf) ; Zos., II, 31 ; Codinus, *De Originibus Constantinopolitanis*, in *Excerpta de Antiquitatibus Const.*, p. 16, ed. Bekkeri (Bonn) ; Maurice, *Les Origines de Constantinople* in *Vol. du Centenaire de la Soc. N. des Antiquaires de France*, Paris, 1904 ; *id.*, *Num. Const.*, II, pp. 481–92 ; *id.*, *Constantin le Grand*, pp. 199–215 ; Duchesne, *op. cit.*, II, pp. 67–70.

[42] Maurice, *Num. Const.*, II, pp. 488–9.

[43] *Vita Const.*, III, 48, 2 ; a rescript of Constantius II (*Cod. Theo.*,

XVI, 10, 2) also refers to a law of his father which forbade sacrifices, but the latter has not survived, and its scope is therefore doubtful.

⁴⁴ *Vita Const.*, III, 64–65 ; IV, 9–13 ; Baynes, *Constantine and the Christian Church*, pp. 25–9.

⁴⁵ *Vita Const.*, IV, 61.

⁴⁶ Schwartz, *Kaiser Constantin und die Christliche Kirche* (Leipzig, 1913) ; Burckhardt, *Die Zeit Constantins des Grossen* (3rd ed., Leipzig, 1898).

⁴⁷ Boissier, *La Fin du Paganisme*, I, p. 11 ; Lot, *La Fin du Monde Antique*, p. 34.

⁴⁸ This view is represented by Salvatorelli, *La politica religiosa e la religiosità di Costantino*, in *Ricerche religiose*, IV (1928), pp. 289–328, and by Piganiol, *L'Empereur Constantin* (1932), pp. 133–48.

⁴⁹ Baynes, *Constantine and the Christian Church*, pp. 95–103.

⁵⁰ Among the works of modern historians which I have consulted, the following appear to me to have given the most convincing interpretations of Constantine's religion : Baynes, *Constantine and the Christian Church* (Raleigh Lecture) ; Boissier, *La Fin du Paganisme*, I, pp. 1–84 ; Duchesne, *op. cit.*, II, pp. 45–71 ; Funk in *Kirchengeschichtliche Abhandlungen und Untersuchungen*, Paderborn, 1899, vol. 2, pp. 1–23 ; Lot, *op. cit.*, pp. 31–44 ; Maurice in *Num. Const.*, II, pp. xlix–xciii ; Müller in *Historische Zeitschrift*, 140 (1929), pp. 261–78 ; Schultze, *Geschichte des Untergangs des griechisch-römischen Heidentums*, I, pp. 28–67.

CHAPTER VII

¹ Hydatius for A.D. 326 (*Chron. Min.*, I, p. 232) ; cf. the issue of *Adventus* coins, Maurice, *op. cit.*, II, p. 494 ; III, pp. 57, 207 ; and the poems of Optatianus Porphyrius pleading for his reinstatement in imperial favour. The reasons for his disgrace are unknown. (*Carmina*, IV, 1 ; V, 8 ; IX, 35 ; XIX, 33, ed. Müller).

² Zos., II, 29, 2 ; Zon., XIII, 2, III, p. 179 ; Eutrop., X, 6 ; Vict. *Epit.*, 41, 11–12 ; Ammianus, XIV, 11, 20 ; Philostorgius, II, 4.

³ As in n. 2 and *Cod. Theo.*, IX, 9, 1, of May 29th, A.D. 326.

⁴ Zos., II, 29, 3–5 ; Maurice (*Constantin le Grand*, pp. 175–9) attaches, in my opinion, quite a disproportionate importance to the death of Crispus. The influence which he supposes it to have exercised over Constantine's dynastic schemes is for the most part purely hypothetical.

⁵ *Cod. Theo.*, XIV, 13 (*ius Italicum*) ; XIV, 16, 2 (*annona*) ; Maurice *Num. Const.*, I, p. cliii.

⁶ *Anon. Val.*, 6, 30 ; Themistius *Or.*, III, p. 48 A. ; Zos., II, 31, 3.

⁷ Seeck, *Regesten*, p. 478.

⁸ "*valuerit igitur in fundis patrimonialibus sitis per Asianam dioecesim, sitis per Ponticam in diem praesentem . . . lex divae memoriae Constantini, quae aedes per Constantinopolitanam urbem sacratissimam dominos exigebat*" (*Nov. Theod.*, V, 1, 1, of A.D. 438). For *annona civica*, *Cod. Theo.*, XIV, 17, 9–13, especially 12.

⁹ Maurice, *op. cit.*, II, pp. 536–7.

¹⁰ Seeck, *Untergang*, IV², pp. 380–1.

¹¹ *Anon. Val.*, 6, 30–1 ; Hydatius for A.D. 332 (*Chron. Min.*, 1, p. 234) ; Eutrop., X, 7 ; Vict. *de Caes.*, 41, 13 ; *Vita Const.*, IV, 5, 1.

¹² For the breach of faith, Ammianus, XVII, 13, 1 ; *Anon. Val.*, 6, 31 ; for the name, Argaragantes, *Hieron. Chron.*, p. 315, Fotheringham ; for the rebellion, *Vita Const.*, IV, 6 ; *Anon. Val.*, 6, 32 ; Hydatius for A.D. 334 (*Chron. Min.*, 1, p. 234) ; Amm., XVII, 12, 18.

¹³ Vict. *de Caes.*, 41, 11 ; *Chron. Pasch.* for A.D. 335 (*Chron. Min.*, I, p. 235).

¹⁴ For Delmatius, *Anon. Val.*, 6, 35 ; Hydatius for A.D. 335 ; for Constans, Hydatius for A.D. 333 (*Chron. Min.*, I, p. 234).

¹⁵ Eutrop., X, 6, 3 ; *Cod. Theo.*, IV, 6, 2 and 3 (*ad fin.*).

¹⁶ Julian, *Or.*, 1, 15 (ed. Hertlein) ; Euseb., *Laud. Const.*, 3, 4.

¹⁷ This account is taken from Faustus of Byzantium, III, 20 ff. (*FHG*, V, 2, pp. 230–2), on which see Baynes, *Rome and Armenia in the Fourth Century*, in *EHR*, 1910, pp. 625–43 at pp. 627–8. For Hannibalianus, *Anon. Val.*, 6, 35 ; Ammianus, XIV, 1, 2 ; Maurice, *Num. Const.*, II, p. 547.

¹⁸ *Anon. Val.*, 6, 35 ; Zos., II, 39, 1 ; Zon., XIII, 4, III, pp. 186–7 ; Vict. *de Caes.*, 41, 16 ; *Vita Const.*, IV, 64, 1.

¹⁹ *Vita Const.*, IV, 61, 2–3.

²⁰ Vict. *de Caes.*, 41, 20.

GENEALOGICAL TABLES

A. *The Dynasty of the Severi.*

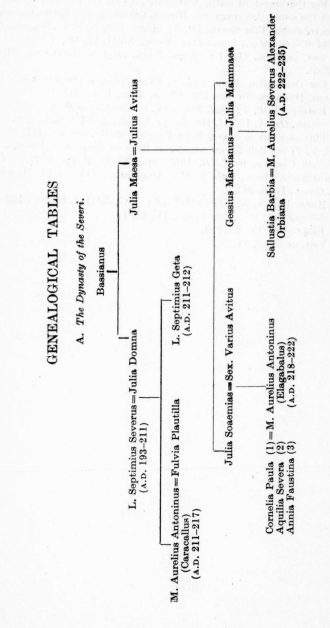

Bassianus

L. Septimius Severus = Julia Domna
(A.D. 193–211)

Julia Maesa = Julius Avitus

M. Aurelius Antoninus = Fulvia Plautilla
(Caracallus)
(A.D. 211–217)

L. Septimius Geta
(A.D. 211–212)

Gessius Marcianus = Julia Mammaea

Sallustia Barbia = M. Aurelius Severus Alexander
Orbiana
(A.D. 222–235)

Julia Soaemias = Sex. Varius Avitus

Cornelia Paula (1) = M. Aurelius Antoninus
Aquilia Severa (2)   (Elagabalus)
Annia Faustina (3)   (A.D. 218–222)

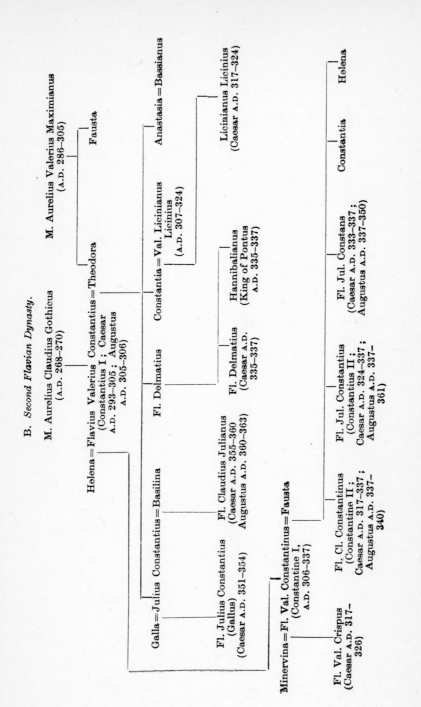

B. *Second Flavian Dynasty.*

M. Aurelius Claudius Gothicus (A.D. 268–270)

M. Aurelius Valerius Maximianus (A.D. 286–305)

Helena = Flavius Valerius Constantius = Theodora (Constantius I ; Caesar A.D. 293–305 ; Augustus A.D. 305–306)

Fausta

Fl. Delmatius

Constantia = Val. Licinianus Licinius (A.D. 307–324)

Anastasia = Bassianus

Licinianus Licinius (Caesar A.D. 317–324)

Galla = Julius Constantius = Basilina

Fl. Claudius Julianus (Caesar A.D. 355–360 Augustus A.D. 360–363)

Fl. Delmatius (Caesar A.D. 335–337)

Hannibalianus (King of Pontus A.D. 335–337)

Fl. Julius Constantius (Gallus) (Caesar A.D. 351–354)

Minervina = Fl. Val. Constantinus = Fausta (Constantine I, A.D. 306–337)

Fl. Val. Crispus (Caesar A.D. 317–326)

Fl. Cl. Constantinus (Constantine II ; Caesar A.D. 317–337 ; Augustus A.D. 337–340)

Fl. Jul. Constantius (Constantius II ; Caesar A.D. 324–337 ; Augustus A.D. 337–361)

Fl. Jul. Constans (Caesar A.D. 333–337 ; Augustus A.D. 337–350)

Constantia

Helena

CHRONOLOGICAL TABLE OF THE EMPERORS

Dates.

Names of Emperors.

138–161. T. Aurelius Fulvus Boionius Arrius Antoninus (Antoninus Pius).

161–169. M. Aurelius Antoninus.
Lucius Aurelius Verus.

169–177. M. Aurelius Antoninus.

177–180. M. Aurelius Antoninus.
M. Commodus Antoninus.

180–193. M. Commodus Antoninus.

193. P. Helvius Pertinax.

193. M. Didius Julianus.

193–198. L. Septimius Severus.

198–208. L. Septimius Severus.
M. Aurelius Antoninus (Caracallus).

208–211. L. Septimius Severus.
M. Aurelius Antoninus (Caracallus).
L. Septimius Geta.

211–212. M. Aurelius Antoninus (Caracallus).
L. Septimius Geta.

212–217. M. Aurelius Antoninus (Caracallus).

217–218. M. Opellius Macrinus.

218. M. Opellius Macrinus.
M. Opellius Diadumenianus.

218–222. M. Aurelius Antoninus (Elagabalus).

222–235. M. Aurelius Severus Alexander.
235–238. C. Julius Verus Maximinus.

238. D. Caelius Calvinus Balbinus.
M. Clodius Pupienus Maximus.

238–244. M. Antonius Gordianus (Gordian III).

Dates.

A.D.   Names of Emperors.

244–248.   M. Julius Philippus.

248–249.   M. Julius Philippus.
           M. Julius Philippus (his son).

249–251.   C. Messius Quintus Decius Traianus.

251–253.   C. Vibius Trebonianus Gallus.
           C. Vibius Afinius Gallus Veldumnianus Volusianus (his son).

253.   M. Aemilius Aemilianus.

253–260.   P. Licinius Valerianus.
           P. Licinius Gallienus.

260–268.   P. Licinius Gallienus.

268–270.   M. Aurelius Claudius (Gothicus).

270.   M. Aurelius Claudius Quintillus.

270–275.   L. Domitius Aurelianus.

275.   *Interregnum* lasting about a month.

275–276.   M. Claudius Tacitus.

276.   M. Annius Florianus.

276–282.   M. Aurelius Probus.

282–283.   M. Aurelius Carus.

283–284.   M. Aurelius Carinus.
           M. Aurelius Numerianus.

284–286.   C. Aurelius Valerius Diocletianus.

286–305.   C. Aurelius Valerius Diocletianus.
           M. Aurelius Valerius Maximianus.

305–306.   Flavius Valerius Constantius (Chlorus).
           Galerius Valerius Maximianus (Galerius).

306–307.   G. Valerius Maximianus (Galerius).
           Fl. Valerius Severus.

307–308.   G. Valerius Maximianus (Galerius).
           Fl. Valerius Constantinus.
           [M. Aurelius Valerius Maximianus.
           M. Valerius Maxentius.]

308–310.   G. Valerius Maximianus (Galerius),
           Valerius Licinianus Licinius.

Dates.

A.D. Names of Emperors.

310–311. G. Valerius Maximianus (Galerius).
Valerius Licinianus Licinius.
Galerius Valerius Maximinus (Daia).
Fl. Valerius Constantinus.

311–313. Valerius Licinianus Licinius.
G. Valerius Maximinus (Daia).
F. Valerius Constantinus.

313–324. Fl. Valerius Constantinus.
Valerius Licinianus Licinius.

324–337. Fl. Valerius Constantinus.

MODERN BIBLIOGRAPHY

(This list is not intended to be comprehensive, but contains the works which have been found of value in the composition of this book. Articles in Encyclopædias and Periodicals are not included, but reference will be found to them in the notes.)

A. GENERAL

Albertini, E.	*L'Empire Romain (Peuples et Civilisations*, IV).	Paris 1929.
Bury, J. B.	*The History of the later Roman Empire* (2nd ed.).	London, 1923.
von Domaszewski, A.	*Geschichte der römischen Kaiserzeit.*	Leipzig, 1909.
Gibbon, E.	*The Decline and Fall of the Roman Empire* (ed. J. B. Bury).	London, 1896.
Homo, L.	*L' Empire Romain,*	Paris, 1925.
„	*La Civilisation Romaine.*	Paris, 1930.
Jones, Sir H. Stuart.	*Companion to Roman History*	Oxford, 1912.
„	*The Roman Empire* (2nd ed.).	London, 1909.
Lot, F.	*La Fin du Monde antique.*	Paris, 1927.
Pelham, H. F.	*Essays on Roman History.*	Oxford, 1911.
Schiller, H.	*Geschichte der römischen Kaiserzeit.*	Gotha, 1883.
Seeck, O.	*Geschichte des Untergangs der antiken Welt* (Vol. I, 4th ed.; Vols. II–IV, 2nd ed.).	Stuttgart, 1921–2.
Stein, E.	*Geschichte des spät-römischen Reiches*, Vol. I.	Vienna, 1928.

B. CONSTITUTIONAL AND ADMINISTRATIVE

Abbott, F. F., and Johnson, A. C.	*Municipal Administration in the Roman Empire.*	Princeton, 1926.
Assmann, J.	*De Coloniis oppidisque quibus imperatoria nomina vel cogmomina imposita sunt.*	Langensalza, 1905.
Bickermann, E.	*Das Edikt des Kaisers Caracalla. Diss.*	Berlin, 1926.

Bruns, C. G.	*Fontes Juris Romani* (7th ed.)	Strassburg, 1908.
Capocci, V.	*La Constitutio Antoniniana.*	Rome, 1925.
Clinton, H. F.	*Fasti Romani.*	Oxford, 1845.
[Daremberg, C., et Saglio, E.]	*Dictionnaire des Antiquités Grecques et Romaines* (various articles).	Paris.
Hirschfeld, O.	*Die kaiserlichen Verwaltungsbeamten bis auf Diokletian* (2nd ed.).	Berlin, 1905.
„	*Kleine Schriften.*	Berlin, 1913.
Keyes, C. W.	*The Rise of the Equites in the Third Century of the Roman Empire. Diss.*	Princeton, 1915.
Kornemann, E.	*Doppelprinzipat und Reichseinteilung.*	Leipzig and Berlin, 1930.
Marquardt, J.	*Römische Staatsverwaltung* (2nd ed.).	Leipzig, 1881.
Meyer, P. M.	*Juristische Papyri. Erklärung von Urkunden zur Einführung in die juristische Papyri.*	Berlin, 1920.
Mommsen, Th.	*Gesammelte Schriften.*	Berlin, 1905.
„	*Römisches Staatsrecht* (3rd. ed.).	Leipzig, 1887.
„	*Römisches Strafrecht.*	Leipzig, 1899.
[Pauly-Wissowa-Kroll.]	*Real encyclopädie der klassischen Altertumswissenschaft* (various articles).	Stuttgart.
Reid, J. S.	*The Municipalities of the Roman Empire.*	Cambridge, 1913.
Ruggiero, E. de.	*Dizionario epigrafico* (various articles).	Rome.
Schulz, O. Th.	*Vom Prinzipat zum Dominat.*	Paderborn, 1919.
Seeck, O.	*Regesten der Kaiser und Päpste für die Jahre 311 bis 476 n. Chr.*	Stuttgart, 1919.
Stein, E.	*Untersuchungen über das officium der Prätorianerpräfectur seit Diokletian.*	Vienna, 1922.

C. Provincial, etc.

| Brünnow, R. E. und von Domaszewski, A. | *Die Provincia Arabia.* | Strassburg, 1904–9. |
| Cagnat, R. | *L'Armée Romaine d'Afrique* (2nd ed.). | Paris, 1913. |

Chapot, V.	*La Frontière de l'Euphrate.*	Paris, 1907.
Collingwood, R. G.	*Roman Britain* (2nd ed.).	Oxford, 1932.
,,	*The Archaeology of Roman Britain.*	London, 1930.
von Domaszewski, A.	*Die Namen römischen Kastellen am Limes Arabicus,* in *Festschrift für H. Kiepert.*	Berlin, 1898.
Février, J. G.	*Essai sur l'Histoire politique et économique de Palmyre.*	Paris, 1931.
Filow, B.	*Die Legionen der Provinz Moesia von Augustus bis auf Diokletian* (*Klio Beiheft* X).	Leipzig, 1906.
Gelzer, M.	*Studien zur byzantinischen Verwaltung Aegyptens.*	Leipzig, 1909.
Haverfield, F. H., and Macdonald, Sir G.	*The Roman Occupation of Britain.*	Oxford, 1924.
,,	*The Romanisation of Roman Britain* (4th ed.).	Oxford, 1923.
Jullian, C.	*Histoire de la Gaule,* Vols. IV–VIII.	Paris, 1914—26.
Keil, H., und von Premerstein, A.	*Berichte über eine, zweite, dritte Reise in Lydien.*	Vienna, 1911–14.
Lesquier, J.	*L'Armée Romaine d'Égypte d'Auguste à Dioclétien.*	Cairo, 1918.
Macdonald, Sir G.	*The Roman Wall in Scotland* (2nd ed.).	Oxford, 1934.
Mommsen, Th.	*The Provinces of the Roman Empire* (English translation by W. P. Dickson of *Römische Geschichte,* V).	London, 1909.
Ramsay, Sir W. M.	*Studies in the History and Art of the Eastern Provinces of the Roman Empire.*	Aberdeen, 1906.
Rappaport, B.	*Die Einfälle der Goten in das römische Reich.*	Leipzig, 1899.
von Sallet, A.	*Die Fürsten von Palmyra.*	Berlin, 1866.
Stout, S. E.	*The Governors of Moesia.*	Princeton, 1911.
von Wietersheim, E.-Dahn F.	*Geschichte der Völkerwanderung.*	Leipzig, 1880.

D. MILITARY

| Bang, M. | *Die Germanen im römischen Dienst bis zum Regierungantritts Konstantins I.* | Berlin, 1906. |
| Cheesman, G. L. | *The Auxilia of the Roman Imperial Army.* | Oxford, 1914. |

Delbrück, H.	*Geschichte der Kriegskunst im Rahmen der politischen Geschichte* (3rd ed.).	Berlin, 1921.
von Domaszewski, A.	*Die Rangordnung des römischen Heeres.*	Bonn, 1908.
,,	*Die Religion des römischen Heeres.*	Trier, 1895.
Grosse, R.	*Römische Militärgeschichte von Gallienus bis zum Beginn der byzantinischen Themen-verfassung.*	Berlin, 1920.
Kromayer, J., und Veith, G.	*Heerwesen und Kriegführung der Griechen und Römer.*	Munich, 1928.
Mommsen, Th.	*Gesammelte Schriften*, Vol. VI.	Berlin, 1910.
Parker, H. M. D.	*The Roman Legions.*	Oxford, 1928.
Reynolds, P. K. B.	*The Vigiles of Imperial Rome.*	Oxford, 1926.
Ritterling, E.	*Zum römischen Heerwesen des ausgehenden 3 Jahrhundert,* in *Festschrift für O. Hirschfeld.*	Berlin, 1903.
Schenk, D.	*Flavius Vegetius Renatus (Klio Beiheft* XXII).	Leipzig, 1930.

See also Section C.

E. Religion and Philosophy

Baynes, N. H.	*Constantine and the Christian Church* (Raleigh Lecture before the British Academy).	London, 1929
Bigg, C.	*The Christian Platonists of Alexandria* (re-ed. by F. E. Brightman).	Oxford, 1913.
,,	*Neoplatonism.*	S.P.C.K., 1895.
Boissier, G.	*La Fin du Paganisme* (9th ed.).	Paris (undated).
Boulanger, A.	*Aelius Aristide et la Sophistique dans la province d'Asie au 2ème siècle de notre ère.*	Paris, 1923.
Burn, A. E.	*The Council of Nicaea.*	S.P.C.K., 1925.
Cumont, F.	*Les Mystères de Mithra* (3rd ed.).	Brussels, 1913
,,	*Textes et Monuments relatifs aux mystères de Mithra.*	Paris, 1894–1900.
,,	*Les Religions Orientales dans le Paganisme Romain.*	Paris, 1919.
Dill, S.	*Roman Society from Nero to Marcus Aurelius.*	London, 1904.

Duchesne, L.	*The Early History of the Church* (English translation by C. Jenkins).	London, 1924.
Gwatkin, H. M.	*Studies of Arianism.*	Cambridge, 1882.
Harnack, A.	*Die Mission und Ausbreitung des Christentums in den ersten drei Jahrhunderten* (4th ed.). (English translation (2nd ed.), by J. Moffat, London, 1908.)	Leipzig, 1924.
Inge, W. R.	*Christian Mysticism* (Bampton Lectures, 1899).	London, 1899.
Kidd, B. J.	*History of the Church to 461 A.D.*	Oxford, 1922.
„	*Documents illustrative of the History of the Church.*	S.P.C.K., 1933.
Neumann, K. J.	*Der römische Staat und die allgemeine Kirche.*	Leipzig, 1890.
Nock, A. D.	*Conversion.*	Oxford, 1933.
Réville, J.	*La Religion à Rome sous les Sévères.*	Paris, 1886.
Schultze, V.	*Geschichte des Untergangs der griechisch-römischen Heidentums.*	Jena, 1892.
Schwartz, E.	*Zur Geschichte des Athanasius* (*Nachrichten von der Königl. Gesellschaft der Wissenschaften zu Göttingen*, Phil.-hist. Klasse).	1904–5, 1908, 1911.
Seeberg, E.	*Die Synode von Antiochien in Jahre 324–5.* (*Neue Studien zur Geschichte der Theologie und der Kirche*, edd. N. Bonwetsch und R. Seeberg.)	Berlin, 1913.
Seeck, O.	*Geschichte des Untergangs* etc., Vol III (2nd ed.).	Stuttgart, 1921.
von Soden, H.	*Urkunden zur Entstehungsgeschichte des Donatismus* (Lietzmann, Kleine Texte, 122).	Bonn, 1913.
Toutain, J.	*Les Cultes Païens dans l'Empire Romain.*	Paris, 1907–1920.
Weber, W.	*Römische Kaisergeschichte und Kirchengeschichte.*	Stuttgart, 1929.
Whittaker, T.	*Apollonius of Tyana and other Essays.*	London, 1909.

25

Whittaker, T.	*The Neoplatonists* (2nd ed.).	Cambridge, 1928.
Wissowa, G.	*Religion und Kultus der Römer* (2nd ed.).	Munich, 1912.

F. Economic and Numismatic

Bott, H.	*Die Grundzüge der diokletiani-schen Steuerverfassung.*	Frankfurt, 1928.
Cagnat, R.	*Étude historique sur les impôts indirects chez les Romains.*	Paris, 1882.
Clausing, R.	*The Roman Colonate ; the Theories of its Origin.*	New York, 1925.
Cohen, H.	*Description historique des mon-naies frappées sous l'Empire Romain* (2nd. ed.)	Paris, 1880–1892.
Eckhel, J.	*Doctrina numorum veterum,* Vols. VII–VIII.	Vienna, 1828.
Frank, T.	*An Economic History of Rome* (2nd ed.).	Baltimore, 1927.
Mattingly, H.	*Roman Coins.*	London, 1928.
Mattingly, H., and Sydenham, E. A.	*The Roman Imperial Coinage,* Vols. II–III, V (1 and 2).	London, 1923 ff.
Maurice, J.	*Numismatique Constantin-ienne.*	Paris, 1908–12.
Mickwitz, G.	*Geld und Wirtschaft in römi-schen Reich des vierten Jahr-hunderts n. Chr.*	Helsingfors, 1932.
Mitteis, L., und Wilcken, U.	*Grundzüge und Chrestomathie der Papyruskunde.*	Leipzig, 1912.
Oertel, F.	*Die Liturgie.*	Leipzig, 1917.
Piganiol, A.	*L'impôt de Capitation sous le bas-Empire Romain.*	Chambéry, 1916.
Rohde, Th.	*Die Münzen des Kaisers Aurel-ianus, seiner Frau Severina und der Fürsten von Palmyra.*	Miskolcz, 1881.
Rostovtzeff, M.	*The Social and Economic His-tory of the Roman Empire.*	Oxford, 1926.
,,	*Studien zur Geschichte des römischen Kolonates.*	Leipzig, 1910.
von Sallet, A.	*Die Daten der alexandrinischen Kaisermünzen.*	Berlin, 1870.
Vinogradoff, Sir P.	*The Growth of the Manor.*	London, 1905.
Vogt, J.	*Die alexandrinischen Münzen.*	Stuttgart, 1924.
Waltzing, J. P.	*Étude historique sur les Corpora-tions professionelles.*	Louvain, 1895–1900.

Webb, P. H. *The Coins of Carausius.* London, 1908.

G. Archæology and Art

Ashby, T.	*The Roman Campagna in Classical Times.*	London, 1927.
Dessau, H.	*Inscriptiones Latinae Selectae.*	Berlin, 1892–1916.
Diehl, C.	*Manuel d'Art Byzantin.*	Paris, 1910.
,,	*En Méditerranée* (4th ed.).	Paris, 1912.
Platner, S. B., and Ashby, T.	*A Topographical Dictionary of Ancient Rome.*	Oxford, 1929.
Richmond, I. A.	*The City Wall of Imperial Rome.*	Oxford, 1930.
Rivoira, G. T.	*Roman Architecture and its principles of construction under the Empire* (English translation by G. McN. Rushforth).	Oxford, 1925.
Strong, E.	*Art in Ancient Rome* (2nd ed.).	London, 1929.
,,	*Roman Sculpture from Augustus to Constantine.*	London, 1907.
Toynbee, J. M. C.	*The Hadrianic School.*	Cambridge, 1934.
Wickhoff, F.	*Wiener Genesis* (English translation by Mrs. S. A. Strong under the title of *Roman Art*).	London, 1900

H. Monographs on Individual Emperors

Baynes, N.	*The Historia Augusta.*	Oxford, 1926.
Bryant, E. E.	*The Reign of Antoninus Pius.*	Cambridge, 1895.
Burckhardt, J.	*Die Zeit Constantins des Grossen* (3rd ed.).	Leipzig, 1898.
de Ceuleneer, A.	*Essai sur la vie et le règne de Septime Sévère.*	Brussels, 1880.
Crees, J. H. E.	*The Reign of the Emperor Probus.*	London, 1911.
Damarau, P.	*Kaiser Claudius Goticus* (*Klio Beiheft* XXXIII).	Leipzig, 1934.
Hasebroek, J.	*Untersuchungen zur Geschichte des Kaisers Septimius Severus.*	Heidelberg, 1921.
Heer, J. M.	*Der historische Wert der Vita Commodi.*	Leipzig, 1901.
Henderson, B. W.	*The Life and Principate of the Emperor Hadrian.*	London, 1923.

Homo, L.	*De Claudio Gothico.*	Paris, 1903.
,,	*Essai sur le règne de l'Empereur Aurélien.*	Paris, 1904.
Hönn, K.	*Quellenuntersuchungen zu den viten des Heliogabalus und des Severus Alexander.*	Leipzig, 1911.
Hüttl, W.	*Antoninus Pius,* Vol. II.	Prague, 1933.
Hunzinger, A. W.	*Die diokletianische Staatsreform. Diss.*	Rostock, 1899.
Jardé, A.	*Études critiques sur la vie et le règne de Sévère Alexandre.*	Paris, 1925.
Kubitschek, W.	*Zur Geschichte des Usurpators Achilleus* (Akademie der Wissenschaften in Wien, Sitzungsberichte 208, Band I, Abhandlung).	Vienna, 1928.
Lacour-Gayet, G.	*Antonin le Pieux et son temps.*	Paris, 1888.
Lécrivain, C.	*Études sur l'Histoire Auguste.*	Paris, 1904.
Lehmann, K. F. W.	*Kaiser Gordian III. Diss.*	Berlin, 1911.
Maurice, J.	*Constantin le Grand.*	Paris (undated).
Piganiol, A.	*L'Empereur Constantin.*	Paris, 1932.
Platnauer, M.	*The Life and Reign of the Emperor L.Septimius Severus.*	Oxford, 1918.
Renan, E.	*Marc Aurèle et la fin du monde antique.*	Paris, 1882.
Reusch, W.	*Der historische Wert der Caracalla-Vita in SHA. (Klio Beiheft* XXIV.)	Leipzig, 1931,
Schwartz, E.	*Kaiser Constantin und die Christliche Kirche.*	Leipzig, 1913.
Schwendemann, J.	*Der historische Wert der Vita Marci.*	Heidelberg, 1923.
Schulz, O. Th.	*Der römische Kaiser Caracalla.*	Leipzig, 1909.
Sedgwick, H. D.	*The Life of Marcus Aurelius.*	Yale, 1922.
Stade, K.	*Der Politiker Diokletian und die letzte grosse Christenverfolgung.*	Wiesbaden, 1926.
Thiele, W.	*De Severo Alexandro Imperatore.*	Berlin, 1909.
Weber, W.	*Untersuchungen zur Geschichte des Kaisers Hadrians.*	Leipzig, 1907.
von Wilamowitz-Moellendorff, U.	*Kaiser Marcus.*	Berlin, 1931.
Wirth, A.	*Quaestiones Severianae. Diss.*	Leipzig, 1888.

25*

INDEX OF SUBJECTS